Homes
REFERENCE
GUIDE

Second Edition 2009

Copyright

Disclaimer

Trademark

Acknowledgments

The LEED for Homes Reference Guide has been made possible through the efforts of many dedicated volunteers, staff members, and others in the USGBC community. The Reference Guide was managed and implemented by USGBC staff and consultants and included review and suggestions from many Technical Advisory Sub-Committee and Technical Advisory Group members and the LEED for Homes Committee. We extend our deepest gratitude to all of our LEED committee members who participated in the development of this guide, for their tireless volunteer efforts and constant support of the USGBC mission.

LEED for Homes Core Committee

Steve Winter (Chair), Steven Winter Associates
Kristin Shewfelt (Vice-Chair), Architectural Energy Corporation
Scott Blunk, GreenBuilt Construction
Mack Caldwell, Ideal Homes
Dennis Creech, Southface Energy Institute
Jim Crocker, Wianno Realty
Dan Dempsey, Carrier Corporation
Ann Edminster, Design AVEnues
Richard Faesy, Vermont Energy Investment Corporation
Randy Hansell, Earth Advantage Program
Daniele Loffreda, Plateau Enviro
Eric Martin, Florida Solar Energy Center, University of Central Florida
Richard Michal, Richard J. Michal, LLC
Tien Peng, Quadrant Homes
Sam Rashkin, U.S. Environmental Protection Agency, ENERGY STAR for Homes
Kevin Stack, Northeast Natural Homes Contractors and Builders
Dave Ware, Owens-Corning
Walker Wells, Global Green USA

A special thanks to representatives of our key stakeholder organizations, who participated in this process: Joy Altwies, University of Wisconsin–Madison, Program Director; Bill Semple, Canada Mortgage and Housing Corporation; Victoria Schomer, Interior Concerns, Owner; and Richard Schneider, USACE, Project Manager/Research Architect.

A special thanks to Jay Hall and Doug King from Building Knowledge, Inc., for their significant contribution to the LEED for Homes Reference Guide.

LEED Technical Advisory Groups

Sustainable Sites TAG

Bryna Dunn (Chair), Moseley Architects
Susan Kaplan (Vice-Chair), Battery Park City Authority
Michele Adams, Cahill Associates
Gina Baker, Burt Hill
Ted Bardacke, Global Green USA
Stephen Benz, Sasaki Associates
Mark Brumbaugh, Brumbaugh & Associates
Meg Calkins, Ball State University
Laura Case, Emory University Campus Services

Zachary Christeson, the HOK Planning Group
Stew Comstock, MD DEP
Jay Enck, Commissioning & Green Building Services
Ron Hand, E/FECT Sustainable Design Solutions
Richard Heinisch, Lithonia
Michael Lane, Lighting Design Lab
Marita Roos, Andropogon Associates
Zolna Russell, Hord Coplan Macht, Inc.
Alfred Vick, Ecos Environmental Design, Inc.
Eva Wong, EPA Heat Island Reduction Initiative

Water Efficiency TAG

David Sheridan (Chair), Aqua Cura
John Koeller (Vice-Chair), Koeller and Company
Gunnar Baldwin, TOTO USA, Inc.
Neal Billetdeaux, JJR
David Carlson, Columbia University
Bill Hoffman, H. W. (Bill) Hoffman and Associates
Geoff Nara, Civil & Environmental Consultants
Heather Kinkade-Levario, ARCADIS
Shabbir Rawalpindiwala, Kohler Company
Stephanie Tanner, US Environmental Protection Agency
Bill Wall, Clivus New England, Inc.
Bill Wilson, Environmental Planning & Design, LLC

Energy & Atmosphere TAG

Greg Kats (Chair), Good Energies
Marcus Sheffer (Vice-Chair), 7group
Saad Dimachkieh, HOK
Jay Enck, Commissioning & Green Building Services
Donald Fournier, Building Research Council
Ellen Franconi, IPMVP and AEC
Mark Frankel, New Buildings Institute
Jonathan Heller, Ecotope Inc.
Tia Heneghan, Sebesta Blomberg
Rusty Hodapp, DFW, Energy & Transportation Management
John Hogan, Seattle Department of Planning & Development
Bion Howard, Building Environmental Science
Bob Maddox, Sterling Planet
Cheryl Massie, Flack + Kurtz
Brenda Morawa, BVM Engineering, Inc.
Erik Ring, LPA, Inc.
Mick Schwedler, Trane
Gord Shymko, IPMVP and G.F. Shymko & Associates
Greg Thomas, Performance Systems
Michael Zimmer, Thompson Hine LLP

Materials & Resources TAG

Nadav Malin (Chair), BuildingGreen, Inc.
Mark Webster (Vice-Chair), Simpson Gumpertz & Heger
Paul Bertram, NAIMA
Chris Dixon, NBBF
Ann Edminster, Design AVEnues
Lee Gros, independent consultant
Nancy Malone, Siegel & Strain Architects
Dana Papke, California Air Resources Board
Kirsten Ritchie, Gensler
Wayne Trusty, Athena Institute
Denise Van Valkenburg, Steelcase
Gabe Wing, Herman Miller, Inc.

Indoor Environmental Quality TAG

Bob Thompson (Chair), U.S. Environmental Protection Agency, Indoor Environments
Management Branch
Steve Taylor (Vice-Chair), Taylor Engineering
Nancy Clanton, Clanton and Associates
Alexis Kurtz, Ove Arup & Partners
George Loisos, Loisos+ Ubelohde
Prasad Vaidya, The Weidt Group
Daniel Bruck, BRC Acoustics & Tech.
David Lubman, David Lubman & Associates
Charles Salter, Salter Associates
Jude Anders, Johnson Controls, Inc. (retired)
Brian Cloward, Mithun Architects+Designers+Planners
Larry Dykhuis, Herman Miller, Inc.
Francis (Bud) Offerman, Indoor Environmental Engineering
Christopher Schaffner, The Green Engineer
Dennis Stanke, Trane Company

LEED for Homes Technical Advisory Sub-Committees

Location & Linkages, Sustainable Sites, and Water Efficiency TASC

Dave Sheridan (Chair), AquaCura
Gina Baker, Burt Hill Architects
Paul Bassett, Hydrologix Solutions
Jim Crocker, Wiannore REALTORS
Anthony Floyd, City of Scottsdale
Ron Hand, E/FECT Sustainable Design Solutions
Randy Hansell, Earth Advantage
Jennifer Henry, U.S. Green Building Council
Donn Mann, Rain Bird Corp.
Carlos Michelon, MWD of Southern California
Dave Modi, American Standard
Michael Pawlukiewicz, Urban Land Institute
Laura Watchman, Defenders of Wildlife

Energy & Atmosphere TASC

David Meisegeier (Chair), ICF International
Greg Thomas, Performance Systems Development
Joy Altwies, University of Wisconsin
Dan Dempsey, Carrier
Eric Martin, Florida Solar Energy Center
Mark Newey, Center for Ecological Technology
Dave Roberts, Architectural Energy Corp.
Bill Semple, Canada Mortgage & Housing Corp.
Rob Vieira, Florida Solar Energy Center
Steven Winter, Steven Winter & Associates

Materials & Resources TASC

Ann Edminster (Chair), Design Avenues
Nadav Malin, BuildingGreen
Steve Brauneis, Rocky Mountain Institute
Mack Caldwell, Ideal Homes
Nancy Malone, Siegel & Strain Architects
Kathleen O'Brien, O'Brien & Company
David Ware, Owens Corning
Peter Yost, BuildingGreen

Indoor Environmental Quality TASC

Eric Werling (Chair), U.S. Environmental Protection Agency,
    Indoor Environment Division
Brian Cloward, Mithun
Don Fugler, Canada Mortgage & Housing Corp.
Don Stevens, Stevens & Associates
Dan Wildenhaus, Atmosphere
Ellen Tohn, ERT Associates
Richard Faesy, Vermont Energy Investment Corp.
Paul Raymer, Heyoka Solutions
Terry Brennan, Camroden Associates
Victoria Schomer, Interior Concerns
Sam Rashkin, U.S. Environmental Protection Agency

Preface

The built environment has a profound impact on our natural environment, economy, health, and productivity. Breakthroughs in building science, technology, and operations are now available to designers, builders, operators, and owners who want to build green and maximize both economic and environmental performance.

The U.S. Green Building Council (USGBC) is coordinating a national consensus effort to provide the industry with the tools necessary to design, build, and operate buildings that deliver high performance inside and out. Council members work together to develop design and construction practices, guidelines, operating practices and guidelines, policy positions, and educational tools that support sustainable design and building practices. Members also forge strategic alliances with industry and research organizations, federal government agencies, and state and local governments to transform the built environment. As the leading organization that represents the entire building industry on environmental building matters, USGBC's unique perspective and leadership enable our members to effect change in the way buildings are designed, built, operated and maintained.

The LEED Green Building Rating System™ is the nationally accepted benchmark for the design, construction, and operation of high-performance green buildings. LEED gives building owners and operators the tools they need to have an immediate and measurable impact on their buildings' performance. LEED promotes a whole-building approach to sustainability by recognizing performance in sustainable site development, water savings, energy efficiency, materials selection, and indoor environmental quality and it rewards innovation in building design.

USGBC Membership

The Council's greatest strength is the diversity of its membership. USGBC is a balanced, consensus nonprofit organization representing the entire building industry, comprising more than 14,000 companies and organizations. Since its inception in 1993, USGBC has played a vital role in providing a leadership forum and a unique, integrating force for the building industry. USGBC programs are distinguished by several features:

❏ Committee-based

The heart of this effective coalition is the committee structure, in which volunteer members design strategies that are implemented by staff and expert consultants. USGBC committees provide a forum for members to resolve differences, build alliances, and forge cooperative solutions for influencing change in all sectors of the building industry.

❏ Member-driven

Membership is open and balanced and provides a comprehensive platform for carrying out important programs and activities. USGBC targets the issues identified by its members as the highest priority. In annual reviews of achievements, USGBC sets policy, revises strategies, and devises work plans based on members' needs.

❏ Consensus-focused

USGBC members work together to promote green buildings and, in doing so, help foster greater economic vitality and environmental health at lower costs. The various industry segments bridge ideological gaps to develop balanced policies that benefit the entire industry.

Contact the U.S. Green Building Council

U.S. Green Building Council
2101 L Street, NW
Suite 500
Washington, DC 20037
(800) 795-1747 Office
(202) 828-5110 Fax
www.usgbc.org

How to Use This Guide

The LEED for Homes Reference Guide is a supporting document to the LEED for Homes Rating System. It assists construction project teams in understanding the following:

❑ the measures that meet LEED for Homes criteria;

❑ the benefits of achieving each criterion (thereby earning credit toward certification); and

❑ resources that provide additional information on each credit.

This document is designed not to reproduce all available research and information on green homebuilding practices, but rather to guide builders to the most appropriate resources for each measure in the Rating System. Project teams should develop and implement strategies to satisfy the intent of each credit as appropriate to their buildings; the guide cannot list every possible strategy or provide all the information that teams need to determine the applicability of a credit to their circumstances.

The LEED for Homes Reference Guide provides information for builders in these areas:

❑ **Introductory information.** Background on the program, how to participate, and an overview of the LEED for Homes certification process.

❑ **Project checklist.** The point system for the LEED certification levels.

❑ **Information on each credit.** Examples of strategies that can be used in each of the eight credit categories, as well as references and resources that provide more information.

Since the construction process for most new homes is managed by homebuilders, the language used in the Rating System and reference guide is intended to be builder friendly.

Introduction

I. Why Green Homes?

The environmental impact of the residential sector is significant. There are more than 120 million homes in the United States, and about 2 million new homes are constructed each year. According to the U.S. Department of Energy, the residential sector accounts for 22% of the total energy consumed in the U.S. and 7% of the water. Levels of indoor air pollutants can often be four to five times higher than outdoor levels. The residential sector also contributes 21% of U.S. carbon dioxide emissions. The considerable impact on the environment created by homes necessitates a shift toward more sustainable residences.

Green homebuilding addresses these issues by promoting the design and construction of homes that have much higher performance levels than homes built to the minimum building codes. Generally, green homes are healthier, more comfortable, more durable, and more energy efficient and have a much smaller environmental footprint than conventional homes.

Breakthroughs in building science, technology, and operations are now available to designers, builders, operators and owners who want to build green and maximize both economic and environmental performance. Green homes rely upon established, proven design features and technologies that do not have a significantly large cost.

In fact, many green measures, particularly those that involve energy and water efficiency, will reduce long-term costs. Often these reductions in operating costs will more than offset the additional up-front costs of a green home. The homebuilding industry is beginning to recognize the value of healthy homes and environmentally responsible projects. The LEED for

Homes Rating System provides a basis for quantifying the benefits of green homes, thereby facilitating the widespread construction of more sustainable homes.

II. LEED® Green Building Rating Systems

History

Following the formation of the U.S. Green Building Council in 1993, members quickly realized that the sustainable building industry needed a system to define and measure green buildings. USGBC began to research existing green building metrics and rating systems. Less than a year after formation, members established a committee comprising architects, real estate agents, a building owner, a lawyer, an environmentalist and industry representatives to focus on this challenge. This cross section of people and professions added a richness and depth both to the process and to the ultimate product—the LEED green building certification program. The first LEED pilot program, known as LEED Version 1.0, was launched at the USGBC Membership Summit in August 1998. After extensive modifications, the LEED Green Building Rating System Version 2.0 was released in March 2000.

As LEED has evolved and matured, the program has undertaken new initiatives. LEED addresses the different project development and delivery processes that exist in the U.S. building design and construction market.

LEED Today

The LEED Green Building Rating System is a voluntary, consensus-based, market-driven program based on existing, proven technology. It evaluates environmental performance from a whole-building perspective over a building's life cycle, providing a definitive measure for what constitutes a green building. The development of the LEED Green Building Rating System was initiated by USGBC members, involves all segments of the building industry and has been open to public scrutiny.

LEED has five environmental categories: Sustainable Sites, Water Efficiency, Energy & Atmosphere, Materials & Resources, and Indoor Environmental Quality. A sixth category, Innovation in Design, addresses sustainable building expertise as well as design measures not covered under the five environmental categories. LEED for Homes also has two additional categories specific to the residential sector: Locations & Linkages and Awareness & Education.

The measurement system is designed for rating and certifying new and existing commercial, institutional, and residential buildings. It is based on accepted energy and environmental principles and strikes a balance between known, established practices and emerging concepts. It is a performance-oriented system in which points are earned for satisfying criteria that address specific environmental impacts inherent in the design, construction, and operation and maintenance of buildings.

Different levels of LEED green building certification are awarded based on the total points earned. The system is designed to be comprehensive in scope yet simple in operation.

The green design field is growing and changing daily. New technologies and products are coming into the marketplace, and innovative designs are proving

their effectiveness. The Rating Systems and the reference guides are evolving as well. Teams wishing to certify their projects with LEED should comply with the version of the Rating System that is current at the time of their registration. USGBC highlights new developments on its Web site on a continual basis, at www.usgbc.org.

III. LEED for Homes Overview and Process

LEED for Homes is a national, voluntary certification system, developed by national experts and experienced builders, that promotes the design and construction of high-performance green homes and encourages the adoption of sustainable practices by the homebuilding industry.

The LEED for Homes Rating System is part of the suite of nationally recognized LEED Green Building Rating Systems administered by USGBC. Like all LEED Rating Systems, it is the market's leadership system, targeting the top 25% of home building practices in terms of environmental responsibility. LEED provides industry resources and tools on how to "green" any new home.

With LEED, homebuilders can differentiate their structures as meeting the highest performance measures, and homebuyers can readily identify high-quality green homes. LEED provides national consistency in defining the features of a green home, enables builders anywhere in the country to obtain a green rating on their homes, and assures homebuyers of the quality of their purchases, all based on a recognized national brand.

Program Scope and Project Eligibility

LEED for Homes addresses several types of new residential construction. Project types that are eligible for LEED certification are listed below, subject to the conditions described.

1. **Single-family homes.** Single-family homes include both attached and detached homes, and may be production, affordable, or custom. Townhomes that share a common vertical wall are considered single-family residences. Duplexes or other stacked housing units that share a common ceiling or floor are considered multifamily residences.

2. **Low-rise multifamily.** Low-rise multifamily buildings are defined as one-, two-, or three-story buildings with at least two dwelling units. Townhomes that share a common vertical wall are considered single-family residences. Duplexes or other stacked housing units that share a common ceiling or floor are considered multifamily residences. Multifamily buildings are eligible to use the LEED for Homes Sampling Protocol for Multi-Family Buildings to reduce verification costs if the builder is able to demonstrate consistency in construction practices.

3. **Mid-rise multifamily.** LEED for Homes has a pilot program for mid-rise multifamily projects. Projects must be 4-6 above-grade occupiable stories, at least 50% residential, and include at least 2 dwelling units to be eligible for the pilot. Projects in the pilot program must follow separate guidelines with sector-specific prerequisites and credits. Contact your LEED for Homes Provider for details.

4. **Production homes.** LEED for Homes recognizes the unique needs of high volume homebuilders who use a mass-production process to achieve a consistent level of quality. Within a given community or subdivision, production builders need assurance that every home built to a certain specification will be certified. Under LEED for Homes, a builder can use a community-scale specification and a simple compliance pathway for all comparable homes. Further, the LEED for Homes Sampling Protocols enable production builders to reduce verification costs if they are able to demonstrate consistency in their construction practices.

5. **Affordable homes.** LEED for Homes can be applied to both affordable single-family and affordable low-rise (one, two, or three stories) multifamily projects.

6. **Manufactured and modular housing.** Manufactured and modular homes are homes that are primarily constructed in a production plant, not on the home site. Certification of these projects requires the involvement of the plant manager or owner and may necessitate on-site plant inspections, particularly for energy performance. Further guidance on manufactured and modular housing is available from Providers.

7. **Existing homes.** Major "gut" rehab projects can participate in LEED for Homes, but partial rehab or renovation projects cannot. To be considered a major rehab project, the home must be stripped to the studs on at least one side of all external walls and the exterior ceiling, to expose the interstitial space for insulation installation and inspection. The American Society of Interior Designers' Foundation and the U.S. Green Building Council have partnered on the development of best practice guidelines and targeted educational resources for sustainable residential remodeling projects. This program will increase understanding of sustainable renovation project practices and benefits among homeowners, residents, design professionals, product suppliers and service providers to build both demand and industry capacity. More information is available at www.regreenprogram.org.

All LEED homes, regardless of type, must meet the prerequisites listed in the LEED for Homes Rating System. All LEED projects must establish a relationship with a Provider before beginning construction, preferably early in the design stage.

Rating and Certification

The strength of the program is its third-party verification. LEED homes are rated by LEED for Homes Certification Providers. These are local and regional organizations with U.S. Green Building Council demonstrated experience, expertise in their market, and a proven record of supporting builders in the construction of high-performance, sustainable homes. A Provider manages a team of Green Raters and works under contract with USGBC. USGBC reviews and completes certifications.

A Green Rater is an individual who conducts field inspections and performance testing, whether as part of the Provider's in-house staff or as a subcontractor.

USGBC has expanded its network of Providers throughout the country. Homebuilders may contact any LEED for Homes Provider to discuss participation. An updated list of Providers is maintained on the USGBC Web site, at http://www.usgbc.org/leed/homes.

Credit Categories

LEED certification is based on 18 prerequisites and 67 credits. The prerequisites are basic performance standards: they are mandatory for every project, and no points are awarded for meeting them. To achieve certification, builders earn credit points by exceeding the minimum standards of the prerequisites. In total, 136 credit points are available.

Prerequisites and points are classified in eight credit categories:

1. **Innovation in Design (ID) Process.** Special design methods, unique re-gional credits, measures not currently addressed in the Rating System, and exemplary performance levels.

2. **Location & Linkages (LL).** The placement of homes in socially and environmentally responsible ways in relation to the larger community.

3. **Sustainable Sites (SS).** The use of the entire property so as to minimize the project's impact on the site.

4. **Water Efficiency (WE).** Water conservation practices, both indoor and outdoor.

5. **Energy & Atmosphere (EA).** Energy efficiency, particularly in the building envelope and heating and cooling design.

6. **Materials & Resources (MR).** Efficient utilization of materials, selection of environmentally preferable materials, and minimization of waste during construction.

7. **Indoor Environmental Quality (EQ).** Improvement of indoor air quality by reducing the creation of and exposure to pollutants.

8. **Awareness & Education (AE).** The education of homeowner, tenant, or multifamily building manager about the operations and maintenance of the green features of a LEED Home.

Certification Levels

The LEED for Homes Rating System works by requiring a minimum level of performance through prerequisites and rewarding improved performance in each of the above categories. The level of performance is indicated by four performance tiers—Certified, Silver, Gold, and Platinum—according to the number of points earned (**Table 1**).

Table 1. LEED for Homes Certification Levels

	Required points
Certified	45–59
Silver	60–74
Gold	75–89
Platinum	90–136
Total available points	136

The number of points for each certification level is adjusted for smaller-than-average and larger-than-average homes using the Home Size Adjustment.

The Rating System guarantees minimum levels of sustainable practice through the 18 prerequisites in the eight credit categories. At the same time, projects enjoy flexibility with the wide variety of credits available to achieve certification. Credit Interpretation Requests are available to project teams that seek clarification or special consideration on specific credits.

How to Participate in LEED for Homes

There are five basic steps for a builder to follow in participating in LEED for Homes:

1. Contact a LEED for Homes Provider and register the project with USGBC.

2. Identify a project team.

3. Build the home to the stated goals and have green measures verified by a Green Rater and qualified energy rater.

4. Achieve certification as a LEED home.

5. Post-certification PR and marketing support.

These steps and the builder's and Provider's roles are summarized in **Table 2** and briefly described below.

Step 1: Contact a LEED for Homes Provider and Join the Program

Every participating builder or project manager starts by selecting a LEED for Homes Provider. A Provider can offer orientation and up-front technical assistance to builders, although some builders—particularly those with experience in green homebuilding—may not need these services.

Once the builder and the Provider have agreed to work in partnership on the project, each project must be registered with USGBC.

Step 2: Identify a Project Team

The builder identifies the project team that will plan, design, and build the home. The team should include professionals with both knowledge and experience in the eight LEED for Homes credit categories. These professionals work together to develop the project goals, identify potential challenges, and determine how best to contribute to the success of the project.

The project team starts by articulating the sustainability goals of the project and determining the specific strategies and systems integration required to meet them.

The LEED for Homes Provider or Green Rater then conducts a preliminary review of the home's current design and determines its projected score in the LEED for Homes Rating System. This review should include the following:

❑ completion of a preliminary project checklist

❑ a preliminary estimate of the LEED for Homes score and certification level

Depending on the projected score, the project team may identify additional green measures to be pursued and add them to the project checklist.

The success of a green homebuilding project is tied to how effectively the green measures are integrated into a home's design and how well the subcontractors understand these measures' installation. For that reason, green designers and consultants may also be critical members of some project teams. They can provide the necessary support to integrate green measures into home designs and ensure that these designs are appropriately constructed by each subcontractor.

Table 2. Roadmap for Participation

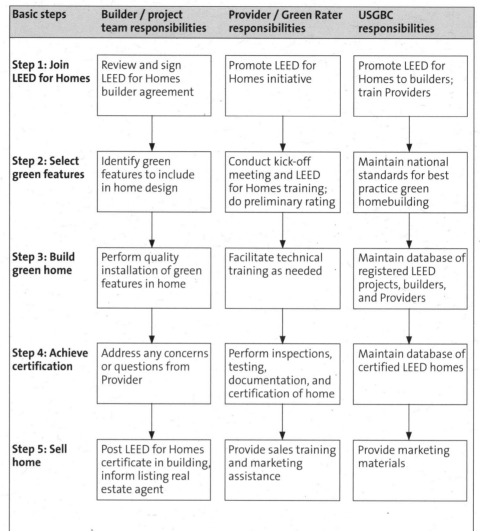

Basic steps	Builder / project team responsibilities	Provider / Green Rater responsibilities	USGBC responsibilities
Step 1: Join LEED for Homes	Review and sign LEED for Homes builder agreement	Promote LEED for Homes initiative	Promote LEED for Homes to builders; train Providers
Step 2: Select green features	Identify green features to include in home design	Conduct kick-off meeting and LEED for Homes training; do preliminary rating	Maintain national standards for best practice green homebuilding
Step 3: Build green home	Perform quality installation of green features in home	Facilitate technical training as needed	Maintain database of registered LEED projects, builders, and Providers
Step 4: Achieve certification	Address any concerns or questions from Provider	Perform inspections, testing, documentation, and certification of home	Maintain database of certified LEED homes
Step 5: Sell home	Post LEED for Homes certificate in building, inform listing real estate agent	Provide sales training and marketing assistance	Provide marketing materials

An integrated design approach is the most effective in integrating green measures into construction, since each change may introduce both expected and unexpected challenges. With an integrated design process, all project team members can examine the problems and solutions. Design charrettes are often used on large projects to bring together stakeholders with strong interests in the potential impacts of a given project.

Step 3: Build the Home

The LEED for Homes program provides project teams with guidance on both green design and green construction practices. Green homebuilding often requires that the trades learn new ways of doing things. Subcontractors who are new to green construction practices may need to be trained in different installation practices for certain measures. The builder is encouraged to work with consultants who specialize in training tradesworkers.

The Green Rater is expected to conduct on-site performance tests and visual inspections of the new home. These tests and inspections are essential to maintaining the rigor and integrity of the program. Typically, two on-site inspections are required for each project: one is conducted during construction of the home, usually just prior to drywall installation, and one is conducted upon completion of the home.

The Provider and Green Rater work with the construction team and trades to schedule and complete the inspections. During the construction process, the builder can contact the Green Rater if questions, problems, or changes arise. The Green Rater can rescore the project if major changes are made during construction.

Not all measures require an inspection by the Green Rater. Many measures in the LEED for Homes Rating System have a substantial design component (e.g., HVAC system sizing) or may be difficult to visually verify (e.g., species of plants). The professional who designed and installed such measures assumes responsibility for compliance with the requirements by signing an Accountability Form. The Accountability Form shifts the responsibility for verification from the Green Rater to the professional responsible for that specific LEED measure.

Credits that require an Accountability Form are noted on the project checklist with the " ➤ " symbol.

Step 4: Certify the Home

The certification process for the completed new home involves three components: visual verification, supporting documentation/calculation review, and performance testing. The Green Rater conducts a final inspection of the green measures on the project's LEED for Homes checklist, visually verifying that everything listed on the checklist is installed. Any calculations or supporting documentation from the project team will also be reviewed. The Green Rater will also conduct performance tests. A complete list of performance tests is presented in **Table 3**.

After conducting the site inspection, documentation/calculation review, and performance tests, the Green Rater sends the project documentation package to their LEED for Homes Provider. The package includes the following:

1. The completed and signed LEED for Homes checklist

2. The competed and signed Accountability Forms

3. The completed and signed Durability Evaluation Form and Durability Inspection checklist (see Innovation and Design topic area 2)

4. Any additional calculations and supporting documentation listed in the Verification and Submittal Guidelines.

The LEED for Homes Provider may ask the Green Rater, who in turn may ask the project team, for additional clarifying information or supporting documentation.

Once the Provider reviews the documentation package and affirms that it is complete, they submit it to USGBC for certification. USGBC notifies the Provider and builder upon final certification. USGBC mails the official notification and a LEED for Homes certificate to the builder.

Table 3. Performance Tests

Category	Measure	Tester	Prerequisite	Credit
Energy & Atmosphere	1.1 Meet performance of ENERGY STAR home	Green Rater	x	
	3 Envelope leakage	Green Rater	x	
	5 Duct leakage	Green Rater	x	
	6.1 Refrigerant charge test	HVAC	x	
Indoor Environmental Quality	4.3 Outdoor air flow test	Green Rater		x
	5.3 Local exhaust	Green Rater		x
	6.2 Supply air flow test	Green Rater		x

Step 5: Market and Sell the LEED Home

Builders may market their LEED-certified homes with support from USGBC, including PR toolkits, signage and collateral pieces that highlight the LEED achievement. Please contact USGBC for more information.

Consistency and Quality

The level of rigor and consistency of LEED for Homes ratings is ensured through four quality assurance processes.

1. **Third-party verification process.** The Green Rater inspects each LEED home and verifies each prerequisite and credit according to the guidance in the Verification and Submittals section of each credit in this Reference Guide. The Provider compiles the documentation and submits it to USGBC, who certifies the home as meeting the LEED for Homes standards.

2. **Training of Providers.** Each Provider organization is chosen because of its experience and expertise. All Providers undergo training by USGBC.

3. **Auditing of Green Raters by Providers.** The Provider is responsible for hiring, training, and overseeing the Green Raters. USGBC requires that each Provider have a quality assurance protocol for its Green Raters. This protocol must have the following minimums:

   1. 10% paper review (including project documentation files) of all LEED for Homes ratings for each Green Rater, conducted by a third party on an annual basis; and

   2. 1% field re-rating (including performance testing) of all LEED for Homes ratings for each Green Rater, conducted by a third party on an annual basis.

4. **Auditing of Providers by USGBC.** The Provider maintains records for each Green Rater, including training completed, LEED ratings completed, builder or homebuyer complaints, all project files, and results of quality assurance checking. USGBC spotchecks these records for each Green Rater on an annual basis.

The above quality assurance procedures are similar to those recently adopted by the Home Energy Rating System for energy raters. Additional information on the HERS Enhanced Rater Quality Assurance Procedures can be found in the "Adopted Enhancements to the Mortgage Industry National Home Energy Rating Standards," on the RESNET Web site, at http://www.resnet.us/standards/mortgage/default.htm.

IV. Supporting Verification Materials

Although some elements of a green home can be easily verified through simple observation, many of the specific LEED for Homes requirements are difficult to verify without additional information – product specifications, contractor calculations, etc. The term "supporting verification materials" refers to the additional information that Green Raters may need in order to fully verify that the home has met the criteria for LEED certification.

Supporting verification materials are not formal submittals, and no outside consultant should be needed to assist with the compilation of these materials. In some cases, these materials may not be required; in other cases, additional information may be requested, subject to the discretion of the verification team.

The supporting verification materials for each prerequisite and credit are described throughout this Reference Guide.

V. Home Size Adjustment

To compensate for the effect of home size on resource consumption, LEED adjusts the award thresholds (points for Certified, Silver, Gold, and Platinum) for home size. The adjustments are based on the material and energy impacts as described below. The LEED checklist automatically makes this adjustment when the home size and number of bedrooms are entered.

The effect of the adjustment on the award thresholds can also be determined by consulting **Tables 4 and 5** and **Equation 1**, as described below. For multifamily buildings, see "Multifamily Adjustment" below.

Rationale

All else equal, a large home consumes more materials and energy than a small home over its life cycle (including pre-construction, construction, use, and demolition or deconstruction). LEED compensates for these impacts by adjusting the threshold for each award level. Thresholds for smaller-than-average homes are lowered, and thresholds for larger-than-average homes are raised.

Data published by the U.S. Census Bureau in the American Housing Survey for 2005 show a strong correlation between number of bedrooms and number of occupants. Although a home may serve many different households over its lifespan, in general, a home with more bedrooms will serve more people. The adjustment is therefore based on the number of bedrooms.

The relationship between home size and certification points is based on estimated energy and materials impacts within the context of the LEED for Homes Rating System. Published data and informal studies of energy and materials usage in homes reveal two critical relationships:

❏ A 100% increase in home size yields an increase in annual energy usage of 15% to 50%, depending on the design, location, and occupants of the home.

❏ A 100% increase in home size yields an increase in materials usage of 40% to 90%, depending on the design and location of the home.

These figures were simplified and generalized to the assumption that as home size doubles, energy consumption increases by roughly one-quarter, and material consumption increases by roughly onehalf; combined, this amounts to an increase in impact of roughly one-third with each doubling in home size. Thus the point adjustment equates to one-third of the points available in the Materials & Resources and the Energy & Atmosphere categories combined for each doubling in home size.

Adjustment for Single-Family Homes

1. Calculate the area of the home in square feet. Follow the calculation method laid out in ANSI Standard Z765 but include all directly conditioned square footage, whether finished or not, that meets building code requirements for living space (e.g., head room, egress).

2. Determine the number of bedrooms in the home. A "bedroom," for purposes of this adjustment, is any room or space that could be used or is intended to be used for sleeping purposes and meets local fire and building code requirements. It is advantageous to

Table 4. Neutral Home Size

Bedrooms	≤1	2	3	4	5	6 or more
Neutral home size (ft²)	900	1,400	1,900	2,600	2,850	250 ft² more for each additional bedroom

Note: For homes with more than 5 bedrooms, "neutral home size" is defined as follows: 2850 + [250 ∗ (number of bedrooms − 5)].

Table 5. Threshold Adjustment (point range: −10 to +10)

Maximum home size (ft²) by number of bedrooms					Adjustment to award thresholds*
≤ 1 bedroom	2 bedrooms	3 bedrooms	4 bedrooms	5 bedrooms	
610	950	1290	1770	1940	−10
640	990	1340	1840	2010	−9
660	1030	1400	1910	2090	−8
680	1070	1450	1990	2180	−7
710	1110	1500	2060	2260	−6
740	1160	1570	2140	2350	−5
770	1200	1630	2230	2440	−4
800	1250	1690	2320	2540	−3
830	1300	1760	2400	2640	−2
860	1350	1830	2500	2740	−1
900	**1400**	**1900**	**2600**	**2850**	**0 ("neutral")**
940	1450	1970	2700	2960	+1
970	1510	2050	2810	3080	+2
1010	1570	2130	2920	3200	+3
1050	1630	2220	3030	3320	+4
1090	1700	2300	3150	3460	+5
1130	1760	2390	3280	3590	+6
1180	1830	2490	3400	3730	+7
1220	1910	2590	3540	3880	+8
1270	1980	2690	3680	4030	+9
1320	2060	2790	3820	4190	+10
For larger homes or homes with more bedrooms, see below.					

Example: An adjustment of −5 means that the threshold for a Certified LEED Home is 40 points (rather than 45 points for an average-sized home). Silver certification would require a minimum of 55 points rather than 60 points, Gold would require a minimum of 70, and Platinum, 85.

count as bedrooms all rooms that meet this definition. When in doubt, consider whether the room in question might be used as a bedroom if another member were added to the household (e.g., new baby, nanny, grandparent, exchange student); if the answer is yes, count the room as a bedroom.

3. If there are five bedrooms or fewer, find the size of the home in the appropriate column in **Table 5**. Read across the row to find the number of points to add or subtract. If the home is larger than the size shown in the bottom row of the applicable column, refer to **Table 4** to estimate the threshold adjustment, or to **Equation 1** to calculate the adjustment.

4. If there are six or more bedrooms, use

Table 4 or **Equation 1** to calculate the adjustment.

5. Add the adjustment to the number of points needed to earn the desired award level (Certified, Silver, Gold, or Platinum). A negative adjustment (for homes that are smaller than average) lowers the threshold for each award level (making it easier to achieve); positive adjustments raise the thresholds.

Definition

A **bedroom**, for purposes of this adjustment, is any room or space that could be used or is intended to be used for sleeping purposes and meets local fire and building code requirements.

Neutral home size — as used in **Equation 1**, should be determined from **Table 5**.

Equation 1. Threshold Adjustment Equation

Threshold adjustment = 18 * log (actual home size / neutral home size) / log (2)

Table 6. Threshold Adjustment (point range: −10 to +10)

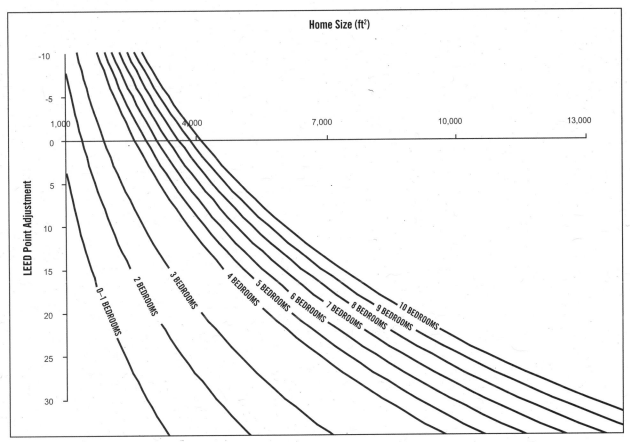

Adjustment for Multifamily Homes

The home size adjustment for multifamily buildings is slightly different. For each unit type (0, 1, 2, 3 bedrooms, etc.),

Weighted Average Home Size Adjustment for Building

= [Σ by unit type (Home Size Adjustment for Unit * Units of That Type in Project)

/ Total Units in Project]

where Home Size Adjustment for Unit = point adjustment from **Table 5** or **Figure 1** above, based on the average floor area for all units of that type

For example,

1-bedroom units

Units	10
Total floor area for 1BR units	8,250 SF
Average area / unit	825 SF
Home size adjustment (1 bedroom)	-2 points

2-bedroom units

Units	10
Total floor area for 2BR units	14,000 SF
Average area / unit	1,400 SF
Home size adjustment (2 bedrooms)	0 points

3-bedroom units

Units	30
Total floor area for 3BR units	51,000 SF
Average area / unit	1,700 SF
Home size adjustment (3 bedrooms)	-3 points

Overall home size adjustment

Weighted average home size adjustment

= [(1BR score * 1BR units) + (2BR score * 2BR units) + (3BR score * 3BR units)] / total units

= [(-2 * 10) + (0 * 10) + (-3 * 30)] / 50

= -2.2 (round to -2.0)

Thus, the LEED for Homes award thresholds for this multifamily building are 43 points for Certified, 58 points for Silver, 73 points for Gold, and 88 points for Platinum.

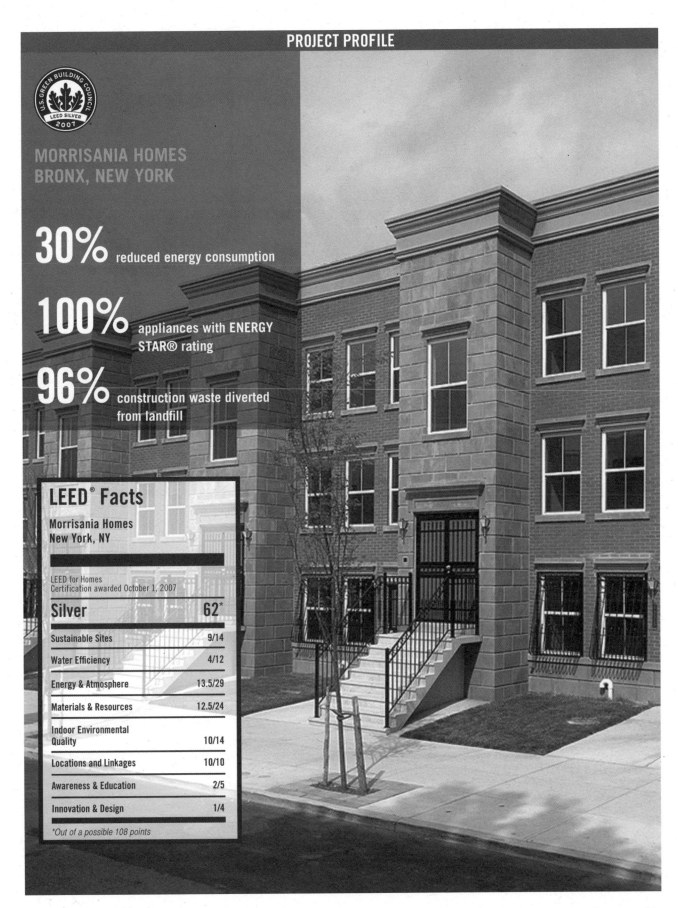

MORRISANIA HOMES
BRONX, NEW YORK

30% reduced energy consumption

100% appliances with ENERGY STAR® rating

96% construction waste diverted from landfill

LEED® Facts

Morrisania Homes
New York, NY

LEED for Homes
Certification awarded October 1, 2007

Silver	62*
Sustainable Sites	9/14
Water Efficiency	4/12
Energy & Atmosphere	13.5/29
Materials & Resources	12.5/24
Indoor Environmental Quality	10/14
Locations and Linkages	10/10
Awareness & Education	2/5
Innovation & Design	1/4

*Out of a possible 108 points

MORRISANIA HOMES IN BRONX, NEW YORK

Affordability Meets Sustainability

PROJECT BACKGROUND

Affordable homes can be green, as demonstrated by the Morrisania Homes development in the South Bronx, New York. This project is an innovative new living environment with a strong focus on protecting the health of its residents and of the surrounding environment. Morrisania Homes is the state of New York's first affordable-housing project to achieve LEED® for Homes certification. Funding for the project came from a partnership between state, city and private investors – a truly collaborative effort that shows how attention to detail can make a big difference in a home's livability and sustainability. Built by Blue Sea Development with the help of architecture and engineering research and consulting firm Steven Winter Associates, the 28-building, 78-unit mix of two- and three-family homes garners most of its greenness from its smart selection of building materials, fixtures and appliances.

DESIGNING FOR GREEN

Like Morrisania Homes, many affordable projects can earn credit in LEED for Homes simply by designing with simplicity, functionality, and accessibility in mind. Projects with smaller-than-average units in high-density developments generally use less material and have a smaller environmental footprint. Consequently, these types of projects can earn up to 16 points or deductions in the home size adjuster and the SS category.

Locating a home in an existing community with access to public transit or nearby stores, churches, and other community resources can earn a project up to 9 points in the LL category. This kind of development not only reduces environmental impacts, but also provides convenience to the occupants.

LOW-HANGING FRUIT

There are numerous credits in the Rating System that are attianable at little or no cost to the project. Many affordable projects will work with suppliers to identify products such as framing lumber, flooring, roofing, etc. that are harvested and processed locally. Purchasing local products reduces the impact of shipping and supports the local economy, and there is often little or no premium for them.

Designing a home with no fireplace and no attached garage will help to improve the indoor environmental quality, and can earn a project up to 5 points in the EQ category. Sealing off the ductwork during construction and flushing out the home after construction is completed can reduce the level of particulates in the home, improving the air quality inside and earning a project 2 points. These simple strategies are common in the affordable community – more than Ð of the affordable projects in the LEED for Homes Pilot Program earned all of these points.

AFFORDABLE LIVING

Many of the credits in LEED for Homes will not only save energy, water, and waste, but will also save the occupants money. Since one of the core missions of many affordable projects is to assist low-income families, it's no surprise that many of the biggest energy- and water-saving measures are commonly adopted.

All the Morrisania homes are stocked with 100 percent ENERGY STAR® rated appliances, as well as efficient boilers and lighting fixtures that will reduce the occupant energy bills. Each unit is also equipped with dual-flush toilets, 2-gallon-per-minute shower heads and 1.5-gallon-per-minute sink faucets to dramatically cut back on the homes' water use. These strategies are common among affordable projects, as developers recognize that the true long-term cost of home ownership does not end with a sticker price.

"This successful development proves that we can have it both ways – we can increase the number of affordable homes, which is essential for working New Yorkers to achieve economic security, and we can do so in a way that also protects the environment and increases energy efficiency."

New York Gov. Eliot Spitzer

Builder: Blue Sea Development Company
LEED for Homes Provider: Steven Winter Associates
Project Size: 107,792 square feet
Project Cost: $10,457,774

ABOUT LEED

The LEED® Green Building Rating System™ is the national benchmark for the design, construction, and operations of high-performance green buildings. Visit the U.S. Green Building Council's web site at www.usgbc.org to learn more about how you can make LEED work for you.

© 2007 U.S. Green Building Council.

Printed on 100% post consumer recycled, process chlorine-free paper with non-toxic soy inks.

www.usgbc.org
202 828-7422

LEED for Homes Checklist

Builder Name:	*Blue Sea Construction*
Project Team Leader (if different):	*Les BlueStone, Blue Sea Construction*
Home Address (Street/City/State):	*784 Jennings Place, New York, NY*

Project Description:

Building Type: *Multi-family*

\# of Units: *2*

Project type: *Affordable*

Avg. Home Size Adjustment: *9*

Adjusted Certification Thresholds

Certified: *36.5* Gold: *66.5*

Silver: *51.5* Platinum: *81.5*

Project Point Total: **56.5**	ID: *1*	SS: *10*	EA: *12*	EQ: *10*
Certification Level: **Silver**	LL: *10*	WE: *4*	MR: *8*	AE: *2*

Notes:
1. Detailed information on measures below are provided in the LEED for Homes Rating System
2. ✍ Indicates measures that must be documented using the Accountability Form

					Max Points Available	Project Points		
Innovation and Design Process (ID) (No Minimum Points Required)						Y / Pts	No	Maybe
1.	Integrated Project Planning		1.1	Preliminary Rating	Prerequisite	Y		
			1.2	Integrated Project Team	1	1		
			1.3	Professional Credentialed with Respect to LEED for Homes	1			
			1.4	Design Charrette	1			
			1.5	Building Orientation for Solar Design	1			
2.	Durability Management		2.1	Durability Planning	Prerequisite	Y		
	Process		2.2	Durability Management	Prerequisite	Y		
			2.3	Third-Party Durability Management Verification	3			
3.	Innovative or Regional	✍	3.1	Innovation #1	1			
	Design	✍	3.2	Innovation #2	1			
		✍	3.3	Innovation #3	1			
		✍	3.4	Innovation #4	1			
				Sub-Total for ID Category:	11	1		

					OR		Y / Pts	No	Maybe
Location and Linkages (LL) (No Minimum Points Required)									
1.	LEED ND		1	LEED for Neighborhood Development	LL2-6	10			
2.	Site Selection	✍	2	Site Selection		2	2		
3.	Preferred Locations		3.1	Edge Development		1			
			3.2	Infill	LL 3.1	2	2		
			3.3	Previously Developed		1	1		
4.	Infrastructure		4	Existing Infrastructure		1	1		
5.	Community Resources		5.1	Basic Community Resources / Transit		1			
			5.2	Extensive Community Resources / Transit	LL 5.1, 5.3	2			
			5.3	Outstanding Community Resources / Transit	LL 5.1, 5.2	3	3		
6.	Access to Open Space		6	Access to Open Space		1	1		
				Sub-Total for LL Category:		10	10		

					OR		Y / Pts	No	Maybe
Sustainable Sites (SS) (Minimum of 5 SS Points Required)									
1.	Site Stewardship		1.1	Erosion Controls During Construction		Prerequisite	Y		
			1.2	Minimize Disturbed Area of Site		1	1		
2.	Landscaping	✍	2.1	No Invasive Plants		Prerequisite	Y		
		✍	2.2	Basic Landscape Design	SS 2.5	2	2		
		✍	2.3	Limit Conventional Turf	SS 2.5	3			
		✍	2.4	Drought Tolerant Plants	SS 2.5	2			
		✍	2.5	Reduce Overall Irrigation Demand by at Least 20%		6			
3.	Local Heat Island Effects	✍	3	Reduce Local Heat Island Effects		1			
4.	Surface Water	✍	4.1	Permeable Lot		4	1		
	Management		4.2	Permanent Erosion Controls		1			
			4.3	Management of Run-off from Roof		2			
5.	Nontoxic Pest Control		5	Pest Control Alternatives		2	2		
6.	Compact Development		6.1	Moderate Density		2			
			6.2	High Density	SS 6.1, 6.3	3			
			6.3	Very High Density	SS 6.1, 6.2	4	4		
				Sub-Total for SS Category:		22	10		

				OR	Max Points Available	Project Points Y / Pts	No	Maybe
Water Efficiency (WE) (Minimum of 3 WE Points Required)								
1.	Water Reuse	1.1	Rainwater Harvesting System	WE 1.3	4			
		1.2	Graywater Reuse System	WE 1.3	1			
		1.3	Use of Municipal Recycled Water System		3			
2.	Irrigation System	2.1	High Efficiency Irrigation System	WE 2.3	3			
		2.2	Third Party Inspection	WE 2.3	1			
		2.3	Reduce Overall Irrigation Demand by at Least 45%		4			
3.	Indoor Water Use	3.1	High-Efficiency Fixtures and Fittings		3	2		
		3.2	Very High Efficiency Fixtures and Fittings		6	2		
				Sub-Total for WE Category:	15	4		
Energy and Atmosphere (EA) (Minimum of 0 EA Points Required)				OR		Y / Pts	No	Maybe
1.	Optimize Energy Performance	1.1	Performance of ENERGY STAR for Homes		Prerequisite	Y		
		1.2	Exceptional Energy Performance		34	0		
7.	Water Heating	7.1	Efficient Hot Water Distribution		2			
		7.2	Pipe Insulation		1			
11.	Residential Refrigerant Management	11.1	Refrigerant Charge Test		Prerequisite	Y		
		11.2	Appropriate HVAC Refrigerants		1			
				Sub-Total for EA Category:	38	11.5		
Materials and Resources (MR) (Minimum of 2 MR Points Required)				OR		Y / Pts	No	Maybe
1.	Material-Efficient Framing	1.1	Framing Order Waste Factor Limit		Prerequisite	Y		
		1.2	Detailed Framing Documents	MR 1.5	1			
		1.3	Detailed Cut List and Lumber Order	MR 1.5	1			
		1.4	Framing Efficiencies	MR 1.5	3	0.5		
		1.5	Off-site Fabrication		4			
2.	Environmentally Preferable Products	2.1	FSC Certified Tropical Wood		Prerequisite	Y		
		2.2	Environmentally Preferable Products		8	4.5		
3.	Waste Management	3.1	Construction Waste Management Planning		Prerequisite	Y		
		3.2	Construction Waste Reduction		3	3		
				Sub-Total for MR Category:	16	8		
Indoor Environmental Quality (EQ) (Minimum of 6 EQ Points Required)				OR		Y / Pts	No	Maybe
1.	ENERGY STAR with IAP	1	ENERGY STAR with Indoor Air Package		13			
2.	Combustion Venting	2.1	Basic Combustion Venting Measures	EQ 1	Prerequisite	Y		
		2.2	Enhanced Combustion Venting Measures	EQ 1	2	2		
3.	Moisture Control	3	Moisture Load Control	EQ 1	1			
4.	Outdoor Air Ventilation	4.1	Basic Outdoor Air Ventilation	EQ 1	Prerequisite	Y		
		4.2	Enhanced Outdoor Air Ventilation		2			
		4.3	Third-Party Performance Testing	EQ 1	1			
5.	Local Exhaust	5.1	Basic Local Exhaust	EQ 1	Prerequisite	Y		
		5.2	Enhanced Local Exhaust		1			
		5.3	Third-Party Performance Testing		1	1		
6.	Distribution of Space Heating and Cooling	6.1	Room-by-Room Load Calculations	EQ 1	Prerequisite	Y		
		6.2	Return Air Flow / Room by Room Controls	EQ 1	1			
		6.3	Third-Party Performance Test / Multiple Zones	EQ 1	2	2		
7.	Air Filtering	7.1	Good Filters	EQ 1	Prerequisite	Y		
		7.2	Better Filters		1			
		7.3	Best Filters	EQ 7.2	2			
8.	Contaminant Control	8.1	Indoor Contaminant Control during Construction	EQ 1	1	1		
		8.2	Indoor Contaminant Control		2			
		8.3	Preoccupancy Flush	EQ 1	11	1		
9.	Radon Protection	9.1	Radon-Resistant Construction in High-Risk Areas	EQ 1	Prerequisite	Y		
		9.2	Radon-Resistant Construction in Moderate-Risk Areas	EQ 1	1			
10.	Garage Pollutant Protection	10.1	No HVAC in Garage	EQ 1	Prerequisite	Y		
		10.2	Minimize Pollutants from Garage	EQ 1	2			
		10.3	Exhaust Fan in Garage	EQ 1	1			
		10.4	Detached Garage or No Garage	EQ 1, 10.2, 10.3	3	3		
				Sub-Total for EQ Category:	21	10		
Awareness and Education (AE) (Minimum of 0 AE Points Required)						Y / Pts	No	Maybe
1.	Education of the Homeowner or Tenant	1.1	Basic Operations Training		Prerequisite	Y		
		1.2	Enhanced Training		1	1		
		1.3	Public Awareness		1	1		
2.	Education of Building Manager	2	Education of Building Manager		1			
				Sub-Total for AE Category:	3	2		
				LEED for Homes Point Totals:	136	56.5		
				(Certification level)		Silver		

Project Checklist, Addendum A
Prescriptive Approach for Energy and Atmosphere (EA) Credits

Points cannot be earned in both the Prescriptive (below) and the Performance Approach (pg 2) of the EA section

Energy and Atmosphere (EA) (No Minimum Points Required)				OR	Max Points Available	Y / Pts	No	Maybe
2. Insulation		2.1	Basic Insulation		Prerequisite	Y		
		2.2	Enhanced Insulation		2			
3. Air Infiltration		3.1	Reduced Envelope Leakage		Prerequisite	Y		
		3.2	Greatly Reduced Envelope Leakage		2	2		
		3.3	Minimal Envelope Leakage	EA 3.2	3			
4. Windows		4.1	Good Windows		Prerequisite	Y		
		4.2	Enhanced Windows		2	2		
		4.3	Exceptional Windows	EA 4.2	3			
5. Heating and Cooling Distribution System		5.1	Reduced Distribution Losses		Prerequisite	Y		
		5.2	Greatly Reduced Distribution Losses		2			
		5.3	Minimal Distribution Losses	EA 5.2	3			
6. Space Heating and Cooling Equipment	✎	6.1	Good HVAC Design and Installation		Prerequisite	Y		
		6.2	High-Efficiency HVAC		2			
		6.3	Very High Efficiency HVAC	EA 6.2	4			
7. Water Heating	✎	7.1	Efficient Hot Water Distribution		2			
		7.2	Pipe Insulation		1			
		7.3	Efficient Domestic Hot Water Equipment		3	2		
8. Lighting		8.1	ENERGY STAR Lights		Prerequisite	Y		
		8.2	Improved Lighting		2			
		8.3	Advanced Lighting Package	EA 8.2	3	3		
9. Appliances		9.1	High-Efficiency Appliances		2	1.5		
		9.2	Water-Efficient Clothes Washer		1			
10. Renewable Energy	✎	10	Renewable Energy System		10			
11. Residential Refrigerant Management		11.1	Refrigerant Charge Test		Prerequisite	Y		
		11.2	Appropriate HVAC Refrigerants		1	1		
			Sub-Total for EA Category:		38	11.5		

By affixing my signature below, the undersigned does hereby declare and affirm to the USGBC that the LEED for Homes requirements, as specified in the LEED for Homes Rating System, have been met for the indicated credits and will, if audited, provide the necessary supporting documents.

Project Team Leader	*Les BlueStone*	Company	*Blue Sea Construction*
Signature		Date	

By affixing my signature below, the undersigned does hereby declare and affirm to the USGBC that the required inspections and performance testing for the LEED for Homes requirements, as specified in the LEED for Homes Rating System, have been completed, and will provide the project documentation file, if requested.

Rater's Name		Company	*Steven Winter Associates*
Signature		Date	

By affixing my signature below, the undersigned does hereby declare and affirm to the USGBC that the required inspections and performance testing for the LEED for Homes requirements, as specified in the LEED for Homes Rating System, have been completed, and will provide the project documentation file, if requested.

Provider's Name		Company	*Steven Winter Associates*
Signature		Date	

LEED SILVER 2006 · U.S. GREEN BUILDING COUNCIL

PLEASANT HILL HOME
FREEPORT, MAINE

45% more energy efficient

66% lower heating bills

Exceptional indoor air quality

LEED® Facts

Pleasant Hill Home
Freeport, ME

LEED for Homes
Certification awarded May 12, 2006

Silver	51*
Sustainable Sites	10.5/14
Water Efficiency	1/12
Indoor Environmental Quality	10/14
Materials & Resources	5.5/24
Location & Linkages	3/10
Energy & Atmosphere	15.5/29
Homeowner Awareness	1/1
Innovation & Design	4/4

*Out of a possible 108 points

PLEASANT HILL (PANISH RESIDENCE)

Building a Dream, While Building Green

REWARDING EXCELLENCE

LEED for Homes certification was a natural fit for Taggart Construction. LEED® is a comprehensive framework for the integrated design approach that is the key to high-performance building, and also offers the builder recognition and validation. As Peter Taggart explains, "Some of the most important details of green construction will never be seen. LEED certification recognizes the value in those choices and rewards you for making them." LEED certification gives both homebuilder and homeowner confidence that the home is built to the highest standards, will perform as expected, and is healthy for people and the environment.

PROGRAM FLEXIBILITY

Like many custom home projects, the Pleasant Hill Home was driven by the homeowners and reflected their values and priorities. The LEED for Homes Rating System was designed to give project teams the freedom to make design decisions that reflect the uniqueness of the homebuyer while still providing guidance on the best strategies for achieving the goals of the project.

The performance pathway in the EA category is an excellent example of this flexibility. Using a simulation model, project teams can work with a qualified energy rater to identify the best design strategies and construction elements to best suit the preferred style, layout, and climatic conditions of the home. The Pleasant Hill Home provides a good example of regionalized design[1]; the home is oriented along the east-west axis and incorporates roof overhangs into the design to maximize solar gains in the winter but limit exposure to the high summer sun. Low-E, argon-filled windows are installed throughout the house, and windows on the south side allow sunlight to enter the space in winter, storing radiant heat in the thick tile floor.

LOCATION, LOCATION, LOCATION

Many of the custom homes in the program have earned significant points in the Location & Linkages section by simply building on desirable, low-impact lots. A project can earn 8 to 10 points by building on an infill lot with existing infrastructure that is located near community resources or public transit.

SELL THE VIRTUES OF GREEN

Most green homebuyers will want to understand the environmental and human health benefits of their new LEED certified home. That's why most custom projects earn the Advanced Training credit, which rewards the project team for teaching the homebuyer about the various green features that are unique to their new home.

Some green measures are visible, and custom projects often incorporate these visibly green elements to give the homeowner a sense of pride and act as a constant reminder of their commitment. Photovoltaic and solar hot water systems, dual-flush toilets, high-efficiency lighting, rainwater capture systems, and native landscaping are just a few examples of strategies that rewarded in the Rating System. The Pleasant Hill Home includes a photovoltaic system that looks great, but also produces up to 3 megawatts worth of clean, renewable electricity.

Many of the virtues of a green home are invisible to the naked eye, but still very important to homebuyers. The Pleasant Hill Home earned the EPA's Indoor Air Package label, which helps the homeowners know that their home is not only beautiful and environmentally responsible, but also healthy.

> "Living in a LEED home is the best of both worlds. We're doing the right thing for the environment, and we still get to live in the home we've always wanted."
>
> Mort Panish
> Homeowner

Owner: Mort and Evelyn Panish
Architectural Designer: Curt Jensch, Taggart Construction
Mechanical Engineer: Pat Coon at Energy Works
Contractor: Peter Taggart
LEED for Homes Provider representative: Danuta Drozdwicz, Fore Solutions
Landscape Designer: Curt Jensch, Taggart Construction
Project size: 2,250 square feet
Project cost: $625,000

Photography courtesy of Peter W. Taggart

ABOUT LEED

The LEED® Green Building Rating System™ is the national benchmark for the design, construction, and operations of high-performance green buildings. Visit the U.S. Green Building Council's Web site at www.usgbc.org to learn more about how you can make LEED work for you.

© 2006, 2008 U.S. Green Building Council.

Printed on 100% post consumer recycled, process chlorine-free paper with non-toxic soy inks.

www.usgbc.org
202 828-7422

---

[1] The Pleasant Hill Home did use energy modeling to earn credits in the EA category. However, because this home was certified using a now-retired methodology, the Project Checklist on the following page shows the prescriptive EA measures that were earned.

LEED for Homes Checklist

Builder Name:	*Taggart Construction*
Project Team Leader (if different):	*Taggart Construction*
Home Address (Street/City/State):	*Freeport, ME*

Project Description:

Building Type: *Single, detached*

\# of Bedrooms: *3*

Project type: *Custom*

Floor Area: *2,250*

Adjusted Certification Thresholds

Certified: *49.5* Gold: *79.5*

Silver: *64.5* Platinum: *94.5*

Project Point Total:	**70**	ID:	**7**	SS:	**12.5**	EA:	**22**	EQ:	**13**
Certification Level:	***Silver***	LL:	**3**	WE:	**4**	MR:	**7.5**	AE:	**1**

Notes:
1. Detailed information on measures below are provided in the LEED for Homes Rating System
2. ✍ Indicates measures that must be documented using the Accountability Form

					Max Points Available	Project Points		

Innovation and Design Process (ID) (No Minimum Points Required)

					Max Points Available	Y / Pts	No	Maybe
1.	Integrated Project Planning		1.1	Preliminary Rating	Prerequisite	Y		
			1.2	Integrated Project Team	1			
			1.3	Professional Credentialed with Respect to LEED for Homes	1			
			1.4	Design Charrette	1			
			1.5	Building Orientation for Solar Design	1			
2.	Durability Management		2.1	Durability Planning	Prerequisite	Y		
	Process		2.2	Durability Management	Prerequisite	Y		
			2.3	Third-Party Durability Management Verification	3	3		
3.	Innovative or Regional	✍	3.1	Innovation #1	1	1		
	Design	✍	3.2	Innovation #2	1	1		
		✍	3.3	Innovation #3	1	1		
		✍	3.4	Innovation #4	1	1		
				Sub-Total for ID Category:	**11**	**7**		

Location and Linkages (LL) (No Minimum Points Required)

					OR	Max Points Available	Y / Pts	No	Maybe
1.	LEED ND		1	LEED for Neighborhood Development	LL2-6	10			
2.	Site Selection	✍	2	Site Selection		2	2		
3.	Preferred Locations		3.1	Edge Development		1			
			3.2	Infill	LL 3.1	2			
			3.3	Previously Developed		1			
4.	Infrastructure		4	Existing Infrastructure		1			
5.	Community Resources		5.1	Basic Community Resources / Transit		1			
			5.2	Extensive Community Resources / Transit	LL 5.1, 5.3	2			
			5.3	Outstanding Community Resources / Transit	LL 5.1, 5.2	3			
6.	Access to Open Space		6	Access to Open Space		1	1		
				Sub-Total for LL Category:		**10**	**3**		

Sustainable Sites (SS) (Minimum of 5 SS Points Required)

					OR	Max Points Available	Y / Pts	No	Maybe
1.	Site Stewardship		1.1	Erosion Controls During Construction		Prerequisite	Y		
			1.2	Minimize Disturbed Area of Site		1	1		
2.	Landscaping	✍	2.1	No Invasive Plants		Prerequisite	Y		
		✍	2.2	Basic Landscape Design	SS 2.5	2	2		
		✍	2.3	Limit Conventional Turf	SS 2.5	3	3		
		✍	2.4	Drought Tolerant Plants	SS 2.5	2	1		
		✍	2.5	Reduce Overall Irrigation Demand by at Least 20%		6			
3.	Local Heat Island Effects	✍	3	Reduce Local Heat Island Effects		1			
4.	Surface Water	✍	4.1	Permeable Lot		4	3		
	Management		4.2	Permanent Erosion Controls		1	1		
			4.3	Management of Run-off from Roof		2			
5.	Nontoxic Pest Control		5	Pest Control Alternatives		2	1.5		
6.	Compact Development		6.1	Moderate Density		2			
			6.2	High Density	SS 6.1, 6.3	3			
			6.3	Very High Density	SS 6.1, 6.2	4			
				Sub-Total for SS Category:		**22**	**12.5**		

				OR	Max Points Available	Project Points		

Water Efficiency (WE) (Minimum of 3 WE Points Required)				OR		Y / Pts	No	Maybe
1.	Water Reuse	1.1	Rainwater Harvesting System	WE 1.3	4			
		1.2	Graywater Reuse System	WE 1.3	1			
		1.3	Use of Municipal Recycled Water System		3			
2.	Irrigation System	2.1	High Efficiency Irrigation System	WE 2.3	3	3		
		2.2	Third Party Inspection	WE 2.3	1	1		
		2.3	Reduce Overall Irrigation Demand by at Least 45%		4			
3.	Indoor Water Use	3.1	High-Efficiency Fixtures and Fittings		3			
		3.2	Very High Efficiency Fixtures and Fittings		6			
			Sub-Total for WE Category:		**15**		**4**	

Energy and Atmosphere (EA) (Minimum of 0 EA Points Required)				OR		Y / Pts	No	Maybe
1.	Optimize Energy Performance	1.1	Performance of ENERGY STAR for Homes		Prerequisite	Y		
		1.2	Exceptional Energy Performance		34	0		
7.	Water Heating	7.1	Efficient Hot Water Distribution		2			
		7.2	Pipe Insulation		1			
11.	Residential Refrigerant Management	11.1	Refrigerant Charge Test		Prerequisite	Y		
		11.2	Appropriate HVAC Refrigerants		1			
			Sub-Total for EA Category:		**38**		**22**	

Materials and Resources (MR) (Minimum of 2 MR Points Required)				OR		Y / Pts	No	Maybe
1.	Material-Efficient Framing	1.1	Framing Order Waste Factor Limit		Prerequisite	Y		
		1.2	Detailed Framing Documents	MR 1.5	1			
		1.3	Detailed Cut List and Lumber Order	MR 1.5	1			
		1.4	Framing Efficiencies	MR 1.5	3	0.5		
		1.5	Off-site Fabrication		4			
2.	Environmentally Preferable Products	2.1	FSC Certified Tropical Wood		Prerequisite	Y		
		2.2	Environmentally Preferable Products		8	6		
3.	Waste Management	3.1	Construction Waste Management Planning		Prerequisite	Y		
		3.2	Construction Waste Reduction		3	1		
			Sub-Total for MR Category:		**16**		**7.5**	

Indoor Environmental Quality (EQ) (Minimum of 6 EQ Points Required)				OR		Y / Pts	No	Maybe
1.	ENERGY STAR with IAP	1	ENERGY STAR with Indoor Air Package		13	13		
2.	Combustion Venting	2.1	Basic Combustion Venting Measures	EQ 1	Prerequisite	Y		
		2.2	Enhanced Combustion Venting Measures	EQ 1	2			
3.	Moisture Control	3	Moisture Load Control	EQ 1	1			
4.	Outdoor Air Ventilation	4.1	Basic Outdoor Air Ventilation	EQ 1	Prerequisite	Y		
		4.2	Enhanced Outdoor Air Ventilation		2			
		4.3	Third-Party Performance Testing	EQ 1	1			
5.	Local Exhaust	5.1	Basic Local Exhaust	EQ 1	Prerequisite	Y		
		5.2	Enhanced Local Exhaust		1			
		5.3	Third-Party Performance Testing		1			
6.	Distribution of Space Heating and Cooling	6.1	Room-by-Room Load Calculations	EQ 1	Prerequisite	Y		
		6.2	Return Air Flow / Room by Room Controls	EQ 1	1			
		6.3	Third-Party Performance Test / Multiple Zones	EQ 1	2			
7.	Air Filtering	7.1	Good Filters	EQ 1	Prerequisite	Y		
		7.2	Better Filters		1			
		7.3	Best Filters	EQ 7.2	2			
8.	Contaminant Control	8.1	Indoor Contaminant Control during Construction	EQ 1	1			
		8.2	Indoor Contaminant Control		2			
		8.3	Preoccupancy Flush	EQ 1	11			
9.	Radon Protection	9.1	Radon-Resistant Construction in High-Risk Areas	EQ 1	Prerequisite	Y		
		9.2	Radon-Resistant Construction in Moderate-Risk Areas	EQ 1	1			
10.	Garage Pollutant Protection	10.1	No HVAC in Garage	EQ 1	Prerequisite	Y		
		10.2	Minimize Pollutants from Garage	EQ 1	2			
		10.3	Exhaust Fan in Garage	EQ 1	1			
		10.4	Detached Garage or No Garage	EQ 1, 10.2, 10.3	3			
			Sub-Total for EQ Category:		**21**		**13**	

Awareness and Education (AE) (Minimum of 0 AE Points Required)						Y / Pts	No	Maybe
1.	Education of the Homeowner or Tenant	1.1	Basic Operations Training		Prerequisite	Y		
		1.2	Enhanced Training		1	1		
		1.3	Public Awareness		1			
2.	Education of Building Manager	2	Education of Building Manager		1			
			Sub-Total for AE Category:		**3**		**1**	
			LEED for Homes Point Totals:		**136**		**70**	
			(Certification level)				**Silver**	

Project Checklist, Addendum A
Prescriptive Approach for Energy and Atmosphere (EA) Credits

Points cannot be earned in both the Prescriptive (below) and the Performance Approach (pg 2) of the EA section

					Max Points Available	Y / Pts	No	Maybe
Energy and Atmosphere (EA) (No Minimum Points Required)				OR				
2.	**Insulation**	2.1	Basic Insulation		Prerequisite	Y		
		2.2	Enhanced Insulation		2	2		
3.	**Air Infiltration**	3.1	Reduced Envelope Leakage		Prerequisite	Y		
		3.2	Greatly Reduced Envelope Leakage		2			
		3.3	Minimal Envelope Leakage	EA 3.2	3	3		
4.	**Windows**	4.1	Good Windows		Prerequisite	Y		
		4.2	Enhanced Windows		2			
		4.3	Exceptional Windows	EA 4.2	3			
5.	**Heating and Cooling Distribution System**	5.1	Reduced Distribution Losses		Prerequisite	Y		
		5.2	Greatly Reduced Distribution Losses		2	2		
		5.3	Minimal Distribution Losses	EA 5.2	3			
6.	**Space Heating and Cooling Equipment**	6.1	Good HVAC Design and Installation		Prerequisite	Y		
		6.2	High-Efficiency HVAC		2			
		6.3	Very High Efficiency HVAC	EA 6.2	4			
7.	**Water Heating**	7.1	Efficient Hot Water Distribution		2			
		7.2	Pipe Insulation		1			
		7.3	Efficient Domestic Hot Water Equipment		3	2		
8.	**Lighting**	8.1	ENERGY STAR Lights		Prerequisite	Y		
		8.2	Improved Lighting		2	1.5		
		8.3	Advanced Lighting Package	EA 8.2	3			
9.	**Appliances**	9.1	High-Efficiency Appliances		2	0.5		
		9.2	Water-Efficient Clothes Washer		1			
10.	**Renewable Energy**	10	Renewable Energy System		10	10		
11.	**Residential Refrigerant Management**	11.1	Refrigerant Charge Test		Prerequisite	Y		
		11.2	Appropriate HVAC Refrigerants		1	1		
			Sub-Total for EA Category:		38	22		

By affixing my signature below, the undersigned does hereby declare and affirm to the USGBC that the LEED for Homes requirements, as specified in the LEED for Homes Rating System, have been met for the indicated credits and will, if audited, provide the necessary supporting documents.

Project Team Leader		Company	*Taggart Construction*
Signature		Date	

By affixing my signature below, the undersigned does hereby declare and affirm to the USGBC that the required inspections and performance testing for the LEED for Homes requirements, as specified in the LEED for Homes Rating System, have been completed, and will provide the project documentation file, if requested.

Rater's Name		Company	*ForeSolutions*
Signature		Date	

By affixing my signature below, the undersigned does hereby declare and affirm to the USGBC that the required inspections and performance testing for the LEED for Homes requirements, as specified in the LEED for Homes Rating System, have been completed, and will provide the project documentation file, if requested.

Provider's Name		Company	*ForeSolutions*
Signature		Date	

CARSTEN CROSSINGS
OAKGROVE MODEL
ROCKLIN, CALIFORNIA

$1,400 yearly savings on utilities

75% minimum construction waste diverted from landfill, by weight

65% lower utility bills

LEED® Facts

Carsten Crossings Oakgrove Model
Rocklin, CA

LEED for Homes
Certification awarded January 18, 2007

Certified	36.5*
Sustainable Sites	4/14
Water Efficiency	2/12
Energy & Atmosphere	14.5/29
Materials & Resources	5/24
Indoor Environmental Quality	6/14
Locations and Linkages	4/10
Awareness & Education	1/1
Innovation & Design	0/4

*Out of a possible 108 points

CARSTEN CROSSINGS OAKGROVE MODEL IN ROCKLIN, CALIFORNIA

A Green Home Among Many

Carsten Crossings is first U.S. subdivision made up entirely of LEED homes

PROJECT BACKGROUND

Grupe's 144-home Carsten Crossings subdivision in Rocklin, California, is the country's first to be built with a commitment to certifying all of its homes under the LEED® for Homes Green Building Rating System. The subdivision includes several different models of varying size and shape, but the same commitment to environmental and health concerns.

Carsten Crossings grew out of Grupe's efforts to build a home that goes above and beyond what builders typically offer and to see just how successful such a home could be. The results spoke volumes: Carsten Crossings homes outsold the competition in the area at a rate of 2:1.

THE VALUE OF VERIFICATION

Grupe officials knew building a subdivision full of LEED homes would help them in their goal of building energy-efficient homes that are both affordable and marketable. What they didn't expect were the unforeseen benefits of third-party verification: Grupe experienced a major reduction in customer calls and complaints because the third-party reviewer was able to catch potential problems before buyers closed on the homes.

In addition to required duct leakage and envelope leakage tests, there are various optional credits in LEED for Homes that reward performance testing. Third-party performance testing of the ventilation intake, exhaust output, and room-by-room air supply can increase homeowner comfort, reduce call-backs, save energy, and earn a project up to 4 points in the EQ category. A project can also earn 3 points for the Third-Party Durability Management Verification credit, which can help a production builder like Grupe confirm that the important durability measures included in the home design were actually implemented in the field.

COMMUNITY FOCUS

There are a variety of credits in LEED for Homes that reward production builders for encouraging a community-based approach to development. By creating developments that are near or within existing communities, have access to public transit and open spaces and do not infringe on ecologically sensitive areas, production builders can have a positive impact on both the local and broader community. Carsten Crossings' proximity to open space, walking paths and parks adds to its appeal – not to mention the reduced fuel costs that come when you can walk to your recreation. This master-planned community has an onsite high school and plans for two onsite elementary schools, making it even easier for residents to minimize their car use.

TEAM EFFORT

Production builders can more easily transition to green building when they leverage the capabilities of their in-house experts. As the entire project team becomes trained in green building and integrated into the design process, many of the credits in LEED for Homes can be earned without significant cost. Up-front design changes that improve the efficiency of the framing, hot water distribution system, and landscape and irrigation design can earn a project several points, while significantly improving the energy- and water-efficiency of the home. These kinds of design changes can require a considerable investment of time and will, but once the process has been transformed, the long-term benefits to your customers and your business will far outweigh the initial cost of training and re-design.

During the pilot phase, production homes were consistently pursuing these strategies and typically earning 1 to 2 points in the ID category (see Integrated Project Planning), 10 to 12 points in the SS category (see Landscaping and Surface Water Management), 2 to 3 points in the WE category (see Irrigation System), 1 to 2 points in the EA category (see Water Heating), and 1 to 2 points in the MR category (see Material-Efficient Framing).

> "Thinking 'green' is good for the environment and good for the long-term appeal and livability of Carsten Crossings."
>
> Mark Fischer
> Grupe Senior Vice President of Operations

Energy Consultant: Davis Energy Group
Marketing: PowerLight Corporation
Lighting Review: University of California-Davis Lighting Technology Center
Project Size (One Home): 2,543 square feet
Site Costs: $128,500 per lot
Construction Costs: $70 per square foot

Photography Grupe Company

ABOUT LEED

The LEED® Green Building Rating System™ is the national benchmark for the design, construction, and operations of high-performance green buildings. Visit the U.S. Green Building Council's web site at www.usgbc.org to learn more about how you can make LEED work for you.

www.usgbc.org
202 828-7422

LEED for Homes Checklist

Builder Name:	*Grupe*
Project Team Leader (if different):	*Grupe*
Home Address (Street/City/State):	*Carsten Crossings, Rocklin, CA*

Project Description:

Building Type: *Single, detached*

# of Bedrooms: *4*

Project type: *Production*

Floor Area: *2,543*

Adjusted Certification Thresholds

Certified: *44.5*   Gold: *74.5*

Silver: *59.5*   Platinum: *89.5*

Project Point Total: **57**	ID: **0**	SS: **7**	EA: **25**	EQ: **11**
Certification Level: ***Certified***	LL: **4**	WE: **4**	MR: **6**	AE: **1**

Notes:
1. Detailed information on measures below are provided in the LEED for Homes Rating System
2. ✍ Indicates measures that must be documented using the Accountability Form

					Max Points Available	Y / Pts	No	Maybe
Innovation and Design Process (ID) (No Minimum Points Required)								
1.	Integrated Project Planning		1.1	Preliminary Rating	Prerequisite	Y		
			1.2	Integrated Project Team	1			
			1.3	Professional Credentialed with Respect to LEED for Homes	1			
			1.4	Design Charrette	1			
			1.5	Building Orientation for Solar Design	1			
2.	Durability Management		2.1	Durability Planning	Prerequisite	Y		
	Process		2.2	Durability Management	Prerequisite	Y		
			2.3	Third-Party Durability Management Verification	3			
3.	Innovative or Regional	✍	3.1	Innovation #1	1			
	Design	✍	3.2	Innovation #2	1			
		✍	3.3	Innovation #3	1			
		✍	3.4	Innovation #4	1			
				Sub-Total for ID Category:	**11**		**0**	

					OR	Max Points Available	Y / Pts	No	Maybe
Location and Linkages (LL) (No Minimum Points Required)									
1.	LEED ND		1	LEED for Neighborhood Development	LL2-6	10			
2.	Site Selection	✍	2	Site Selection		2	2		
3.	Preferred Locations		3.1	Edge Development		1			
			3.2	Infill	LL 3.1	2			
			3.3	Previously Developed		1			
4.	Infrastructure		4	Existing Infrastructure		1	1		
5.	Community Resources		5.1	Basic Community Resources / Transit		1			
			5.2	Extensive Community Resources / Transit	LL 5.1, 5.3	2			
			5.3	Outstanding Community Resources / Transit	LL 5.1, 5.2	3			
6.	Access to Open Space		6	Access to Open Space		1	1		
				Sub-Total for LL Category:		**10**		**4**	

					OR	Max Points Available	Y / Pts	No	Maybe
Sustainable Sites (SS) (Minimum of 5 SS Points Required)									
1.	Site Stewardship		1.1	Erosion Controls During Construction		Prerequisite	Y		
			1.2	Minimize Disturbed Area of Site		1	1		
2.	Landscaping	✍	2.1	No Invasive Plants		Prerequisite	Y		
		✍	2.2	Basic Landscape Design	SS 2.5	2	2		
		✍	2.3	Limit Conventional Turf	SS 2.5	3			
		✍	2.4	Drought Tolerant Plants	SS 2.5	2			
		✍	2.5	Reduce Overall Irrigation Demand by at Least 20%		6			
3.	Local Heat Island Effects	✍	3	Reduce Local Heat Island Effects		1	1		
4.	Surface Water	✍	4.1	Permeable Lot		4	1		
	Management		4.2	Permanent Erosion Controls		1	1		
			4.3	Management of Run-off from Roof		2	1		
5.	Nontoxic Pest Control		5	Pest Control Alternatives		2			
6.	Compact Development		6.1	Moderate Density		2			
			6.2	High Density	SS 6,1, 6.3	3			
			6.3	Very High Density	SS 6.1, 6.2	4			
				Sub-Total for SS Category:		**22**		**7**	

					Max Points Available	Project Points Y/Pts	No	Maybe

Water Efficiency (WE) (Minimum of 3 WE Points Required)

				OR	Max Points Available	Y / Pts	No	Maybe
1.	Water Reuse	1.1	Rainwater Harvesting System	WE 1.3	4			
		1.2	Graywater Reuse System	WE 1.3	1			
	✍	1.3	Use of Municipal Recycled Water System		3			
2.	Irrigation System	✍ 2.1	High Efficiency Irrigation System	WE 2.3	3	3		
		2.2	Third Party Inspection	WE 2.3	1	1		
	✍	2.3	Reduce Overall Irrigation Demand by at Least 45%		4			
3.	Indoor Water Use	3.1	High-Efficiency Fixtures and Fittings		3			
		3.2	Very High Efficiency Fixtures and Fittings		6			
				Sub-Total for WE Category:	15	4		

Energy and Atmosphere (EA) (Minimum of 0 EA Points Required)

				OR	Max Points Available	Y / Pts	No	Maybe
1.	Optimize Energy Performance	1.1	Performance of ENERGY STAR for Homes		Prerequisite	Y		
		1.2	Exceptional Energy Performance		34	0		
7.	Water Heating	✍ 7.1	Efficient Hot Water Distribution		2			
		7.2	Pipe Insulation		1			
11.	Residential Refrigerant Management	11.1	Refrigerant Charge Test		Prerequisite	Y		
		11.2	Appropriate HVAC Refrigerants		1			
				Sub-Total for EA Category:	38	24.5		

Materials and Resources (MR) (Minimum of 2 MR Points Required)

				OR	Max Points Available	Y / Pts	No	Maybe
1.	Material-Efficient Framing	1.1	Framing Order Waste Factor Limit		Prerequisite	Y		
		1.2	Detailed Framing Documents	MR 1.5	1			
		1.3	Detailed Cut List and Lumber Order	MR 1.5	1			
		1.4	Framing Efficiencies	MR 1.5	3			
		1.5	Off-site Fabrication		4			
2.	Environmentally Preferable Products	✍ 2.1	FSC Certified Tropical Wood		Prerequisite	Y		
		✍ 2.2	Environmentally Preferable Products		8	3		
3.	Waste Management	3.1	Construction Waste Management Planning		Prerequisite	Y		
		3.2	Construction Waste Reduction		3	2.5		
				Sub-Total for MR Category:	16	5.5		

Indoor Environmental Quality (EQ) (Minimum of 6 EQ Points Required)

				OR	Max Points Available	Y / Pts	No	Maybe
1.	ENERGY STAR with IAP	1	ENERGY STAR with Indoor Air Package		13			
2.	Combustion Venting	2.1	Basic Combustion Venting Measures	EQ 1	Prerequisite	Y		
		2.2	Enhanced Combustion Venting Measures	EQ 1	2	1		
3.	Moisture Control	3	Moisture Load Control	EQ 1	1	1		
4.	Outdoor Air Ventilation	✍ 4.1	Basic Outdoor Air Ventilation	EQ 1	Prerequisite	Y		
		4.2	Enhanced Outdoor Air Ventilation		2	2		
		4.3	Third-Party Performance Testing	EQ 1	1	1		
5.	Local Exhaust	✍ 5.1	Basic Local Exhaust	EQ 1	Prerequisite	Y		
		5.2	Enhanced Local Exhaust		1			
		5.3	Third-Party Performance Testing		1			
6.	Distribution of Space Heating and Cooling	✍ 6.1	Room-by-Room Load Calculations	EQ 1	Prerequisite	Y		
		6.2	Return Air Flow / Room by Room Controls	EQ 1	1	1		
		6.3	Third-Party Performance Test / Multiple Zones	EQ 1	2	2		
7.	Air Filtering	7.1	Good Filters	EQ 1	Prerequisite	Y		
		7.2	Better Filters		1			
		7.3	Best Filters	EQ 7.2	2			
8.	Contaminant Control	✍ 8.1	Indoor Contaminant Control during Construction	EQ 1	1	1		
		8.2	Indoor Contaminant Control		2			
		✍ 8.3	Preoccupancy Flush	EQ 1	11			
9.	Radon Protection	✍ 9.1	Radon-Resistant Construction in High-Risk Areas	EQ 1	Prerequisite	Y		
		✍ 9.2	Radon-Resistant Construction in Moderate-Risk Areas	EQ 1	1			
10.	Garage Pollutant Protection	10.1	No HVAC in Garage	EQ 1	Prerequisite	Y		
		10.2	Minimize Pollutants from Garage	EQ 1	2	2		
		10.3	Exhaust Fan in Garage	EQ 1	1			
		10.4	Detached Garage or No Garage	EQ 1, 10.2, 10.3	3			
				Sub-Total for EQ Category:	21	11		

Awareness and Education (AE) (Minimum of 0 AE Points Required)

					Max Points Available	Y / Pts	No	Maybe
1.	Education of the Homeowner or Tenant	✍ 1.1	Basic Operations Training		Prerequisite	Y		
		✍ 1.2	Enhanced Training		1	1		
		✍ 1.3	Public Awareness		1			
2.	Education of Building Manager	✍ 2	Education of Building Manager		1			
				Sub-Total for AE Category:	3	1		
				LEED for Homes Point Totals:	136	57		
				(Certification level)		Certified		

Project Checklist, Addendum A
Prescriptive Approach for Energy and Atmosphere (EA) Credits

Points cannot be earned in both the Prescriptive (below) and the Performance Approach (pg 2) of the EA section

				OR	Max Points Available	Y / Pts	No	Maybe
Energy and Atmosphere (EA) (No Minimum Points Required)								
2.	**Insulation**	2.1	Basic Insulation		Prerequisite,	Y		
		2.2	Enhanced Insulation		2	2		
3.	**Air Infiltration**	3.1	Reduced Envelope Leakage		Prerequisite	Y		
		3.2	Greatly Reduced Envelope Leakage		2	2		
		3.3	Minimal Envelope Leakage	EA 3.2	3			
4.	**Windows**	4.1	Good Windows		Prerequisite	Y		
		4.2	Enhanced Windows		2	2		
		4.3	Exceptional Windows	EA 4.2	3			
5.	**Heating and Cooling**	5.1	Reduced Distribution Losses		Prerequisite	Y		
	Distribution System	5.2	Greatly Reduced Distribution Losses		2			
		5.3	Minimal Distribution Losses	EA 5.2	3			
6.	**Space Heating and Cooling**	6.1	Good HVAC Design and Installation		Prerequisite	Y		
	Equipment	6.2	High-Efficiency HVAC		2			
		6.3	Very High Efficiency HVAC	EA 6.2	4	3		
7.	**Water Heating**	7.1	Efficient Hot Water Distribution		2	2		
		7.2	Pipe Insulation		1			
		7.3	Efficient Domestic Hot Water Equipment		3			
8.	**Lighting**	8.1	ENERGY STAR Lights		Prerequisite	Y		
		8.2	Improved Lighting		2			
		8.3	Advanced Lighting Package	EA 8.2	3	3		
9.	**Appliances**	9.1	High-Efficiency Appliances		2	0.5		
		9.2	Water-Efficient Clothes Washer		1			
10.	**Renewable Energy**	10	Renewable Energy System		10	10		
11.	**Residential Refrigerant**	11.1	Refrigerant Charge Test		Prerequisite	Y		
	Management	11.2	Appropriate HVAC Refrigerants		1			
			Sub-Total for EA Category:		**38**	**24.5**		

By affixing my signature below, the undersigned does hereby declare and affirm to the USGBC that the LEED for Homes requirements, as specified in the LEED for Homes Rating System, have been met for the indicated credits and will, if audited, provide the necessary supporting documents.

Project Team Leader		Company	*Grupe*
Signature		Date	

By affixing my signature below, the undersigned does hereby declare and affirm to the USGBC that the required inspections and performance testing for the LEED for Homes requirements, as specified in the LEED for Homes Rating System, have been completed, and will provide the project documentation file, if requested.

Rater's Name		Company	*Davis Energy Group*
Signature		Date	

By affixing my signature below, the undersigned does hereby declare and affirm to the USGBC that the required inspections and performance testing for the LEED for Homes requirements, as specified in the LEED for Homes Rating System, have been completed, and will provide the project documentation file, if requested.

Provider's Name		Company	*Davis Energy Group*
Signature		Date	

Innovation in Design Process

Overview

Sustainable design strategies and measures are constantly evolving and improving. New technologies are continually introduced to the marketplace, and up-to-date scientific research influences building design strategies. Occasionally, a strategy results in building performance that greatly exceeds that required in an existing LEED credit. Other strategies may not be addressed by any LEED prerequisite or credit but warrant consideration for their sustainability benefits.

Green homebuilding strategies and techniques are most effectively implemented as part of an integrated design process, with input from individuals involved in each phase of the project. Good design can keep costs down and ensure proper integration of green techniques and achievement of project goals.

One aspect of home design that is often overlooked is the assessment and mitigation of long-term durability risks to the home. Durability failures are a significant cost and cause of stress for both builders and homeowners, but many easy and low-cost strategies are often overlooked because builders do not consider durability in the up-front design.

The Innovation in Design Process (ID) credit category encourages project planning and design to improve the coordination and integration of the various elements in a green home. This category also creates an opportunity for projects to earn credit for implementing strategies or measures not addressed in the current LEED for Homes Rating System. Credits can be earned for innovative designs, exemplary performance, or regional best practices that can be shown to produce quantifiable environmental and human health benefits.

The three Innovation in Design Process topic areas in the LEED for Homes Rating System—Integrated Project Planning, Durability Management Process and Innovative or Regional Design—are summarized in **Table 1** and described in the following sections.

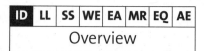
Table 1. Overview of Innovation in Design (ID) Process Category

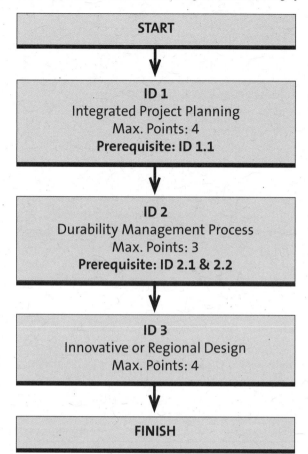

ID 1: Integrated Project Planning

Intent

Maximize opportunities for integrated, cost-effective adoption of green design and construction strategies.

Requirements

Prerequisite

1.1 **Preliminary Rating.** As early as practical, conduct a preliminary LEED for Homes meeting, with the participation of the Provider and key members of the project team. As part of the meeting, create an action plan that identifies the following:

❑ The targeted LEED award level (Certified, Silver, Gold, or Platinum).

❑ The LEED for Homes credits that have been selected to meet the targeted award level.

❑ The party accountable for meeting the LEED for Homes requirements for each selected credit.

Credits

1.2 **Integrated Project Team** (1 point). Assemble and involve a project team to meet the three criteria below:

a) Include team members, in addition to the builder and Verification Team, whose capabilities include at least three of the following skill sets:

❑ architecture or residential building design;

❑ mechanical or energy engineering;

❑ building science or performance testing;

❑ green building or sustainable design; and

❑ civil engineering, landscape architecture, habitat restoration, or land-use planning.

b) Actively involve all team members referenced above in at least three of the following phases of the home design and construction process:

❑ conceptual or schematic design;

❑ LEED planning;

❑ preliminary design;

❑ energy and envelope systems analysis or design;

❑ design development;

❑ final design, working drawings or specifications; and

❑ construction.

c) Conduct meetings with the project team at least monthly to review project status, introduce new team members to project goals, discuss problems encountered, formulate solutions, review responsibilities and identify next steps.

1.3 **Professional Credentialed with Respect to LEED for Homes** (1 point). At least one principal member of the project team shall be a professional who is credentialed with respect to LEED for Homes as determined by the U.S. Green Building Council.

1.4 **Design Charrette** (1 point). No later than the design development phase and preferably during schematic design, conduct at least one full-day integrated design workshop with the project team defined in ID 1.2. Use the workshop to integrate green strategies across all aspects of the building design, drawing on the expertise of all participants.

1.5 **Building Orientation for Solar Design** (1 point). Design the home such that all of the following requirements are met:

a) The glazing area on the north- and south-facing walls of the building is at least 50% greater than the sum of the glazing area on the east- and west-facing walls.

b) The east-west axis of the building is within 15 degrees of due east-west.

c) The roof has a minimum of 450 square feet of south-facing area that is oriented appropriately for solar applications.

d) At least 90% of the glazing on the south-facing wall is completely shaded (using shading, overhangs, etc.) at noon on June 21 and unshaded at noon on December 21.

Synergies and Trade-Offs

This credit is intended to promote an integrated, system-oriented approach to green project design and development. The selected green home-building strategies and technologies in the Rating System should each be fully integrated into a home's design.

ID 1.1: Preliminary Rating

ID 1.2: Integrated Project Team

ID 1.3: LEED Accredited Professional

ID 1.4: Design Charrette

Green building experts commonly agree that the most cost-effective and successful green projects result from early and frequent interactions among all key team members. Incorporating green measures through a comprehensive, holistic design can yield synergies and improve the overall performance of the home. Even conventional designs can significantly benefit from integrated project planning that coordinates the different stages and elements of construction (e.g., framing, HVAC, insulation, plumbing, electrical).

These credits are intended to promote an integrated, systems-oriented approach to green project design and development.

Approach and Implementation

Initiate integrated project planning and integrated design as early as possible. Use an iterative process that refines the design as the scope and details of the project evolve.

During the preliminary rating, set specific goals for the project, including the certification level being sought. Work with the project team to identify individual measures within the rating system that are definitely or possibly achievable. Once a certification goal has been established, aim to earn roughly five points more than necessary so that the goal can still be met if the project fails to achieve certain measures or performance thresholds.

The integrated project team may include members with expertise outside the list provided in ID 1.2(a). For example, projects with a photovoltaic system will require a PV installation contractor. No member of the verification team may be counted as a member of the integrated project team for ID 1.2. An individual working for the Provider organization can be counted as a member of the integrated project team only if he or she has been hired separately to provide consulting services on the project and is not serving as a member of the verification team. With approval of the Provider and Verification Team, a project team may undergo multiple half-day charrettes if the entire project team is involved and the focus of the charrettes is to optimize integration of the various aspects (e.g., framing, HVAC, insulation, plumbing) of the project.

ID 1.3 can be awarded for participation of someone with the LEED AP Homes credential on the following conditions:

1) The person with the credential must be a principal member of the project team, and not a member of the verification team (e.g., not the Green Rater for the project).

2) The person with the credential must play an ongoing role on the project team, including participation in meetings, etc.

3) The credential must be earned prior to the project's preliminary rating. There are currently no credentials or levels of experience that are considered equivalent to LEED AP Homes.

Calculations

No calculations are required.

Exemplary Performance

No additional points are available for exemplary performance.

Verification and Submittals

Supporting Verification Materials, made available by the Project Team

ID 1.2: Integrated Project Team

❑ Present a list of project team members to the Verification Team.

❑ Present a list of meeting dates or plans for regularly scheduled meetings to the Verification Team.

ID 1.3: Professional Credentialed with Respect to LEED for Homes

❑ Identify the Professional Credentialed with Respect to LEED for Homes to the Verification Team.

ID 1.4: Design Charrette

❑ Present information about the charrette (dates, participants, etc.) to the Verification Team.

Verification Team

ID 1.1: Preliminary Rating

❑ Participate in the preliminary LEED for Homes rating, or verify participation by the LEED for Homes Provider.

ID 1.2: Integrated Project Team

❑ Visually verify the list of project team members and meeting dates.

ID 1.3: Professional Credentialed with Respect to LEED for Homes

❑ Verify participation of a Professional Credentialed with Respect to LEED for Homes on the project team.

ID 1.4: Design Charrette

❑ Visually verify the list of project team members and meeting dates.

Considerations

Economic Issues

Improved up-front design can often yield significant environmental benefits at a much lower cost than a high-technology alternative. Examples are provided in various credits throughout the Rating System and include measures like advanced framing techniques, compact plumbing design, low-maintenance landscaping, passive solar design, and proper building orientation.

Designing and constructing a home using an integrated approach can also reduce the frequency and significance of errors in design. It is not uncommon for the various trades to act independently, leading to ad hoc on-site fixes that are inefficient and sometimes ineffective. Integrated project planning improves coordination, leading to reduced construction costs and fewer problems that lead to call-backs.

ID 1.1 and ID 1.4 correspond to the Green Development Plan, which is a mandatory measure in the Enterprise Community Partners' Green Communities Initiative. Affordable housing projects that participate in LEED for Homes and also complete the mandatory components of the Green Communities Initiative may be eligible for financial and technical assistance from the Enterprise Foundation. Contact Enterprise Community Partners for further information at www.enterprise.org.

Resources

Web Sites

U.S. Department of Energy, Integrated Building Design for Energy Efficiency

www.eere.energy.gov/buildings/info/design/integratedbuilding

This Web site is part of the department's Energy Efficiency and Renewable Energy "Building Toolbox." The site outlines principles of integrated energy design and includes resources on the design, modeling, and construction of energy-efficient homes.

Whole Building Design Guide

www.wbdg.org/wbdg_approach.php

This Web site describes the core elements of "whole building design," which includes the combination of an integrated design approach and an integrated team process. This site helps users identify design objectives and organize their processes to meet those objectives.

ID 1.5: Building Orientation for Solar Design

Successful solar home design begins with the building orientation and layout. Proper roof orientation enables photovoltaic and solar hot water systems to function optimally. Proper window orientation, together with shading designs, can help reduce cooling loads in the summer and heating loads in the winter.

Builders and designers are encouraged to adopt other passive solar techniques to reduce energy use and improve occupants' comfort. Homes with passive solar design elements can earn additional points by incorporating these designs into the energy simulation model under Energy & Atmosphere 1.2.

Approach and Implementation

The location on the site and orientation of the home should be chosen during the earliest phases of the project because they affect all other aspects of design and construction. In large developments, take building orientation into consideration when laying out the streets.

Where possible and appropriate for the climate, plant deciduous trees around the home to provide valuable shading in the summer but allow sunlight through in winter. Shading can be provided by vegetation, exterior shading devices (overhangs and awnings), and integral window-shading devices. Temporary shading, such as indoor blinds and shades, are not acceptable for this credit.

Projects planning to adopt additional passive solar design elements should use the performance pathway in the Energy & Atmosphere category. Since the optimal passive solar techniques vary based on the location, climate, and specific design of a home, project teams are encouraged to involve a solar design expert and use en-ergy models to identify the best practices. Modeling the energy use in a home provides critical feedback on the effectiveness of different passive solar strategies.

Calculations

Four calculations are required for this credit.

1. Calculate the ratio of glazing area on the north- and south-facing walls to the glazing area on the east- and west-facing walls.

2. Calculate the precise orientation of the home. Using a compass, detailed map, GIS calculations, or an alternative method, demonstrate that the east-west axis of the building is within 15 degrees of due east-west.

3. Calculate the area of the roof that is south facing. Flat roof area can be included.

4. Provide simulation data or calculations to demonstrate that at least 90% of all south-facing glazing area is unshaded at noon on December 21 and completely shaded at noon on June 21. Information about tools for conducting this calculation can be found under "Resources," below. Visual inspection by the Verification Team at the designated times are an acceptable substitute for calculations.

Exemplary Performance

No additional points are available for exemplary performance.

Verification and Submittals

Supporting Verification Materials, made available by the Project Team

❑ Present any calculations or simulation results to the Verification Team.

Verification Team

- ❑ Visually verify that calculations or simulations were performed to meet the credit requirements.
- ❑ Visually verify any relevant design elements (e.g., trees, overhangs, awnings).

Considerations

Economic Issues

Proper building orientation and window-shading design can help reduce cooling costs in summer and heating costs in winter. Building orientation also facilitates active solar design (i.e., photovoltaic systems) and advanced passive solar design, which can further reduce space heating and cooling and lighting costs.

Once a home has been constructed, the orientation of the walls, windows, and overhangs cannot be changed. Designing the home with the proper orientation will significantly reduce the cost and increase the efficacy of incorporating new solar technologies and strategies in the future.

Regional Variances

Use of this credit depends on the location and climate of the home. Any additional passive solar strategies should be developed with consideration for the local climate and seasonal variations.

Resources

Web Sites

U.S. Department of Energy, Building Technologies Program

www.eere.energy.gov/buildings/info/design/integratedbuilding/passive.html

A part of the department's "Building Toolbox," this site includes tips and techniques for passive solar heating, passive solar cooling, thermal storage, and daylighting.

Building Energy Software Tools Directory

www.eere.energy.gov/buildings/tools_directory

This site includes information on numerous building software tools for evaluating energy performance in buildings. To find tools for passive solar design, choose "Tools by Subject" and select "Solar / Climate Analysis."

Sustainable by Design, Overhang Design Tool

www.susdesign.com/overhang/index.php

This site includes a tool that calculates the effect of shading devices based on the design of the window, the design of the overhang, the window orientation, and the time of day.

Florida Solar Energy Center

www.fsec.ucf.edu/en/consumer/buildings/homes/windows/shading.htm

This site provides information on window orientation and shading, including various shading strategies.

Print Media

High-Performance Home Technologies: Solar Thermal and Photovoltaic Systems. Prepared by Pacific Northwest National Laboratory and Oak Ridge National Laboratory for the US Department of Energy. Report # NREL/TP-550-41085. June 4, 2007. Available at www.eere.energy.gov/buildings/building_america

Passive Solar Design for the Home, U.S. Department of Energy Office of Energy Efficiency and Renewable Energy. Report # DOE/GO-102001-1105. February, 2001. Available from the U.S. Office of Scientific and Technical Information (www.osti.gov), or on-line at www.nrel.gov/docs/fy01osti/27954.pdf.

ID	LL	SS	WE	EA	MR	EQ	AE
			1.5				

ID 2: Durability Management Process

Intent

Promote durability and high performance of the building enclosure and its components and systems through appropriate design, materials selection, and construction practices.

Requirements

Note: USGBC and its representatives are responsible only for verifying the completion of LEED for Homes requirements; such verification in no way constitutes a warranty as to the appropriateness of the selected durability measures or the quality of implementation (see Disclaimer, page 2).

Prerequisites

2.1 **Durability Planning.** Prior to construction, the project team shall do the following:

   a) Complete the Durability Risk Evaluation Form to identify all moderate and high-risk durability issues for the building enclosure.

   b) Develop specific measures to respond to those issues.

   c) Identify and incorporate all the applicable indoor moisture control measures listed in **Table 1**.

   d) Incorporate the measures from 2.1(b) and (c), above, into project documents (drawings, specifications, and/or scopes of work, as appropriate).

   e) List all the durability measures and indicate their locations in the project documents in a durability inspection checklist. Include the checklist in project documents for use in verification.

2.2 **Durability Management.** During construction, the builder shall have a quality management process in place to ensure installation of the durability measures. This prerequisite can be satisfied by having the builder inspect and check off each measure in the durability inspection checklist created for 2.1(e), above.

Table 1. Indoor Moisture Control Measures

Location or equipment	Required moisture control measure
Tub, showers, and spa areas	Use nonpaper-faced backer board on walls.
Kitchen, bathroom, laundry rooms, and spa areas	Use water-resistant flooring; do not install carpet.
Entryway (within 3 feet of exterior door)	Use water-resistant flooring; do not install carpet.
Tank water heater in or over living space	Install drain and drain pan.
Clothes washer in or over living space	Install drain and drain pan, or install accessible single-throw supply valve.
Conventional clothes dryer	Exhaust directly to outdoors.
Condensing clothes dryer	Install drain and drain pan.

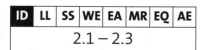
Credits

2.3 **Third-Party Durability Management Verification** (3 points). Have the Verification Team inspect and verify each measure listed in the durability inspection checklist created for 2.1(e), above.

Synergies and Trade-Offs

Many of the credits in the LEED for Homes Rating System can serve as durability strategies and may be used in the creation of a durability inspection checklist. If this is done, the home can still receive LEED points for those credits.

ID 2.1: Durability Planning

ID 2.2: Durability Management

ID 2.3: Third-Party Durability Management Verification

All homes eventually suffer problems or failures because of moisture (indoor or outdoor, too much or too little), pests, and/or storm damage. Builders who evaluate and address durability risks during the design process are more likely to produce a home with fewer failures, and any failures that do occur will be less damaging and less expensive for the occupant to fix.

This credit emphasizes four basic elements of designing for durability:

1. Evaluate the durability risks for a specific home in a specific site.

2. Incorporate strategies into the home design to counteract the greatest long-term durability risks.

3. Manage construction of the home to ensure that design strategies for durability are actually implemented during construction.

4. Have a third party inspect the home to verify that design strategies for durability have been implemented during construction.

Those guidelines do not guarantee a high-quality home, nor do they guarantee that failures or call-backs will not occur. However, they do offer a methodology for addressing durability concerns.

This section is designed to inspire builders to examine project-specific durability concerns and seek site-appropriate solutions to mitigate the highest durability risks.

Approach and Implementation

Durability management is designed to ensure that the design decisions related to durability are implemented properly during construction. For this reason, durability management processes should go hand-in-hand with on-site training of trades and crew members.

Complete each of the measures in this credit as early in the process as possible. If a design charrette (ID 1.3) is held, address durability evaluation, planning, and management with the team.

Complete and submit a Durability Evaluation Form. Seek assistance from consultants as necessary. Rank each durability risk as low, medium or high. The principal durability risks are the following:

❑ exterior water;

❑ interior moisture loads;

❑ air infiltration;

❑ interstitial condensation;

❑ heat loss;

❑ ultraviolet radiation;

❑ pests; and

❑ natural disasters (e.g., hurricane winds, earthquakes).

Once the evaluation has been completed, develop a list of measures and strategies to address the greatest durability risks. Include the measures listed in Table ID 2. The list may also include measures that are awarded elsewhere in the LEED for Homes Rating System (e.g., improved air sealing, improved ventilation).

Use the list of strategies as a checklist to facilitate inspections, and incorporate each strategy into project documents.

A template version of the durability inspection checklist is available from your Provider. A project team that does not use the template provided by USGBC must include the following elements in

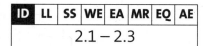
the durability inspection checklist:

❑ A signed, dated declaration indicating that the builder has evaluated the project's durability risks, incorporated appropriate measures into the design, and inspected to verify that the durability measures were installed or implemented appropriately.

❑ Basic information about the project, including site address, builder's name and the third-party inspector's name and affiliation.

❑ A checkbox or other way for both the internal and the third-party verifier to indicate that each measure was inspected and verified.

Conduct a durability evaluation for each new project, since many durability risks are site-specific.

Increasingly, homebuilders are developing and implementing quality management programs as part of their risk management activities. Quality management programs are typically aimed at assuring consistent performance across a company's operations, and emphasize in-field compliance with drawings, specifications and/or scopes of work.

If a builder chooses not to develop an inhouse quality management plan, ID 2.2 can be satisfied by having someone on the project team (other than the Provider or Verification Team) inspect and check off the measures on the durability inspection checklist. This inspection should be done as early as possible, depending on the measures being implemented, so that any problems that are identified can be easily remedied.

Third-party verification of the durability measures is an optional credit. This verification should be conducted by the Verification Team and should consist of inspections and observations of each measure on the durability inspection checklist. The Verification Team can provide feedback and insight about the du-

rability measures, but it is not the role of the Verification Team to verify or validate either the choice of durability measures or the effectiveness with which they are implemented. In signing the durability inspection checklist, the Verification Team is only verifying that the home includes each of the measures listed.

Calculations

No calculations are required.

Exemplary Performance

No additional points are available for exemplary performance.

Verification and Submittals

Supporting Verification Materials, made available by the Project Team

ID 2.1: Durability Planning

❑ Complete and submit the Durability Evaluation Form to the Verification Team.

❑ Include durability measures in project documents.

❑ Develop and submit a completed durability inspection checklist.

ID 2.2: Durability Management

❑ Present documentation of quality management processes to the Verification Team or conduct an inspection of durability measures in the home and indicate the completion of the inspection on the durability inspection checklist.

❑ Ensure that all applicable measures in Table 1 were installed.

Verification Team

ID 2.1: Durability Planning

❑ Verify completion of the Durability Evaluation Form and durability inspection checklist.

ID 2.2: Durability Management

❑ Visually verify documentation of quality management process or verify that the project team conducted on-site inspection of durability measures and indicated its completion on the durability inspection checklist.

❑ Visually verify that all applicable measures in Table 1 were installed.

ID 2.3: Third-Party Verification

❑ Visually verify that strategies listed on the durability inspection checklist were incorporated into the home.

❑ Upon verification, check off and sign the durability inspection checklist.

Considerations

Economic Issues

Some durability measures will increase the initial cost of construction, but incorporating such measures can reduce the builder's long-term costs, since durability failures regularly lead to call-backs from new occupants and necessitate expensive repairs that could have been avoided through improved design and construction.

Durability measures can reduce repair costs for the occupant and enhance system performance, lowering heating and cooling costs.

Regional Variances

Durability risks vary significantly by location and climate. The durability evaluation is a critical step in understanding the regional and local durability concerns and identifying the areas of focus.

Resources

Web Sites

ASTM E2136-01: Standard Guide for Specifying and Evaluating Performance of Single Family Attached and Detached Dwellings - Durability

www.astm.org

According to ASTM, "this guide gives examples of performance statements for durable in-place materials, products, components, subsystems, and systems for single family attached and detached dwellings, considering the effects of normal degradation factors to which they are anticipated to be subjected over their service lives."

Building America Best Practice Handbooks

www.eere.energy.gov/buildings/building_america

This site includes links to the Best Practice Handbooks, which include detailed information about design and construction practices following building science principles. There are five climate-specific volumes, all available for free download.

Building for Environmental and Economic Sustainability (BEES)

www.bfrl.nist.gov/software/bees

The BEES software assists the user in selecting building products based on their total life-cycle costs and environmental impacts. The software is free to download.

Building Science Resources

www.buildingscienceconsulting.com/resources/resources.htm

This site, managed and maintained by Building Science Consulting, contains technical building science information on various building components.

Canadian Standards Association, CSA S478-95: Guideline on Durability in Buildings

www.shopcsa.ca

According to CSA, "this guideline considers the agents and mechanisms related to durability, and provides advice for incorporating requirements for durability into the design, operation, and maintenance provisions for buildings and their components."

Durability by Design: A Guide for Residential Builders and Designers

www.huduser.org/publications/destech/durdesign.html

This site contains a full download of this durability guide, written by the National Association of Homebuilders and distributed by the U.S. Department of Housing and Urban Development. The guide provides a comprehensive assessment of practices and measures to improve durability.

Energy & Environmental Building Association, Houses that Work Series

www.eeba.org/housesthatwork/index.html

This site includes information on the "Houses that Work" series, including how to sign up for courses, conferences, and other events.

Energy & Environmental Building Association, Builders' Guides

www.eeba.org/bookstore

The EEBA Builder Guides, written by Joe Lstiburek, provide detailed step-bystep guidance on design and construction based on building science and best-practice construction techniques. There are four climate-specific guides: hot and humid; cold; mixed humid; and mixed dry.

Firewise Communities

www.firewise.org/resources/homeowner.htm

This site includes information and re-sources on preparing for the risks of wildfires, particularly at the interface between communities and wilderness.

Forest Products Laboratory, Advanced Housing Research Center

www.fpl.fs.fed.us/ahrc

This site houses research published by the Advanced Housing Research Center, which is funded by the U.S. Department of Agriculture. This site includes research on mold, wildfire mitigation, paints and finishes, and other durability-related topics.

National Economic Service-life Tools (NEST)

www.pathnet.org/sp.asp?id=9714

This tool was developed by the Partnership for Advancing Housing Technology (PATH). According to PATH, this set of tools "combines regionally specific economic conditions with the regionally specific durability to produce accurate, specific local estimates of the savings associated with increased durability."

National Housing Quality Certified Builder Program

www.nahbrc.org/builder/quality

The National Association of Home Builders Research Center offers this quality management program. The program addresses both builders and trade contractors.

National Climatic Data Center's Climate Atlas of the United States

www.gis.ncdc.noaa.gov/website/ims-climatls/index.html

This site contains a free interactive atlas that enables the user to view maps of the United States by geographic area, element type (e.g., temperature, precipitation, wind), and specific data type (e.g., mean wind speed, occurrence of high winds).

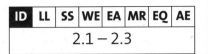

National Renewable Energy Laboratory Maps and Data

www.nrel.gov/gis/maps.html

This site includes links to data sets and interactive maps of relative solar radiation and wind throughout the United States. These maps were designed as tools for renewable energy development, but they can be used to identify durability risks from solar radiation and wind.

Natural Resources Conservation Service Wind Maps

www.wcc.nrcs.usda.gov/climate/windrose.html

This site includes data and visual depictions of "wind roses" for cities throughout the United States. Wind rose images present the distribution of wind, including speed, direction, and frequency. The data are free.

Radon Zone Map

www.epa.gov/iaq/radon/zonemap.html

This site contains basic information on radon risks and includes a link to state maps showing the relative risk of radon for each county.

Print Media

The Scopes of Work Program, by Linda Haas Davenport. NAHB Builder Press, 2000.

Baseline Measures for Improving Housing Durability, by Robert Chapman and Christine Izzo. Report # NISTIR 6870. National Institute of Standards and Technology, September 2002. Available online, at www.fire.nist.gov/bfrlpubs/build02/PDF/b02159.pdf.

Water Management Guide, by Joseph Lstiburek. Third edition. Energy & Environmental Building Association. Available online, at www.eeba.org/bookstore.

ID 3: Innovative or Regional Design

Intent

Minimize the environmental impact of the home by incorporating additional green design and construction measures that have tangible and demonstrable benefits beyond those in the LEED for Homes Rating System.

Requirements

Prerequisites

None.

Credits

3.1 **Innovation 1** (1 point). Prepare a written Innovative Design Request, to be submitted by the LEED for Homes Provider to USGBC, explaining the merits of the proposed measure. This point cannot be counted until LEED for Homes has ruled on the request. All written submittals must contain the following:

- ❑ the intent of the proposed measure;
- ❑ the proposed requirement for compliance;
- ❑ the proposed documentation to demonstrate compliance; and
- ❑ a description and an estimate of the benefit or impact provided by the proposed measure.

3.2 **Innovation 2** (1 point).

3.3 **Innovation 3** (1 point).

3.4 **Innovation 4** (1 point).

Synergies and Trade-Offs

This credit rewards innovative or regional measures that are not addressed elsewhere in the Rating System. A project can also receive 1 LEED point for exceeding the performance requirements of existing credits.

ID 3.1: Innovation 1

ID 3.2: Innovation 2

ID 3.3: Innovation 3

ID 3.4: Innovation 4

The homebuilding industry continues to develop innovations in design and construction. Complementary industries and technical fields, such as glass and glazing, paints and coatings, materials research, and waste management, also continue to produce new products that affect the homebuilding sector.

LEED for Homes embraces and rewards the development and adoption of new technologies and strategies that can produce quantifiable environmental and human health benefits. This credit category also creates an opportunity for projects to earn points for implementing strategies or measures not addressed in the current LEED for Homes Rating System. Points can be earned not only for innovative designs but also for exemplary performance or regional best practices.

Approach and Implementation

Points can be earned under this credit for any of three types of green homebuilding measures.

1. Exemplary performance: Exceeding the requirements for a credit already awarded in the LEED for Homes Rating System.

2. Innovative design: Implementation of an innovative technology, design, or construction practice that is not currently awarded in the LEED for Homes Rating System.

3. Regional design: Implementing a technology, design, or construction technique that is not currently awarded in the LEED for Homes Rating System and addresses a regional environmental or human health concern.

The requirements for earning an exemplary performance credit are listed for each credit in this Reference Guide. Exemplary performance credit is not available for every credit but is typically reserved for credits where exceeding the current requirements will yield a substantial environmental or human health benefit. If a credit does not list a threshold for exemplary performance, an ID request may be submitted through the Provider.

All requests for innovative design credits must be submitted through a LEED for Homes Provider and must be ruled upon and approved by USGBC before any points are awarded to the project. Innovative design credits awarded for one project at a specific point in time do not constitute automatic approval for similar strategies in a future project. Innovative design credits are not granted for a particular product or design strategy that simply aids in the achievement of an existing LEED for Homes credit.

Innovative design requests should include the following information, similar to the structure of all LEED for Homes credits:

❑ Intent: an explanation of why this innovation is being installed and the general environmental benefits it yields.

❑ Measures: a succinct explanation of the proposed technology or design measure, as well as its application in a specific project.

❑ Proposed metric: a method or metric (preferably quantitative) for assessing the impacts of the innovation.

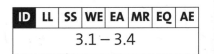

❑ Verification and submittals: an explanation of how the proposed measures will be verified in the field.

❑ Proposed benefits: an explanation of how the measure will yield environmental, human health or other benefits, and an estimate of the net benefits compared with standard building practice and other LEED for Homes credits.

An explanation of how the estimate was calculated must also be included. Wherever possible, provide references to published material, including third-party research (preferred) and/or manufacturer's estimates. Most requests will be judged using metrics similar to those used to justify existing LEED for Homes credits.

Regional design credits are available for green measures or strategies that are unique to a climate or region. As with innovative design credits, these measures must be outside the current scope of LEED for Homes and must have a measurable, demonstrable environmental or human health benefit. A request for a regional design credit must be submitted through a LEED for Homes Provider and approved by USGBC.

Calculations

Calculations may be required to demonstrate the value of a proposed innovative design measure.

Exemplary Performance

All exemplary performance points earned under other credits must be scored under this credit.

Verification and Submittals

Supporting Verification Materials, made available by the Project Team

❑ Notify the LEED for Homes Provider as early as possible about the intent to submit an innovation request.

❑ Complete a formal innovative or regional design request.

❑ Sign an Accountability form to indicate that you met the requirements of the Innovation Credit.

Verification Team

❑ Review the innovative or regional design request and verify that all elements are installed in the home.

❑ Submit the request to USGBC for review.

❑ Provide feedback to the project team about the ruling.

❑ For each Innovation credit, verify that the Accountability Form has been signed by the responsible party.

Location & Linkages

Overview

Homebuilding projects have substantial site-related environmental effects, in terms of both the impact to the site itself and the impacts that stem from the location of the site. The next chapter (Sustainable Sites) focuses on the former; this chapter describes how best to choose site locations that promote environmentally responsible land-use patterns and neighborhoods.

Location & Linkages (LL) credits reward builders for selecting home sites that have more sustainable land-use patterns and offer environmental advantages over conventional developments. Fragmentation of farmland and forest and other natural areas is minimized by locating new development within and near existing developed areas. Well-sited developments need less infrastructure, especially roads and water and sewer lines. And such developments promote a range of sustainable transportation options, including walking, cycling, and mass transit, thereby reducing dependence on personal automobiles.

LL credits can be earned in either of two ways, summarized in **Table 1** and described in the following sections.

Pathway 1: LL 1, LEED for Neighborhood Development. The LEED for Neighborhood Development Rating System integrates the principles of smart growth, new urbanism, and green building into a national standard for neighborhood design. The pilot phase of this program is expected to conclude in late 2008, after which new projects can register with the LEED for Neighborhood Development program, and homes can receive credit for selecting a site in a certified development.

Pathway 2: LL 2–6. Projects that either cannot or choose not to participate in the LEED for Neighborhood Development program can earn points in this category by pursuing the following strategies:

LL 2: Site Selection

LL 3: Preferred Locations

LL 4: Infrastructure

LL 5: Community Resources / Transit

LL 6: Access to Open Space

Table 1. Overview of Location & Linkages (LL) Category

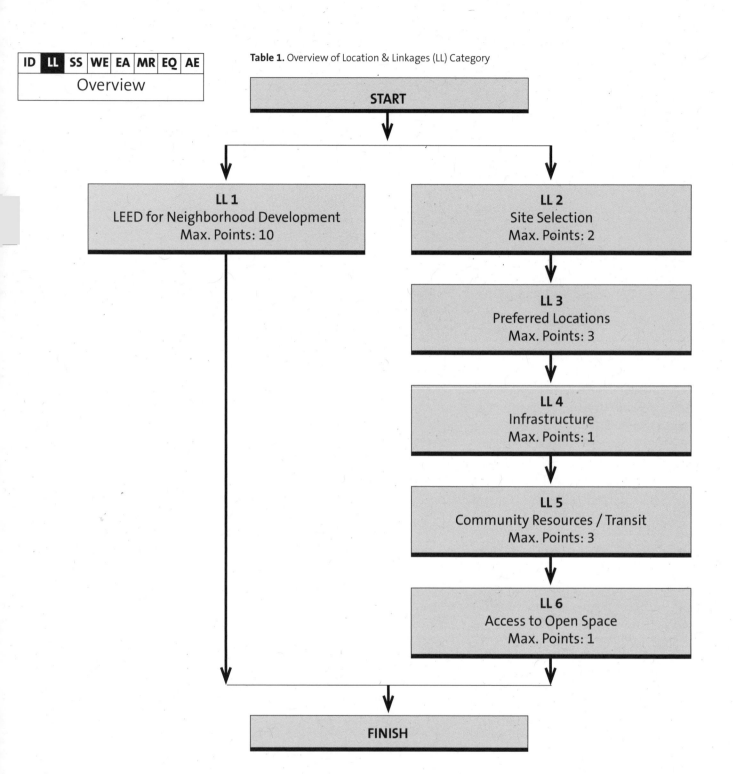

LL 1: LEED for Neighborhood Development

Intent

Minimize the environmental impact of land development practices by building homes in LEED for Neighborhood Development certified developments.

Requirements

Prerequisites

None.

Credits

1 **LEED for Neighborhood Development** (10 points). Complete the requirements of the LEED for Neighborhood Development (LEED-ND) certification program.

Synergies and Trade-Offs

A project receiving points for LL 1 is not eligible for points under LL 2–6, and vice versa.

LL 1. LEED for Neighborhood Development

The USGBC's LEED for Neighborhood Development Rating System (in its pilot phase during 2007–2008) is designed to certify communities that emphasize environmentally responsible planning and layout of the infrastructure and buildings that together constitute a neighborhood. LEED for Neighborhood Development certified neighborhood developments are those that will incorporate the principles of smart growth and pedestrian-oriented design, offer many benefits over conventional developments, including:

❏ more efficient use of land,

❏ reduced development and fragmentation of farmland and wilderness,

❏ reduced need for infrastructure extension, and

❏ a wider and more sustainable range of transportation options—including walking, biking, or access to mass transit.

This credit rewards builders who choose to build their homes in certified LEED for Neighborhood Development neighborhoods.

Approach and Implementation

Projects do not need to complete LEED-ND certification before earning this credit, but the requirements of Stage 2 must be met.

New projects will be able to register for LEED for Neighborhood Development at completion of the pilot phase of the program. At that time, credit for selection of a home site in a LEED neighborhood development will become available.

To determine whether LEED for Neighborhood Development may be appropriate, review the Rating System on the Web site, paying particular attention to the prerequisites. Projects that cannot or choose not to pursue LEED for Neighborhood Development certification can pursue similar strategies using LL 2 – 6. LEED for Neighborhood Development projects may constitute whole neighborhoods, portions of neighborhoods, or multiple neighborhoods. Homes built in small infill projects that are single use but complement existing neighboring uses can earn certification as well as homes in larger, mixed-use developments.

Information on the LEED Neighborhood Development program and updates can be found at www.usgbc.org/leed/nd.

Calculations

No calculations are required for this credit.

Exemplary Performance

No additional points are available for exemplary performance.

Verification and Submittals

Supporting Verification Materials, made available by the Project Team:

❏ Demonstrate LEED for Neighborhood Development certification or that requirements for Stage 2 have been met.

Verification Team:

❏ Verify LEED for Neighborhood Development certification or that requirements for Stage 2 have been met.

Resources

Please see the USGBC Web site, at www. usgbc.org/resources, for more specific resources on materials sources and other technical information. The LEED for Neighborhood Development Rating System can be found at www.usgbc.org/leed/nd.

Web Sites

LEED for Neighborhood Development

U.S. Green Building Council (USGBC)

www.usgbc.org/leed/nd

USGBC, in partnership with the Congress for the New Urbanism and the Natural Resources Defense Council, is developing the LEED for Neighborhood Development Rating System. This rating system integrates the principles of smart growth, new urbanism, and green building into the first national standard for neighborhood design. LEED certification provides independent, third-party verification that a development's location and design meet accepted high standards for environmentally responsible, sustainable development.

The Congress for the New Urbanism (CNU)

www.cnu.org/

CNU is working with the U.S. Green Building Council and the Natural Resources Defense Council to lay the groundwork for a more coordinated and powerful environmental strategy: sustainability at the scale of neighborhoods and communities.

Natural Resources Defense Council (NRDC)

www.nrdc.org/cities/smartgrowth/default.asp

This site highlights the critical elements of smart growth. The Web site includes case study examples of smart growth, including Sacramento and Nashville.

ID	LL	SS	WE	EA	MR	EQ	AE
				1			

LL 2: Site Selection

Intent

Avoid development on environmentally sensitive sites.

Requirements

Prerequisites

None.

Credits

2 **Site Selection** (2 points). Do not develop buildings, built structures, roads, or parking areas on portions of sites that meet any of the following criteria:

a) Land whose elevation is at or below the 100-year floodplain as defined by FEMA.

b) Land that is specifically identified as habitat for any species on federal or state threatened or endangered lists.

c) Land within 100 feet of any water, including wetlands as defined by U.S. Code of Federal Regulations 40 CFR, Parts 230–233 and Part 22, and isolated wetlands or areas of special concern identified by state or local rule, or land within distances given in applicable state or local regulations, whichever is more stringent. New wetlands constructed as part of stormwater mitigation or other site restoration efforts are exempt from this part of the requirement.

d) Land that prior to acquisition for the project was public parkland, unless land of equal or greater value as parkland is accepted in trade by the public landowner (park authority projects are exempt).

e) Land that contains "prime soils," "unique soils," or "soils of state significance," as identified in state Natural Resources Conservation Service soil surveys. Verification of soil types should be conducted by the project civil engineer, wetlands engineer, or biologist. If no project team member is qualified to verify this requirement, follow the steps laid out in the LEED for Homes Reference Guide. Sites that are previously developed are exempt from this requirement.

Synergies and Trade-Offs

A project receiving points for LL 1 is not eligible for points under LL 2–6, and vice versa.

LL 2. Site Selection

Builders and project leaders who seek to minimize environmental impact should avoid locations that contribute to the degradation or loss of our agricultural and natural resource lands. As suburban and exurban development increases, the importance of wise site selection increases as well. Prevention of habitat encroachment is an essential element of sustainable site selection. By avoiding environmentally sensitive areas, communities can help preserve land that might function as a corridor for wildlife, recreational open space, or wildlife sanctuary.

Careful community designs can integrate the natural surroundings with the neighborhood, providing a strong connection between the built and natural environments and minimizing adverse impacts on the nonbuilt portions of the site.

This credit rewards builders for choosing building sites that avoid environmentally sensitive areas or contain precious resources (e.g., prime farmland, unaltered land, wildlife habitat).

Approach and Implementation

The best strategy for meeting this credit is to build new homes on previously developed infill lots. This practice not only avoids disruption and fragmentation of habitat and farmland but also increases the chances that the neighborhood will grow in a more compact pattern, facilitating the use of more sustainable modes of transportation, such as walking, cycling, and mass transit. Projects that are constructed in previously developed and/or infill lots are awarded points in LL 3.

Evaluate communities for potential building sites that have the above criteria prior to purchasing the land and ensure that the criteria are addressed by the designer during the conceptual design phase. Utilize professionals, such as planners, landscape architects, ecologists, environmental engineers, and/or civil engineers, for the screening process.

To find soil data, follow these steps:

1. Download GIS data from www. soildatamart.nrcs.usda.gov for the appropriate state and county.

2. Alternatively, visit www.websoilsurvey.nrcs.usda.gov/app. In the "Area of Interest" tab, choose "Soil Survey Area" and select the appropriate state, county, and soil survey area. Choose the "Soil Map" tab. Use the map to zoom in on the home site. Choose the "Layers" tab and make sure "Soil Survey Areas" is selected.

3. If soil data are unavailable, contact the state or regional Natural Resources Conservation Service office. State Web sites are listed at www. nrcs.usda.gov/about/organization/regions.html.

4. To determine whether the site soil type is "prime," "unique," or of "state significance," refer to state or local Natural Resources Conservation Service guidebooks or contact the agency's state or regional office.

Calculations

At least 95% of the site must meet the criteria listed above.

Exemplary Performance

No additional points are available for exemplary performance.

Verification and Submittals

Supporting Verification Materials, made available by the Project Team:

❑ Provide all necessary soil and site data to Verification Team.

❑ Sign an Accountability Form averring that the site meets all the stipulations of the credit.

Verification Team:

❑ Verify site data, floodplain maps, soil data maps, or other supporting verification materials.

❑ Verify that the Accountability Form has been signed by the responsible party.

Considerations

Environmental Issues

Habitat preservation is the most effective means to meet the requirements of the Endangered Species Act and to minimize development impacts on indigenous wildlife. Avoiding building on inappropriate sites preserves these areas for wildlife, recreation, and ecological balance. Building in floodplains can be detrimental to ecosystems.

Wetlands provide very important wildlife habitat because they tend to be biologically rich. Development on wetlands or floodplains presents particularly serious environmental challenges because it not only alters wildlife habitats but can also reduce water quality and increase the likelihood of erosion and flooding. Undisturbed, these natural areas retain stormwater for slow release into rivers and aquifers and protect lakes and streams by collecting sediment from stormwater and floodwater.

Economic Issues

Minimizing disruption of natural drain-age patterns is generally less expensive up-front and avoids costly construction and maintenance of elaborate drainage systems. Preserving native trees and vegetation also saves landscaping costs in the short and long term. Some plants can and should be replanted elsewhere on or off the site.

Siting a home at or below the FEMA 100-year floodplain puts the home at significantly higher risk for flood damage. Such locations, as well as sites near a large body of water, may necessitate different construction techniques and safeguards that increase costs.

Resources

Web Sites

Inhabitat.com

www.inhabitat.com/2006/07/05/green-building-101-sustainable-sites/

Inhabitat.com is devoted to the future of design, tracking innovations in technology, practices, and materials that promote a more sustainable future. The site offers good discussions, plus links to materials and energy-related information.

BuildingGreen, Inc.

www.buildinggreen.com/auth/article.cfm?fileName=040501a.xml

This Web site, maintained by an independent publishing company committed to presenting accurate, unbiased, and timely green design information, includes steps and sample strategies for selecting sustainable building sites.

Building Siting

U.S. Department of Energy, Building Technologies Program

www.eere.energy.gov/buildings/info/design/buildingsiting/index.html

This Web site addresses the following siting topics: rehabilitation or infill versus undeveloped site, site planning, design to minimize impacts to site, parking and pavement, exterior water management, and water efficiency.

Environmental Systems Research Institute, Inc. (ESRI)

www.esri.com/

This software company creates tools for GIS mapping. Its Web site includes an option to make a map of all of the flood areas within a user-defined location.

Digital Q3 Flood Data Availability, States Map

Federal Emergency Management Agency (FEMA), Map Service Center

(800) 358-9616

http://msc.fema.gov

FEMA's national flood information map.

Information Resources

Green Communities

www.greencommunitiesonline.org/resources.asp

A resource for publications on general and affordable housing development, including siting and site development issues.

NatureServe

www.natureserve.org

NatureServe is a nonprofit conservation organization that provides the scientific information and tools needed to help guide effective conservation action. It represents an international network of biological inventories—known as natural heritage programs or conservation data centers—operating in all 50 U.S. states, Canada (www.natureserve-canada.ca), Latin America, and the Caribbean.

State Natural Heritage Programs

www.natureserve.org/visitLocal/index.jsp

This Web site indexes NatureServe Natural Heritage programs operating in all 50 U.S. states, 11 Canadian provinces and territories, and countries and territories in Latin America and the Caribbean.

Print Media

Constructed Wetlands in the Sustainable Landscape, by Craig Campbell and Michael Ogden. John Wiley & Sons, 1999.

Holding Our Ground: Protecting America's Farms and Farmland, by Tom Daniels and Deborah Bowers. Island Press, 1997.

Saved by Development: Preserving Environmental Areas, Farmland, by Rick Pruetz. Arje Press, 1997.

Wetland Indicators: A Guide to Wetland Identification, Delineation, Classification, and Mapping, by Ralph W. Tiner. Lewis Publishers, 1999.

LL 3: Preferred Locations

Intent

Encourage the building of LEED homes near or within existing communities.

Requirements

Prerequisites

None.

Credits

3.1 **Edge Development** (1 point). Select a lot such that at least 25% of the perimeter immediately borders previously developed land. In the case of a multihome new development, each home in the development is awarded this point if at least 25% of the development site immediately borders previously developed land.

OR

3.2 **Infill** (2 points). Select a lot such that at least 75% of the perimeter immediately borders previously developed land. In the case of a multihome new development, each home in the development is awarded these points if at least 75% of the development site immediately borders previously developed land.

AND/OR

3.3 **Previously Developed** (1 point). Build on a previously developed lot. In the case of a multihome new development, each home in the development is awarded this point if at least 75% of the development site is built on previously developed land.

Synergies and Trade-Offs

A project receiving points for LL 1 is not eligible for points under LL 2–6, and vice versa.

LL 3.1 Edge Development Site

LL 3.2 Infill Site

LL 3.3 Previously Developed Site

The location of a new development can have a large environmental impact. The best strategies are to avoid developing previously undisturbed areas, to build on vacant infill sites within existing neighborhoods, or to build immediately adjacent to existing communities in "edge developments." This minimizes environmental impact because it prevents further loss or fragmentation of wetlands and habitat and minimizes the need for new impervious cover that increases stormwater runoff.

Frequently, new developments are located remote from existing communities. Such communities, sometimes called "leapfrog" developments, often fragment habitat or farmland, usually require extensive expansion of basic infrastructure and community services, and typically force their residents to rely solely on cars for all transportation needs. Edge developments, located immediately adjacent to existing communities, have a lesser impact. Generally, infill sites, within existing neighborhoods, have an even lower environmental impact.

Research has shown that the maximization of sites in urbanized areas of the United States would result in a need for only 350,000 acres, rather than 1.2 million acres, of undeveloped farmland and open space to accommodate overall housing needs. This credit is designed to promote the efficient use and reuse of land and to minimize alteration of previously undeveloped land by encouraging builders to locate projects in environmentally preferable locations.

Approach and Implementation

Locating a site is obviously the first step for any project. Seek opportunities to build near or within existing communities. Incorporate smart growth principles into the overall business model.

For the purposes of LEED for Homes, projects are categorized according to their location with respect to existing communities and the state of land being built upon. Edge development and infill sites refer to the state of the surrounding community. Whether a specific site is previously developed relates to the history of development on the site. Some sites, particularly multihome developments, will have a mix of land that is previously developed and undeveloped.

An infill site is not necessarily previously developed, and vice versa. A project can earn points for being previously developed even if it is not an edge development or infill site, and vice versa.

Calculations

For LL 3.1 and LL 3.2, estimate the percentage of the total site that immediately borders previously developed land. To qualify as previously developed, the development must be at least 5 years old.

Where the term "borders previously developed land" is used, the land itself must be developed. Being located adjacent to a lot with development located on it is not sufficient unless the development is immediately adjacent to the LEED project.

Any fraction of the perimeter that borders waterfront is excluded from the total perimeter. Roadways and sidewalks do not count as adjoining previously developed land in determining whether a site is an infill or edge site. In other words, a project site with four roads around its perimeter but farmland on the other side of the roads would not be considered an infill site. Land across the road that is built-out residential land instead of farmland could contribute toward classification as an infill site.

For LL 3.3, estimate the percentage of the total site that is previously developed. If the home is located in a new develop-

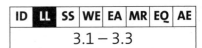
Figure 1. Qualifying Edge Development Site

FARMLAND FARMLAND

Portion of perimeter adjacent to undeveloped land

PROJECT SITE

Portion of perimeter adjacent to previously developed land

Figure 2. Qualifying Infill Site

Garfield Avenue

PROJECT SITE

(100% of project boundary borders previously developed land)

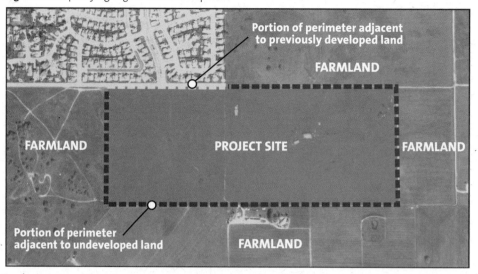

Figure 3. Nonqualifying Edge or Infill Development

Portion of perimeter adjacent to previously developed land

FARMLAND

FARMLAND

PROJECT SITE

FARMLAND

Portion of perimeter adjacent to undeveloped land

FARMLAND

Figure 4. Qualifying Previously Developed Site

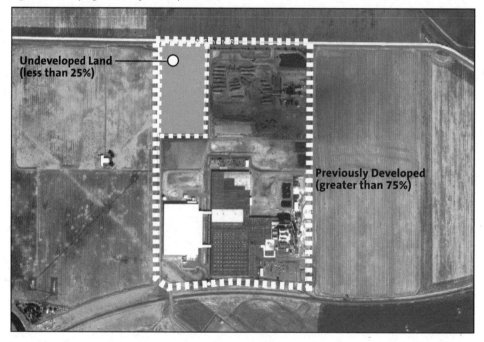

Undeveloped Land
(less than 25%)

Previously Developed
(greater than 75%)

ment, then the development site includes all of the new home sites in that new development, not just the one building site that is to be certified.

LL 3.1. Edge Development Site. 25% or more of the perimeter immediately borders previously developed land (**Figures 1** and **3**).

LL 3.2. Infill Site. 75% or more of the perimeter borders previously developed land (**Figures 1** and **2**).

LL 3.3. Previously Developed Site. At least 75% of the site was previously developed, defined as having preexisting paving, construction, or altered landscapes (**Figure 4**). Landscapes altered by current agricultural use, forestry use, or use as preserved natural area do not count as previously developed land.

Exemplary Performance

No additional points are available for exemplary performance.

Verification and Submittals

Supporting Verification Materials, made available by the Project Team:

❑ Present any relevant calculations to the Verification Team.

Verification Team:

❑ Visually verify that calculations are complete and satisfy the credit requirements; and/or

❑ Visually verify that the site meets the credit requirements.

Considerations

Environmental Issues

Sprawling development has led to increased fragmentation and loss of habitat and is a serious threat to many species of plants and animals. Building within or adjacent to existing development can minimize habitat fragmentation.

Exurban development has also led to intrusion onto prime agricultural land. Prime agricultural land is typically the most resource efficient and therefore environmentally sound location for farming, requiring less fertilizer and irrigation. Development takes such land out of agricultural production, possibly fragmenting farming communities and consequently reducing the viability of the local agricultural economy. Most of the fruits, vegetables, and dairy products in the United States are produced close to our metropolitan areas, in the path of development.

Economic Issues

Construction on infill or previously developed sites can cost more because of site preparation (e.g., demolition, removal of toxins) and construction constraints (e.g., permitting, legal requirements). Land costs are typically higher for infill sites, but this may be offset by increased desirability and marketability for prospective buyers. If the previously developed land is considered a brownfield, its purchase cost may be lower or even subsidized by state or regional development agencies.

Affordable housing projects are often located on infill sites, and these projects may be eligible for support from financial institutions and federal, state, and local housing and urban development agencies.

Regional Variances

In some cities, current residents oppose the additional population and buildings that come with infill projects, but when redevelopment is done well, it can enhance a neighborhood. Building on infill sites can drive up nearby land values, potentially displacing existing rental units, particularly in low-income areas. Community interaction and consideration of public comments can help the builder be responsive to these concerns and work to achieve a positive community reaction.

Resources

Web Sites

Brownfields Cleanup and Redevelopment

U.S. Environmental Protection Agency

www.epa.gov/brownfields/index.html

On this site, you can find information about EPA's Brownfields Program, including the brownfields law, EPA Brownfields Grants, technical tools and resources, and information on brownfield projects across the country.

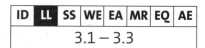

Infill Development Strategies for Shaping Livable Neighborhoods

Municipal Research and Services Center of Washington

www.mrsc.org/Publications/textfill.aspx

This site, sponsored by the State of Washington, contains an overview of strategies for encouraging and implementing infill development patterns. The principal audience is policymakers and developers in Washington, but the insights are broadly applicable.

Greyfields into Goldfields: Dead Malls Become Living Neighborhoods

The Congress for the New Urbanism (CNU)

www.cnu.org/malls

A 2002 study on the opportunity for converting dead shopping malls into new neighborhoods.

National Vacant Properties Campaign

www.vacantproperties.org/

This Web site provides information, resources, tools, and assistance to support vacant property revitalization efforts.

Natural Resources Defense Council

www.nrdc.org/cities/smartgrowth/default.asp

This site highlights the critical elements of smart growth. The Web site includes case study examples of smart growth, including Sacramento and Nashville.

Smart Growth America

www.smartgrowthamerica.org

This coalition of organizations from around the country posts the latest smart growth news and supports smart growth initiatives across the United States.

Smart Growth Network

www.smartgrowth.org

The Web site outlines smart growth principles, provides a guide through smart growth terms and technical concepts, and hosts a searchable catalogue of reports, Web sites, tools, and case studies.

Print Media

Strategies for Successful Infill Development, 2001. Northeast-Midwest Institute and The Congress for the New Urbanism. Available at www.nemw.org/infillbook.htm.

Designing Healthy Cities: Prescriptions, Principles, and Practice, by Joseph Aicher. Krieger Publishing, 1998.

Planning and Urban Design Standards. American Planning Association. John Wiley & Sons, 2006.

Planning the Built Environment, by Larz Anderson. American Planning Association Press, 2000.

Crossroads, Hamlets, Village, Town: Design Characteristics of Traditional Neighborhoods, Old and New, by Randall Arendt. American Planning Association, 1999.

Travel by Design: The Influence of Urban Form on Travel, by Marlon Boarnet. Oxford Press, 2001.

The Next American Metropolis, by Peter Calthorpe. Princeton Architectural Press, 1993.

SmartCode. Duany Plater-Zyberk & Company. New Urban Publications, undated (version 9.0 expected in 2007), also available for download at www.smartcodefiles.com.

LL 4: Infrastructure

Intent

Encourage the building of LEED homes in developments that are served by or are near existing infrastructure (i.e., sewers and water supply).

Requirements

Prerequisites

None.

Credits

4   **Existing Infrastructure** (1 point). Select a lot that is within ½ mile of existing water service lines and sewer service lines. In the case of a multihome new development, each home in the development is awarded this point if the center of the development site is within ½ mile of existing water service lines and sewer service lines.

Synergies and Trade-Offs

A project receiving points for LL 1 is not eligible for points under LL 2–6, and vice versa.

LL4: Infrastructure

Locating near existing infrastructure reduces or obviates the need for further infrastructure development, which saves materials and embedded energy. Sites near existing water and sewer lines are also likely to have other infrastructure, including roads, electric power, and natural gas.

LL 3.3, Previously Developed Site, addresses project sites that have existing paved roads, preexisting structures (e.g., brownfields or grayfields), or altered landscapes. LL 4 concerns proximity to water and sewer lines.

This credit rewards the selection of a home site within a community that has existing municipal water and sewer lines.

Approach and Implementation

During the site selection process, give preference to home sites that are located in communities that have public sewer and water lines in place. This credit is not automatically earned through the use of private wells or septic systems. Projects with private wells or septic systems can earn this credit, but the home must be located within ½ mile of central water and sewer service lines; the home does not need to be connected to the central water and sewer service.

For multihome developments, this credit can be earned if the development boundary meets the criteria. In large developments, it is good practice to label storm drains and storm inlets to indicate where the water leads, so as to discourage dumping. For example, use a painted stencil that reads "Caution – leads to [name of body of water]."

Calculations

Calculate the distance from the home to the nearest existing water and sewer hookup.

Exemplary Performance

No additional points are available for exemplary performance.

Verification and Submittals

Supporting Verification Materials, made available by the Project Team:

❑ If necessary, present local maps and documents to the Verification Team demonstrating the proximity of the home to existing water and sewer infrastructure.

Verification Team:

❑ Visually verify (using maps, documents, or on-site observation) that the home is within ½ mile of existing water and sewer infrastructure.

Considerations

Environmental Issues

Locating in places that already have utilities and roads reduces the environmental impacts, including materials and embedded energy use, associated with construction of new infrastructure.

Economic Issues

The cost of extending existing infrastructure is very high because of the time, materials, and energy involved with laying new pipe underground. Locating near existing water and sewer lines also increases the likelihood that other costly infrastructure, including roads, electric power, and natural gas lines, are accessible.

Regional Variances

The availability of existing infrastructure varies considerably by region. In some areas, water and sewer infrastructure is extensive. In other areas, especially those that are remote and less developed, this credit may be available only for infill projects.

Resources

Web Sites

Environment and Energy Study Institute

www.eesi.org/publicationsaceee%20paper.pdf

This Web site links to an article published in 2006 by the American Council for an Energy-Efficient Economy, titled "It's About How and Where We Build: Connecting Energy and Smart Growth." The article focuses on efficiently locating home sites to reduce the amount of energy needed for transportation and other infrastructure. It concludes that greater use of energy-efficient design and smart growth land use will help achieve the goals of environmental protection, economic prosperity, and community livability.

Smart Growth Network

www.smartgrowth.org

This network of nonprofit organizations and governmental agencies promotes smart growth practices. The Web site outlines smart growth principles, provides a guide to smart growth terms and technical concepts, and hosts a searchable catalogue of reports, Web sites, tools, and case studies.

Print Media

Our Built and Natural Environments: A Technical Review of the Interactions between Land Use, Transportation, and Environmental Quality. U.S. Environmental Protection Agency, Development, Community, and Environment Division, 2001.

LL 5: Community Resources / Transit

Intent

Encourage the building of LEED homes in development patterns that allow for walking, biking, or public transit (thereby minimizing dependency on personal automobiles and their associated environmental impacts).

Requirements

Prerequisites

None.

Credits

Note: For new multihome developments, the distances below can be measured from the center of the community as long as the distance from the center of the community to the farthest home does not exceed ¼ mile. Using this approach, whole communities can qualify for this credit. For any homes farther than ¼ mile from the center of the community, distances must be recalculated for each home.

5.1 **Basic Community Resources / Transit** (1 point). Select a site that meets one of the following criteria:

   a) Located within ¼ mile of four basic community resources (**Table 1**).

   b) Located within ½ mile of seven basic community resources (**Table 1**).

   c) Located within ½ mile of transit services that offer 30 or more transit rides per weekday (combined bus, rail, and ferry).

OR

5.2 **Extensive Community Resources / Transit** (2 points). Select a site that meets one of the following criteria:

   a) Located within ¼ mile of seven basic community resources (**Table 1**).

   b) Located within ½ mile of 11 basic community resources (**Table 1**).

   c) Located within ½ mile of transit services that offer 60 or more transit rides per weekday (combined bus, rail, and ferry).

OR

5.3 **Outstanding Community Resources / Transit** (3 points). Select a site that meets one of the following criteria:

   a) Located within ¼ mile of 11 basic community resources (**Table 1**).

   b) Located within ½ mile of 14 basic community resources (**Table 1**).

   c) Located within ½ mile of transit services that offer 125 or more transit rides per weekday (combined bus, rail, and ferry).

Transit rides per weekday are calculated as follows: (1) within a ½ mile radius, count all the transit stops; (2) multiply each transit stop by the number of buses, trains, and ferries that pass through that stop per day; (3) add the total number of rides available at each stop within ½ mile together. Example: If there are four bus stops, and at each

bus stop the service frequency is half-hourly (48 times per day), the total transit rides per day is 192.

Table 1. Types of Basic Community Resources

- ❑ Arts and entertainment center
- ❑ Bank
- ❑ Community or civic center
- ❑ Convenience store
- ❑ Daycare center
- ❑ Fire station
- ❑ Fitness center or gym
- ❑ Laundry or dry cleaner
- ❑ Library
- ❑ Medical or dental office
- ❑ Museum
- ❑ Pharmacy
- ❑ Police station
- ❑ Post office
- ❑ Place of worship
- ❑ Restaurant
- ❑ School
- ❑ Supermarket
- ❑ Other neighborhood-serving retail
- ❑ Other office building or major employment center

Note: Up to two of each type of community resource may be counted. For example, two restaurants within ¼ mile may be counted as two community resources; four restaurants also count as two.

Synergies and Trade-Offs

A project receiving points for LL 1 is not eligible for points under LL 2–6, and vice versa.

LL 5.1 Basic Community Resources / Transit

LL 5.2 Extensive Community Resources / Transit

LL 5.3 Outstanding Community Resources / Transit

Locating housing in communities with nearby existing resources reduces the number of cars that households need and therefore reduces a family's overall expenses and time spent in the car. It also creates more vibrant neighborhoods with better access to employment centers, transportation systems, schools, shopping, general services, and civic amenities. Increasing numbers of people enjoy in-town living or residing in and around mixed-use communities.

Living near community resources or mass transit options reduces the number and length of daily auto trips. According to the Bureau of Transportation Statistics, vehicle use in the United States nearly tripled, from 1 trillion to 2.99 trillion miles per year, between 1970 and 2005. Vehicles are responsible for more than 20 percent of U.S. greenhouse gas emissions (Energy Information Administration, Emissions of Greenhouse Gases in the United States 2005). Vehicle emissions contribute to climate change, smog, and particulate pollution, which all are harmful to human health and natural ecosystems. Neighborhoods with clusters of community services also tend to be more walkable and encourage a more active lifestyle.

In this credit, points are given to projects located near abundant local community resources, such as shops or services within walking distance or mass transit options like buses and rail. Homeowners in such communities are more likely to live near their workplaces and within easy reach of nearby activity centers.

Approach and Implementation

Where possible, build new homes on sites that are within or near existing communities that have resources in walking distance of access to mass transit options like buses and light rail. In semiurban and suburban communities, locate near bus routes, railways, and other mass transit corridors.

Design mixed-use projects by including commercial and other nonresidential spaces in any multifamily developments. Community resources that are included in the development can be counted in the calculation for these credits.

Contact the local transit agency to obtain information on existing or planned transit routes and the headways of each route that meet the thresholds in the requirements. Ideally, this information will be provided in a geo-referenced format. Using a GIS buffer analysis, identify sites that have adequate transit service per the requirements. Also get information about the frequency of transit stops for use in calculating total transit stops.

Contact local agencies, including chambers of commerce, to identify community resources near the project site or to find a potential project site with sufficient concentrations of community resources. In many cases, an online map program such as Google Maps can identify certain kinds of community resources; resources identified in this way must be verified on the ground, since these web pages are not always current.

In multi-home developments, incorporate walkways and bike paths throughout the development—both near the streets and

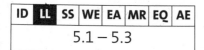
between green spaces—that enable easy pedestrian access to the broader community beyond the development.

Calculations

The distance requirements must be calculated based on possible walking distances, not "as the crow flies". For example, if a resource is within ½ mile on a map, but requires >½ mile of walking because of highways or other obstructions, the resource should not be counted.

Count the total number of community resources that are within ¼ mile and ½ mile. Up to two of each type of community resource may be counted. For example, in LL 5.1, two restaurants can count for two of the four community resources within ¼ mile. A project that wants to count a community resource that is not listed must submit a Credit Interpretation Request to USGBC.

Developers of larger communities can measure the distance to the community resource from the center of the community, as long as the distance from the center to the farthest home does not exceed ¼ mile. Using this approach, whole communities can be qualified for this credit. For any homes farther than ¼ mile from the center of the community, distances must be recalculated for each home.

Calculate *transit rides per weekday* as follows:

1. Count all transit stops that are within ½ mile of the home. Multiple transit stops can only be counted if they are for different transit lines. For example, a single bus that stops just north of the home, in front of the home, and just south of the home, should only be counted as one stop. Stops for the same line that travel in different directions (e.g., an inbound bus and an outbound bus) count as different stops. In the case of large

developments, count the distance from the center of the development;

2. For each transit stop, count the number of times a bus, train, or ferry stops per day. If the number of rides varies over the year (e.g., the project is in an academic campus or a seasonal resort), the average rides per weekday should be used;

3. Sum the total number of rides per day for each stop within ½ mile.

Example: If there are four bus stops, and at each bus stop the service frequency is half-hourly (48 times per day), the total transit rides per day would be 192.

Exemplary Performance

Projects that are located within 1/2 mile of transit services that offer 250 or more transit rides per weekday may be awarded 1 point for exemplary performance, to be counted under Innovation in Design Process Credit 3.

Verification and Submittals

Supporting Verification Materials, made available by the Project Team:

❑   Present maps and/or a list of community resources or transit modes to the Verification Team.

❑   If applicable, present calculations for transit rides to the Verification Team.

Verification Team:

❑   Visually verify (using maps, lists provided by the project team, and/or on-site observation) the presence of community resources or transit rides, as per the credit requirements.

❑   If applicable, visually verify calculations for transit rides.

Considerations

Economic Issues

Although the cost of land near community resources may be higher, access to abundant transportation choices and other community resources can significantly increase the value and marketability of a home.

Environmental Issues

Increased automobile travel is one of the most damaging consequences of sprawl. People living and working in outlying developments tend to drive greater distances. Vehicle emissions contribute to climate change, smog, and particulate pollution, which are harmful to human health and natural ecosystems. In addition, the parking and roadway surfaces required to support vehicle travel consume land and nonrenewable resources, disrupt natural stormwater flow, and enlarge urban heat islands.

Regional Variances

The availability of community resources and public transit varies considerably by region. In some regions of the country, public transit is extensive and community resources are clustered. In regions not well served by transit, this credit will likely be available only for projects located near existing town centers.

Resources

Web Sites

Best Workplaces for Commuters

www.bestworkplacesforcommuters.gov/index.htm

(888) 856-3131

This program, established by the Environmental Protection Agency and the Department of Transportation, publicly recognizes employers for exemplary commuter benefits programs. It provides tools, guidance, and promotions to help employers incorporate commuter benefits into their employee benefits plan, reap financial benefits, and gain national recognition.

Victoria Transportation Policy Institute

www.vtpi.org

This independent research organization provides consulting and publicly available research about solutions to emerging transportation issues, such as transportation demand management.

Print Media

"The Influence of Land Use on Travel Behavior: Empirical Strategies," by Reid Ewing and Robert Cervero. *Transportation Research, Policy and Practice* 35: 823–45, 2001.

Hidden in Plain Sight: Capturing the Demand for Housing Near Transit. Center for Transit-Oriented Development. Reconnecting America, 2004.

Our Built and Natural Environments: A Technical Review of the Interactions between Land Use, Transportation, and Environmental Quality. Development, Community, and Environment Division. U.S. Environmental Protection Agency, 2001.

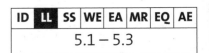

ID	LL	SS	WE	EA	MR	EQ	AE
	5.1 – 5.3						

LL 6: Access to Open Space

Intent

Provide open spaces to encourage walking, physical activity, and time spent outdoors.

Requirements

Prerequisites

None.

Credits

6   **Access to Open Space** (1 point). Select a location within ½ mile of a publicly accessible or community-based open space that is at least ¾ acre in size. The open space requirement can be met by either one large open space or two smaller spaces totaling ¾ acre.

Note: Open spaces must consist predominantly of softscapes such as soil, grass, shrubs, and trees. These include natural open spaces; city, county, and state parks; play areas; and other community open spaces specifically intended for recreational use. Areas around ponds can be counted as open space if they have usable, accessible recreational space such as walking or bicycle paths. Private lands open to the public for passive recreation are also acceptable provided there is deeded public access or a history of allowable public use and anticipated continued future public use for at least 10 years.

Synergies and Trade-Offs

A project receiving points for LL 1 is not eligible for points under LL 2–6, and vice versa.

LL 6. Access to Open Space

Publicly accessible green spaces promote outdoor activity and recreation and provide calming and restorative settings, community gathering places, and space for environmental education. Open spaces also facilitate outdoor activity, leading to improved human health. Locating new open spaces close to communities and locating new housing close to existing open spaces can reduce residents' need to drive to enjoy outdoor recreational activities.

Green spaces with shrubs and trees also provide ecological benefits, such as cooling to offset heat island effects, windbreaks in winter, erosion control, stormwater absorption, and habitat for wildlife. And because they are aesthetically pleasing and offer amenities that people want, they can raise property values.

This credit rewards builders for selecting a home site that is located near publicly accessible open space or for including open space in a multihome development.

Approach and Implementation

Use local maps and geographic surveys to identify building sites that are located near open spaces. Information on existing parks can also be obtained from the local planning department, parks and recreation department, or similar entities. Design walking and bicycle pathways to increase accessibility to nearby open spaces.

The design of large developments should incorporate publicly accessible open space, including small parks, playgrounds, or other recreation areas. Work with the local government to facilitate public access and/or management of the open spaces.

Calculations

No calculations are required for this credit.

Exemplary Performance

Projects that are located within 1/2 mile of transit services that offer 250 or more transit rides per weekday may be awarded 1 point for exemplary performance, to be counted under Innovation in Design Process Credit 3.

Verification and Submittals

Supporting Verification Materials, made available by the Project Team:

❑   Present maps and/or directions to the Verification Team.

Verification Team:

❑   Visually verify (using maps and/or on-site observation) the presence of open spaces that meet the requirements of the credit.

Considerations

Economic Issues

Green space can have a significant positive effect on property values. Access to open space and places for outdoor recreation are amenities that people seek in making location decisions.

Constructing homes that have access to open space translates to value for builders, homeowners, and entire communities. Bond ratings are beginning to reflect the fact that unlimited or mismanaged growth can threaten a community's fiscal health, whereas land conservation and sound planning can help sustain it. Land conservation is increasingly a sound investment.

Regional Variances

The availability of open spaces varies considerably by region. In some areas, publicly accessible open space is extensive. In other areas, the builder may have to create public open spaces.

Resources

Web Sites

National Recreation and Park Association

www.nrpa.org

NRPA provides educational resources, frequent conferences, recommended accreditation programs, community initiatives, and published research about parks.

Municipal Research Services Center of Washington

www.mrsc.org/Subjects/Parks/parkplanpg.aspx

This Web site provides an overview of the park planning, design, and open space elements required in a sample state's comprehensive planning guidelines for local governments.

Print Media

Green Infrastructure: Linking Landscapes and Communities, by Mark A. Benedict and Edward T. McMahon. Island Press, 2006.

Neighborhood Pattern & Design 172, by J. Mertes et al. Park, Recreation, Open Space and Greenway Guidelines. National Recreation and Park Association, 1995.

Designing Small Parks: A Manual for Addressing Social and Ecological Concerns, by Ann Forsyth and Laura Musacchio. Planners Book Service.

Urban Open Space, by Mark Francis. Island Press, 2003.

Parks, Recreation, and Open Space: A Twenty-First Century Agenda, by Alexander Garvin. APA Planning Advisory Service, 2001.

ID	LL	SS	WE	EA	MR	EQ	AE
			6				

Sustainable Sites

Although the focus of green building is typically on the built structures located on a site, the design of the site and its natural elements can have a significant environmental impact. The Location & Linkages category rewards projects for choosing a preferable site location; the Sustainable Sites category rewards projects for designing the site to minimize adverse impacts.

Early decisions about how to incorporate the home into the site can have significant long-term effects on local and regional ecosystems, as well as on demand for water, chemicals, and pesticides for site management. Good design decisions can result in attractive, easy-to-maintain landscaping that protects native plant and animal species and contributes to the health of local and regional habitats.

The way in which a home is, or is not, integrated into the site can have various effects. Rain that falls on a site can be either a detriment, causing soil erosion and runoff of chemicals and pesticides, or an opportunity to offset potable water demand and recharge underground aquifers. Plant growth can be a burden, requiring regular upkeep, watering, and chemicals, or an enhancement that provides shade and improved occupant comfort, aesthetic value, habitat for native species, and a mechanism for absorbing carbon and enriching the soil.

Site design should take into consideration not only the aesthetic and functional preferences of the occupants but also long-term management needs, preservation principles, and potential impacts on local and regional ecosystems.

The six Sustainable Sites (SS) credits in the LEED for Homes Rating System—Site Stewardship, Landscaping, Local Heat Island Effects, Surface Water Management, Nontoxic Pest Control, and Compact Development—are summarized in **Table 1** and described in the following sections.

Table 1. Overview of Sustainable Sites (SS) Category

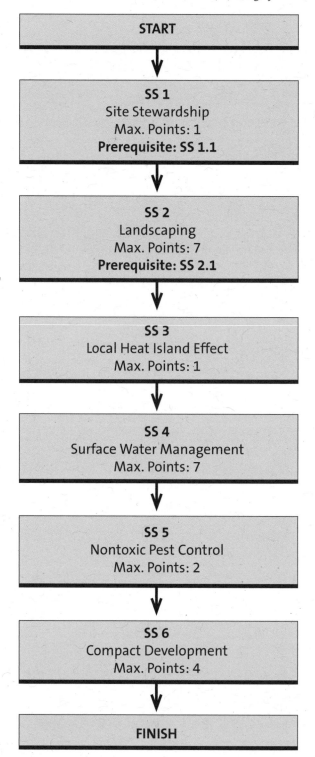

IMPORTANT NOTE:
*A minimum of **5 points** must be achieved in the SS category.*

SS 1: Site Stewardship

Intent

Minimize long-term environmental damage to the building lot during the construction process.

Requirements

Prerequisites

1.1 **Erosion Controls During Construction.** Prior to construction, design and plan appropriate erosion control measures. During construction, implement these measures. Erosion control measures must include all of the following:

a) Stockpile and protect disturbed topsoil from erosion (for reuse).

b) Control the path and velocity of runoff with silt fencing or comparable measures.

c) Protect on-site storm sewer inlets, streams, and lakes with straw bales, silt fencing, silt sacks, rock filters, or comparable measures.

d) Provide swales to divert surface water from hillsides.

e) If soils in a sloped area (i.e., 25%, or 4:1 slope) are disturbed during construction, use tiers, erosion blankets, compost blankets, filter socks and berms, or some comparable approach to keep soil stabilized.

Credits

1.2 **Minimize Disturbed Area of Site** (1 point). Minimize disturbance to the site by meeting the following:

Where the site is not previously developed:

a) Develop a tree or plant preservation plan with "no-disturbance" zones clearly delineated on drawings and on the lot (see Note 1 below).

b) Leave at least 40% of the buildable lot area undisturbed, not including area under roof. Only softscapes can be counted toward this credit; projects cannot receive credit for preserving preexisting hardscapes, such as driveways.

OR

Where the site is previously developed:

c) Develop a tree or plant preservation plan with "no-disturbance" zones clearly delineated on drawings and on the lot (see Note 1 below), and rehabilitate the lot by undoing any previous soil compaction, removing existing invasive plants, and meeting the requirements of SS 2.2 (see Note 2, below).

OR

d) Build on site with a lot area of less than 1/7 acre, or with housing density for the project that is equal to or greater than 7 units per acre. For multifamily buildings, the average lot size shall be calculated as the total lot size divided by the number of units.

Notes: *1. Any "no-disturbance" zones must also be protected from parked construction vehicles and building material storage. Soils compacted by vehicles or stored materials can cause major difficulties in establishing any new landscaping.*

2. Homes on previously developed lots that disturb the entire lot during construction can earn this credit by meeting the requirements in part (c) above.

Synergies and Trade-Offs

SS 4.2 rewards homes for the installation of permanent erosion controls.

If the project does not include full landscaping, homeowner association or other rules must require homeowners to have the site fully landscaped within one year; see SS 2. Erosion controls and soil stabilization measures must be robust enough to function until landscaping is in place (i.e., up to one year).

SS 1.1 Erosion Controls (During Construction)

Site clearing and earth moving can contribute to considerable runoff, leading to soil erosion and alteration of natural drainage patterns both on- and off-site. Each year, roughly 80 to 100 tons of soil per acre are lost because of construction. This runoff can carry pollutants and debris to regional lakes and streams and damage stormwater management infrastructure. Compacted soils from parked vehicles can cause major difficulties in establishing any new landscaping.

Proper measures can prevent soil erosion and preserve the quality of water in the surrounding areas. This prerequisite requires that all projects take measures prior to and during construction to limit soil erosion of surface areas surrounding the building site.

Approach and Implementation

Prior to construction, design a plan for the entire site that addresses erosion control, no-disturbance zones for tree or plant preservation (if applicable), and placement for construction material (see SS 1.2).

Conduct an informal survey of the site to identify site elements and determine a strategy to control runoff and erosion. Incorporate the specific elements of the plan into the construction drawings and specifications, with clear instructions on responsibilities. All erosion control strategies must be clearly articulated, shared with the project team, and carried out. Educate crews on the purpose and implementation of the erosion control measures. Conduct regular inspections, particularly before and after storm events.

On large sites (more than 1 acre), a stormwater pollution prevention plan (SWPPP) may be required by the National Pollutant Discharge Elimination System (NPDES) or local regulations. Determine whether the project needs to comply. Even if an SWPPP is not required, use the NPDES standard as a guideline on how to develop and implement an erosion control plan.

Acceptable approaches are listed in the prerequisite, SS 1.1. Stabilize and protect soil by using mulches, permanent seeding, sod, or soil roughening. Keeping heavy machinery off the site can prevent or reduce soil compaction. Preserving existing vegetation is also encouraged for erosion control and is rewarded in SS 1.2.

Maintain existing vegetation for as long as possible, even if it will be removed, to provide erosion control during construction. In a large development, phase grading of the site to limit the extent and duration of exposure. Avoid grading during wet months.

Restore the landscape promptly once construction has been completed. Install landscaping in phases when areas become accessible, rather than waiting for all phases of construction to be completed.

Calculations

No calculations are required.

Exemplary Performance

No additional points are available for exemplary performance.

Verification and Submittals

Supporting Verification Materials, made available by the Project Team:

❏   Ensure that required erosion control measures have been installed.

Verification Team:

- ☐ Visually verify that the required erosion control measures have been installed.

Considerations

Environmental Issues

The most significant on-site consequence of erosion is the loss of topsoil. Loss of topsoil greatly reduces the soil's ability to support plant life, regulate water flow, and maintain the biodiversity of soil microbes and insects that control disease and pest outbreaks.

Erosion from developed sites causes a variety of water quality problems. Runoff can carry pollutants, sediments, and surplus nutrients that interfere with aquatic habitats. The increase in sediment in stream channels can lessen flow capacity, increasing the risk of flooding.

Economic Issues

There are minor expenses associated with installing and inspecting erosion and sediment control measures on construction sites. The cost depends on the type, location, topography, and soil conditions of the project. The measures can save costs for cleanup, replacing soil, and loosening soil after compaction.

Runoff that ends up in the surrounding streets, storm drains, and drainage ditches increases maintenance costs for local governments. The additional cost is passed on to taxpayers in the form of higher taxes or stormwater utility fees.

Regional Variances

All sites that are at least 1 acre (or less than 1 acre but part of a larger common plan of development or sale) are subject to the National Pollutant Discharge Elimination System stormwater permit requirements. However, depending on decisions made by the permitting authority, small sites (those less than 5 acres) may be eligible for permit waivers or may not need to submit a Notice of Intent. States and municipalities may have similar permit requirements and stipulations.

Resources

Please see the USGBC Web site, at www.usgbc.org/resources, for more specific resources on materials sources and other technical information.

In addition to the resources below, check with state and local organizations for information on minimizing disturbance to the site and erosion and sedimentation control specific to your region.

Web Sites

CPESC Inc.

www.cpesc.net

Search the directory on this Web site to find certified erosion and sedimentation control professionals in your state.

EPA Erosion and Sediment Control Model Ordinances

www.epa.gov/owow/nps/ordinance/erosion.htm

This resource, developed by the Environmental Protection Agency, is geared toward helping municipalities draft ordinances for erosion and sedimentation control and might serve as a helpful tool in developing company policies for meeting the SS 1.1 prerequisite.

Erosion Control Technology Council

www.ectc.org

This nonprofit organization develops performance standards, testing procedures, and guidance on the application and installation of erosion control products.

International Erosion Control Association

www.ieca.org

This organization's mission is to connect,

educate, and develop the worldwide erosion and sediment control community.

Soil Erosion and Sedimentation in the Great Lakes Region

www.great-lakes.net/envt/pollution/erosion.html

This resource from the Great Lakes Information Network provides links to education and training opportunities, materials, manuals, maps, and other resources related to soil erosion, sedimentation, and watershed management.

Vermont Department of Environmental Conservation, Water Quality Division

www.vtwaterquality.org/stormwater/docs/construction/sw_low_risk_site_handbook.pdf

This Web site links to the Low Risk Site Handbook for Erosion Prevention and Sediment Control, an easy-to-follow guide that describes specific strategies, including diagrams and photos.

SS 1.2: Minimize Disturbed Area of Site

In addition to causing soil erosion, construction can unnecessarily kill natural vegetation, including shrubs and trees, destroying habitat and displacing wildlife. Construction vehicles and stored materials can compact soils, making it difficult to reestablish vegetation. Even with extensive efforts at rehabilitation, it may take years for the site to fully recover from this unnecessary damage.

This credit rewards projects that avoid causing long-term or permanent environmental and ecological damage during the construction phase. It encourages preservation of existing vegetation to minimize destruction of habitat.

Approach and Implementation

This credit is automatically granted to high-density construction, in recognition of the fact that compact development enables communities to set aside land for conservation. A project built on a previously developed site must earn this point by rehabilitating the site rather than preserving it.

The placement of the home on the building site can have a considerable and lasting impact on drainage patterns. Locate the home to take advantage of natural features on the site. For example, deciduous trees are an excellent source of shade, and existing plant and terrain features can provide natural swales to manage water runoff.

Carefully schedule construction in phases to minimize disturbance of the site. Include contractual requirements that subcontractors minimize site disturbance, and establish contractual penalties for the removal of trees and disturbance of protected zones.

Prior to construction, identify areas of the site that will be disturbed, including those areas to be affected by heavy equipment and vehicles and the places where construction materials will be stored. Clearly mark construction and disturbance boundaries on drawings, including delineation of lay-down, recycling, and disposal areas. Use areas to be paved as staging areas.

Maintain existing vegetation for as long as possible, even if it is scheduled to be removed, to provide erosion control on-site. Salvage existing plants, especially desirable native species, from the building site so that they can be replanted.

On sites that have been previously developed, preservation may not be the appropriate strategy. For example, brownfield sites may have unwanted paved areas or structures. In these cases, a project can earn points by remediating or rehabilitating the portion of the site unaffected by construction.

Calculations

Part (a) and (b) apply only to sites that are not previously developed or "disturbed". Undeveloped sites with substantial amounts of garbage and/or invasive weeds should be treated as previously developed sites.

For SS 1.2 (b), calculate the percentage of the buildable lot area that is left undisturbed during construction as follows:

Step 1. Calculate the buildable lot area and subtract the area under roof. The buildable lot area refers to the entire lot area except public streets or rights-of-way or land excluded from residential development by law.

Step 2. Calculate the buildable lot area that is being preserved during construction and subtract any preserved hardscapes (e.g., driveways, walkways).

Step 3. Divide #2 by #1 to find the percentage of the buildable lot area left undisturbed. This value must be at least 40%.

Exemplary Performance

No additional points are available for exemplary performance.

Verification and Submittals

Supporting Verification Materials, made available by the Project Team:

❑ For SS 1.2(a) and (c), present a tree and plant preservation plan and/or site drawings to the Verification Team.

❑ For SS 1.2(b), present calculations for the undisturbed area of the site to the Verification Team.

❑ For SS 1.2(d), present calculations that the lot is less than 1/7 of an acre, or that the site's density is at least 7 units an acre.

Verification Team:

❑ Visually verify the tree and plant preservation plan and/or site drawings.

❑ Visually verify that the calculations are completed.

❑ Visually verify that no-disturbance zones are marked on-site.

Considerations

Environmental Issues

Preserving existing vegetation can have significant environmental benefits, in both the short term and the long term. During construction, on-site vegetation helps minimize erosion and runoff that can damage nearby bodies of water. Preserving existing vegetation provides continuity to the site's habitat, reducing disruption or destruction of local wildlife.

Economic Issues

Native or adapted plantings generally have lower maintenance costs over their lifetime since, once established, they require little or no irrigation, mowing, or inputs of fertilizers and pesticides. In many cases, trees and vegetation grown off-site are costly to purchase and may not survive transplanting. Additional trees and other landscaping, as well as soil remediation and water elements, impose significant up-front costs.

Regional Variances

The appropriate strategies depend on the state of the site prior to construction and the type of development. If a project is built on an already developed site, it must be rehabilitated because prior development likely means that the soil is compacted and the existing vegetation is not environmentally preferable.

Resources

Please see the USGBC Web site, at www. usgbc.org/resources, for more-specific resources on materials sources and other technical information.

In addition to the resources below, check with state and local organizations for information on minimizing disturbance to the site and erosion and sedimentation control specific to your region.

Web Sites

American Society of Landscape Architects

www.asla.org

ASLA is the national professional association representing landscape architects. The Web site provides information about products, services, publications, and events.

Ecological Restoration

www.ecologicalrestoration.info

This quarterly print and online publica-

ID	LL	SS	WE	EA	MR	EQ	AE
		1.2					

tion from the University of Wisconsin–Madison Arboretum provides a forum for people interested in all aspects of ecological restoration.

Lady Bird Johnson Wildlife Center

www.wildflower.org

The center, located in Austin, Texas, has the mission of educating people about the environmental necessity, economic value, and natural beauty of native plants. The Web site offers a number of resources, including a nationwide native plant information network and a national suppliers directory.

North American Native Plant Society

www.nanps.org

A nonprofit association dedicated to the study, conservation, cultivation, and restoration of native plants. Its Web site contains links to state and provincial associations.

Plant Native

www.plantnative.org

This organization is dedicated to moving native plants and nature-scaping into mainstream landscaping practices.

Society for Ecological Restoration International

www.ser.org

Nonprofit consortium of scientists, planners, administrators, ecological consultants, landscape architects, engineers, and others with the mission of promoting ecological restoration as a means of sustaining the diversity of life and reestablishing an ecologically healthy relationship between nature and culture.

Soil and Water Conservation Society

www.swcs.org

An organization focused on fostering the science and art of sustainable soil, water, and related natural resources management.

Print Media

Design for Human Ecosystems: Landscape, Land Use and Natural Resources, by John Tillman Lyle. Island Press, 1999.

This text explores landscape design that functions like natural ecosystems.

Landscape Restoration Handbook by Donald Harker, Marc Evans, Gary Libby, Kay Harker, and Sherrie Evans. Lewis Publishers, 1999.

This comprehensive guide to natural landscaping and ecological restoration provides information on 21 ecological restoration types.

SS 2: Landscaping

Intent

Design landscape features to avoid invasive species and minimize demand for water and synthetic chemicals.

Requirements

Prerequisites

2.1 **No Invasive Plants.** Introduce no invasive plant species into the landscape.

Note: Invasive plant species vary by region. Consult the local Cooperative Extension Service or state agencies. A list of regional resources is available from the U.S. Department of Agriculture, at www.invasivespeciesinfo.gov/unitedstates/state.shtml. Not all nonnative species are considered invasive.

Credits

Note: Points shown below are for homes that are fully landscaped. A project that has not completed the designed landscaping may earn up to 50% of the points for each credit as long as 50% or more of the designed landscaping is completed upon certification. In this case, 100% completion of the landscaping must be required by homeowner association or other rules within a specific time period not to exceed one year after occupancy. Erosion controls and soil stabilization measures must be robust enough to be effective for one year. The builder or project team must also develop a landscaping plan that meets the requirements in SS 2 and provide it to the homeowner.

2.2 **Basic Landscape Design** (2 points). Meet all of the following requirements for all designed landscape softscapes:

a) Any turf must be drought-tolerant.

b) Do not use turf in densely shaded areas.

c) Do not use turf in areas with a slope of 25% (i.e., 4:1 slope).

d) Add mulch or soil amendments as appropriate.

Mulch is defined as a covering placed around plants to reduce erosion and water loss and to help regulate soil temperature. In addition, upon decomposition, organic mulches serve as soil amendments. The type of mulch selected can affect soil pH.

e) All compacted soil (e.g., from construction vehicles) must be tilled to at least 6 inches.

AND/OR

2.3 **Limit Conventional Turf** (maximum 3 points, as specified in **Table 1**). Limit the use of conventional turf in the designed landscape softscapes.

AND/OR

2.4 **Drought-Tolerant Plants** (maximum 2 points, as specified in **Table 2**). Install drought-tolerant plants.

Table 1. Limited Conventional Turf

Percentage of designed landscape softscape area that is conventional turf	Points
41–60%	1
21–40%	2
20% or less	3

Table 2. Drought-Tolerant Plants

Percentage of installed plants that are drought-tolerant	Points
45–89%	1
90% or more	2

OR

2.5 **Reduce Overall Irrigation Demand by at Least 20%** (maximum 6 points, as specified in **Table 3**). Design the landscape and irrigation system to reduce overall irrigation water usage. The estimates must be calculated and prepared by a landscape professional, biologist, or other qualified professional using the method outlined below.

Table 3. Reduction in Water Demand

Reduction in estimated irrigation water usage	SS 2.5 points	WE 2.3 points	Total points
20–24%	2	0	2
25–29%	3	0	3
30–34%	4	0	4
35–39%	5	0	5
40–44%	6	0	6
45–49%	6	1	7
50–54%	6	2	8
55–59%	6	3	9
60% or more	6	4	10

Method for Calculating Reduction in Irrigation Demand

Step 1. Calculate the baseline irrigation water usage:

Baseline Usage = Landscaped Area * ET_0 * 0.62

where ET_0 = Baseline Evapotranspiration Rate (available from local and state Departments of Agriculture)

Step 2. Calculate the design case irrigation water usage:

Design Case Usage = (Landscaped Area * ET_L ÷ IE) * CF * 0.62

where ET_L = ET_0 * K_L and K_L = K_S * K_{MC}. Refer to **Tables 4 and 5** for values for K_S and K_{MC}, and to **Table 6** for values for IE. For CF, use estimated value based on manufacturer's specifications for percentage water savings.

Step 3. Calculate the percentage reduction in irrigation water usage:

Percentage Reduction = (1 − Design Case Usage ÷ Baseline Usage) * 100

Step 4. Refer to **Table 3**, above, to determine points earned.

Table 4. Species Factor

Vegetation type	Species factor (K_S)		
	Low	Average	High
Trees	0.2	0.5	0.9
Shrubs	0.2	0.5	0.7
Groundcover	0.2	0.5	0.7
Turf	0.6	0.7	0.8

Table 5. Microclimate Factor

Example microclimate impacts	Microclimate factor (K_{MC})		
	Low	Average	High
Shading	0.5	0.8	1.0
High sun exposure	1.0	1.2	1.5
Protection from wind	0.8	0.9	1.0
Windy area	1.0	1.2	1.5

Table 6. Irrigation Efficiency

Irrigation type	Irrigation efficiency (IE)	
	Low	High
Fixed spray	0.4	0.6
Impact and microspray	0.5	0.7
Rotors	0.6	0.8
Multistream rotators	0.6	0.8
Low volume and point source (e.g., drip)	0.7	0.9

Synergies and Trade-Offs

A project receiving points in SS 2.5 should also refer to WE 2.3.

Any measures chosen in SS 2 should be integrated with irrigation system design, which is addressed in WE 2. Rainwater and graywater reuse systems (WE 1) should also be included in landscaping design.

SS 2.1: No Invasive Plants

Conventional building practices rarely include ecological protection as a priority. As a result, native plants on building lots are rarely preserved. Where a building site is disrupted, the choice of plantings and groundcover can have significant long-term environmental consequences, both on the site and regionally.

An invasive plant is defined in U.S. Executive Order 13112 as any species that is nonnative (or alien) to the ecosystem under consideration and whose introduction causes or is likely to cause economic or environmental harm or harm to human health.

Invasive species cause economic, environmental, and sometimes even human harm by killing established trees, clogging drainage systems, overtaking and destroying the natural plant ecosystem, including wetlands, and resisting control without toxic herbicides. According to the U.S. Department of Agriculture, the United States spends more than $100 billion annually on containing or managing the effects of invasive species infestations. Nearly half of endangered species and endangered ecosystems in the country are significantly affected by invasive species.

Not all nonnative species are considered invasive. This prerequisite allows the use of nonnative species but prohibits the use of invasive plants.

Approach and Implementation

The first step in fulfilling this prerequisite is to choose plantings and groundcover for the site. Where possible, preserve existing vegetation by minimizing disturbance to the site (see SS 1.2). When selecting plantings and groundcover for the site, use native or adapted plantings and avoid any turf except mixes of native grasses.

Prior to installation, consult experts—landscape professionals, local and regional governmental agencies, subject experts, educational facilities, or native plant organization staff—to identify appropriate native or adapted plant materials. If nonnative plants are selected, consult lists of local or regional invasive species and noxious weeds to ensure that none are used on the site.

This prerequisite applies to all designed landscape. Areas of the site that are left undisturbed by construction (see SS 1.2) are not required to undergo inspection. Projects are nevertheless strongly encouraged to replace any known invasive species on the site, since invasive vegetation will creep onto the remainder of the site.

Calculations

No calculations are required.

Exemplary Performance

No additional points are available for exemplary performance.

Verification and Submittals

Supporting Verification Materials, made available by the Project Team:

❑ Present a list of plants being used and a list of local invasive plants (and/or list of noninvasive plants) to the Verification Team.

❑ If no landscape professional is involved in the project, sign an Accountability Form to indicate that the plants that are installed match those on the list provided to the Verification Team.

Verification Team:

- ❑ Visually verify, using the two lists provided by the builder or project team leader, that none of the plants being used are considered invasive.

- ❑ Verify that an Accountability Form has been signed by the responsible party.

Considerations

Environmental Issues

Invasive species tend to reproduce at very high rates and outcompete native species for space, water, and nutrients. Infestations can disrupt local ecosystems and cause a significant loss of biodiversity. Broader long-term effects include extirpation of local wildlife populations and disruption of critical ecosystem functions. By contrast, native plants promote biodiversity and habitat sustainability by providing food and shelter for indigenous wildlife.

Economic Issues

Control of invasive species can be costly for individual property owners and entire communities.

Preserving existing vegetation is less expensive than installing vegetation grown off-site. In many cases, trees and other vegetation raised off-site are costly to purchase and may not survive transplanting, so preserving existing vegetation is preferable. Additional trees and other landscaping, as well as soil remediation and water elements, can incur first costs.

Regional Variances

The classification of invasive species varies by region. A plant that is designated as invasive in one area may not be considered invasive elsewhere. Consult local and regional resources to identify both invasive and native species in your area.

Resources

Please see the USGBC Web site, at www.usgbc.org/resources, for more specific resources on materials sources and other technical information.

Lists of local drought-tolerant plants and grasses are available from local USDA Agricultural Cooperative Extension Service offices, as well as through numerous Internet resources. To find local Extension Service offices, go to www.csrees.usda.gov/Extension/index.html.

Web Sites

Agricultural Cooperative Extension Services

www.csrees.usda.gov/Extension/index.html

This site provides links and contacts for local and state Agricultural Cooperative Extension System offices. These offices are staffed by experts who can provide valuable information specific to your region.

Ecological Restoration

www.ecologicalrestoration.info

This quarterly print and online publication from the University of Wisconsin–Madison Arboretum provides a forum for people interested in all aspects of ecological restoration.

Lady Bird Johnson Wildlife Center

www.wildflower.org

The center, located in Austin, Texas, has the mission of educating people about the environmental necessity, economic value, and natural beauty of native plants. The Web site offers a number of resources, including a nationwide native plant information network and a national suppliers directory.

National Invasive Species Information Center

www.invasivespeciesinfo.gov/plants/main.shtml

As part of the USDA's National Agricultural Library, NISIC serves as a reference gateway to information, organizations, and services about invasive species.

North American Native Plant Society

www.nanps.org

A nonprofit association dedicated to the study, conservation, cultivation, and restoration of native plants. Its Web site contains links to state and provincial associations.

Plant Native

www.plantnative.org

This organization is dedicated to moving native plants and nature-scaping into mainstream landscaping practices.

U.S. Forest Service "Celebrating Wildflowers"

www.fs.fed.us/wildflowers/nativegardening/instructions.shtml

A site hosted by the U.S. Forest Service has extensive information on native gardening, selecting appropriate native plants, invasive plant species, and basic instructions for restoration and native landscaping projects.

Print Media

Design for Human Ecosystems: Landscape, Land Use and Natural Resources, by John Tillman Lyle. Island Press, 1999.

This text explores landscape design that functions like natural ecosystems.

Landscape Restoration Handbook by Donald Harker, Marc Evans, Gary Libby, Kay Harker, and Sherrie Evans. Lewis Publishers, 1999.

This comprehensive guide to natural landscaping and ecological restoration provides information on 21 ecological restoration types.

SS 2.2: Basic Landscape Design

Many conventional practices, such as planting turf in sloped or shaded areas, can lead to an unsustainable site that requires considerable water, chemicals, and time to maintain. The use of drought-tolerant species and the application of mulch reduce irrigation demand and conserve local and regional potable water resources.

SS 2.2 applies to the area of the lot that is disturbed during construction.

Approach and Implementation

Develop a site map showing existing or planned structures, topography, orientation, sun and wind exposure, use of space, and existing vegetation. Perform shadow profiles of landscape areas for each season, based on midday conditions, and illustrate the plant selection within the profiles.

Work with a landscape or irrigation professional to design landscaping that minimizes the need for irrigation and chemicals. Install climate-appropriate landscaping that is attractive and functional (e.g., it provides shading, water runoff management, pest control). Avoid designs with sharp angles or tight curves and bends that can be difficult to maintain and irrigate. Simplicity in the design will ensure ease of maintenance and water-use efficiency.

Design landscaping with climate-tolerant plants that, once established, can survive on natural rainfall quantities. Contour the land to direct rainwater runoff through the site to give vegetation an additional water supply. Minimize the amount of site area covered with turf and use mulches and other techniques that improve water retention and help foster optimal soil conditions.

Plant turf grasses only for functional benefits, such as recreation and pedestrian use, or specifically for soil conservation. Where possible, use mixed native grasses rather than conventional turf.

Shading can be a valuable element of the landscape design, helping cool the home and reduce local heat island effects. Rather than eliminate it, plant appropriate vegetation beneath tree canopies.

Keep landscape areas mulched to conserve moisture and prevent evaporative water loss from the soil surface to reduce the need for supplemental irrigation during periods of limited rainfall. Mulch is a covering placed around plants to reduce erosion and water loss and help regulate the soil temperature. In addition, upon decomposition, organic mulches serve as soil amendments. The type of mulch selected can affect soil pH.

Avoid using peat moss or shredded hardwood bark as a mulch; once dry, it resists absorbing new moisture and is actually water repellent.

Calculations

No calculations are required.

Exemplary Performance

No additional points are available for exemplary performance.

Verification and Submittals

Supporting Verification Materials, made available by the Project Team:

❑ Sign an Accountability Form to indicate that the requirements of the credit have been met.

Verification Team:

❑ Verify that an Accountability Form has been signed by responsible party.

❑ Verify that turf is not installed in densely shaded or sloped areas.

❑ Verify that compact soil has been tilled.

Considerations

Environmental Issues

Conventional turf requires more water, chemicals, and maintenance than native plantings or groundcover. Turf also has shallow roots, which make it ineffective at managing runoff, particularly on sloped areas. Avoiding turf in shaded and sloped areas will reduce chemical runoff and soil erosion, which can have harmful effects on nearby aquatic environments.

Economic Issues

Planting appropriate vegetation in shaded and sloped areas will significantly reduce long-term maintenance costs.

Regional Variances

The use of native plantings is generally encouraged, but best practice is to choose plantings that are appropriate for the specific features of the project site. Individual project sites and even portions of the same site may vary significantly in soil type, solar exposure, wind, and associated evaporation rates and moisture levels. Where possible, choose plantings that take into consideration both local and microclimate conditions.

Other

Conventional turf is typically a monoculture, which encourages proliferation of certain types of pests. The use of mixed native grasses facilitates a more varied ecosystem that reduces the risk that any one species will become an infestation.

Resources

Please see the USGBC Web site, at www.usgbc.org/resources, for more specific resources on materials sources and other technical information.

Lists of local drought-tolerant plants and grasses are available from local USDA Agricultural Cooperative Extension Service offices, as well as through numerous Internet resources. To find local Extension Service offices, go to www.csrees.usda.gov/Extension/index.html.

Web Sites

American Society of Landscape Architects

www.asla.org

ASLA is the national professional association representing landscape architects. The Web site provides information about products, services, publications, and events.

Lady Bird Johnson Wildlife Center

www.wildflower.org

The center, located in Austin, Texas, has the mission of educating people about the environmental necessity, economic value, and natural beauty of native plants. The Web site offers a number of resources, including a nationwide native plant information network and a national suppliers directory.

North American Native Plant Society

www.nanps.org

A nonprofit association dedicated to the study, conservation, cultivation, and restoration of native plants. Its Web site contains links to state and provincial associations.

Plant Native

www.plantnative.org

This organization is dedicated to moving native plants and nature-scaping into mainstream landscaping practices.

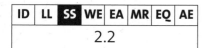
Soil and Water Conservation Society

www.swcs.org

An organization focused on fostering the science and art of sustainable soil, water, and related natural resources management.

Print Media

Design for Human Ecosystems: Landscape, Land Use and Natural Resources, by John Tillman Lyle. Island Press, 1999.

This text explores landscape design that functions like natural ecosystems.

Landscape Restoration Handbook by Donald Harker, Marc Evans, Gary Libby, Kay Harker, and Sherrie Evans. Lewis Publishers, 1999.

This comprehensive guide to natural landscaping and ecological restoration provides information on 21 ecological restoration types.

Most conventional turf is a monoculture with a shallow but tight root system. These qualities prevent it from storing water well and allow heavy rainfall to run off rather than absorb into the surface. Because conventional turf reduces the soil's capacity to store water, keeping it healthy requires considerable watering. As a monoculture, conventional turf can also facilitate the overpopulation of certain insect species, leading to greater risk of infestation. Turf also must be mowed, and homeowners with large lawns are likely to use power equipment, which generates air and noise pollution.

The credit rewards the limited use of conventional turf.

Approach and Implementation

Work with a landscape professional or contact the local Agricultural Cooperative Extension Service office to find out more about designing a landscape that is appropriate to the general climate and specific microclimate of the project site.

Conventional turf is defined as any turf that requires regular mowing, watering, and/or chemicals. Native grass mixes that do not require regular maintenance are not considered conventional turf.

The best approach for limiting conventional turf is to use native plants and groundcovers that require little additional watering or upkeep. Groundcovers are a particularly good substitute for grass on sloped areas. Consider the use of herbaceous perennials, pachysandra, or deciduous or coniferous shrubs.

Plant native drought-tolerant turf where grass is necessary. Native grass mixes that provide many of the benefits of conventional turf but few of the negative environmental impacts are available. Avoid planting turf in sloped or shaded areas.

Calculations

To calculate the number of points earned for this credit, use the following steps. Note that the undisturbed portion of the lot is not used in this calculation.

Step 1. Determine the total designed landscape softscape area, excluding any undisturbed portion of the lot, any public right-of-way, the area under roof, and any hardscapes, such as walkways and driveways. (See area F in **Figure 1**).

Step 2: Estimate the total designed landscape softscape area planted with conventional turf.

Step 3. Calculate the percentage of the total designed landscape softscape area that is planted with conventional turf.

Step 4. Refer to **Table 3**, above, to determine points earned. If more than 60% of the designed landscape softscape area is conventional turf, no points are earned.

Exemplary Performance

No additional points are available for exemplary performance.

Verification and Submittals

Supporting Verification Materials, made available by the Project Team:

❑ Present calculations to the Verification Team demonstrating the percentage of the site's landscape softscape area that is covered by conventional turf.

❑ Sign an Accountability Form to indicate that the vegetation planted is not conventional turf.

ID	LL	SS	WE	EA	MR	EQ	AE
				2.3			

Verification Team:

- ❑ Visually verify that all relevant calculations are completed.

- ❑ Verify limited conventional turf is installed, as per the calculations provided.

- ❑ Verify that an Accountability Form has been signed by the responsible party.

Considerations

Environmental Issues

Conventional turf is typically a monoculture, which encourages proliferation of certain types of pests. The use of mixed native grasses facilitates a more varied ecosystem. Conventional turf requires more water, chemicals, and maintenance than native plantings or groundcover. Turf also has shallow roots that make it ineffective at managing runoff, particularly on sloped areas. Avoiding turf in shaded and sloped areas will reduce chemical runoff and soil erosion, which can have harmful effects on nearby aquatic environments.

Economic Issues

Planting climate-appropriate vegetation that includes groundcover, shrubs, and other plants rather than turf will significantly reduce long-term maintenance costs.

Regional Variances

Best practice is to choose plantings that are appropriate for the specific features of the project site. Individual project sites and even portions of the same site may vary significantly in soil type, solar exposure, wind, and associated evaporation rates and moisture levels. Take into consideration both local and microclimate conditions when selecting plant materials. The use of native plant species is generally encouraged.

Other

Conventional turfgrass is typically a monoculture, which encourages proliferation of certain types of pests. The use of mixed native grasses facilitates a more varied ecosystem that reduces the risk that any one species will become an infestation.

Figure 1.

Example areas:
A: House
B: Garage
C: Driveway
D: Walkway
E: Fountain
F: Landscaped softscapes
G: Undisturbed softscapes
H: Public right-of-way
I: Public road

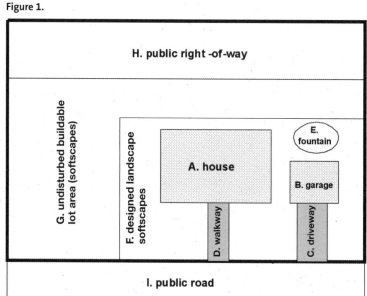

Resources

Please see the USGBC Web site, at www.usgbc.org/resources, for more specific resources on materials sources and other technical information.

Lists of local drought-tolerant plants and grasses are available from local USDA Agricultural Cooperative Extension Service offices, as well as through numerous Internet resources. To find local Extension Service offices, go to www.csrees.usda.gov/Extension/index.html

Web Sites

American Society of Landscape Architects

www.asla.org

ASLA is the national professional association representing landscape architects. The Web site provides information about products, services, publications, and events.

Ecological Restoration

www.ecologicalrestoration.info

This quarterly print and online publication from the University of Wisconsin–Madison Arboretum provides a forum for people interested in all aspects of ecological restoration.

Lady Bird Johnson Wildlife Center

www.wildflower.org

The center, located in Austin, Texas, has the mission of educating people about the environmental necessity, economic value, and natural beauty of native plants. The Web site offers a number of resources, including a nationwide native plant information network and a national suppliers directory.

North American Native Plant Society

www.nanps.org

A nonprofit association dedicated to the study, conservation, cultivation, and restoration of native plants. Its Web site

contains links to state and provincial associations.

Plant Native

www.plantnative.org

This organization is dedicated to moving native plants and nature-scaping into mainstream landscaping practices.

Society for Ecological Restoration International

www.ser.org

The mission of this nonprofit consortium of scientists, planners, administrators, ecological consultants, landscape architects, engineers, and others is to promote ecological restoration as a means of sustaining the diversity of life and reestablish an ecologically healthy relationship between nature and culture.

Soil and Water Conservation Society

www.swcs.org

An organization focused on fostering the science and art of sustainable soil, water, and related natural resources management.

U.S. Forest Service "Celebrating Wildflowers"

www.fs.fed.us/wildflowers/nativegardening/instructions.shtml

A site hosted by the U.S. Forest Service that has extensive information on native gardening, selecting appropriate native plants, invasive plant species, and basic instructions for restoration and native landscaping projects.

Print Media

Design for Human Ecosystems: Landscape, Land Use and Natural Resources, by John Tillman Lyle. Island Press, 1999.

This text explores landscape design that functions like natural ecosystems.

Landscape Restoration Handbook by Donald Harker, Marc Evans, Gary Libby, Kay

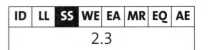

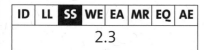

ID	LL	SS	WE	EA	MR	EQ	AE
		2.3					

Harker, and Sherrie Evans. Lewis Publishers, 1999.

This comprehensive guide to natural landscaping and ecological restoration provides information on 21 ecological restoration types.

SS 2.4: Drought-Tolerant Plants

The use of drought-tolerant plants helps reduce the need for irrigation. Since the provision and distribution of potable water is costly and energy intensive, particularly during dry periods, a more sensible strategy is to design landscaping that requires less potable water. Minimizing the need for irrigation during droughts also helps protect soil quality and regional water quality by reducing runoff of topsoil, pesticides, and fertilizers.

This credit rewards the use of native or adapted drought-resistant plants.

Weeds can overtake even a well-designed landscape. Because weeds grow rapidly and have big root systems, they can outcompete installed plants, particularly when water is scarce. Remove the weeds before and during landscaping so that the new plants will have sufficient water.

Drought-tolerant plantings may not be appropriate for certain areas of the site. For example, in regions with consistent rainfall, it is appropriate to use plants that need considerable water at the bottom of slopes or in rain gardens.

Approach and Implementation

Work with a landscape professional or contact the local Agricultural Cooperative Extension Service office to find out more about designing a landscape that is drought tolerant.

Choose plantings that are not only drought tolerant but also appropriate to the local climate and microclimate of the site. Take an integrated approach to the choice of plantings, groundcover, trees, and grasses so as to design the landscaping for maximum durability without watering or chemicals.

Landscaping should contain drought-resistant plants and grasses and native woody plants when possible. Plant trees and shrubs that are water savers. The use of native or adapted plants is an excellent approach because water conservation is built in, not dependent on high-tech equipment and controls.

If irrigation is necessary, zone the landscaping to use the optimal irrigation techniques for each type of vegetation. Use drip irrigation around plantings to minimize evapotranspiration losses and wasted water.

Calculations

Calculate the number of installed drought-tolerant plants as a percentage of the total installed plants. Include only newly installed, not existing, plants.

Exemplary Performance

No additional points are available for exemplary performance.

Verification and Submittals

Supporting Verification Materials, made available by the Project Team:

❏ Present calculations to the Verification Team demonstrating the percentage of installed plants that is drought tolerant.

❏ Present a list of plants being used and a list of local or regional drought-tolerant plants to the Verification Team.

❏ Sign an Accountability Form to indicate that the installed plants match those on the list provided to the Verification Team.

Verification Team:

❑ Visually verify that the calculations are completed.

❑ Visually verify, using the two lists provided by the builder or project team leader, that any plants counted toward this credit are drought tolerant.

❑ Verify that an Accountability Form has been signed by the responsible party.

Considerations

Environmental Issues

The use of drought-tolerant plants, particularly in dry regions, can significantly reduce demand for water, chemicals, and maintenance. Avoiding irrigation during dry periods can also reduce runoff that not only damages topsoil but also can carry chemicals and fertilizers into nearby aquatic environments.

Economic Issues

In some climates, it is possible to eliminate the need for permanent irrigation through the use of drought-tolerant plants and improved landscape design. In other climates, irrigation costs can be cut by half or more simply by selecting site-appropriate plants.

Regional Variances

The use of drought-tolerant plants is generally encouraged, but best practice is to choose plants that are appropriate for the specific features and characteristics of the project site, such as soil type, orientation, exposure to wind, and moisture levels. Where possible, take into consideration both local and microclimate conditions.

Resources

Please see the USGBC Web site, at www.usgbc.org/resources, for more specific resources on materials sources and other technical information.

Lists of local drought-tolerant plants and grasses are available from local USDA Agricultural Cooperative Extension Service offices, as well as through numerous Internet resources. To find local Extension Service offices, go to www.csrees.usda.gov/Extension/index.html

Web Sites

American Society of Landscape Architects

www.asla.org

ASLA is the national professional association representing landscape architects. The Web site provides information about products, services, publications, and events.

Lady Bird Johnson Wildlife Center

www.wildflower.org

The center, located in Austin, Texas, has the mission of educating people about the environmental necessity, economic value, and natural beauty of native plants. The Web site offers a number of resources, including a nationwide native plant information network and a national suppliers directory.

North American Native Plant Society

www.nanps.org

A nonprofit association dedicated to the study, conservation, cultivation, and restoration of native plants. Its Web site contains links to state and provincial associations.

Plant Native

www.plantnative.org

This organization is dedicated to moving native plants and nature-scaping into mainstream landscaping practices.

Soil and Water Conservation Society

www.swcs.org

An organization focused on fostering the science and art of sustainable soil, water, and related natural resources management.

Print Media

Design for Human Ecosystems: Landscape, Land Use and Natural Resources, by John Tillman Lyle. Island Press, 1999.

This text explores landscape design that functions like natural ecosystems.

Landscape Restoration Handbook by Donald Harker, Marc Evans, Gary Libby, Kay Harker, and Sherrie Evans, Lewis Publishers, 1999.

This comprehensive guide to natural landscaping and ecological restoration provides information on 21 ecological restoration types.

SS 2.5: Reduce Overall Irrigation Demand by At Least 20%

Landscape irrigation practices consume large quantities of potable water. According to one estimate, a typical suburban lawn requires 10,000 gallons of irrigation water each year.[1] Irrigation typically uses potable water, even though nonpotable water (e.g., rainwater, graywater, recycled water) is equally effective. A holistic approach to landscape design can significantly reduce potable water consumption by using site-appropriate vegetation to reduce demand and by designing high-efficiency irrigation to reduce wasted supply.

This credit rewards projects that can demonstrate less overall irrigation water demand compared with a conventional landscape and irrigation design in a comparable site.

Approach and Implementation

This credit, together with Water Efficiency 2.3, is a performance-based alternative to the prescriptive measures in SS 2.2, 2.3, and 2.4, as well as WE 2.1 and 2.2. Projects that use the performance approach cannot earn points for prescriptive measures in SS 2.3, SS 2.4, WE 2.1, or WE 2.2, and can earn only partial credit in SS 2.2. However, the measures and strategies listed in each of those credits are an excellent guide for how to reduce irrigation water demand.

The performance approach provides more flexibility but requires a higher level of verification using site-specific calculations (see "Calculations," below). Projects cannot earn the points in this credit simply by being located in an area with considerable rainfall.

This credit requires a minimum reduction in irrigation water demand of 20% and rewards a reduction of up to 45%. If a project reduces water demand by more than 45%, it is eligible to earn points in WE 2.3. Significant reduction in water demand is most easily met by a combination of landscape design and efficient irrigation water use.

Choose appropriate vegetation that requires little irrigation. Work with a landscape professional and/or irrigation specialist to choose trees, shrubs, and groundcover that are well suited to the local soil and climate. Avoid turfgrass and any species that require regular watering.

Use high-efficiency irrigation techniques, including those listed in WE 2.1, to provide only as much water to the plants as needed and to minimize evaporative losses and leaks.

Ensure that both the landscaping plan and the irrigation system are installed in accordance with the design. Have the designer and installer work closely together and use a third party to verify that the system is functioning properly after installation.

Any rainwater, graywater, or recycled water system should be integrated with the landscape design and irrigation system. However, these systems are rewarded in WE 1.1, 1.2, and 1.3, and any water demand being met by these systems must still be counted in the calculation for this credit.

Calculations

A guidance document and accompanying calculator have been developed for performing the calculation for this credit. Please contact your LEED for Homes

---

1 U.S. Environmental Protection Agency, Office of Water. *Water-Efficient Landscaping*. EPA Publication 832-F-02-002, September 2002. 21 January 2005.

Provider for these resources. Calculate the percentage reduction in irrigation demand for this credit using the four-step process outlined below. When calculating water use, do not subtract water from rainwater, graywater, or recycled water systems; these elements are rewarded in other credits.

A landscape professional must perform the calculation. This includes individuals with certification, licensure, formal training (higher education), or at least 10 years of professional experience.

If insufficient data prevent use of the prescribed method, a landscape professional can submit a modified method as a Credit Interpretation Request.

Standard assumptions and variables

❑ All calculations are based on irrigation during the month of July.

❑ All estimates for water use must be based on expected demand when the plantings are fully mature.

❑ If the landscape is divided into zones, calculate each zone separately. The average for the entire site should be calculated by weighting the results for each zone based on its proportion to the total landscaped area.

❑ Landscape Coefficient (K_L) indicates the volume of water lost via evapotranspiration. This value is dependent on the landscape species, the microclimate, and the planting density. The formula for determining the landscape coefficient is given in Step 2, below.

❑ Species Factor (K_S) accounts for the water requirements of different plant species. The species factor can be divided into three categories (high, average, and low) depending on the plant species considered. To determine the most appropriate category for a plant species, use plant manuals and professional experience. This

factor is somewhat subjective, but landscape professionals should have a general idea of the water needs of particular plant species. See **Table 7** for sample values.

❑ Microclimate Factor (K_{MC}) accounts for environmental conditions specific to the landscape, including temperature, wind, and humidity. The average K_{MC} is 1.0; it refers to conditions where the landscape evapotranspiration rate is unaffected by buildings, pavements, reflective surfaces, and slopes. Higher K_{MC} conditions occur where evaporative potential is increased because of proximity to heat-absorbing and reflective surfaces or exposure to wind.

❑ Baseline Evapotranspiration Rate (ET_0) represents the rate of water loss for a particular climate or region. Use a published value for ET_0 that corresponds to the climate of the project site. The ET_0 value for July must be used in this calculation because the highest evapotranspiration rates and, therefore, the greatest irrigation demands occur during that month. Published ET_0 values are available from various sources, including state and local departments of agriculture.

❑ Landscape Evapotranspiration Rate (ET_L) is the site-specific rate, which is calculated based on other variables (see equation, Step 2, below).

❑ Irrigation Efficiency (IE) is based on the type of irrigation equipment installed. Some manufacturers provide a distribution uniformity, which can be used here. Otherwise, refer to **Table 9** for sample values.

❑ Control Factor (CF) is based on the type of controls installed, such as weather-based or moisture sensor-based systems. If no moisture sensor, rain-delay controller, or flow-control sensor is used, CF = 1.0. A controller that is estimated to reduce overall irrigation has a CF of 1 minus the fraction of *overall* irrigation water saved. For example, a controller that saves 10% has a CF of 0.90. This number must be supported by either manufacturer's documentation or calculations by a landscape professional.

Estimating the percentage reduction in water usage for irrigation

Step 1. Calculate the baseline irrigation water usage:

Baseline Usage = Landscaped Area * ET_0 * 0.62

where ET_0 = Baseline Evapotranspiration Rate (available from local and state departments of agriculture)

Step 2. Calculate the design case irrigation water usage:

Design Case Usage = (Landscaped Area * $ET_L \div IE$) * CF * 0.62

where $ET_L = ET_0 * K_L$ and $K_L = K_S * K_{MC}$. Refer to **Tables 7** and **8** for values for K_S and K_{MC}, and to **Table 9** for values for IE. For CF, use estimated value based on manufacturer's specifications for percentage water savings.

Step 3. Calculate the percentage reduction in irrigation water usage:

Percentage Reduction = (1—Design Case Usage ÷ Baseline Usage) * 100

Step 4. Refer to **Table 3**, above, to determine points earned.

Table 7. Species Factor

Vegetation type	Species factor (K_s)		
	Low	Average	High
Trees	0.2	0.5	0.9
Shrubs	0.2	0.5	0.7
Groundcover	0.2	0.5	0.7
Turf	0.6	0.7	0.8

Table 8. Microclimate Factor

Example microclimate impacts	Microclimate factor (K_{MC})		
	Low	Average	High
Shading	0.5	0.8	1.0
High sun exposure	1.0	1.2	1.5
Protection from wind	0.8	0.9	1.0
Windy area	1.0	1.2	1.5

Table 9. Irrigation Efficiency

Irrigation type	Irrigation efficiency (IE)	
	Low	High
Fixed spray	0.4	0.6
Impact and microspray	0.5	0.7
Rotors	0.6	0.8
Multistream rotators	0.6	0.8
Low volume and point source (e.g., drip)	0.7	0.9

Verification and Submittals

Supporting Verification Materials, made available by the Project Team:

❏ Present calculations to the Verification Team.

❏ Present a list of plants being used to the Verification Team.

❏ Sign an Accountability Form to indicate that the installed landscape and irrigation system corresponds to the design used in the calculation.

Verification Team:

❏ Visually verify that the calculations are completed.

❏ If drought-tolerant plants are claimed ([Ks] less than 0.4), use a list of installed plants provided by the project team and a list of drought-tolerant plants created by a third-party entity (e.g. ag. cooperative extension) to verify that installed plants in that zone are drought-tolerant.

❏ Verify that the calculation was performed by a qualified individual (e.g., certified or licensed landscape architect).

❏ Conduct on-site verification of any water-saving items identified in the calculation, including high-efficiency irrigation measures and high/low shading conditions.

❏ Verify that an Accountability Form has been signed by the responsible party.

Exemplary Performance

A project that earns SS 2.5 can earn 1 point, to be counted under Innovation & Design Process Credit 3, for fulfilling SS 2.2 parts b, c, and d. See the Exemplary Performance section under WE 2.3 for additional credit for projects that demonstrate exemplary outdoor water savings.

Considerations

Economic Issues

The most effective strategy to reduce the cost of irrigation is to design landscaping adapted to the local climate and the site's microclimate, with careful plant selection and layout. Although the additional design cost for a drip irrigation system may make it more expensive than a conventional system, a drip system usually costs less to install and has lower water use and maintenance requirements.

Many municipalities offer rebates or incentives for water-efficient irrigation systems, dedicated water meters, and rain or moisture sensors. Check with the regional or state water authority for information on possible incentives.

Environmental Issues

The use of native or adapted landscaping and the avoidance of conventional turf can reduce the demand for fertilizer and pesticides as well as irrigation. The use of native landscaping can also provide habitat for native wildlife and create a site that is integrated with its natural surroundings.

Regional Variances

The need for an irrigation system will depend on the type of landscaping used, the microclimate effects on evapotranspiration rates, and the amount and frequency of rainfall. Water-efficient landscaping helps conserve local and regional potable water resources. Local water authorities may require irrigation measures, especially in areas where water resources are scarce. A project that uses the measures in this credit as part of code compliance is still eligible to earn LEED points.

Resources

Note that several of the resources included in WE 1.1 and 1.2 can assist in integrating

rainwater harvesting and graywater with landscape irrigation systems.

Web Sites

American Society of Landscape Architects

www.asla.org

ASLA is the national professional association representing landscape architects. The Web site provides information about members, products, services, publications, and events.

International Center for Water Technology

www.icwt.net

The International Center for Water Technology is a consortium of public and private entities, led by the efforts of California State University–Fresno. This Web site is the more technical counterpart to Wateright; it includes research papers and educational materials about cutting-edge progress in water-saving technologies.

The Irrigation Association

www.irrigation.org

This nonprofit organization provides education for and certification of irrigation system designers, installers, and auditors. It also promotes systems and products that efficiently use water in turf and landscape irrigation applications.

Wateright

www.wateright.org/duie.asp

This is a consumer-friendly Web site developed by the Center for Irrigation Technology at California State University–Fresno with support from the U.S. Bureau of Reclamation. This webpage includes a good explanation of distribution uniformity and irrigation efficiency.

U.S. EPA WaterSenseSM: Efficiency Made Easy

www.epa.gov/owm/water-efficiency/pp/irrprof.htm

This site provides information on the Environmental Protection Agency's Water-Sense labeling program for water-efficient landscape irrigation products plus tips and recommendations for water-efficient irrigation. Follow the link to "Weather-or Sensor-Based Irrigation Control Technologies" for related information on high-efficiency irrigation controllers.

Water-Efficient Landscaping

www.muextension.missouri.edu/xplor/agguides/hort/g06912.htm

This Web site has general descriptions and strategies for water efficiency in gardens and landscapes.

Water-Efficient Landscaping: Preventing Pollution and Using Resources Wisely

www.epa.gov/owm/water-efficiency/docs/water-efficient_landscaping_508.pdf

This manual from the Environmental Protection Agency provides information about reducing water consumption through creative landscaping techniques.

Water Wiser: The Water Efficiency Clearinghouse

www.awwa.org/waterwiser/

This clearinghouse provides articles, reference materials, and papers on all forms of water efficiency.

Print Media

Landscape Irrigation: Design and Management, by Stephen W. Smith. John Wiley and Sons, 1996.

This text is a comprehensive guide to landscape irrigation strategies, techniques, and hardware.

Turf Irrigation Manual, by Richard B. Choate and Jim Watkins. Fifth edition. Telsco Industries, 1994.

This manual covers all aspects of turf and landscape irrigation.

SS 3: Local Heat Island Effects

Intent

Design landscape features to reduce local heat island effects.

Requirements

Prerequisites

None.

Credits

3   **Reduce Local Heat Island Effects** (1 point). Do one of the following:

    a)   Locate trees or other plantings to provide shading for at least 50% of sidewalks, patios, and driveways within 50 feet of the home. Shading should be calculated for noon on June 21, when the sun is directly overhead, based on five years' growth.

    b)   Install light-colored, high-albedo materials or vegetation for at least 50% of sidewalks, patios, and driveways within 50 feet of the home. Acceptable strategies include the following:

        i.   White concrete

        ii.   Open pavers (counting only the vegetation, not the pavers); and

        iii.   Any material with a solar reflectance index (SRI) of at least 29.

Synergies and Trade-Offs

Shading hardscapes around the home can reduce irrigation needs as well as temper the home's outdoor environment and reduce cooling loads.

Providing shade is addressed in two other credits: EA 1.2 (Exceptional Energy Performance) and SS 4.3(b) and (c) (Vegetated Roof).

Locating fences, trees, shrubs, or other plantings appropriately can capture or deflect seasonal breezes.

SS 3: Local Heat Island Effects

"Heat island effect" refers to the absorption of heat by hardscapes, such as pavement and buildings, and its radiation to the surrounding areas. Particularly in urban areas, other sources may be present, such as heat and exhaust from cars and trucks, air-conditioners, and street equipment. The heat island effect causes higher temperatures, leading to increased demand for air-conditioning and potential disruption of local ecosystems.

Reduction of the heat island effect minimizes disturbance of local microclimates and reduces summer cooling loads, which in turn reduce energy use, ground-level ozone, greenhouse gas and smog generation, and infrastructure requirements.

This credit rewards projects that implement strategies to reduce heat islands.

Approach and Implementation

Take local heat island effects into consideration when designing the home and use of the site. This credit focuses on new and existing sidewalks, patios, and driveways within 50 feet of the home, but the strategies included in this credit can and should be applied to the garage and home. Where possible, reduce the size of the home and garage.

Design the landscaping with trees or vegetated overhangs that shade the house and any hard surfaces. Deciduous trees can provide shading during the summer and allow solar heat gain during the winter months. Where tree planting is not possible, use architectural shading devices with vines or other vegetation to block direct sunlight.

Minimize paved areas. Use cool paving materials for any sidewalks, patios, or driveways to minimize the absorption of solar heat and the subsequent transfer of this heat to the surroundings. Options include white concrete, vegetation within open pavers, or any material with a solar reflectance index of 29 or more. Porous or permeable paving materials are encouraged and rewarded in SS 4.1 but are not acceptable strategies for this credit.

Use microsurfaces and coatings over asphalt pavement to attain the desired solar reflectance index value. Use coatings and integral colorants in cementitious pavers or cast-in-place parking surfaces to improve solar reflectance.

In multifamily buildings, this credit is awarded to a project that places at least 50% of the paving (i.e., parking garage) underneath the building.

Encourage building managers and homeowners to keep all light-colored surfaces clean. Dirty surfaces have a lower effective solar reflectance index.

Calculations

At least 50% of the sidewalks, patios, and driveways must be shaded or comprised of materials that meet the requirements in part (b). For multi-home developments, common roads should not be included in this calculation. Use one of the following calculations:

1. Percentage of Nonroof Shaded Hardscape = Shaded Area of Hardscape ÷ Total Area of Hardscape

where Shaded Area is the area in shade at noon on June 21 at five years' growth. Assume that the sun is directly overhead. Some estimating may be necessary to determine the coverage expected by the vegetation at five years' growth. Additional methods for meeting the requirements include: parking that is beneath the home or under a vegetated deck, or lower levels of a multi-level garage.

2. Percentage of Nonroof Light-Colored Hardscape = Light-Colored Hardscape ÷ Total Area of Hardscape

where light-colored materials includes white concrete, vegetation between pavers, or any material with an SRI of 29 or more.

Exemplary Performance

Projects that meet the credit requirements for 100% of sidewalks, patios, and driveways within 50 feet of the home may be awarded ½ point for exemplary performance, to be counted under Innovation & Design Process Credit 3.

Verification and Submittals

Supporting Verification Materials, made available by the Project Team:

❏ Present calculations to the Verification Team demonstrating the percentage of the sidewalks, patios, and driveways that is shaded, high albedo, and/or vegetated.

❏ For part (b), present specifications or test results demonstrating the SRI value.

❏ Sign an Accountability Form to indicate that any shading designs or materials choices meet the requirements of the credit.

Verification Team:

❏ Visually verify that the calculations are completed.

❏ Conduct on-site verification of trees and plantings installed to provide shade, and high-albedo products, as per the calculations provided.

❏ Verify that an Accountability Form has been signed by the responsible party.

Considerations

Environmental Issues

The heat island effect causes higher temperatures, leading to increased demand for air-conditioning and potential disruption of local ecosystems. Where solar radiation is significant, increasing shading from vegetation can provide various additional environmental benefits.

Economic Issues

Cooling a home is expensive, and reducing the heat island can lower this cost. Installation of additional trees and architectural shading devices may require higher initial costs, but these items have an acceptable payback when integrated into a whole-systems approach that maximizes energy savings.

According to the American Concrete Pavement Association, concrete made with white cement may cost up to twice as much as that made with gray cement. However, some blended cements (e.g., slag cements) are very light in color and cost the same as conventional cement.

Resources

Please see the USGBC Web site, at www. usgbc.org/resources, for more specific resources on materials sources and other technical information.

Web Sites

American Concrete Pavement Association

www.pavement.com

(847) 966-2272

A national association representing concrete pavement contractors, cement companies and equipment, and material manufacturers and suppliers. See the R&T Update No. 3.05, June 2002, "Albedo: A Measure of Pavement Sur-

ID	LL	SS	WE	EA	MR	EQ	AE
				3			

face Reflectance" (www.pavement.com/Downloads/RT/RT3.05.pdf).

American Society of Landscape Architects

www.asla.org

ASLA is the national professional association representing landscape architects. The Web site provides information about products, services, publications, and events.

Heat Island Group

Lawrence Berkeley National Laboratory

www.eetd.lbl.gov/HeatIsland

The Lawrence Berkeley National Laboratory conducts research to find, analyze, and implement solutions to minimizing heat island effects; its current efforts focus on the study and development of more reflective surfaces for roadways and buildings.

Heat Island Effect

U.S. Environmental Protection Agency

www.epa.gov/heatisland

(202) 343-9343

Basic information about heat island effect, its social and environmental costs, and strategies to minimize its prevalence, including shading and coloration of hardscapes.

Use of Cool Pavements to Reduce the Urban Heat Island Effect

Town of Gilbert, AZ

www.ci.gilbert.az.us/planning/urbanheatisland.cfm

This online brochure produced by the Town of Gilbert, Arizona, provides guidelines and specific details for addressing heat island effects created by hardscapes.

SS 4: Surface Water Management

Intent

Design site features to minimize erosion and runoff from the home site.

Requirements

Prerequisites

None.

Credits

Note: Certain surface water management strategies may be regulated, restricted, or even prohibited by local water authorities or code requirements.

4.1 **Permeable Lot** (maximum 4 points, as specified in **Table 1**). Design the lot such that at least 70% of the buildable land, not including area under roof, is permeable or designed to capture water runoff for infiltration on-site. Area that can be counted toward the minimum includes the following:

  a) Vegetative landscape (e.g., grass, trees, shrubs).

  b) Permeable paving, installed by an experienced professional. Permeable paving must include porous above ground materials (e.g., open pavers, engineered products) and a 6-inch porous subbase, and the base layer must be designed to ensure proper drainage away from the home.

  c) Impermeable surfaces that are designed to direct all runoff toward an appropriate permanent infiltration feature (e.g., vegetated swale, on-site rain garden, or rainwater cistern).

4.2 **Permanent Erosion Controls** (1 point). Design and install one of the following permanent erosion control measures:

  a) If portions of the lot are located on a steep slope, reduce long-term runoff effects through use of terracing and retaining walls.

  OR

  b) Plant one tree, four 5-gallon shrubs, or 50 square feet of native groundcover per 500 square feet of disturbed lot area (including area under roof).

4.3 **Management of Runoff from Roof** (maximum 2 points). Design and install one or more of the following runoff control measures:

  a) Install permanent stormwater controls (e.g., vegetated swales, on-site rain garden, dry well, or rainwater cistern) designed to manage runoff from the home (1 point).

  b) Install vegetated roof to cover 50% of the roof area (0.5 point).

  OR

  c) Install vegetated roof to cover 100% of the roof area (1 point).

  d) Have the site designed by a licensed or certified landscape design or engineering professional such that all water runoff from the home is managed through an on-site design element (2 points).

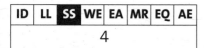
Table 1. Permeable Area

Percentage of buildable land (excluding area under roof) that is permeable	Points
70–79	1
80–89	2
90–99	3
100	4

Synergies and Trade-Offs

SS 1.1 addresses erosion control during construction.

Trees, shrubs, or groundcover installed for erosion control can be designed as drought-tolerant or otherwise preferable; see SS 2 for more information on landscaping. Conventional turf is less permeable than other plantings and consequently less effective at managing runoff.

SS 4.1: Permeable Lot

SS 4.2: Permanent Erosion Controls

Overloading of storm sewers can result in flooding and damage, and stormwater runoff usually leads to erosion, either on the project site or on downstream areas. Transport of fertilizers, chemicals, and sediment into local water bodies can adversely affect water quality and damage ecosystems.

Runoff can be greatly reduced by maintaining a high level of permeability that creates the opportunity for stormwater to infiltrate the ground on the project site. Increased permeability has multiple benefits: reduced burden on stormwater management infrastructure; reduced transport of fertilizer and chemicals in runoff; reduced erosion of valuable topsoil, which is essential for healthy landscape plants; reduced sedimentation of downstream rivers and lakes; and replenishment of underground aquifers.

Approach and Implementation

Early in the process, lay out the home site and landscaping to include large amounts of permeable area. Determine the number and type of trees and shrubs to be planted on the site and locate them to maximize erosion control and shading benefits. Integrate larger erosion control measures with infiltration features and impermeable hardscapes. Build a smaller home and minimize the area of impermeable patios, walkways, and driveways. Where possible, build up rather than out to minimize the footprint of the home.

SS 4.1: Permeable Lot

Where walkways and patios are necessary, use open pavers or engineered porous materials to allow water to be absorbed. Installation of permeable paving may require hiring a professional who can design

the system with the necessary sublayers. If the sublayers are not designed properly, water may drain toward the home, causing leaks or damage.

Where impermeable materials are used, work with a landscape professional and/or civil engineer to design the landscaping to accommodate runoff. Slope the surfaces of any impermeable materials to direct water toward permanent infiltration features, such as vegetated swales or on-site rain gardens. Such infiltration features should be part of an integrated design that also manages erosion control and runoff (see SS 4.2 and 4.3).

Where vegetative swales or rain gardens are used, estimate the expected quantity of runoff from the surfaces being served. Include enough vegetation of the appropriate species to accommodate a typical heavy rainfall.

Conventional turf is much less permeable than native grasses or groundcover. Although it can be counted as vegetation for this credit, conventional turf is discouraged.

Non-vegetated groundcover (e.g., bare mulch, pinestraw), can be used to earn credit SS 4.1, but these areas must meet the requirements under SS 4.1 (b). This includes areas where the soil below is not expected to be compacted.

SS 4.2: Permanent Erosion Controls

Establish and install permanent erosion controls concurrently with earthwork, final grading, and turf establishment operations.

On steep slopes that have been disturbed, install terracing, benching, retaining walls, and drainage systems as needed to prevent erosion or remove subsurface water. These measures should be installed prior to installation of soil stabilization measures.

Plant trees, shrubs, and/or groundcover on the area disturbed during construction. Replant disturbed areas quickly with closely spaced plants. Choose appropriate vegetation to surround trees and tall shrubs, taking into consideration the availability of sunlight and water.

Calculations

SS 4.1: Permeable Lot

Use the following steps:

Step 1. Calculate the total buildable land area, not including the area under roof. The total buildable land includes the entire lot except areas that are unbuildable because of public rights-of-way, etc. In **Figure 1** below, this step would include sections C, D, E, F, and G.

Step 2. Estimate the percentage of the area calculated in Step 1 that is vegetated, covered with permeable paving, and/or designed with runoff features, as per the credit requirements.

Step 3. Refer to **Table 3**, above to determine points earned.

4.2 Permanent Erosion Controls

No calculations are required for SS 4.2(a). For SS 4.2(b), calculate the number of trees, shrubs, or groundcover plants as follows:

Trees required = total disturbed lot area ÷ 500 ft²

or

Shrubs required = (total disturbed lot area ÷ 500 ft²) x 4

or

Native groundcover plants required = 10% * total disturbed lot area

A combination of trees, shrubs, and groundcover can be used to meet the credit requirements. For example, for a project with 4,000 square feet of disturbed land, the installation of two trees, eight 5-gallon shrubs, and 200 square feet of groundcover would earn 1 point.

Trees installed should be mature enough to have a caliper (trunk thickness) of at least 1.5 inches. Also, it is acceptable to use ten 2-gallon shrubs rather than four 5-gallon shrubs per 500 sf."

Figure 1. Determining Total Buildable Land Area

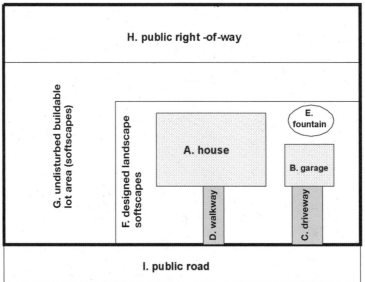

Exemplary Performance

No additional points are available for exemplary performance.

Verification and Submittals

4.1 Permeable Lot

Supporting Verification Materials, made available by the Project Team:

❏ Present calculations to the Verification Team demonstrating the percentage of the built area that is permeable or designed with infiltration features.

❏ Sign an Accountability Form to indicate that the landscape features that have been installed match those in the design.

Verification Team:

❏ Visually verify that the calculations are completed.

❏ Conduct on-site verification of permeable elements, as per the calculations provided.

❏ Verify that an Accountability Form has been signed by the responsible party.

4.2 Permanent Erosion Controls

Supporting Verification Materials, made available by the Project Team:

❏ For SS 4.2(b), present calculations to the Verification Team demonstrating the number of trees or shrubs or area of groundcover required by the credit.

Verification Team:

❏ For SS 4.2(b), visually verify that the calculations are completed.

❏ Visually verify that the appropriate measures (terraces, retaining walls, trees, shrubs, groundcover) have been installed.

Considerations

Economic Issues

The most cost-effective approach for improving permeability is to simply reduce the amount of impermeable surfaces on the lot. The use of open pavers for walkways is a low-cost, attractive solution. Vegetated infiltration features can be highly economical, depending on the level of landscaping expertise on the project team. Engineered solutions tend to be the most expensive approach.

Regional Variances

The choice and location of plantings will depend on the regional climate and microclimate conditions.

Resources

Please see the USGBC Web site, at www.usgbc.org/resources, for more specific resources on materials sources and other technical information.

Web Sites

Maryland Stormwater Management Program

Maryland Department of the Environment

www.mde.state.md.us/Programs/Water-Programs/SedimentandStormwater

This site includes an explanation of the impacts of runoff, as well as various useful resources. This page has a link to the 2000 Maryland Stormwater Design Manual, which includes specific guidance for designing a site to manage stormwater.

2001 Stormwater Management Manual for Western Washington: Volume II, Construction Stormwater Pollution Prevention

www.ecy.wa.gov/biblio/9912.html

The objective of this manual is to provide a commonly accepted set of technical

ID	LL	SS	WE	EA	MR	EQ	AE
		4.1 & 4.2					

standards and guidance on stormwater management measures that will control the quantity and quality of stormwater produced by new development and re-development.

American Society of Landscape Architects

www.asla.org

ASLA is the national professional association representing landscape architects. The Web site provides information about products, services, publications, and events.

Erosion Control Technology Council

www.ectc.org

(651) 554-1895

This nonprofit organization develops performance standards, testing procedures, and guidance on the application and installation of erosion control products.

International Erosion Control Association

www.ieca.org

(800) 455-4322

This organization's mission is to connect, educate, and develop the worldwide erosion and sediment control community.

NAHB Research Center ToolBase Services: Permeable Pavement

www.toolbase.org/Technology-Inventory/Sitework/permeable-pavement

In a resource provided through a partnership with the Department of Housing and Urban Development, the Partnership for Advancing Technology in Housing (PATH), and the National Association of Home Builders Research Center, this site provides details, lists of manufacturers, and related information on permeable paving options.

Stormwater Best Management Practice Design Guide. EPA/600/R-04/121A.

September, 2004.

www.epa.gov/ORD/NRMRL/pubs/600r04121/600r04121a.pdf

This document is Volume 2 of a three-volume document that provides guidance on the selection and design of stormwater management best management practices (BMPs). It provides specific design guidance for a group of on-site BMP control practices that are referred to as vegetative biofilters, including the following BMP control practices: grass swales, filter and buffer strips, and bioretention cells.

The Center for Watershed Protection's Storm Water Center

www.stormwatercenter.net

The Stormwater Manager's Resource Center is designed specifically for stormwater practitioners, local government officials, and others who need technical assistance on stormwater management issues.

SS 4.3: Management of Runoff from Roof

Erosion problems are worsened by storm-water runoff from impervious surfaces, such as rooftops, decks, driveways, and paved walkways. Runoff not only erodes the soil but also collects sediment containing nutrients from fertilizers and toxic chemicals from pesticides, all of which pollute the environment and lead to property damage, loss of fish and wildlife habitat, and reduced water quality in our lakes and streams.

This credit rewards projects that install permanent runoff control measures (e.g., vegetated swales, roof garden, dry well, rainwater cistern) that are specifically designed to manage rainfall collected from the roof of a home.

Approach and Implementation

Assess rainwater runoff once the home and its roof have been designed. As part of the durability management process, assess where rainwater will flow from the roof.

Design the home with less roof area. A two-story house has less rooftop area than a rambler with the same interior square footage. A smaller footprint means more permeable area and less runoff.

Consider a vegetated roof. Vegetated roofs can be used in small-scale residential developments, but they require planning and proper integration with the rest of the home design. Bring a vegetated roof expert onto the project team early so that the roof is designed appropriately and any code requirements can be addressed prior to construction.

Vegetated roofs are complex structures that require consideration of the load-bearing capacity (dead and live loads) of roof decks. Waterproofing must be resistant to biological and root attack. Frequently, an additional root-fast layer must be installed to protect the primary

waterproofing membrane from plant roots.

Rainwater harvesting can help manage runoff from the roof while also providing a source of water for irrigation and certain indoor applications. Find a landscape professional or rainwater harvest expert to help design and install the system. A rainwater harvesting system can be used to fulfill SS 4.3(a) or (d). See Water Efficiency 1.1 for more information on rainwater harvesting.

If runoff from the roof is going to be handled through permanent vegetative stormwater controls, work with a landscape professional to design an integrated approach to runoff from all impermeable surfaces on the site (see also SS 4.1). Estimate the expected quantity of runoff for the entire roof. Include enough vegetation of appropriate species to accommodate a typical heavy rainfall.

SS 4.3(a) does not require a landscape professional (although it is recommended) and can be earned for managing some of the runoff from the roof of the home.

Calculations

For SS 4.3(b) and (c), estimate the percentage of the total roof area covered by vegetation.

Exemplary Performance

No additional points are available for exemplary performance.

Verification and Submittals

Supporting Verification Materials made available by the Project Team:

For SS 4.3(d), sign an Accountability Form to indicate that the features on the site are designed to manage all water runoff from the building.

Verification Team:

❑ Visually verify that all relevant measures are installed on the site.

❑ For SS 4.3(d), verify that an Accountability Form has been signed by the responsible party.

Considerations

Economic Issues

A vegetated roof can be costly to design and install and may require design changes to the structure. Vegetated roofs can reduce heating and cooling costs considerably but are often chosen simply because they are attractive and enhance the sales value, particularly for buildings with accessible rooftops.

On a community scale, on-site rainwater management measures provide a useful function in reducing the burden on municipal stormwater management systems.

Regional Variances

In areas that experience frequent high-intensity rainstorms, the stormwater management infrastructure is often overloaded. On-site rainwater management strategies help reduce this burden, which can also lessen the risk of flooding in nearby waterways.

Waterfront properties play a considerable role both in generating harmful stormwater runoff and in its control.

Resources

Please see the USGBC Web site, at www.usgbc.org/resources, for more specific resources on materials sources and other technical information.

Web Sites

The Center for Watershed Protection's Storm Water Center

www.stormwatercenter.net

The Stormwater Manager's Resource Center is designed specifically for stormwater practitioners, local government officials, and others who need technical assistance on stormwater management issues.

Greenroofs.com

www.greenroofs.com

This green roof industry resource portal offers basic information, a product and service directory, and research links.

Penn State Center for Green Roof Research

www.hortweb.cas.psu.edu/research/greenroofcenter/

The center has the mission of demonstrating and promoting green roof research, education, and technology transfer in the northeastern United States.

Maryland Stormwater Management Program

Maryland Department of the Environment

www.mde.state.md.us/Programs/WaterPrograms/SedimentandStormwater

This site includes an explanation of the impacts of runoff, as well as various useful resources. This page has a link to the 2000 Maryland Stormwater Design Manual, which includes specific guidance for designing a site to manage stormwater.

Stormwater Best Management Practice Design Guide. EPA/600/R-04/121A.

September, 2004.

www.epa.gov/ORD/NRMRL/pubs/600r04121/600r04121a.pdf

This document is Volume 2 of a three-volume document that provides guidance on the selection and design of stormwater management best management practices (BMPs). It provides specific design guidance for a group of on-site BMP control practices that are referred to as vegetative biofilters, including the following BMP control practices: grass swales, filter and buffer strips, and bioretention cells.

Rain Gardens

Wisconsin Department of Natural Resources

www.dnr.state.wi.us/org/water/wm/nps/rg/index.htm

This site has information about designing and installing rain gardens. It includes a link to "Rain Gardens: A How-to Manual for Homeowners," as well as other useful resources.

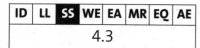

SS 5: Nontoxic Pest Control

Intent

Design home features to minimize the need for poisons for control of insects, rodents, and other pests.

Requirements

Prerequisites

None.

Credits

5   **Pest Control Alternatives** (½ point each, maximum 2 points). Implement one or more of the measures below. All physical actions (for pest management practices) must be noted on construction plans.

    a)   Keep all wood (i.e., siding, trim, structure) at least 12 inches above soil (code typically requires 8 inches).

    b)   Seal all external cracks, joints, penetrations, edges, and entry points with caulking. Where openings cannot be caulked or sealed, install rodent- and corrosion-proof screens (e.g., copper or stainless steel mesh). Protect exposed foundation insulation with moisture-resistant, pest-proof cover (e.g., fiber cement board, galvanized insect screen).

    c)   Include no wood-to-concrete connections or separate any exterior wood-to-concrete connections (e.g., at posts, deck supports, stair stringers) with metal or plastic fasteners or dividers.

    d)   Install landscaping such that all parts of mature plants will be at least 24 inches from the home.

    e)   In areas marked "moderate to heavy" through "very heavy" on the termite infestation probability map (**Figure 1**), implement one or more of the following measures (½ point each):

        i)   Treat all cellulosic material (e.g., wood framing) with a borate product to a minimum of 3 feet above the foundation.

        ii)   Install a sand or diatomaceous earth barrier.

        iii)   Install a steel mesh barrier termite control system.

        iv)   Install nontoxic termite bait system.

        v)   Use noncellulosic (i.e., not wood or straw) wall structure.

        vi)   Use solid concrete foundation walls or masonry wall with top course of solid block bond beam or concrete-filled block.

Synergies and Trade-Offs

Limiting conventional turf and installing native plants (SS 2) can help reduce the need for fertilizers and pesticides that contain toxic chemicals.

Figure 1. Termite Infestation Probability Map

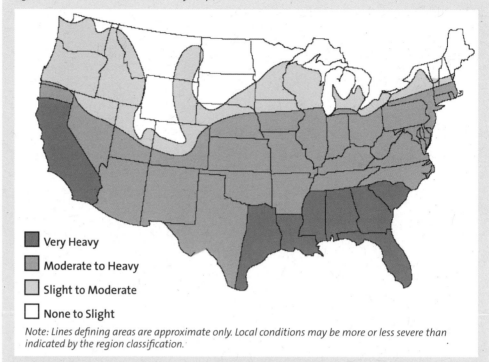

■ Very Heavy

■ Moderate to Heavy

□ Slight to Moderate

□ None to Slight

Note: Lines defining areas are approximate only. Local conditions may be more or less severe than indicated by the region classification.

Source: Excerpted from the 2000 International Residential Building Code™.
Portions of this publication reproduce sections from the *2000 International Residential Code*.
International Code Council, Inc., Country Club Hills, IL. Reproduced with Permission. All Rights Reserved.

Keeping plants away from the home makes it unnecessary to irrigate close to the home and risk leaking moisture into the home's foundation.

The thermal bypass inspection, required in the EA credit category, addresses cracks, joints, and penetrations in the building envelope.

Toxic chemicals, frequently used to control pests in homes, expose occupants to harmful or hazardous chemicals and practices. However, alternatives are available. Proper placement and installation of physical barriers can help protect homes from termites, ants, mice, and other pests.

This credit rewards homes that use one or more of the listed pest control alternatives to minimize the need for poisons.

Approach and Implementation

The first step in controlling pests is to assess the risks associated with different pests. Identify the types of local pests and determine whether the project is in an area where termites are a problem (**Figure 1**, above). This assessment should be done as part of durability planning (see Innovation & Design 2.1).

Select from the following nontoxic pest control strategies during the design phase, since they may require an alternative construction approach:

❑ Use solid concrete foundation walls or concrete-filled block.

❑ Use noncellulosic wall structure.

❏ Keep all wood (i.e., siding, trim, structure) at least 12 inches above soil (code typically requires 8 inches). This requirement only applies to wood within the built structure; it does not apply to material stored on-site during construction. This requirement applies to wood that is directly exposed to soil or air, including non-structural elements such as trim and siding. Internal framing that is separated from soil or air by foundation walls does not need to comply. It does not apply to porches or decks; these are handled in part (c).

❏ Include no wood-to-concrete connections or separate any exterior wood-to-concrete connections with metal or plastic dividers. SS 5 (c) applies to all exterior elements, including the façade and exterior framing over foundations.

Most of the following strategies are focused on limiting points and means for entry by pests:

❏ Limit landscaping immediately adjacent to the house. Maintaining a buffer zone between landscaping plants and the house perimeter limits the habitat suitable for insect infestation. To earn SS 5 (d), all structures that connect to the home without a gap (e.g., porches, steps) must be at least 24" from mature plant parts.

❏ Seal any external cracks and penetrations and use screens and other pest-proof covers on any potential access points. This may include sheet metal or metal mesh termite shields on the foundation stem wall.

❏ Install physical barriers, such as sand or diatomaceous earth, outside the home foundation to prevent penetrations through foundations and slabs. These barriers are particularly effective against termites.

❏ Treat lumber and cellulose with borate, a natural chemical alternative that controls insects but is benign to humans.

The following other strategies are not rewarded in this credit but are encouraged:

❏ Use a sealed-to-the-wall vapor barrier for homes with crawl spaces on the floor or beneath a concrete slab to limit moisture intrusion and suitable habitat for insects.

❏ Design and install plastic barrier systems around pipes and electrical conduit extending through slab foundations.

❏ Install plantings and landscaping elements that repel pests and encourage biodiversity. Monocultures, such as turfgrass, are more likely to host a single type of insect that can become an infestation risk.

Many of the above measures also have general durability benefits, such as reducing the risk of water damage and decay.

Calculations

No calculations are required.

Exemplary Performance

Projects that implement more than four of the measures listed in SS 5 should be awarded exemplary performance credit, to be counted under Innovation & Design 3. Each additional measure is worth ½ point, with a maximum of 1 exemplary performance point total.

Verification and Submittals

Verification Team:

❏ Visually verify that all relevant measures are complete.

ID	LL	SS	WE	EA	MR	EQ	AE
			5				

Considerations

Environmental Issues

In addition to posing health risks for occupants, toxins can leach into soils and disrupt local ecosystems.

Economic Issues

Initial costs of nontoxic pest prevention can be higher than chemical controls. However, such costs are frequently offset by the long-term effectiveness of structural solutions. Many pest control measures have the additional benefit of improving the durability of the home, which helps maintain performance and reduce maintenance and eventual repairs.

Regional Variances

The type and threat of pest infestations vary by region and even locale. Investigate the most common pests of concern for the project site and use the nontoxic pest control measures that are appropriate.

Resources

Please see the USGBC Web site, at www. usgbc.org/resources, for more specific resources on materials sources and other technical information.

Web Sites

Biointensive Integrated Pest Management

www.attra.org/attra-pub/ipm.html

This site provides background on biointensive IPM, including specific strategies. The site focuses primarily on agricultural applications but provides an exhaustive list of references and definitions of terms and practices.

Bio-Integral Resource Center

www.birc.org

This nonprofit organization specializes in the development and communication of least-toxic, sustainable, and environmen-tally sound integrated pest management methods.

Integrated Pest Management Practitioners Association

www.ipmaccess.com

A source of background information, systems, and products for integrated pest management.

Statewide Integrated Pest Management Program, University of California

www.ipm.ucdavis.edu/WATER/U/index. html

This site has some basic information on the risks associated with pesticides, as well as tips for alternative pest management strategies.

Print Media

Common Sense Pest Control, by William Olkowski, Shiela Daar, and Helga Olkowski. Taunton Press, 1991.

SS 6: Compact Development

Intent

Make use of compact development patterns to conserve land and promote community livability, transportation efficiency, and walkability.

Requirements

Prerequisites

None.

Credits

6.1 **Moderate Density** (2 points). Build homes with an average housing density of 7 or more dwelling units per acre of buildable land. A single home on $1/7$-acre buildable lot qualifies.

OR

6.2 **High Density** (3 points). Build homes with an average housing density of 10 or more dwelling units per acre of buildable land. A single home on $1/10$-acre buildable lot qualifies.

OR

6.3 **Very High Density** (4 points). Build homes with an average housing density of 20 or more dwelling units per acre of buildable land. A single home on $1/20$-acre buildable lot qualifies.

Note: Buildable land area is calculated as follows:

❑ *Exclude public streets or public rights-of-way, land occupied by nonresidential structures, public parks, and land excluded from residential development by law.*

❑ *For multiple-lot developments, include only the sum of the lot areas for homes being built for LEED for Homes.*

❑ *The numerator is the number of housing units in the project, and the denominator is the buildable land area included in the project (subject to the above exclustions). Both relate to the project only, not the surrounding area.*

Synergies and Trade-Offs

SS 1.2 is automatically granted to moderate, high, or very high-density homes because of the reduced impact of compact development.

SS 6.1: Moderate Density
SS 6.2: High Density
SS 6.3: Very High Density

Smart, sustainable growth means using land more efficiently and preserving those lands that are most environmentally sensitive. Compact development achieves the goal: it protects undeveloped land that has streams, forests, and wildlife and reduces overall land-use impacts. Compact development also encourages pedestrian activity and bicycling and enables mass transit use, all of which reduce vehicle miles traveled.

It is more cost-effective to provide and maintain services like water, sewer, electricity, and other utilities in compact neighborhoods than in dispersed communities.

Approach and Implementation

This credit is awarded to any of the following project types:

- ❑ a single-family home on a small lot;

- ❑ row houses on small lots; and

- ❑ a multifamily, multistory building on a small to medium lot (credit threshold is measured against lot size divided by number of units).

Since development on a small lot generally precludes having a large yard or green space on-site, try to locate compact development projects near public open spaces. For large developments, incorporate publicly accessible green spaces into the layout. Proximity to publicly accessible open space is awarded a point in Location & Linkages 6.

For multihome developments, this credit can be earned if the average density for all of the homes in the development exceeds the credit requirements. Increase the density of the development by clustering homes together and setting aside and deeding land for public use (e.g. parks, bicycle paths). Providing a variety of housing types has other advantages in creating a more complete community as well since it enables households with a variety of income levels to coexist in closer proximity.

Locate high-density housing within existing communities or near public transportation options (see Location & Linkages 5). This increases the use of community resources and reduces the environmental impacts associated with transportation.

Calculations

Calculate average housing density as follows, whether the project is a single home or a large development:

Average Density = Housing Units ÷ Acres of Buildable Land

Note that buildable land includes subdivision covenant setbacks, unless they meet the exclusion requirements described in the Note for calculating buildable area.

Exemplary Performance

Projects with a density greater than 40 dwelling units per acre of buildable land should be awarded 1 point, to be counted under Innovation & Design 3.

Verification and Submittals

Supporting Verification Materials, made available by the Project Team:

- ❑ Present calculations to the Verification Team demonstrating the average housing density of the project.

Verification Team:

❑ Visually verify the housing density calculations.

Considerations

Environmental Issues

In addition to the benefits of reduced land consumption and car-dependence described above, compact development also reduces the per capita area of impervious surfaces, which reduces the overall volume of stormwater runoff and increases aquifer recharge. Stormwater runoff is a significant environmental problem because it carries pollutants from yards, roofs, and roads into aquatic environments. Permeable surfaces and appropriate erosion controls in residential construction allow stormwater to be absorbed instead of overloading storm sewers and waterways.

Economic Issues

Compact development can reduce costs by efficiently using existing infrastructure. Wherever land is a significant cost of new construction, compact development can improve the economics of a project.

Regional Variances

In some cases, multifamily housing may require different zoning and permitting.

Resources

Please see the USGBC Web site, at www. usgbc.org/resources, for more specific resources on materials sources and other technical information.

Web Sites

Affordable Housing Design Advisor

www.designadvisor.org

While this Web site targets affordable housing, it can serve as a tool, resource, idea bank, and step-by-step guide to good design for any moderate- to high-density

housing, and has a section devoted to "Demystifying Density." The site is supported by the U.S. Department of Housing and Urban Development.

The Congress for the New Urbanism

www.cnu.org

This nonprofit organization provides tools and resources for promoting walkable, neighborhood-based development as an alternative to sprawl.

Smart Growth Network

www.smartgrowth.org

This Web site outlines smart growth principles, provides a guide through smart growth terms and technical concepts, and hosts a searchable catalogue of reports, Web sites, tools, and case studies dating from 1997 to today.

Urban Land Institute

ULI Washington

www.washington.uli.org

The Urban Land Institute is a nonprofit organization based in Washington, D.C., that promotes the responsible use of land to enhance the total environment. ULI's online bookstore includes numerous publications regarding compact and higher-density development.

Print Media

Changing Places: Rebuilding Community in the Age of Sprawl, by Richard Moe and Carter Wilkie. Henry Holt & Company, 1999.

Density by Design: New Directions in Residential Development, by Steven Fader. Urban Land Institute, 2000.

Green Development: Integrating Ecology and Real Estate, by Alex Wilson et al. John Wiley & Sons, 1998.

Once There Were Greenfields: How Urban Sprawl Is Undermining America's Environment, Economy and Social Fabric, by F. Kaid Benfield et al. Natural Resources Defense Council, 1999.

ID	LL	**SS**	WE	EA	MR	EQ	AE
		6.1 – 6.3					

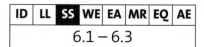

ID	LL	SS	WE	EA	MR	EQ	AE
		6.1 – 6.3					

Suburban Nation: The Rise of Sprawl and the Decline of the American Dream, by Andres Duany et al. North Point Press, 2000.

Water Efficiency

In the United States, approximately 340 billion gallons of fresh water is withdrawn per day from rivers and reservoirs to support residential, commercial, industrial, agricultural, and recreational activities. This accounts for about one-fourth of the nation's total supply of renewable fresh water. Almost 65 percent of this water is discharged to rivers, streams, and other water bodies after use and, in some cases, treatment. Additionally, water is withdrawn from underground aquifers. In some parts of the United States, water levels in these aquifers have dropped more than 100 feet since the 1940s.

On an annual basis, the water deficit in the United States is currently estimated at about 3,700 billion gallons. In other words, Americans extract 3,700 billion gallons per year more than they return to the natural water system to recharge aquifers and other water sources.

Water for domestic use may be delivered from a public supplier or be self-supplied (i.e., by a well). Self-supplied domestic withdrawals are an estimated 3,590 million gallons per day.[1]

The Energy Policy Act of 1992 mandated the use of water-conserving plumbing fixtures and fittings to reduce water use in residential, commercial, and institutional buildings. Water efficiency measures in new homes can easily reduce water usage by 30% or more. In a typical home, savings of 30,000 gallons of water a year can be achieved very cost-effectively. This results in average annual water utility savings of about $100 per year.

As communities grow, increased demand for water leads to additional maintenance and higher costs for municipal supply and treatment facilities. New homes that use water efficiently have lower water use fees and reduced sewage volumes. Many water conservation strategies involve either no additional cost or short-term paybacks, whereas other strategies, such as rainwater harvesting and graywater plumbing systems, often involve more substantial investment.

The Water Efficiency (WE) category in the LEED for Homes Rating System has three kinds of credits—Water Reuse, Irrigation Systems, and Indoor Water Use—which are summarized in **Table 1** and described in the following sections.

---

1 U.S. Geological Survey, Estimated Use of Water in the United States in 2000, www.pubs.usgs.gov/circ/2004/circ1268/

Table 1. Overview of Water Efficiency (WE) Category

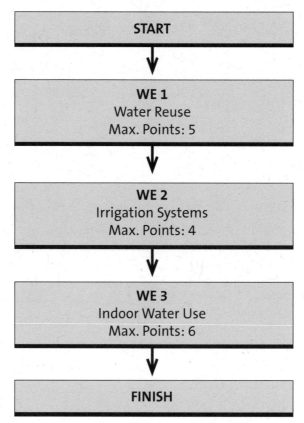

IMPORTANT NOTE:
*A minimum of **3 points** must be achieved in the WE category.*

WE 1: Water Reuse

Intent

Use municipal recycled water or offset central water supply through the capture and controlled reuse of rainwater and/or graywater.

Requirements

Prerequisites

None.

Credits

Note: Rainwater and graywater capture systems are subject to local codes and may require special permits. Note that the water quality should meet local standards, and consult manufacturers' recommendations to determine the compatibility of plumbing fixtures with graywater. Many states and regulatory agencies require that water going into a toilet or sink meet potable water standards; builders should comply with local codes.

1.1 **Rainwater Harvesting System** (maximum 4 points, as specified in **Table 1** below). Design and install a rainwater harvesting and storage system (including surface runoff and/or roof runoff) for landscape irrigation use or indoor water use. The storage system must be sized to hold all the water from a 1-inch rainfall event (equivalent to 0.62 gallons per square foot of roof area used for capture), taking into consideration the size of the harvest system (i.e., 50% or 75% of total roof area, depending on the measure chosen from **Table 1** below).

AND/OR

1.2 **Graywater Reuse System** (1 point). Design and install a graywater reuse system for landscape irrigation use (i.e., not a septic system) or indoor water use. The system must include a tank or dosing basin that can be used as part of the irrigation system. Graywater must be collected from at least one of the following:

❏ clothes washer;

❏ showers;

❏ some combination of faucets and other sources estimated to exceed 5,000 gallons per year.

OR

1.3 **Use of Municipal Recycled Water System** (3 points). Design the plumbing such that irrigation system water demand is supplied by municipal recycled water. This is applicable only in communities with a municipal recycled water program.

Note: A home using a municipal recycled water system cannot receive points under WE 1.2 (Graywater Reuse System) or WE 1.1 (Rainwater Harvesting System) for outdoor applications.

Table 1. Rainwater Harvesting

System Size	Application	Points
≥ 50% of roof area	Indoor only	2
≥ 50% of roof area	Outdoor only	3
≥ 75% of roof area	Both indoor & outdoor	4

Synergies and Trade-Offs

A project receiving points for WE 1.3 must skip WE 1.1 and WE 1.2.

Rainwater harvesting and graywater reuse irrigation systems should be integrated with resource-efficient landscape (SS 2) and irrigation system design (WE 2).

WE 1.1: Rainwater Harvesting System

A rainwater harvesting system captures rainwater from a home site and stores it for future use in a large tank or cistern. Such a system can significantly reduce or completely eliminate the amount of potable water used for irrigation or select indoor uses, such as toilets and clothes washers.

Rainwater harvesting also helps manage runoff from the house, which reduces the risk of on-site flooding and erosion and eases the strain on stormwater management systems. Rainwater is good for landscaping because it has lower salt content and higher nitrogen content than treated potable water.

Rainwater should not be used for drinking unless the system is carefully designed for that purpose and it has been approved by the local water authority and/or health department.

Approach and Implementation

The site and the goals of the rainwater harvesting system will determine how this credit is achieved.

Projects located in areas with substantial year-round rainfall may find rainwater harvesting more useful for indoor applications and runoff management. Projects located in areas with rainfall spikes may use harvesting for evening out the availability of irrigation water and mitigating on-site erosion.

The design of a rainwater harvesting system should take into consideration both the volume and the frequency of local rainfall events annually and seasonally, as well as the landscaping and its irrigation needs.

A rainwater capture system has the following basic components:

❑ Catchment area: the surface area on a roof that captures rainwater for harvesting.

❑ Conveyance system: the gutters, downspouts, and diverters that connect the roof to the storage tank.

❑ Storage system: tanks and cisterns, which should be opaque and kept out of direct sunlight to discourage growth of algae and bacteria, and covered to keep out pests and debris.

❑ Distribution system: the piping and/or pumps that connect the storage system to the end-use fixtures and fittings.

More sophisticated systems, particularly those for indoor applications, may require filtration and disinfection components. The storage, conveyance, and any filtration systems should be inspected and maintained regularly to ensure proper operation and sanitation.

Although rainwater harvesting system components can be purchased off-the-shelf, the design and installation are generally customized for each home and require the involvement of an experienced professional.

Rainwater collection systems can be designed and implemented on the scale of a small community or housing development. A home in a development can earn points in this credit if water from the project site is captured and stored as part of the community system.

Calculations

Step 1. Determine the rainwater harvest system size as a percentage of the total area of the roof (including any porches and attached garage), using the following equation and referring to **Table 1**, above:

System Size (%) = Harvest Area ÷ Total Roof Area

For example, if the total roof area is 1,200 square feet and the system harvests water from 800 square feet, then the system is sized for 67% of the roof area and can earn either 2 or 3 points, depending on whether the water is used for indoor or outdoor applications.

Step 2. Determine the minimum storage capacity requirement as follows:

Storage Capacity = 0.62 Gal/ft² x Harvest Area

where the rooftop harvest area is given in square feet. For example, if the rooftop harvest area is 800 square feet, the storage tank must be at least 496 gallons (0.62 Gal/ft² x 800 ft²).

Partial Credit

artial Credit (1 point) can be awarded if a system is installed that only collects water from 25-50% of the roof area, but a storage tank must be installed to collect water for a 1-inch rain event falling on 50% of the roof area.

Exemplary Performance

Projects that install a system sized to capture water from 100% of the roof area and can demonstrate a demand for this water can apply for 1 additional point, to be counted under Innovation in Design 3. This application must be submitted by the Provider and approved by USGBC before the point can be counted.

Verification and Submittals

Supporting Verification Materials, made available by the Project Team:

❑ Present calculations for the rainwater harvesting system size and storage capacity to the Verification Team.

❑ Include any rainwater harvesting system equipment literature in the occupant's operations and maintenance manual.

Verification Team:

❑ Visually verify that all calculations related to this credit are completed.

❑ Visually verify that the rainwater harvesting system has been installed.

Considerations

Environmental Issues

Generally, rainwater is preferable to potable water for the purposes of irrigation. Rainwater with high mineral content or acidity may damage systems or plantings, but pollutants can be filtered out by soil or mechanical systems prior to being applied to plantings.

Economic Issues

Depending on the amount of local rainfall, a bioswale or rain garden is an alternative to a large-capacity rainwater storage tank. Bioswales and rain gardens are not rewarded in WE 2, but they are rewarded in SS 4. A rainwater harvesting system is substantially more expensive but provides more water storage.

Regional Variances

Projects in areas with substantial year-round rainfall may find rainwater harvesting more useful for indoor applications and runoff management. Projects in areas with rainfall spikes may use harvesting to even out the availability of irrigation water and mitigate on-site erosion.

Resources

Web Sites

American Rainwater Catchment Systems Association

www.arcsa.org

An industry association with extensive links and resources for rainwater harvesting products, systems, and consultants.

City of Tucson, Arizona, Tucson Water

www.ci.tucson.az.us/water/conservation.htm

The Tucson Water Department has developed programs and published literature for customers to use in their efforts to use water resources wisely and efficiently.

City of Tucson Water Harvesting Guidance Manual

www.dot.ci.tucson.az.us/stormwater/education/waterharvest.cfm

Advocating an integrated site design process, this manual is primarily directed toward site development and design for rainwater harvesting and reuse, including extensive site details and design examples.

National Climatic Data Center

www.ncdc.noaa.gov/oa/climate/aasc.html

A useful site for researching local climate data, such as rainfall data for rainwater harvesting calculations, it includes links to state climate offices.

The Texas Manual on Rainwater Harvesting, 2005

Texas Water Development Board

www.twdb.state.tx.us/iwt/rainwater.asp

www.twdb.state.tx.us/publications/reports/InfoSheets.asp

This third edition of the manual covers rainwater harvesting systems design, components, water quality and treatment, harvesting guidelines, and cost estimation and includes several case studies.

Water Use It Wisely

www.wateruseitwisely.com/toolsLinks/index.shtml

This site provides extensive lists of links and related resources concerning water conservation in addition to a series of links to rainwater harvesting and gray-water systems. Scroll down to the "Gray-water, Reuse, and Rainwater Harvesting" section of the list of links and resources.

Print Media

Harvesting Rainwater for Landscape Use, by Patricia H. Waterfall. Revised edition. University of Arizona, 2006.

www.cals.arizona.edu/pubs/water/az1344.pdf or www.azwater.gov

This document may be ordered from the Arizona Department of Water Resources, Tucson Active Management Area, 400 W. Congress, Suite 518, Tucson, AZ 85701, (520) 770-3800.

Rainwater Harvesting for Drylands, by Brad Lancaster. Volume 1. Rainsource Press, 2006. Available through www.harvestingrainwater.com.

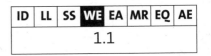

ID	LL	SS	**WE**	EA	MR	EQ	AE
			1.1				

WE 1.2: Graywater Reuse System

Graywater is defined by the Uniform Plumbing Code as "untreated household wastewater which has not come into contact with toilet waste." It includes used water from bathtubs, showers, wash basins, and clothes washers and laundry tubs, but not wastewater from kitchen sinks or dishwashers.

Graywater should not be confused with black water, the wastewater from toilets. Black water must not be reused.

Graywater can be used for various applications to offset the demand for potable water, but the most common application is for landscape irrigation. This credit rewards the reuse of least 5,000 gallons of graywater per year.

Approach and Implementation

Graywater systems must meet state and local health codes and standards, and these regulations often limit the use of graywater to particular applications, such as irrigation. Graywater systems might also require inspection and approval by local health officials.

The use of graywater in fixtures and fittings or appliances, such as toilets, can void the manufacturer's warranty. Check the manuals and ask the manufacturer whether there are stipulations or conditions for the use of graywater.

A graywater system has several components:

❏ Plumbing system: piping to capture the graywater at its source, transfer it to the storage tank, and distribute it to end-use applications.

❏ Surge tank: the storage container, sized to hold at least one week of graywater (roughly 100 gallons), with a regulator, overflow pipe, and venting system.

❏ Filtration system: graywater treatment, if necessary, to minimize odors and bacteria growth.

A graywater system should be designed by plumbing and/or landscape contractors and should be integrated with the landscape and irrigation design. Take into account how much graywater will be produced by the home and how this graywater will be captured. Also consider how much water is needed for the landscape design; avoid oversizing or undersizing the system.

Calculations

If graywater is collected from faucets and other sources, use the following approach to estimate the number of gallons of graywater collected per year:

1. 1.Estimate frequency-of-use for graywater sources, based on # of daily uses, duration of use, and # of occupants. **See Table 2** for use assumptions to be used in this calculation.

2. Identify flow rates (GPM) for graywater sources, based on fixture specifications, etc.

3. Multiply frequency of use by flow rate to estimate total # of gallons collected per year.

Table 2. Standard Fixture Usage

Fixture Type	Use assumption
Water closet	5 times per day per occupant
Shower	5 minutes per day per occupant
Kitchen sink faucets	4 minutes per day per occupant
Lavatory faucet	1.25 minutes per day per occupant

Exemplary Performance

Projects that install a graywater system that collects water from multiple elements (e.g., clothes washers, showers, and wash basin faucets) and can demonstrate a demand for this water can apply for 1 additional point, to be counted under Innovation in Design 3. This application must be submitted by the Provider and approved by USGBC before the point can be counted.

Verification and Submittals

Supporting Verification Materials, made available by the Project Team:

❑ Present calculations for the graywater reuse system and surge tank size to the Verification Team.

❑ Include any system equipment information in the occupant's operations and maintenance manual.

Verification Team:

❑ Visually verify that all calculations related to this credit are completed.

❑ Visually verify that the graywater reuse system has been installed.

Considerations

Environmental Issues

Depending on its source, graywater can contain chemicals and have a higher pH than is optimal for certain types of plants. Graywater is also not suitable for irrigation of fruit and vegetable gardens unless the system includes appropriate filtration and treatment. Work with a landscape professional to ensure that the graywater reuse system is integrated into the landscape and irrigation system design.

Regional Variances

Graywater systems must meet state and local health codes and standards. Check with local code officials.

Resources

Web Sites

California Graywater Systems, Title 24, Part 5, CA Administrative Code

www.owue.water.ca.gov/docs/Revised_Graywater_Standards.pdf

The revised California Graywater Standards include code requirements, details, and systems design standards for installation and use of graywater systems.

Graywater Guide: Using Graywater in Your Home Landscape

California State Department of Water Resources

www.owue.water.ca.gov/docs/graywater_guide_book.pdf

This guide was prepared to help homeowners and landscape and plumbing contractors understand the California Graywater Standards and design, install, and maintain graywater systems.

Greywater Fact Sheet

Washington State Department of Health, Division of Environmental Health

www.doh.wa.gov/ehp/ts/WW/greywater/Greywater-1.htm

and

www.doh.wa.gov/ehp/ts/WW/GreywaterFact.PDF

A web-based and PDF document that describes graywater uses, applications, cautions, and irrigation system installation guidelines.

Water Use It Wisely

www.wateruseitwisely.com/toolsLinks/index.shtml

This site provides extensive lists of links and related resources concerning water conservation in addition to a series of links to graywater resources and sites. Scroll down to the "Greywater, Reuse,

and Rainwater Harvesting" section of links and resources.

Print Media

Create an Oasis with Greywater, by Art Ludwig. Fifth edition. Oasis Design, 2006.

Available at www.oasisdesign.net/greywater/createanoasis/index.htm.

Builder's Greywater Guide, by Art Ludwig. Oasis Design, 2006. Available at www.oasisdesign.net/greywater/buildersguide/index.htm.

WE 1.3: Use of Municipal Recycled Water System

Municipalities across the country, particularly in arid regions, have begun to develop infrastructure for tertiary treatment of wastewater and stormwater. Such water is generally called recycled or reclaimed. This approach enables communities to meet their water demand without having to further divert rivers and streams or drain critical underground aquifers.

To ensure public safety, recycled water undergoes various treatment processes. Depending on the level of treatment, recycled water can be used to satisfy almost any type of water demand. The U.S. Environmental Protection Agency regulates wastewater treatment and drinking water quality, and most states have guidelines or regulations pertaining to the application and reuse of recycled water.

This credit rewards a home that uses only municipal recycled water for 100% of its irrigation needs.

Approach and Implementation

Design the plumbing system to make use of recycled water from the municipal supply. Most municipal water recycling systems treat the water only well enough to be used for irrigation. To use recycled water, the home must be plumbed to separate potable water from recycled water intake. The recycled water is typically distributed through "purple line," to distinguish the system from the potable water supply system.

Consult the local water authority and plumbing codes. In all cases, the home must be plumbed according to the applicable guidelines.

Calculations

No calculations are required for this credit.

Exemplary Performance

A project that meets WE 1.3 and also installs a rainwater or graywater harvest system to offset indoor water loads may apply for exemplary performance credit. This application must be submitted by the Provider and approved by USGBC before any points can be counted."

Verification and Submittals

Supporting Verification Materials, made available by the Project Team:

❑ Provide evidence from the municipality that a municipal recycled water system is in place.

❑ Include any system equipment information in the occupant's operations and maintenance manual.

Verification Team:

❑ Visually verify that the home is plumbed to receive recycled water from a municipal recycled water system.

Considerations

Economic Issues

Although this measure may increase the cost of plumbing the home, in some municipalities recycled water is provided at a lower rate, so the occupant will realize savings over the long term.

Regional Variances

Not every municipality has a wastewater or stormwater recycling system. In areas without water recycling, consider installing a rainwater capture system (WE 1.1) or graywater reuse system (WE 1.2).

ID	LL	SS	WE	EA	MR	EQ	AE
			1.3				

Resources

Web Sites

Environmental Protection Agency, Region 9 Water Program

www.epa.gov/region09/water/recycling/index.html

This site provides basic information on water recycling, as well as contacts and case studies. It also provides information about text resources.

City of San Diego Water Department

www.sandiego.gov/water/recycled/index.shtml

This site provides detailed information about the City of San Diego's recycled water program. It includes insights for governments and consumers interested in learning about developing and operating a recycled water program. The site also includes links to other water recycling projects across the United States.

WE 2: Irrigation System

Intent

Minimize outdoor demand for water through water-efficient irrigation.

Requirements

Prerequisites

None.

Credits

Note: Points shown below are for irrigation systems installed throughout the designed landscape. If only 50% of the designed landscape includes these measures, then only 50% of the points are available. Even if part of the yard is not landscaped, the irrigation system must be stubbed to that part of the yard, as appropriate.

2.1 **High-Efficiency Irrigation System** (1 point each, maximum 3 points). Design and install a high-efficiency irrigation system (based on overall landscaping plans, including measures adopted in SS 2) such that any of the following are met:

a) Install an irrigation system designed by an EPA WaterSense certified professional.

b) Design and install an irrigation system with head-to-head coverage.

c) Install a central shut-off valve.

d) Install a submeter for the irrigation system.

e) Use drip irrigation for at least 50% of landscape planting beds to minimize evaporation.

f) Create separate zones for each type of bedding area based on watering needs.

g) Install a timer or controller that activates the valves for each watering zone at the best time of day to minimize evaporative losses while maintaining healthy plants and obeying local regulations and water use guidance.

h) Install pressure-regulating devices to maintain optimal pressure and prevent misting.

i) Utilize high-efficiency nozzles with an average distribution uniformity (DU) of at least 0.70. This may include conventional rotors, multistream rotors, or high-efficiency spray heads, but the DU must be verified by manufacturer documentation or third-party tests. A point source (drip) irrigation system should be counted as having a DU of 0.80.

j) Check valves in heads.

k) Install a moisture sensor controller or rain delay controller. For example, "smart" evapotranspiration controllers receive radio, pager, or Internet signals to direct the irrigation system to replace only the moisture that the landscape has lost because of heat, wind, etc.

AND/OR

2.2 **Third-Party Inspection** (1 point). Perform a third-party inspection of the irrigation system in operation, including observation of all of the following:

a) All spray heads are operating and delivering water only to intended zones.

b) Any switches or shut-off valves are working properly.

c) Any timers or controllers are set properly.

d) Any irrigation systems are located at least 2 feet from the home.

e) Irrigation spray does not hit the home.

OR

2.3 **Reduce Overall Irrigation Demand by at Least 45%** (maximum 4 points, as specified in **Table 1**). Design the landscape and irrigation system to reduce the overall irrigation water demand water budget. The estimates must be calculated and prepared by a landscape professional, biologist, or other qualified professional using the method outlined below.

Note: A project must earn full points in SS 2.5 before receiving points for this credit.

Table 1. Reduction in Water Demand

Reduction in estimated irrigation water usage	WE 2.3 points	SS 2.5 points	Total points
45–49%	1	6	7
50–54%	2	6	8
55–59%	3	6	9
60% or more	4	6	10

Method for Calculating Reduction in Irrigation Demand

Step 1. Calculate the baseline irrigation water usage:

Baseline Usage = Landscaped Area * ET_0 * 0.62

where ET_0 = Baseline Evapotranspiration Rate (available from local and state departments of agriculture)

Step 2. Calculate the design case irrigation water usage:

Design Case Usage = (Landscaped Area * ET_L ÷ IE) * CF * 0.62

where ET_L = ET_0 * K_L and K_L = K_S * K_{MC}. Refer to **Tables 2 and 3** for values for K_S and K_{MC}, and to **Table 4** for values for IE. For CF, use estimated value based on manufacturer's specifications for percentage water savings.

Step 3. Calculate the percentage reduction in irrigation water usage:

Percentage Reduction = (1 − Design Case Usage ÷ Baseline Usage) * 100

Step 4. Refer to **Table 1**, above, to determine points earned.

Table 2. Species Factor

Vegetation type	Species factor (K_S)		
	Low	Average	High
Trees	0.2	0.5	0.9
Shrubs	0.2	0.5	0.7
Groundcover	0.2	0.5	0.7
Turf	0.6	0.7	0.8

Table 3. Microclimate Factor

Example microclimate impacts	Microclimate factor (K_{MC})		
	Low	Average	High
Shading	0.5	0.8	1.0
High sun exposure	1.0	1.2	1.5
Protection from wind	0.8	0.9	1.0
Windy area	1.0	1.2	1.5

Table 4. Irrigation Efficiency

Irrigation type	Irrigation efficiency (IE)	
	Low	High
Fixed spray	0.4	0.6
Impact and microspray	0.5	0.7
Rotors	0.6	0.8
Multistream rotators	0.6	0.8
Low volume and point source (e.g., drip)	0.7	0.9

Synergies and Trade-Offs

A project receiving points for WE 2.3 must skip WE 2.1 and 2.2.

A project receiving points for WE 2.3 must achieve full points in SS 2.5.

This irrigation system design must address all aspects of the landscape design, including any features from SS 2, as well as any rainwater harvesting or graywater reuse system (WE 1).

Landscape irrigation practices in the United States consume large quantities of potable water. Outdoor uses, primarily landscaping, account for 30% of the 26 billion gallons of water consumed daily in the United States.[2] Irrigation typically uses potable treated water, even though nonpotable rainwater, graywater, or recycled water is equally effective.

The measures listed in these credits improve the efficiency of irrigation systems by limiting overwatering, evaporation, and leaks and losses. A well-designed irrigation system addresses all three problems while providing plantings with only as much water as necessary.

A home may not need an irrigation system. These credits reward any necessary irrigation systems that are designed and installed to be highly efficient.

Approach and Implementation

Determine whether an irrigation system is necessary. Consider the local and regional climate conditions and evapotranspiration losses and work with a landscape professional to design the site so that irrigation needs are minimized. Depending on the type of landscaping being used, irrigation systems may not be necessary. If a site is designed not to require irrigation, a project can earn credit under SS 2.5 and WE 2.3. No points may be earned in WE 2.1 or WE 2.2.

If a temporary irrigation system is installed below ground , it should be treated as permanent and it can be awarded points under WE 2.1. If an irrigation system is installed above ground, it should be treated as temporary and it cannot be awarded points under WE 2.1

Rather than choosing a landscape first and fitting the irrigation system to it, design the landscape to minimize demand for water and chemicals. Avoid turf. Install plants that stay healthy and attractive without regular irrigation.

If irrigation is needed, bring in a certified irrigation professional to design the system. Certifications for irrigation specialists include the U.S. Environmental Protection Agency's WaterSense Program and the Irrigation Association. This strategy is awarded in WE 2.1(a). Even licensed landscape professionals may not have adequate training to design and install an irrigation system.

A well-designed system uses head-to-head coverage and high-efficiency nozzles or drip irrigation to ensure that plantings receive enough water but no more than necessary. Strategies for taking into consideration the moisture requirements of the installed plants are awarded in WE 2.1(b), (e), and (i).

Controls, timers, and sensors enable "smart" irrigation systems to operate only when water is needed and conditions are optimal for watering. Flow sensors can also identify leaks or breaks. These strategies are awarded in WE 2.1(g), (h), and (k).

Valves are generally managed by the controls but also enable the system to be manually shut off when a leak or problem occurs. The heads that distribute water vary in effectiveness. The best strategies are awarded in WE 2.1(c) and (j).

---

2 United States Environmental Protection Agency, Office of Water. Water-Efficient Landscaping. EPA Publication 832-F-02-002, September 2002. 21 January 2005. www.epa.gov/owm/water-efficiency/final_final.pdf

Use multiple irrigation zones if the site is designed with different types of landscaping or if shading and wind exposure create different microclimates on the site. A zoned irrigation system enables the occupant to deliver the appropriate amounts of water to different types of plantings. These strategies are awarded in WE 2.1(f) and (k).

Install the irrigation system properly. Poor installation can cause equipment failures, leading to leaks and inefficient distribution. Water should not hit any impermeable surfaces, especially the house, because it is wasteful and can cause durability problems. WE 2.2 rewards projects that pass a third-party inspection after installation.

It is a good idea to create a map of the entire irrigation system for the occupant. Having a permanent record of the system layout is important for conducting system repairs, as well as any future activity that might require excavation.

Consult WaterSense (see "Resources," below) to find a certified irrigation professional or high-efficiency equipment. A voluntary partnership program sponsored by the U.S. Environmental Protection Agency, WaterSense seeks to protect the nation's water supply by promoting water-efficient products and services across the country. The WaterSense label identifies high-efficiency products that have been verified for performance. WaterSense currently has a certification program for irrigation professionals, and a specification for weather- or sensor-based controls is under development.

Calculations

No calculations are required for this credit.

Verification and Submittals

Supporting Verification Materials, made available by the Project Team:

WE 2.1 High-Efficiency Irrigation System

❑ Present any system equipment information and design plans to the Verification Team.

❑ Include any system equipment information in the occupant's operations and maintenance manual.

❑ Sign an Accountability Form to indicate that the installed system meets the requirements of the credit.

Verification Team:

WE 2.1 High-Efficiency Irrigation System

❑ Where appropriate, visually verify that all applicable elements of the irrigation system (e.g., controls, sensors, meters) are installed.

❑ Verify that an Accountability Form has been signed by responsible party.

WE 2.2 Third-Party Inspection

❑ Conduct an on-site verification that the irrigation system is operating.

❑ If performed by someone other than the Verification Team, verify that an Accountability Form has been signed by the responsible party.

Exemplary Performance

Projects that install more than 3 of the measures listed in WE 2.1 should be awarded exemplary performance credit, to be counted in Innovation in Design 3 (ID 3).

Projects with only landscaping beds (i.e., no turf) that are served only by low-volume and point source irrigation (e.g., drip) can earn 0.5 point of exemplary performance credit, to be counted in Innovation in Design 3.

Each additional measure is worth ½ point, for a maximum of 2 exemplary performance points total.

Considerations

Economic Issues

The most effective way to avoid escalating water costs for irrigation is to design landscaping adapted to the local climate and the site's microclimate. The cost of irrigation can be reduced or eliminated through thoughtful planning and careful plant selection and layout.

Although a drip irrigation system may be more expensive to design than a conventional system, it usually costs less to install and has lower water use and maintenance requirements.

Many municipalities offer rebates or incentives for water-efficient irrigation systems, dedicated water meters, and rain or moisture sensors.

Environmental Issues

The use of native plants and the avoidance of conventional turfgrass can reduce the demand for irrigation. This approach also reduces demand for fertilizer and pesticides, provides habitat for native wildlife, and creates a home that is integrated with its natural surroundings.

Regional Variances

The need for an irrigation system depends on the type of landscaping used, the microclimate effects on evapotranspiration rates, and the amount and frequency of rainfall. Local water authorities may require irrigation measures, especially where water resources are scarce. A project that

uses measures as part of code compliance is still eligible to earn LEED points.

Resources

Note that several of the resources included in WE Credits 1.1 and 1.2, above, also include references to integrating rainwater harvesting and graywater with landscape irrigation systems.

Web Sites

American Society of Landscape Architects

www.asla.org

ASLA is the national professional association representing landscape architects. The Web site provides information about members, products, services, publications, and events.

Wateright

www.wateright.org/duie.asp

This is a consumer-friendly Web site developed by the Center for Irrigation Technology at California State University–Fresno with support from the U.S. Bureau of Reclamation. This site includes a good explanation of distribution uniformity and irrigation efficiency.

International Center for Water Technology

www.icwt.net

The International Center for Water Technology is a consortium of public and private entities, led by the efforts of California State University–Fresno. This Web site is the more technical counterpart to Wateright; it includes research papers and educational materials about cutting-edge progress in water-saving technologies.

The Irrigation Association

www.irrigation.org

This nonprofit organization provides education for and certification of irrigation system designers, installers, and auditors.

It also promotes systems and products that efficiently use water in turf and landscape irrigation applications.

U.S. EPA WaterSense℠: Efficiency Made Easy

www.epa.gov/owm/water-efficiency/pp/irrprof.htm

This site provides information on the Environmental Protection Agency's WaterSense labeling program for water-efficient landscape irrigation products, plus tips and recommendations for water-efficient irrigation. Follow the link to "Weather- or Sensor-Based Irrigation Control Technologies" for related information on high-efficiency irrigation controllers.

University of Missouri Extension, Water-Efficient Landscaping

www.muextension.missouri.edu/xplor/agguides/hort/g06912.htm

This Web site has general descriptions and strategies for water efficiency in gardens and landscapes.

Water-Efficient Landscaping: Preventing Pollution and Using Resources Wisely

www.epa.gov/owm/water-efficiency/docs/water-efficient_landscaping_508.pdf

This manual from the Environmental Protection Agency provides information about reducing water consumption through creative landscaping techniques.

Water Wiser: The Water Efficiency Clearinghouse

www.awwa.org/waterwiser

This clearinghouse provides articles, reference materials, and papers on all forms of water efficiency.

Print Media

Landscape Irrigation: Design and Management, by Stephen W. Smith. John Wiley and Sons, 1996.

This text is a comprehensive guide to landscape irrigation strategies, techniques, and hardware.

Turf Irrigation Manual, by Richard B. Choate and Jim Watkins. Fifth edition. Telsco Industries, 1994.

This manual covers all aspects of turf and landscape irrigation.

Landscape irrigation practices in the United States consume large quantities of potable water. Outdoor uses, primarily landscaping, account for 30% of the 26 billion gallons of water consumed daily in the United States.[3] Irrigation typically uses potable water, even though nonpotable rainwater, graywater, or recycled water is equally effective.

A holistic approach to landscape design can significantly reduce potable water consumption by focusing both on site-appropriate vegetation to reduce demand and on high-efficiency irrigation design to reduce waste.

This credit rewards projects that can demonstrate less overall irrigation water demand compared with a conventional landscape and irrigation design in a comparable site.

Approach and Implementation

This credit, together with SS 2.5, is a performance-based alternative to the prescriptive measures in SS 2.2, 2.3, and 2.4, as well as WE 2.1 and 2.2. Projects that use the performance approach cannot earn points for prescriptive measures in SS 2.3, SS 2.4, WE 2.1, or WE 2.2, and can earn only partial credit in SS 2.2. However, the measures and strategies listed for those credits are an excellent guide for how to reduce irrigation water demand.

The performance approach provides more flexibility but requires a higher level of verification using site-specific calculations (see "Calculations," below). Builders cannot earn the points in this credit simply by building in an area with considerable rainfall.

This credit should be pursued only after all the points in SS 2.5 have been achieved, corresponding to a minimum 45% water savings. Significant reduction in water demand is most easily met by a combination of landscape design and efficient irrigation water use.

Choose appropriate vegetation that requires little irrigation. Work with a landscape professional and/or irrigation specialist to choose trees, shrubs, and groundcover that are well suited to the local soil and climate. Avoid turfgrass and any species that require regular watering.

Use high-efficiency irrigation techniques, including those listed in WE 2.1, to provide only as much water to the plants as needed and to minimize evaporative losses and leaks.

Ensure that both the landscaping plan and the irrigation system are installed in accordance with the design. Have the designer and installer work closely together and use a third party to verify that the system is functioning properly after installation. Landscape design and irrigation system design are different skills. If irrigation is needed, have a certified irrigation professional design the system. Certifications for irrigation specialists include the U.S. Environmental Protection Agency's WaterSense Program and the Irrigation Association.

Any rainwater, graywater, or recycled water system should be integrated with the landscape design and irrigation system. However, these systems are rewarded in WE 1.1, 1.2, and 1.3, and any water demand being met by these systems must still be counted in the calculation for this credit.

---

3 United States Environmental Protection Agency, Office of Water. Water-Efficient Landscaping. EPA Publication 832-F-02-002, September 2002. 21 January 2005. www.epa.gov/owm/water-efficiency/final_final.pdf

Calculations

A guidance document and accompanying calculator have been developed for performing the calculation for this credit. Please contact your LEED for Homes Provider for these resources.

If a temporary irrigation system is installed below ground , it should be treated as permanent and it can be awarded points under WE 2.1. If an irrigation system is installed above ground, it should be treated as temporary and it cannot be awarded points under WE 2.1.

Calculate the percentage reduction in irrigation demand for this credit using the four-step process outlined below. When calculating water use, do not subtract water from rainwater, graywater, or recycled water systems; these elements are rewarded in other credits.

A landscape professional must perform the calculation. This includes individuals with certification, licensure, formal training (higher education), or at least 10 years of professional experience.

If insufficient data prevent use of the prescribed method, a landscape professional can submit a modified method as a Credit Interpretation Request.

Standard assumptions and variables

❑ All calculations are based on irrigation during the month of July.

❑ All estimates for water use must be based on expected demand when the plantings are fully mature.

❑ If the landscape is divided into zones, calculate each zone separately. The average for the entire site should be calculated by weighting the results for each zone based on its proportion to the total landscaped area.

❑ Landscape Coefficient (K_L) indicates the volume of water lost via evapotranspiration. This value is dependent on the landscape species, the microclimate, and the planting density. The formula for determining the landscape coefficient is given in Step 2, below.

❑ Species Factor (K_S) accounts for the water requirements of different plant species. The species factor can be divided into three categories (high, average, and low) depending on the plant species considered. To determine the most appropriate category for a plant species, use plant manuals and professional experience. This factor is somewhat subjective, but landscape professionals should have a general idea of the water needs of particular plant species. See **Table 5** for sample values. (Note: If a species does not require irrigation once it is established, then the effective $K_S = 0$ and the resulting $K_L = 0$.)

❑ Microclimate Factor (K_{MC}) accounts for environmental conditions specific to the landscape, including temperature, wind, and humidity. The average K_{MC} is 1.0; it refers to conditions where the landscape evapotranspiration rate is unaffected by buildings, pavements, reflective surfaces, and slopes. Higher K_{MC} conditions occur where evaporative potential is increased because of proximity to heat-absorbing and reflective surfaces or exposure to wind.

❑ Baseline Evapotranspiration Rate (ET_0) represents the rate of water loss for a particular climate or region. Use a published value for ET_0 that corresponds to the climate of the project site. The ET_0 value for July must be used in this calculation because the highest evapotranspiration rates and, therefore, the greatest irrigation demands occur during that month. Published ET_0 values are available from various sources, including state and local departments of agriculture.

- Landscape Evapotranspiration Rate (ET_L) is the site-specific rate, which is calculated based on other variables (see equation, Step 2, below).

- Irrigation Efficiency (IE) is based on the type of irrigation equipment installed. Some manufacturers provide a distribution uniformity, which can be used here. Otherwise, refer to **Table 7** for sample values.

- Control Factor (CF) is based on the type of controls installed, such as weather-based or moisture sensor-based systems. If no moisture sensor, rain-delay controller, or flow-control sensor is used, CF = 1. A controller that is estimated to reduce overall irrigation has a CF of 1 minus the fraction of *overall* irrigation water saved. For example, a controller that saves 10% has a CF of 0.90. This number must be supported by either manufacturer's documentation or calculations by a landscape professional.

Estimating the percentage reduction in water usage for irrigation

Step 1. Calculate the baseline irrigation water usage:

Baseline Usage = Landscaped Area * ET_0 * 0.62

where ET_0 = Baseline Evapotranspiration Rate (available from local and state departments of agriculture)

ID	LL	SS	**WE**	EA	MR	EQ	AE
			2.3				

Table 5. Species Factor

Vegetation type	Species factor (K_s)		
	Low	Average	High
Trees	0.2	0.5	0.9
Shrubs	0.2	0.5	0.7
Groundcover	0.2	0.5	0.7
Turf	0.6	0.7	0.8

Table 6. Microclimate Factor

Example microclimate impacts	Microclimate factor (K_{MC})		
	Low	Average	High
Shading	0.5	0.8	1.0
High sun exposure	1.0	1.2	1.5
Protection from wind	0.8	0.9	1.0
Windy area	1.0	1.2	1.5

Table 7. Irrigation Efficiency

Irrigation type	Irrigation efficiency (IE)	
	Low	High
Fixed spray	0.4	0.6
Impact and microspray	0.5	0.7
Rotors	0.6	0.8
Multistream rotators	0.6	0.8
Low volume and point source (e.g., drip)	0.7	0.9

Step 2. Calculate the design case irrigation water usage:

Design Case Usage = (Landscaped Area * $ET_L \div IE$) * CF * 0.62

where $ET_L = ET_0 * K_L$ and $K_L = K_S * K_{MC}$. Refer to **Tables 5** and **6** for values for K_S and K_{MC}, and to **Table 7** for values for IE. For CF, use estimated value based on manufacturer's specifications for percentage water savings.

Step 3. Calculate the percentage reduction in irrigation water usage:

Percentage Reduction = (1 – Design Case Usage ÷ Baseline Usage) * 100

Step 4. Refer to **Table 1**, above, to determine points earned.

Verification and Submittals

Supporting Verification Materials, made available by the Project Team:

❏ Present irrigation demand calculations to the Verification Team.

❏ Present a list of the plants being used to the Verification Team.

❏ Sign an Accountability Form to indicate that the installed landscape and irrigation system correspond to the design used in the calculation.

Verification Team:

❏ Visually verify that the calculations are completed.

❏ Verify that an Accountability Form has been signed by the responsible party.

❏ Verify that the calculation was performed by a qualified individual (e.g., certified or licensed landscape architect).

AND

– Collect and submit outdoor water use calculation to USGBC for review.

AND

– If drought-tolerant plants are claimed (i.e., low species factors are claimed), use a list of installed plants provided by the project team and a list of drought-tolerant plants created by a third-party entity (e.g. ag. cooperative extension) to verify that installed plants are drought-tolerant.

AND

– Conduct on-site verification of any water-saving items identified in the calculation, including high-efficiency irrigation measures and high/low shading conditions.

Exemplary Performance

Projects that reduce overall outdoor water demand by 65% or more should be awarded 1 point for exemplary performance, to be counted under Innovation in Design Process Credit 3. A reduction of 70% is worth 2 points; a reduction of 75% is worth 3 points; a reduction of 80% is worth 4 points.

Considerations

Economic Issues

The most effective strategy to reduce the cost of irrigation is to design landscaping adapted to the local climate and the site's microclimate, with careful plant selection and layout. Although the additional design cost for a drip irrigation system may make it more expensive than a conventional system, a drip system usually costs less to install and has lower water use and maintenance requirements.

Many municipalities offer rebates or incentives for water-efficient irrigation systems, dedicated water meters, and rain or moisture sensors. Check with the regional or state water authority for information on possible incentives.

Environmental Issues

The use of native or adapted plants, and the avoidance of conventional turfgrass can reduce the demand for fertilizer and pesticides as well as irrigation. The use of native landscaping can also provide habitat for native wildlife and create a site that is integrated with its natural surroundings.

Regional Variances

The need for an irrigation system will depend on the type of landscaping used, the microclimate effects on evapotranspiration rates, and the amount and frequency of rainfall. Water-efficient landscaping helps conserve local and regional potable water resources. Local water authorities may require irrigation measures, especially in areas where water resources are scarce. A project that uses the measures in this credit as part of code compliance is still eligible to earn LEED points.

Resources

Web Sites

Wateright

www.wateright.org/duie.asp

This is a consumer-friendly Web site developed by the Center for Irrigation Technology at California State University–Fresno with support from the U.S. Bureau of Reclamation. This site includes a good explanation of distribution uniformity and irrigation efficiency.

International Center for Water Technology

www.icwt.net

The International Center for Water Technology is a consortium of public and private entities, led by the efforts of California State University–Fresno. This Web site is the more technical counterpart to Wateright; it includes research papers and educational materials about cutting-edge progress in water-saving technologies.

The Irrigation Association

www.irrigation.org

This nonprofit organization provides education for and certification of irrigation system designers, installers, and auditors. It also promotes systems and products that efficiently use water in turf and landscape irrigation applications.

U.S. EPA WaterSense^{SM}: Efficiency Made Easy

www.epa.gov/owm/water-efficiency/pp/irrprof.htm

This site provides information on the Environmental Protection Agency's WaterSense labeling program for water-efficient landscape irrigation products, plus tips and recommendations for water-efficient irrigation. Follow the link to "Weather- or Sensor-Based Irrigation Control Technologies" for related information on high-efficiency irrigation controllers.

ID	LL	SS	WE	EA	MR	EQ	AE
			2.3				

WE 3: Indoor Water Use

Intent

Minimize indoor demand for water through water-efficient fixtures and fittings.

Requirements

Prerequisites

None.

Credits

Note: Compensating shower valves and conventional, non-compensating shower valves may not work properly when low-flow showerheads (restricting water flow below 2.5 gpm) are installed. Installing low-flow showerheads where compensating valves or conventional, non-compensating valves are installed can increase the risk of scalding (or other types of injuries, such as slips and falls due to thermal shock) when the plumbing system experiences pressure changes. Make sure any low-flow showerhead is installed with a valve that has been designed, tested, and verified to function safely at the reduced flow rate. If in doubt, consult the manufacturer of the valve before installing a low-flow showerhead.

3.1 **High-Efficiency Fixtures and Fittings** (1 point each, maximum 3 points). Meet one or more of the following requirements by installing high-efficiency (low-flow) fixtures or fittings. A project cannot earn points in both WE 3.1 and WE 3.2 for the same fixture type (e.g., faucet, shower, or toilet).

a) The average flow rate for all lavatory faucets must be ≤ 2.00 gpm.

b) The average flow rate for all showers must be ≤ 2.00 gpm per stall.

c) The average flow rate for all toilets must be ≤ 1.30 gpf

OR

toilets must be dual-flush and meet the requirements of ASME A112.19.14
OR

toilets must meet the U.S. EPA WaterSense specification and be certified and labeled accordingly.

3.2 **Very High Efficiency Fixtures and Fittings** (2 points each, maximum 6 points). Meet one or more of the following requirements by installing very high efficiency fixtures or fittings. A project cannot earn points in both WE 3.1 and WE 3.2 for the same fixture type (e.g., faucet, shower, or toilet).

a) The average flow rate for all lavatory faucets must be ≤ 1.50 gpm

OR

lavatory faucets must meet the U.S. EPA WaterSense specification and be certified and labeled accordingly.

b) The average flow rate for all showers must be ≤ 1.75 gpm per stall.

c) The average flow rate for all toilets must be ≤ 1.10 gpf.

Synergies and Trade-Offs

Indoor water savings also can be achieved with more efficient water distribution systems and appliances. Points for indoor water distribution-related savings are available under EA 7.1, and points for appliance-related water savings are available under EA 9.

Low-flow showerheads and faucets will reduce demand for hot water and resulting energy use for water heating. Credits in EA 7 address water heating efficiency.

WE 3.1 High-Efficiency Fixtures and Fittings
WE 3.2 Very High Efficiency Fixtures and Fittings

Faucets, showers, baths, and toilets typically account for two-thirds of a home's indoor water use and one-third of its total water use. Installing high-efficiency fixtures and fittings is an easy strategy for reducing indoor water use: the most efficient fixtures and fittings use less than half the water of the conventional alternatives. High-efficiency fixtures and fittings can also significantly reduce the energy demand associated with domestic water heating. Since indoor water use varies with occupancy, the actual water and energy savings will depend on the number of occupants in the home, as well as water use habits.

Kitchen faucets are not included in this credit because studies have shown that most water consumption in the kitchen is volume-based (e.g., filling glasses or pots). Low-flow faucets installed in a kitchen only increase the amount of time required to complete a filling task.

This credit rewards installation of either high-efficiency or very high efficiency fixtures and fittings in bathrooms.

Approach and Implementation

High-efficiency fixtures and fittings are sold side-by-side with conventional fixtures and fittings. From the consumer standpoint, they generally look and operate the same way as conventional fixtures and fittings but use less water and have a lower rated water use in gallons per minute (gpm) or gallons per flush (gpf). Low-flow faucets achieve savings through the use of aerators, which combine air with water to give the user the feeling of an equivalent water pressure but with less water.

Flow restrictors are an acceptable strategy

to earn WE 3, if the flow-restrictors are hardware that cannot easily be removed.

Low-flow showerheads, especially those with flow volumes of less than 1.75 gpm, should be installed with proper thermostatic mixing valves that have been designed, tested, and verified to function safely at the reduced flow rate. The use of conventional or compensating shower valves can increase the risk of scalding when the plumbing system experiences pressure changes. Study showerhead manufacturers' information on the performance of the high-efficiency and very high efficiency showerheads (including testing for scalding and thermal shock) before making a selection.

High-efficiency toilets (HETs) have an average or effective flush volume of 1.28 gallons or less. HETs generally accomplish this by employing improved hydraulic designs, improved technologies, better valving, and in some cases smaller tanks. Some HET designs include multiple flush settings or pressure assistance to reduce water demand. For example, dual-flush toilets have a normal flush rate for solid waste but a much reduced flush rate for liquid waste. Pressure-assist toilets achieve the highest water efficiency by using pressure rather than gravity to remove the waste. Note that flush-valve conversion devices and toilet tank bags cannot be used to earn credit under WE 3.

Not all high-efficiency toilets operate equally well, and poor design can lead to ineffective flushing and the need for multiple flushes. The U.S. Environmental Protection Agency's WaterSense program certifies toilets that achieve both water efficiency and operational effectiveness. The WaterSense label identifies high-efficiency products that have been verified for performance. WaterSense currently la-

look for

bels high-performing, water-efficient toilets and bathroom faucets. Specification for showerheads is under development. Low-flow showerheads and faucets will reduce both the hot water consumption and the rate at which hot water reaches the fixtures. If low-flow showerheads and faucets are installed, a smaller water heater and smaller-diameter piping can be used. To make up for the lower flow rate associated with low-flow showerheads and faucets, design the water distribution system to be compact (EA 7.1).

If the home will use any graywater or recycled water indoors, consider its quality in fixture selection. Determine whether manufacturers have set minimum supply water quality standards for specific fixtures and fittings. If rainwater or graywater will be used with plumbing fixtures and fittings designed for municipally supplied potable water, verify that the supply water quality is acceptable and will not compromise long-term fixture performance or void the manufacturer's warranty.

Calculations

If a project includes multiple fixtures and fittings with different efficiencies, use a straight-line average to determine the overall average efficiency of each fixture type. For example, if two lavatory faucets have flow rates of 1.5 gpm and a third is rated for 2.1 gpm, the average overall flow rate is equal to $(1.5 + 1.5 + 2.1) \div 3$, or 1.7 gallons per minute. For the purposes of this calculation, the flow rate of dual-flush toilets can be calculated using the following formula (high and low volumes must be verified):

Avg. volume = [(high volume flush) + 2* (low volume flush)] ÷ 3

Using this approach, dual-flush toilets can be used to meet WE 3.2 if the average flow rate for all toilets in the home is ≤ 1.10 gpf. If the high and low volume cannot be verified, a value of 1.25 gallons per flush must be used.

Average flow rates must be calculated to the hundredths place. For example, if the average flow rate is 1.13, this cannot be rounded down to 1.10.

Verification and Submittals

Supporting Verification Materials, made available by the Project Team:

❑ Include any equipment literature in the occupant's operations and maintenance manual.

Verification Team:

❑ Visually verify that all fixtures and fittings meet the appropriate requirements.

Exemplary Performance

Projects that can demonstrate flow rates that are substantially lower than those in WE 3.2 can apply for an additional point, to be counted under Innovation in Design 3. This application must be submitted by the Provider and approved by USGBC before the point can be counted.

Considerations

Economic Issues

State and local water authorities may provide incentives or rebates for high-efficiency fixtures and fittings. In some cases, these programs cover the entire additional cost of high-efficiency alternatives.

High-efficiency fixtures and fittings will save the occupants money on utility costs for water and water heating over the life of the home.

Regional Variances

Water conservation has become increasingly important in certain parts of the country, and some local water authorities require indoor water conservation measures. A project that uses measures as part of code compliance is still eligible to earn LEED points.

Resources

Please see the USGBC Web site, at www.usgbc.org/resources, for more specific resources on materials sources and other technical information.

Web Sites

Maximum Performance (MaP™) TESTING California Urban Water Conservation Council

www.cuwcc.org/maptesting.lasso

The Maximum Performance (MaP™) testing project was initiated in 2003 to test toilet models' performance. This testing protocol simulates real-world use to help consumers identify high-efficiency toilets that not only save water but also work well. The current MaP testing report provides performance information on 470 toilet models. This site provides access to the complete listings of the tested toilets.

California Urban Water Conservation Council Product News

www.cuwcc.org/products_tech.lasso

This site provides a variety of information on toilets, urinals, faucets, and showerheads, including high-efficiency models, state and national standards, and other essentials for choosing the right fixtures and fittings.

Choosing a Toilet

www.taunton.com/finehomebuilding/pages/h00042.asp

This Fine Homebuilding article includes several varieties of water-efficient toilets.

Composting Toilet Reviews

www.buildinggreen.com/features/mr/waste.html

An Environmental Building News article discusses commercial composting toilets.

Terry Love's Consumer Toilet Reports

www.terrylove.com/crtoilet.htm

This Web site offers a plumber's perspective on many of the major low-flow and composting toilets used in commercial and residential applications.

Water Closet Performance Testing

www.ebmud.com/conserving_&_recycling/toilet_test_report/default.htm

This site provides two reports on independent test results for flush performance and reliability for a variety of toilets.

U.S. EPA's WaterSense^SM Program

www.epa.gov/owm/water-efficiency

This Web site provides an overview of the U.S. Environmental Protection Agency's WaterSense water-use efficiency program and information about EPA WaterSense-labeled high-efficiency toilets and bathroom sink faucets.

Water Use It Wisely

www.wateruseitwisely.com/toolsLinks/index.shtml

This site provides extensive lists of links and related resources concerning water conservation in addition to a series of links to plumbing fixture and faucet resources and sites. Scroll down to the "Fixtures and Appliances" section of links and resources.

Water Wiser: The Water Efficiency Clearinghouse

www.awwa.org/waterwiser

This web clearinghouse provides articles, reference materials, and papers on all forms of water efficiency.

Energy & Atmosphere

Data from the homebuilding industry indicate that roughly 1.5 million new homes are built each year and that the average size of new homes has doubled in the past 50 years. As a result, total U.S. fossil fuel use in homes has been steadily increasing. The average American consumes 5 times more energy than the average global citizen, 10 times more than the average Chinese person, and nearly 20 times more than the average Indian.[1]

Conventional fossil-based generation of electricity releases carbon dioxide (CO_2), which contributes to global climate change. Coal-fired electric utilities emit almost one-third of the country's anthropogenic nitrogen oxides, the precursor of smog, and two-thirds the sulfur dioxide, which causes acid rain. They also emit more fine particulate material than any other activity in the United States. Because the human body is incapable of clearing fine particles from the lungs, these emissions are contributing factors in tens of thousands of cancer and respiratory illness–related deaths annually. Natural gas, nuclear fission, and hydroelectric generators all have adverse environmental impacts as well. Natural gas is a major source of nitrogen oxides and greenhouse gas emissions. Nuclear power increases the potential for catastrophic accidents and raises significant waste transportation and disposal issues. Hydroelectric generating plants disrupt natural water flows, disturbing aquatic habitat and reducing fish populations.

Buildings consume approximately 37% of the energy and 68% of the electricity produced in the United States annually, according to the U.S. Department of Energy. In 2006, total emissions from residential buildings were responsible for 1.2 billion metric tons of CO_2 emissions, or 20% of the U.S. total.

Scientists predict that left unchecked, emissions of CO_2 and other greenhouse gases from human activities will raise global temperatures by 2.5ºF to 10ºF over the 21st century. The effects will be profound and may include rising sea levels, more frequent floods and droughts, and increased spread of infectious diseases. To address the threat of climate change, greenhouse gas emissions must be slowed, stopped, and reversed. Meeting the challenge will require dramatic advances in technologies and a shift in how the world economy generates and uses energy.

Absent significant improvements in environmental performance, the residential building sector will be a major contributor of global CO_2 emissions. Homes have a lifespan of 50 to 100 years, during which they continually consume energy and produce CO_2 emissions. Further, the U.S. population and economy are projected to grow significantly over the coming decades, increasing the need for new homes. To meet this demand, approximately 12 million new homes are projected to be constructed by 2015.

Building green homes is one of the best strategies for meeting the challenge of climate change because the technology to make substantial reductions in energy and CO_2 emissions already exists. The average certified LEED home uses 30% to 40% less electricity and saves more than 100 metric tons of CO_2 emissions over its lifetime. Modest investments in energy-saving and other climate-friendly technologies can yield homes and communities that are healthier and more comfortable, durable, energy-efficient,

---

1 Making Better Energy Choices, Worldwatch, www.worldwatch.org/node/808#1

and environmentally responsible places to live.

The average mix of end uses of energy in U.S. homes is summarized in **Figure 1**. The actual percentages vary with climate and location—homes in the North use proportionally more energy for space heating and less for electric air-conditioning than homes in the South, and vice versa—but these uses nevertheless represent the primary target areas for energy efficiency improvements.

Table 1 shows the two parallel pathways through the Energy & Atmosphere (EA) credit category in the LEED for Homes Rating System. The first (beginning with EA 1) is a performance pathway that requires the use of an approved energy analysis software program to demonstrate the overall energy performance of the home's design. The second (EA 2–10) is a prescriptive pathway that enables a project to achieve LEED points without the need for energy modeling. The project may instead demonstrate that each of the prescriptive requirements of EA 2–10 has been achieved. A handful of credits can be earned using either approach. The 11 topic areas in the EA credit category are described in the following sections.

Figure 1. Energy Use in U.S. Homes

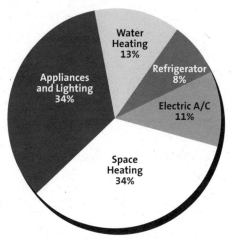

Source: 2005 Building Energy Data Book, Table 4.2.1.

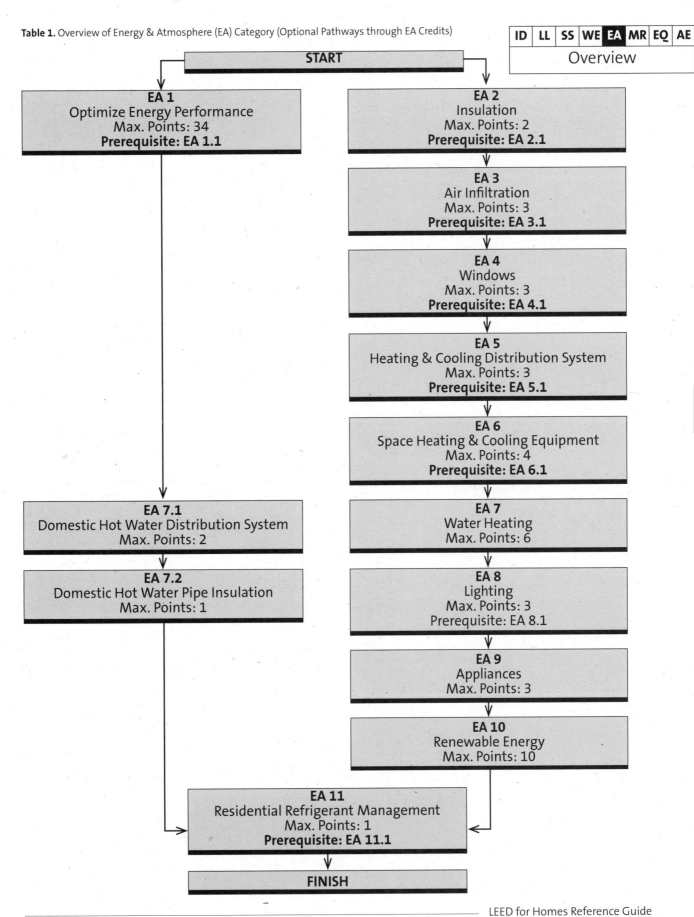

EA 1: Optimize Energy Performance

Intent

Improve the overall energy performance of a home by meeting or exceeding the performance of an ENERGY STAR labeled home.

Requirements

Prerequisites

1.1 **Performance of ENERGY STAR for Homes.** Meet the performance requirements of ENERGY STAR for Homes, including third-party inspections.

Credits

1.2 **Exceptional Energy Performance** (maximum 34 points). Exceed the performance of ENERGY STAR for Homes. Use the equations below relating the Home Energy Standards (HERS) Index to the appropriate number of LEED points.

South

$$\text{LEED Pts} = \{ [\text{Log} (100 - \text{HERS Index})] / 0.024 \} - 48.3$$

North

$$\text{LEED Pts} = \{ [\text{Log} (100 - \text{HERS Index})] / 0.021 \} - 60.8$$

Figure 1. HERS Index Values and LEED Points

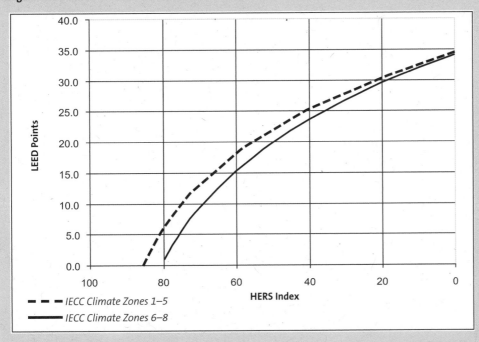

Table 1. HERS Index and LEED Points

IECC Climate Zones 1–5			IECC Climate Zones 6–8		
HERS Index	Percent Above IECC 2004	LEED for Homes Points	HERS Index	Percent Above IECC 2004	LEED for Homes Points
100	0		100	0	
95	5		95	5	
90	10		90	10	
85	15		85	15	
84	16	2.0	84	16	
83	17	3.0	83	17	
82	18	4.0	82	18	
81	19	5.0	81	19	
80	20	6.0	80	20	
79	21	7.0	79	21	2.0
78	22	7.5	78	22	3.0
77	23	8.5	77	23	4.0
76	24	9.0	76	24	5.0
75	25	10.0	75	25	6.0
74	26	10.5	74	26	6.5
73	27	11.6	73	27	7.5
72	28	12.0	72	28	8.0
71	29	12.5	71	29	9.0
70	30	13.0	70	30	9.5
69	31	14.0	69	31	10.0
68	32	14.5	68	32	11.0
67	33	15.0	67	33	11.5
66	34	15.5	66	34	12.0
65	35	16.0	65	35	12.5
64	36	16.5	64	36	13.5
63	37	17.0	63	37	14.0
62	38	17.5	62	38	14.5
61	39	18.0	61	39	15.0
60	40	18.5	60	40	15.5
55	45	20.5	55	45	18.0
50	50	22.5	50	50	20.0
45	55	24.2	45	55	22.0
40	60	26.0	40	60	24.0
35	65	27.0	35	65	25.5
30	70	28.5	30	70	27.0
25	75	30.0	25	75	28.5
20	80	31.0	20	80	30.0
15	85	32.0	15	85	31.0
10	90	33.0	10	90	32.0
5	95	33.5	5	95	33.0
0	100	34.0	0	100	34.0

Synergies and Trade-Offs

A project receiving points for this credit must skip credits EA 2–6, 7.3, and 8–10.

Passive solar designs must be modeled and can take credit using the approach laid out in EA 1.

Shading and the reduction of local heat island effects (SS 3) can reduce energy demands for space cooling. Similarly, vegetated roofs (SS 4.3) can reduce both space heating and cooling loads.

High-efficiency appliances and fixtures (WE 3) can reduce hot water demand.

Reduced framing (MR 1) can allow for more insulation and fewer thermal breaks.

Proper design and verification of space heating and cooling distribution systems (EQ 6) can help provide thermal comfort with minimized waste. In hot and humid climates, effective dehumidification (EQ 3) can significantly reduce cooling loads.

EA 1.1: ENERGY STAR for Homes

EA 1.2: Exceptional Energy Performance

EA 1 is a performance pathway that requires the builder to use an approved energy analysis software program to demonstrate the overall energy performance of the home's design (in combination with credits EA 7.1, 7.2, and 11).

The overall energy performance of a new home cannot be measured until after the home has been built. Thus, the energy performance of a new home design must be predicted using energy analysis software. The Residential Energy Services Network (RESNET) has developed a nationally accepted set of guidelines for assessing the relative energy performance of homes, known as the Home Energy Rating System (HERS).

For EA 1, HERS software must be used to assess the energy efficiency of the home compared with the 2004 version of the International Energy Conservation Code (IECC). The HERS software assigns each modeled home a HERS index as an indicator of its energy efficiency. A home that is designed to comply with the 2004 version of IECC receives a HERS index of 100. Each additional HERS index point is roughly equal to a 1% increase in energy use over a home that complies with the IECC standard. A home that is less efficient than the performance levels required under IECC receives a HERS index of greater than 100, and homes that are more efficient receive a HERS index of less than 100. Index values can range down to 0, for a superefficient home that is designed to use no net energy.

In LEED for Homes, a new home is required to meet the minimum energy performance levels specified in the U.S. Environmental Protection Agency's ENERGY STAR for Homes program, Version 2006. An ENERGY STAR qualified home is designed to use 15% to 20% less energy than a comparable home built to the 2004 IECC standard. Using the HERS guidelines, such a home receives a HERS index of 85 to 80.[2]

An ENERGY STAR home must be third-party verified to ensure that the measures designed to improve the energy performance of the home function as intended. This verification includes three types of activities:

❑ thermal bypass inspection (i.e., an insulation inspection before the drywall is installed);

❑ visual inspection of all installed energy efficiency measures; and

❑ performance tests, including overall envelope tightness and duct tightness.

In the LEED for Homes Rating System, higher levels of energy efficiency can earn points, up to a maximum of 34 points for a net-zero energy home.

Approach and Implementation

LEED for Homes addresses the overall energy performance of homes with two interrelated measures, EA 1.1: ENERGY STAR for Homes, and EA1.2: Exceptional Energy Performance. A home that has exceptional energy performance under EA 1.2 will automatically demonstrate compliance with the prerequisite, EA 1.1.

---

2 An ENERGY STAR home located in IECC climate zones 1 through 5 (i.e., warm to moderate states) must achieve a HERS index of no more than 85. An ENERGY STAR home located in IECC climate zones 6 through 8 must achieve a HERS index of no more than 80.

EA 1.1: ENERGY STAR for Homes

The mandatory minimum level of energy performance in the LEED for Homes Rating System requires that a qualifying home be designed to meet the energy performance requirements of ENERGY STAR for Homes, Version 2006. Under this prerequisite, compliance must be demonstrated using a HERS-approved energy analysis software program. Although a home must meet the energy performance requirements of ENERGY STAR for Homes to meet this LEED prerequisite, it is not required to be ENERGY STAR labeled.

Approved HERS software is listed on the RESNET Web site, at www.resnet. us. These energy-modeling programs are available only to HERS-trained qualified qualified energy raters or HERS providers. Thus, projects that plan to use the performance pathway must be modeled by individuals who have access to the HERS-approved software and have been trained in its use. The LEED for Homes Certification Provider can find a qualified HERS-trained energy modeler, and in some cases the Verification Team may also be an qualified qualified energy rater.

As part of the modeling process, every aspect of a home is evaluated and may contribute to its efficiency (or inefficiency). The HERS index reflects insulation levels, air sealing, window size and specifications, distribution system, space heating and cooling equipment size, water heating, lighting, appliances, and even renewable energy.

Work with a qualified energy rater to determine the most appropriate measures for each project; the most economical and effective strategies will vary based on the home design and location. Ideas for efficiency upgrades can be found in the alternative compliance pathway (EA 2–10). Please see the descriptions of each of these measures in the sections below.

An ENERGY STAR home may not get credit for renewable energy systems as a component of the minimum HERS index of 85 for homes located in IECC climate zones 1 through 5 (or a HERS index of 80 for homes located in IECC climate zones 6 through 8).

The use of electric resistance heating will prevent a home from scoring well on the HERS index unless the home has practically no heating demand. If electric heating is preferred or natural gas is unavailable, consider using an electric heat pump.

All homes must meet the following requirements. These requirements are in the prescriptive path, and they must also be met by homes following the performance pathway:

❏ HVAC equipment must be designed and sized using ACCA Manual J, the ASHRAE 2001 Handbook of Fundamentals, or an equivalent computation procedure. See EQ 6.1 for more details.

❏ If a heat pump is installed with a programmable thermostat, the thermostat must be equipped with adaptive recovery. This technology enables the heating equipment to gradually adjust when the thermostat setting changes, preventing overdependence on the less efficient backup heating system.

EA 1.2: Exceptional Energy Performance

Most qualifying LEED homes substantially exceed the minimum requirements of EA 1.1 and thus earn points under EA 1.2. Any home that achieves a HERS index below the ENERGY STAR threshold (85 or 80, depending on zone) is automatically deemed to be in compliance with EA 1.1 (above). Project teams are strongly encouraged to achieve certification by ENERGY STAR, but it is not required under LEED for Homes.

Assess each energy efficiency measure for relative cost-effectiveness. Often, projects cost more than necessary because the most cost-effective measures were overlooked.

Project teams that focus on selecting upgrades to install may sometimes not adequately address the integration of these measures into the home's design. Consider upgrade strategies at the earliest possible part of the design process. For example, one early decision that can greatly affect energy use is the orientation of the home to minimize exposure on east- and west-facing walls.

To achieve exceptional energy efficiency, consider passive or active solar design or the use of renewable forms of electricity generation.

Passive solar home design. A home's windows, walls, and floors can be designed to collect, store, and distribute solar energy in the form of heat in the winter and to reject solar heat in the summer. This is called passive solar design, or climatic design. Passive solar homes range from those heated almost entirely by the sun to those with south-facing windows that take some fraction of the heating load. The difference between a passive solar home and a conventional home is design: The passive solar home takes advantage of the local climate. Such a home has several basic elements.

Solar collectors. Carefully design the windows of the home to serve as the primary areas through which sunlight enters without causing the home to overheat (especially on late-summer afternoons). Other approaches include trombe walls, sunspaces, and clerestories.

Thermal mass. Design a portion of the wall and floor materials to store the heat provided by the sunlight.

Shading control. Shade windows to prevent overheating. Use roof overhangs and interior window blinds to shade the solar aperture area during summer months.

Control underheating and overheating with fans, vents, and dampers that allow or restrict heat flow through the home.

Distribution. Design the home so that the solar heat collected can be circulated to other areas of the house. Combine natural convection flows with fans and ducts.

Active solar home design. Active systems typically use pumps or fans to circulate a fluid that flows from solar collection panels to a storage tank and then to the rooms where heat is needed. Active systems are often used to heat water for domestic use or for heating the home itself (e.g., radiant heat).

Renewable energy sources. Photovoltaic (PV) and wind are two renewable forms of electricity generation. The energy benefits of these systems can be calculated with the HERS software and are accounted for in the HERS index.

Consider how the landscaping design can affect energy use. For example, retaining or planting deciduous trees on the south side allows for shading of the home's windows, walls, and roof in the summer. In the winter, these same trees, now leafless, allow the sun's rays to heat the home.

Calculations

No calculations are needed for this credit beyond those performed by the HERS energy modeling software (including the automated HERS index calculation).

Verification and Submittals

Supporting Verification Materials, made available by the Project Team:

❏ Present any equipment or product literature (e.g., user manuals, brochures, specifications) related to the energy-consuming systems and energy-saving components (e.g., HVAC equipment, windows, insulation, appliances) to the Verification Team.

❏ Include all equipment literature in the occupant's operations and maintenance manual.

Verification Team:

❏ Complete the verification requirements for an ENERGY STAR home, including thermal bypass (insulation) inspection, envelope air leakage testing with a blower door, and duct leakage testing with a duct pressurization fan.

❏ Visually verify all energy-consuming systems and energy-saving components (e.g., HVAC equipment, windows, insulation, appliances) at the home site. Document the relevant metrics (e.g., efficiencies, R-values, percentage fluorescent lights) and provide them to the qualified qualified energy rater for modeling.

❏ Conduct the necessary modeling to produce a HERS index, or have a qualified energy rater conduct the necessary modeling. Verify that the HERS index for the home meets or exceeds the prerequisite.

❏ Include a copy of the HERS rating report in the project documentation file and the occupant's operations and maintenance manual.

Exemplary Performance

The energy models that are used for the performance pathway (EA 1) do not recognize the benefits of water-efficient clothes washers. A project using the performance pathway should be awarded exemplary performance points for meeting the requirements of EA 9.1(d) and 9.2 for clothes washers, to be counted under Innovation in Design 3.

Projects can submit an Innovation in Design Request for commissioning of

building energy systems. These will be considered on a case-by-case basis.

Considerations

Environmental Issues

Reduced fossil fuel–based demand for energy reduces emissions of air pollutants like carbon dioxide, nitrogen oxides, and sulfur dioxide. Many energy-efficiency strategies also improve the indoor environmental quality of the home by maintaining a steady, comfortable temperature with fewer drafts.

Economic Issues

One of the most common misperceptions is that energy-efficiency measures are expensive. Investing in upgrade measures can actually minimize the incremental cost of building an energy-efficient home.

For example, when the home's envelope is made tight with additional insulation and air sealing measures, the heating and cooling loads may be substantially reduced and the heating and cooling equipment can be smaller (and less expensive). The savings on the HVAC equipment may offset the cost of the additional envelope measures.

Additional examples of cost streamlining techniques are available in the cost comparisons in the U.S. Department of Energy's Best Practice Guidelines, at www.eere.energy.gov/buildings/building_america.

Other

In multi-family homes, it is good practice to install individual meters for each unit. This practice will allow occupants and renters to know how much energy they are using and encourage more responsible consumption patterns. Projects using certain types of smart meters may be eligible for an Innovative Design credit (ID 3), subject to review of an ID Request.

Resources

Web Sites

ENERGY STAR® Qualified New Homes Program

U.S. Environmental Protection Agency

www.energystar.gov/homes

ENERGY STAR is a government-industry partnership managed by the U.S. Environmental Protection Agency and the U.S. Department of Energy. The program's Web site provides complete program and verification guidelines along with resources for technical, construction, and marketing support. The guidelines for ENERGY STAR new homes are available at www.energystar.gov/index.cfm?c=bldrs_lenders_raters.homes_guidelns09.

2004 International Energy Conservation Code

International Code Council

www.iccsafe.org

The International Code Council, a membership association dedicated to building safety and fire prevention, develops the codes used to construct residential and commercial buildings, including homes and schools. Most U.S. cities, counties, and states that adopt codes choose the codes developed by the International Code Council. ICC publishes the 2004 International Energy Conservation Code referenced in this credit (the IECC Climate Zones and IECC 2004). The 2003 International Energy Conservation Code and 2004 supplement may be purchased through the ICC online bookstore.

American Council for an Energy Efficient Economy

www.aceee.org

ACEEE is a nonprofit organization dedicated to advancing energy efficiency as a means of promoting both economic prosperity and environmental protection. This organization advances energy efficiency through technical and policy assessments; advising policymakers and program managers; collaborating with businesses, public interest groups, and other organizations; and providing education and outreach through conferences, workshops, and publications.

Building America Program

U.S. Department of Energy

www.eere.energy.gov/buildings/building_america

Building America is a private–public partnership that develops energy solutions for new and existing homes. The Building America project combines the knowledge and resources of industry leaders with the U.S. Department of Energy's technical capabilities. The extensive residential building resources here include climate-specific best practice guidance, building research reports, and additional links to training, high-performance homebuilding, energy efficiency, green building, and other related resources.

Building Energy Codes Program

U.S. Department of Energy

www.energycodes.gov/rescheck

The Building Energy Codes program provides comprehensive resources for states and code users, including news, compliance software, code comparisons, and the Status of State Energy Codes database. The database includes state energy contacts, code status, code history, Department of Energy grants awarded, and construction data. The site also includes RESCHECK, a free software tool with related support materials that have been developed to simplify and clarify code compliance with the Model Energy Code, the International Energy Conservation Code, and several state codes. This compliance tool includes the prescriptive path and trade-off compliance methods.

Energy-10™ Energy Simulation Software

National Renewable Energy Program

www.nrel.gov/buildings/energy10.html

Energy-10™ is an award-winning software tool for designing low-energy buildings. Energy-10™ integrates daylighting, passive solar heating, and low-energy cooling strategies with energy-efficient shell design and mechanical equipment. The program is applicable to small commercial and residential buildings with up to two zones and simple HVAC equipment. The Energy-10™ software was developed by the National Renewable Energy Laboratory under funding from the Office of Building Technologies, Energy Efficiency and Renewable Energy, U.S. Department of Energy. It is distributed by the Sustainable Buildings Industry Council under license to the Midwest Research Institute.

EnergyGauge: Energy and Economic Analysis Software

Florida Solar Energy Center

www.energygauge.com

EnergyGauge is a family of user-friendly PC software tools that allow simple yet detailed performance-based analysis of building energy use and perform economic analysis of proposed energy improvements.

REM Software Series

Architectural Energy Corporation

www.archenergy.com/products/rem/

The REM Software Series home energy analysis software is designed to help homebuilders, home designers, energy consultants, home improvement contractors, utilities, and home energy rating organizations with critical energy analysis for residential structures. AEC features two powerful evaluation tools in the series: REM/Rate™ and REM/Design™. REM/Rate™ produces a home energy rating report based on the RESNET National HERS Technical Standards.

Residential Energy Services Network

www.resnet.us

RESNET is a not-for-profit membership corporation and national standards-making body for energy efficiency rating systems. It provides standards for and listings of RESNET-certified HERS energy raters and accredited providers. This organization's Web site provides extensive resources on the Home Energy Rating System, the HERS index referenced in this credit, related software, home energy mortgages, education, regional and national energy rating organizations and associations, and related articles and web links. The listing of certified HERS qualified qualified energy raters is available at www.resnet.us/directory/raters.aspx.

Print Media

Builder's Guide series for specific North American climate zones: *Cold Climates, Mixed-Humid Climates, Hot-Humid Climates*, and *Hot-Dry & Mixed Dry Climates*, by Joseph Lstiburek, Ph.D., P.Eng. Building Science Press. Using a systems approach to building design and construction, these extensive guides provide climate-specific details and guidelines for residential construction, incorporating most aspects of each construction phase, type of building system, and climate considerations.

"Solar Energy Use." Chapter 33 in *ASHRAE Handbook, HVAC Applications*. American Society of Heating Refrigerating and Air-Conditioning Engineers, 2007.

The Passive Solar Design and Construction Handbook, edited by Steven Winter Associates and Michael J. Crosbie. John Wiley & Sons, 1997.

The Building Environment: Active and Passive Control Systems, by Vaughn Bradshaw. John Wiley & Sons, 2006.

The Solar House: Passive Heating and Cooling, by Daniel Chiras. Chelsea Green

ID	LL	SS	WE	**EA**	MR	EQ	AE
				1.1 & 1.2			

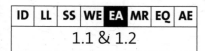

1.1 & 1.2

Publishing Company, 2002.

Solar Engineering of Thermal Processes, by John Duffie and W. Beckman. Third edition. John Wiley & Sons, 2006.

EA 2: Insulation

Intent

Design and install insulation to minimize heat transfer and thermal bridging.

Requirements

Prerequisites

2.1 **Basic Insulation.** Meet all the following requirements:

a) Install insulation that meets or exceeds the R-value requirements listed in Chapter 4 of the 2004 International Energy Conservation Code. Alternative wall and insulation systems, such as structural insulated panels (SIPs) and insulated concrete forms (ICFs), must demonstrate a comparable R-value, but thermal mass or infiltration effects cannot be included in the R-value calculation.

b) Install insulation to meet the Grade II specifications set by the National Home Energy Rating Standards (**Table 1**). Installation must be verified by an qualified qualified energy rater or Verification Team conducting a predrywall thermal bypass inspection, as summarized in **Figure 1**.

Note: For any portion of the home constructed with SIPs or ICFs, the rater must conduct a modified visual inspection using the ENERGY STAR Structural Insulated Panel Visual Inspection Form.

Credits

2.2 **Enhanced Insulation** (2 points). Meet the following requirements:

a) Install insulation that exceeds the R-value requirements listed in Chapter 4 of the 2004 International Energy Conservation Code by at least 5%. Alternative wall and insulation systems, such as structural insulated panels (SIPs) and insulated concrete forms (ICFs), must demonstrate a comparable R-value, but thermal mass or infiltration effects cannot be included in the R-value calculation.

b) Install insulation to meet the Grade I specifications set by the National Home Energy Rating Standards (**Table 1**). Installation must be verified by an qualified energy rater or Verification Team conducting a predrywall thermal bypass inspection as summarized in **Figure 1**.

Note: For any portion of the home constructed with SIPs or ICFs, the rater must conduct a modified visual inspection, using the ENERGY STAR Structural Insulated Panel Visual Inspection Form.

Synergies and Trade-Offs

A project receiving points for EA 1 is not eligible for this credit, and vice versa. A project pursuing this credit must follow the prescriptive pathway and all of the associated prerequisites in EA 2–10. Prerequisite EA 1.1 should be skipped. See the pathway schematic at the beginning of the EA section.

MR 1.2–1.5 address framing efficiency. Efficient framing can create additional spacing in wall cavities, reducing thermal breaks and insulation compaction.

Environmentally preferable insulation is awarded in MR 2.2.

Table 1. Summary of HERS Installation Grades
Please refer to "Adopted Enhancements to the Mortgage Industry National Home Energy Rating Standards," available from RESNET, for a more detailed description.

Grade	Description
I	Meet the requirements of Grade II (below), but allow only very small gaps, and compression or incomplete fill amounts to 2% or less.
II	Moderate to frequent installation defects, gaps around wiring, electric outlets, etc. and incomplete fill amounts to 10% or less. Gaps running clear through the insulation amount to no more than 2% of the total surface area covered by the insulation. Wall insulation is enclosed on all six sides and in substantial contact with the sheathing material on at least one side (interior or exterior) of the cavity.

Figure 1. ENERGY STAR Thermal Bypass Inspection Checklist

ENERGY STAR Qualified Homes
Thermal Bypass Inspection Checklist

Home Address: _____ City: _____ State: _____

Thermal Bypass	Inspection Guidelines	Corrections Needed	Builder Verified	Rater Verified	N/A
1. Overall Air Barrier and Thermal Barrier Alignment	**Requirements:** Insulation shall be installed in full contact with sealed interior and exterior air barrier except for alternate to interior air barrier under item no. 2 *(Walls Adjoining Exterior Walls or Unconditioned Spaces)*				
	All Climate Zones:				
	1.1 Overall Alignment Throughout Home	☐	☐	☐	☐
	1.2 Garage Band Joist Air Barrier (at bays adjoining conditioned space)	☐	☐	☐	☐
	1.3 Attic Eave Baffles Where Vents/Leakage Exist	☐	☐	☐	☐
	Only at Climate Zones 4 and Higher:				
	1.4 Slab-edge Insulation (A maximum of 25% of the slab edge may be uninsulated in Climate Zones 4 and 5.)	☐	☐	☐	☐
	Best Practices Encouraged, Not Req'd.:				
	1.5 Air Barrier At All Band Joists (Climate Zones 4 and higher)	☐	☐	☐	☐
	1.6 Minimize Thermal Bridging (e.g., OVE framing, SIPs, ICFs)	☐	☐	☐	☐
2. Walls Adjoining Exterior Walls or Unconditioned Spaces	**Requirements:** • Fully insulated wall aligned with air barrier at both interior and exterior, **OR** • Alternate for **Climate Zones 1 thru 3**, sealed exterior air barrier aligned with RESNET Grade 1 insulation fully supported • Continuous top and bottom plates or sealed blocking				
	2.1 Wall Behind Shower/Tub	☐	☐	☐	☐
	2.2 Wall Behind Fireplace	☐	☐	☐	☐
	2.3 Insulated Attic Slopes/Walls	☐	☐	☐	☐
	2.4 Attic Knee Walls	☐	☐	☐	☐
	2.5 Skylight Shaft Walls	☐	☐	☐	☐
	2.6 Wall Adjoining Porch Roof	☐	☐	☐	☐
	2.7 Staircase Walls	☐	☐	☐	☐
	2.8 Double Walls	☐	☐	☐	☐
3. Floors between Conditioned and Exterior Spaces	**Requirements:** • Air barrier is installed at any exposed insulation edges • Insulation is installed to maintain permanent contact w/ sub-floor above • Optional until July 1, 2008, insulation is installed to maintain permanent contact with air barrier below				
	3.1 Insulated Floor Above Garage	☐	☐	☐	☐
	3.2 Cantilevered Floor	☐	☐	☐	☐
4. Shafts	**Requirements:** Openings to unconditioned space are fully sealed with solid blocking or flashing and any remaining gaps are sealed with caulk or foam (provide fire-rated collars and caulking where required)				
	4.1 Duct Shaft	☐	☐	☐	☐
	4.2 Piping Shaft/Penetrations	☐	☐	☐	☐
	4.3 Flue Shaft	☐	☐	☐	☐
5. Attic/ Ceiling Interface	**Requirements:** • All attic penetrations and dropped ceilings include a full interior air barrier aligned with insulation with any gaps fully sealed with caulk, foam or tape • Movable insulation fits snugly in opening and air barrier is fully gasketed				
	5.1 Attic Access Panel (fully gasketed and insulated)	☐	☐	☐	☐
	5.2 Attic Drop-down Stair (fully gasketed and insulated)	☐	☐	☐	☐
	5.3 Dropped Ceiling/Soffit (full air barrier aligned with insulation)	☐	☐	☐	☐
	5.4 Recessed Lighting Fixtures (ICAT labeled and sealed to drywall)	☐	☐	☐	☐
	5.5 Whole-house Fan (insulated cover gasketed to the opening)	☐	☐	☐	☐
6. Common Walls Between Dwelling Units	**Requirements:** Gap btwn drywall shaft wall (common wall) and structural framing btwn units is sealed at all exterior boundary conditions				
	6.1 Common Wall Between Dwelling Units	☐	☐	☐	☐

Rater Inspection Date: _____ Builder Inspection Date: _____

Home Energy Rating Provider: _____ Builder Company Name: _____

Home Energy Rater Company Name: _____ Builder Division Name: _____

Home Energy Rater Signature: _____ Builder Employee Signature: _____

EA 2.1: Basic Insulation

EA 2.2: Enhanced Insulation

Approximately one-quarter of a home's heat losses and gains is due to heat flow into or out of the home's insulated thermal envelope—its exterior walls, floor, and attic. The minimum required levels of insulation in new homes are generally governed by model energy codes. The 2004 version of the International Energy Conservation Code is the most commonly used energy code in the United States. Under IECC 2004, the insulation requirements for a new home vary regionally.

R-value is the metric used to measure the thermal effectiveness of insulation. The higher the R-value, the higher the resistance to heat flow through the insulation. The minimum R-values required for exterior walls, floors, attics, and basements are specified in IECC for each of eight climate zones.

RESCHECK, developed by the U.S. Department of Energy, is an easy-to-use software program that determines whether a home's insulation levels meet the IECC (or appropriate local code) requirements. This free software can be downloaded from www.energycodes.gov/rescheck.

Energy-efficient homes may incorporate insulation that is substantially better than the minimum specified in IECC. However, inferior installation of the insulation is no less a problem than insufficient insulation. Common problems in new homes include missing insulation, gaps and voids, thermal bypasses, and thermal bridging. Properly installed, high–R-value insulation can achieve substantial energy savings, plus enhance comfort and improve durability through control of condensation.

This credit rewards homes for improved thermal performance from insulation.

Approach and Implementation

Several types of insulation are available. Detailed information about these choices can be found at the North American Insulation Manufacturers Association Web site, www.naima.org/pages/products/bi.html.

After selecting the type of insulation, determine the proper amounts to install. The level of insulation required in each region of the country is specified by IECC.

Because improper installation of insulation can compromise its effectiveness, study the HERS Type I and Type II recommended insulation installation practices. See also ENERGY STAR's Thermal Bypass Inspection Protocol; a detailed guideline is available online, at www.energystar.gov/index.cfm?c=bldrs_lenders_raters.nh_technical_resources.

For part (b) in historic homes, gut-rehab homes, or other cases where part of an exterior wall cavity is inaccessible, LEED for Homes follows the guidance provided by EPA in Note 1 of the Thermal Bypass Inspection Checklist (TBC): "verification of measures in the thermal bypass inspection checklist (TBC) are subject to the judgment and discretion of the qualified energy rater." If a qualified energy rater is satisfied that the methodology and results of infrared testing on a project meet the TBC requirements, this is acceptable. Similarly, if the qualified energy rater is satisfied that a specific approach to blown-in insulation meets the TBC requirements on a project, this is acceptable.

Train crew members in proper installation techniques. Finally, have the installation inspected by an qualified energy rater or Verification Team.

Additional energy efficiency benefits can be achieved by adding more insulation than is required by IECC 2004 and meeting the installation criteria for HERS Grade I. If not all of the insulation exceeds code by 5%, a home can still meet the requirements of EA 2.2 by demonstrating that the average overall thermal conductance value (UAo) exceeds code by 5%, using the RESCHECK software.

Calculations

No calculations are needed for this credit unless the insulation values are averaged. In this case, an overall thermal conductance can be calculated by hand or demonstrated using the RESCHECK software.

Verification and Submittals

Supporting Verification Materials, made available by the Project Team:

❑ If using RESCHECK to demonstrate overall performance, provide calculations to the Verification Team.

Verification Team:

❑ Visually inspect the installation of insulation, per the thermal bypass inspection checklist above, to confirm that the requirements have been met.

❑ If manual calculations or the RESCHECK software is used to demonstrate overall performance, visually verify the calculations.

Exemplary Performance

No additional points are available for exemplary performance. Projects that exceed the credit requirements are encouraged to use the performance pathway in EA 1.2.

Considerations

Environmental Issues

Environmentally preferable types of insulation, such as products made from recycled cellulose, are available. See MR 2.2 for guidance on insulation materials that are rewarded in LEED for Homes.

Some types of foam insulation contain formaldehyde, a colorless, pungent gas that at elevated levels can cause watery eyes, burning sensations in the eyes and throat, nausea, and difficulty in breathing. High concentrations may trigger attacks in people with asthma. There is evidence that some people can develop a sensitivity to formaldehyde.

Economic Issues

Additional investment in a home's insulation will substantially reduce its heating and cooling loads, perhaps enough to require smaller (and less expensive) heating and cooling equipment. The savings on the HVAC equipment may offset the cost of the additional insulation.

Resources

Web Sites

2004 International Energy Conservation Code

International Code Council

www.iccsafe.org

The International Code Council, a membership association dedicated to building safety and fire prevention, develops the codes used to construct residential and commercial buildings, including homes and schools. Most U.S. cities, counties, and states that adopt codes choose the international codes developed by the International Code Council. ICC publishes the 2004 International Energy Conservation Code (2004 IECC) referenced as a requirement in this credit.

ID	LL	SS	WE	EA	MR	EQ	AE
2.1 & 2.2						

Builder Information

Residential Energy Services Network

www.resnet.us/builder/default.htm

This section of the RESNET Web site includes a tool for finding certified qualified energy raters in your region, along with links to additional resources, including energy codes, RESNET standards, and energy mortgages. The RESNET standards for insulation inspections are in Chapter 3, Section 303.4.1.4, of the 2006 Mortgage Industry National Home Energy Rating Systems Standards, and in Appendix A of the same document under Building Element: Walls—Insulation Inspection, pp. A11–15, www.resnet.us/standards/mortgage/default.htm. A useful PowerPoint on the thermal bypass checklist that includes good details and what-not-to-do images can also be found on the RESNET Web site, at www.resnet.us/rater/checklist/default.htm.

Thermal Bypass Checklist & Checklist Guide and SIPs Inspection Form

ENERGY STAR® Qualified New Homes Program

U.S. Environmental Protection Agency

www.energystar.gov

The ENERGY STAR thermal bypass checklist can be used in meeting part of the insulation credit requirements. A PDF or PowerPoint of the thermal bypass checklist guide may be accessed on this ENERGY STAR Technical Resources webpage, under "Guidelines for ENERGY STAR Qualified Homes," at www.energystar.gov/index.cfm?c=bldrs_lenders_raters.nh_technical_resources. The ENERGY STAR inspection form for structurally insulated panel (SIPs) can be found on the EPA Web site; search for "SIP visual inspection form."

Residential Compliance Using REScheck™

U.S. Department of Energy, Energy Efficiency and Renewable Energy Building Energy Codes Program

www.energycodes.gov/rescheck/download.stm

EERE developed the REScheck materials to simplify and clarify code compliance with the Model Energy Code, the International Energy Conservation Code, and several state codes. This site includes links to download the free software along with additional links and resources for further training and education for the program. The site also includes links to state-specific versions of the software.

Print Media

Builder's Guide series for specific North American climate zones: *Cold Climates, Mixed-Humid Climates, Hot-Humid Climates*, and *Hot-Dry & Mixed Dry Climates*, by Joseph Lstiburek, Ph.D., P.Eng. Building Science Press. See in particular Chapter 4: Insulations, Sheathing and Vapor Barriers, and Chapter 15: Insulation. Using a systems approach to building design and construction, these extensive guides provide climate-specific details and guidelines for residential construction, incorporating most aspects of each construction phase, type of building system, and climate considerations.

EA 3: Air Infiltration

Intent

Minimize energy consumption caused by uncontrolled air leakage into and out of conditioned spaces.

Requirements

Prerequisites

3.1 **Reduced Envelope Leakage.** Meet the air leakage requirements shown in **Table 1**. The air leakage rate must be tested and verified by an qualified energy rater.

Credits

3.2 **Greatly Reduced Envelope Leakage** (2 points). Meet the air leakage requirements shown in **Table 1**. The air leakage rate must be tested and verified by an qualified energy rater.

OR

3.3 **Minimal Envelope Leakage** (3 points). Meet the air leakage requirements shown in **Table 1**. The air leakage rate must be tested and verified by an qualified energy rater.

Table 1: Air Leakage Requirements

LEED Criteria	Performance requirements (in ACH50)			
	IECC Climate Zones 1–2	IECC Climate Zones 3–4	IECC Climate Zones 5–7	IECC Climate Zone 8
EA 3.1: Reduced Envelope Leakage (mandatory)	7.0	6.0	5.0	4.0
EA 3.2: Greatly Reduced Envelope Leakage (optional)	5.0	4.25	3.5	2.75
EA 3.3: Minimal Envelope Leakage (optional)	3.0	2.5	2.0	1.5

Synergies and Trade-Offs

A project receiving points for EA 1 is not eligible for this credit, and vice versa. A project pursuing this credit must follow the prescriptive pathway and meet all the prerequisites in EA 2–10. Prerequisite EA 1.1 should be skipped. See the pathway schematic at the beginning of the EA section.

Natural air leakage through the envelope contributes to the overall ventilation rate of the home. From a health perspective, it is important to not underventilate a home. From an energy perspective, it is also important not to overventilate. EQ 4 addresses the balance between mechanical and natural ventilation.

EA 3.1: Reduced Envelope Leakage

EA 3.2: Greatly Reduced Envelope Leakage

EA 3.3: Minimal Envelope Leakage

Approximately one-quarter of the heating losses and gains in a new home is due to air leakage through the thermal envelope. Substantial reductions in envelope leakage can be obtained using air sealing techniques.

Unless located in a very mild climate, every LEED home must have a mechanical ventilation system. Accordingly, the thermal envelope can be substantially tighter. Homes with tight envelopes use substantially less energy and have much improved comfort (i.e., fewer drafts). More importantly, tighter homes have improved durability through reduced flow of moisture through the envelope and less risk of condensation within the exterior envelope.

Homes in mild climates (i.e., fewer than 4,500 infiltration degree-days) can achieve abundant natural ventilation through open windows most of the year. Tightening up the envelope of such a home can achieve modest energy benefits, but then additional mechanical ventilation capabilities may become necessary.

The standard for this credit is air changes per hour (ACH), a 25-year-old approach based on the Grimsrud-Sherman Model. The ACH approach penalizes small buildings, which tend to have a higher surface area to volume ratio, and it rewards large buildings that are obviously more resource intensive. An alternative approach to measuring envelope air leakage is to normalize the leakage based on the surface area of all six sides of the cube or building enclosure. Comparable envelope leakage rates with this alternative metric (similar but not identical to the air change requirements in **Table 1**, above) are as follows:

0.35 cfm/ft^2 of building enclosure area @ 50 Pa

0.25 cfm/ft^2 of building enclosure area @ 50 Pa

0.15 cfm/ft^2 of building enclosure area @ 50 Pa

This section rewards builders who use air sealing techniques to tighten the envelopes of new homes.

Approach and Implementation

Reducing air leakage is not expensive, but knowing where the primary air leaks are requires training and experience. Generally, seal all leakage locations, including any and all plumbing and electrical penetrations in the exterior envelope (e.g., recessed lights). Leaks are also common where dissimilar construction materials meet (e.g., drywall and flooring, brick fireplace and drywall, foundation and frame wall). Consult the U.S. Environmental Protection Agency's Thermal Bypass Checklist.

A qualified energy rater must verify the air leakage rate using a depressurization (blower door) test. The standard pressure used is 50 Pascals of pressure differential, indoor to outdoor (equivalent to about a 20-mile-per-hour wind buffeting the home). Background information on blower doors can be found at www.oikos.com/tec/.

Leaks are easily seen with the blower door operating. Using a smoke stick, identify major air leaks, seal them, and confirm that these leakage sites have been eliminated.

Inform the HVAC contractor that the home will have enhanced air tightness so that this fact can be entered into the design calculations. Otherwise, the HVAC equipment will likely be oversized (see also EA 6.1).

Most new homes do not have any mechanically driven fresh air ventilation and receive very little natural ventilation during winter and summer weather extremes. Generally, new homes in harsh climates should not be tightened to below about 6.0 air changes per hour at 50 Pascals (6.0 ACH at 50 Pa) unless an alternative means of bringing in fresh air (e.g., a mechanical ventilation system) is designed into the home. The level of tightness promoted for ENERGY STAR homes is generally 4 to 7 ACH at 50 Pa, depending on the climate zone.

Calculations

No calculations are needed for this credit if the blower door test produces a result in ACH50. The ACH50 value can be calculated using the following formula:

ACH 50 = CFM 50 x 60 mins/hr ÷ volume

where the volume is measured in cubic feet.

Verification and Submittals

Qualified Energy Rater:

❑ Perform a blower door depressurization test on the home to determine the envelope leakage.

Exemplary Performance

No additional points are available for exemplary performance. Projects that exceed the credit requirements are encouraged to use the performance pathway in EA 1.2.

Considerations

Economic Issues

The air tightness of the envelope is one of the factors used to assess the size of the heating and cooling equipment needed to meet the peak heating and cooling loads. An additional investment in a home's air sealing will substantially reduce its heating and cooling loads and may allow smaller (and less expensive) heating and cooling equipment. The savings on the HVAC equipment may offset the additional cost of the air sealing tasks.

Resources

Web Sites

Designs That Work: Air Sealing Details

Building Science Corporation

www.buildingscience.com/bsc/designsthatwork/airsealing/default.htm

Available at the Building Science Corporation Web site, this extensive series of practical construction details provides examples of tested air sealing solutions for a variety of building materials and conditions.

Standard 62.2-2007: Ventilation and Acceptable Indoor Air Quality in Low-Rise Residential Buildings, Section 4.1.3

American Society of Heating, Refrigerating and Air-Conditioning Engineers

www.ashrae.org/technology/page/548

ASHRAE is an international organization committed to advancing heating, ventilation, air conditioning, and refrigeration to serve humanity and promote a sustainable world through research, standards writing, publishing, and continuing education. Section 4.1.3 of ASHRAE Standard 62.2 provides specific guidance on balancing mechanical and natural ventilation to avoid both underventilating and overventilating. This standard can be purchased from ASHRAE or previewed for free at the Web site address above.

Blower Door Testing

Pennsylvania Housing Research / Resource Center

www.pct.edu/wtc/Blower-Door-FINAL.pdf

This document was created by PHRC, an affiliate of the Pennsylvania College of Technology. It contains a brief description and explanation of blower door testing for consumers.

Introduction to Blower Doors

Home Energy Magazine Online

www.homeenergy.org/archive/hem.dis.anl.gov/eehem/94/940220.html

This online article, written by David Keefe, provides an in-depth description of blower door testing techniques. It includes definitions of terms and concepts and links to related articles, such as "Building Tightness Guidelines: When Is a House Too Tight" and "Air Sealing in Low-Rise Buildings."

Print Media

Builder's Guide series for specific North American climate zones: *Cold Climates, Mixed-Humid Climates, Hot-Humid Climates*, and *Hot-Dry & Mixed Dry Climates*, by Joseph Lstiburek, Ph.D., P.Eng. Building Science Press. See in particular the construction details and options in Chapter 3: Air Barriers, Chapter 4: Insulations, Sheathing and Vapor Barriers, Chapter 11: Framing, and Chapter 16: Drywall. Using a systems approach to building design and construction, these extensive guides provide climate specific details and guidelines for residential construction, incorporating most aspects of each construction phase, type of building system, and climate considerations.

"Blower Door Guidelines for Cost-Effective Air Sealing," by J. Schlegel. *Home Energy* 7(2), 1990.

EA 4: Windows

Intent

Maximize the energy performance of windows.

Requirements

Prerequisites

4.1 **Good Windows.** Meet all of the following requirements:

a) Design and install windows and glass doors that have NFRC ratings that meet or exceed the window requirements of the ENERGY STAR for Homes national Builder Option Package (**Table 1**).

b) The ratio of skylight glazing to conditioned floor area may not exceed 3%.[3] All skylights must meet the ENERGY STAR performance requirements for skylights, but are exempt from the requirements in **Table 1**.

c) Homes in the Northern or North/Central climate zones that have a total window-to-floor area ratio (WFA) of 18% or more must meet a more stringent U-factor requirement (also applicable to EA 4.2 and 4.3): U-factor = [0.18 / WFA] * [U-factor from **Table 1**].

d) Homes in the Southern or South/Central climate zones that have a total window-to-floor area ratio (WFA) of 18% or more must meet a more stringent solar heat gain coefficient (SHGC) requirement (also applicable to EA 4.2 and 4.3): SHGC = [0.18 / WFA] * [SHGC from **Table 1**].

Note: Up to 0.75% of the window-to-floor area may be used for decorative glass or skylight area that does not meet the U-factor and SHGC requirements above.

Credits

4.2 **Enhanced Windows** (2 points). Design and install windows and glass doors that have NFRC ratings that exceed the window requirements in the ENERGY STAR for Homes national Builder Option Package (**Table 1**).

OR

4.3 **Exceptional Windows** (3 points). Design and install windows and glass doors that have NFRC ratings that substantially exceed the window requirements in the ENERGY STAR for Homes national Builder Option Package (**Table 1**).

Synergies and Trade-Offs

A project receiving points for EA 1 is not eligible for this credit, and vice versa. A project pursuing this credit must follow the prescriptive pathway and meet all of the prerequisites in EA 2–10. Prerequisite EA 1.1 should be skipped. See the pathway schematic at the beginning of the EA section.

Improving the window performance may also reduce heating and/or cooling loads and the energy associated with operating heating and cooling equipment.

---

3 For example, a home with 2,000 square feet of conditioned floor area may not have more than 60 square feet of skylight glazing.

Table 1. ENERGY STAR Requirements for Windows and Glass Doors

	Metric	ENERGY STAR Zone			
		Northern	North Central	South Central	Southern
EA 4.1: Good Windows (prerequisite)	U-factor	≤0.35	≤0.40	≤0.40	≤0.55
	SHGC	Any	≤0.45	≤0.40	≤0.35
EA 4.2: Enhanced Windows (optional, 2 points)	U-factor	≤0.31	≤0.35	≤0.35	≤0.55
	SHGC	Any	≤0.40	≤0.35	≤0.33
EA 4.3: Exceptional Windows (optional, 3 points)	U-factor	≤0.28	≤0.32	≤0.32	≤0.55
	SHGC	Any	≤0.40	≤0.30	≤0.30

Figure 1. Zones for Window Specifications

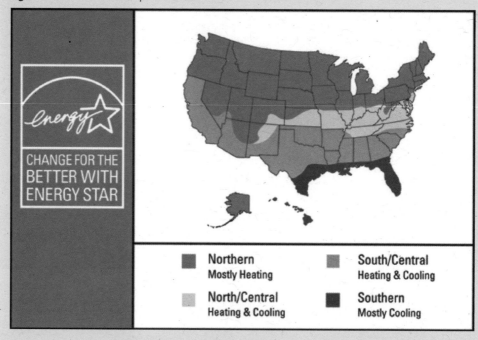

Northern
Mostly Heating

South/Central
Heating & Cooling

North/Central
Heating & Cooling

Southern
Mostly Cooling

EA 4.1: Good Windows

EA 4.2: Enhanced Windows

EA 4.3: Exceptional Windows

Approximately one-quarter of the heat losses and gains in new homes occurs through the windows. High-performance windows can substantially reduce energy use in new homes.

The National Fenestration Rating Council (NFRC) has developed a certified window rating and labeling program that quantifies the thermal performance of windows in terms of U-factor and solar heat gain coefficient (SHGC).

The U-factor is a measure of the thermal resistance to heat flow of the overall window (i.e., the inverse of the R-value). Building codes require U-factors that range from 0.35 in northern states to 1.2 in southern states. The lower the value, the greater the resistance to heat flow.

The solar heat gain coefficient is the ratio of the solar heat gain entering the space through the fenestration assembly to the incident solar radiation. Solar heat gain includes directly transmitted solar heat and absorbed solar radiation that is then released into the space. The lower the SHGC, the less solar energy transmitted to the space.

Two benefits of high window performance are reduced energy use and improved comfort. Better-performing windows reduce the risk of condensation, thereby leading to improved durability of the overall home.

This section rewards the selection and installation of windows with specifications that exceed the ENERGY STAR for Homes window requirements.

Approach and Implementation

Most new windows have an NFRC sticker that explicitly states the U-factor and SHGC. Further, many manufacturers also label their ENERGY STAR windows with an ENERGY STAR sticker as well.

Factors that affect the NFRC rating value are the type of glass, amount of glass (relative to the amount of framing), number of layers of glass (single, double, or triple), frame material (wood composites, vinyl, or fiberglass), number of panes of glass, low-E coating, warm edge spacers, and gas filling (between the layers of glass).

The NFRC labeling process simplifies the window selection process. Look at the label and confirm that the window delivers the performance desired.

When choosing windows, take into consideration the design and location of the home. U-factor is more important in cold climates, whereas SHGC is more important in hot climates. In cold areas, it may be advantageous to install windows with a high SHGC to enable solar gains that can offset heating loads. In all climates, the specifications for the windows and other envelope components should be used by the HVAC contractor to properly size the heating and cooling equipment.

Unless excellent windows are installed, minimize the total window area of the home. Substantial energy savings can be achieved through the interior or exterior shading of windows and by appropriately locating windows in the home relative to the sun's orientation. These benefits are not accounted for in this credit. Projects incorporating shading and other passive solar design strategies are encouraged to follow the performance pathway (EA 1).

Windows that exceed the specifications of EA 4.3 are available throughout the country. Various manufacturers produce cold-climate windows with U-Factors of 0.20 or lower, and warm-climate windows with SHGCs of 0.25 or lower. Projects that use these types of windows are encouraged to follow the performance pathway (EA 1) to take credit for the improved windows.

Install the windows properly to ensure that there is no water leakage—a common problem that usually has nothing to do with the windows themselves. The Water Management Guide (see "Resources," below) offers best practice guidance.

Care should be taken in cold climates when recessing windows in thick walls, as the stagnant air pockets near recessed windows will lower window surface temperatures, thereby increasing the risk of condensation. In such cases, use windows with a very low U-Factor — 0.25 or lower.

Window technologies are emerging to allow optimum use of solar gains through dynamic controls. These technologies include both electrochromic glass (coating that changes from clear to tinted with the application of a small electric current) and products with integral operable shading layers. Achieving the full potential from such products requires effective control systems, either automated, or through dedicated users.

Calculations

Calculations are required for this credit under the following circumstances:

1. If the window-to-floor area ratio (WFA) exceeds 0.18, calculate the WFA using the following equation:

   WFA = Total Glazing Area (ft²) ÷ Total Conditioned Floor Area (ft²)

2. If the WFA exceeds 0.18, the requirements for the prerequisite and each

credit change in the following ways:

In the Northern and North Central zones, meet the following requirement:

U-Factor = (0.18 ÷ WFA) * (U-Factor in **Table 1**)

In the Southern and South Central zones, meet the following requirement:

SHGC = (0.18 ÷ WFA) * (SHGC in **Table 1**)

3. If a solar screen is used to meet the SHGC requirements, the overall SHGC for a window unit with solar screen is determined by the following equation:

$SHGC_{Overall} =$

[(Window SHGC) x (Solar Screen SHGC) X (Percentage of Area Covered)]

+ (Window SHGC x Percentage of Area Not Covered)

For example, a window with an SHGC of 0.5 using a solar screen that provides 70% shading (the equivalent of 0.3 solar heat gain coefficient) and covers 60% of the window has an overall solar heat gain coefficient of

$SHGC_{Overall}$ = (0.5 x 0.3 x 0.6) + (0.5 x 0.4)

= 0.09 + 0.20

= 0.29

Verification and Submittals

Supporting Verification Materials, made available by the Project Team:

❑ Present any equipment literature (e.g., brochures, specifications) to the Verification Team.

❑ Present any calculations related to excess window area, solar screens, or

U-value and SHGC averaging to the Verification Team.

Verification Team:

❑ Verify that installed skylight area does not exceed 3% of conditioned floor area.

❑ Verify that installed skylights are ENERGY STAR labeled.

❑ Verify calculation of the window-to-floor area ratio.

❑ Verify that installed windows meet the U-value and SHGC specifications in the prerequisite and/or credits.

❑ Conduct on-site verification to confirm that installed products match above plans, calculations and product literature.

Exemplary Performance

No additional points are available for exemplary performance. Projects that exceed the credit requirements are encouraged to use the performance pathway in EA 1.2.

Considerations

Economic Issues

An investment in more energy-efficient windows can substantially reduce heating and cooling loads and may allow smaller (and less expensive) heating and cooling equipment. The savings on the HVAC equipment may offset the additional cost of the upgraded windows.

Regional Variances

The approach and benefits of good window design for a home located in a cold climate will be very different from those for a home in a warm or mild climate. A step-by-step guide to selecting energy-efficient windows, broken down by state and city, is available at www.efficientwindows.org/factsheets.cfm.

Resources

Web Sites

Efficient Windows Collaborative

www.efficientwindows.org

Efficient Windows Collaborative members have made a commitment to manufacture and promote energy-efficient windows. This site provides unbiased information on the benefits of energy-efficient windows, descriptions of how they work, and recommendations for their selection and use. This site includes a "Window Selection Tool" that enables users to compare the cost and performance of different windows in cities throughout the United States. The site also includes an excellent primer on the NFRC Window Label (see below), at www.efficientwindows.org/nfrc.cfm.

NFRC Window Label

National Fenestration Rating Council

www.nfrc.org/label.aspx

NFRC is a nonprofit organization that administers the only uniform, independent rating and labeling system for the energy performance of windows, doors, skylights, and attachment products. This site describes the elements contained in the NFRC window label on all rated windows, doors, and skylights.

Residential Windows, Doors, and Skylights

U.S. Environmental Protection Agency ENERGY STAR® Program

www.energystar.gov/index.cfm?c=windows_doors.pr_windows

Like other resources here, the ENERGY STAR site provides good background information on window performance along with a listing of ENERGY STAR Partner window manufacturers, whose products have earned the ENERGY STAR and meet the ENERGY STAR specifications for energy efficiency in the appropriate climate zones. This site also includes the

qualification criteria by climate zone, the ENERGY STAR climate zone map, and a sample ENERGY STAR label for windows, doors, and skylights.

Windows and Daylighting

Lawrence Berkeley National Laboratory

www.windows.lbl.gov

This site provides access to the laboratory's extensive research findings and publications on window performance and selection. Links to window energy use modeling and related software may also be found at www.windows.lbl.gov/software.

Print Media

Water Management Guide, by Joseph Lstiburek. Energy and Environmental Building Association. Available online, at www.eeba.org/bookstore.

EA 5: Heating and Cooling Distribution System

Intent

Minimize energy consumption due to thermal bridges and/or leaks in the heating and cooling distribution system.

Requirements

A. Forced-Air Systems

Prerequisites

5.1 **Reduced Distribution Losses.** Meet the following requirements:

   a) Limit duct air leakage rate to outside the conditioned envelope. The tested duct leakage rate must be ≤ 4.0 cfm at 25 Pascals per 100 square feet of conditioned floor area (for each installed system), verified by the qualified energy rater. Testing is waived if the home meets EA 5.3 (b) or (c).

   b) Do not install ducts in exterior walls unless extra insulation is added to maintain the overall UA for an exterior wall without ducts. Ducts may be run inside interior wall cavities but must be fully ducted (i.e., do not use the wall cavity as the duct).

   c) Use at least R-6 insulation around ducts in unconditioned spaces.

Credits

5.2 **Greatly Reduced Distribution Losses** (2 points). Limit duct air leakage to outside the conditioned envelope. The tested duct leakage rate must be ≤ 3.0 cfm at 25 Pascals per 100 square feet of conditioned floor area (for each installed system), verified by the qualified energy rater.

OR

5.3 **Minimal Distribution Losses** (3 points). Meet one of the following requirements:

   a) Limit duct air leakage to outside the conditioned envelope. The tested duct leakage rate must be ≤ 1.0 cfm at 25 Pascals per 100 square feet of conditioned floor area, verified by the qualified energy rater.

   b) Locate the air-handler unit and all ductwork within the conditioned envelope and minimize envelope leakage (i.e., meet the requirements of EA 3.3).

   c) Locate the air-handler unit and all ductwork visibly within conditioned spaces (i.e., no ductwork hidden in walls, chases, floors, or ceilings).

B. Nonducted HVAC Systems (e.g., Hydronic Systems)

Prerequisites

5.1 **Reduced Distribution Losses.** Use at least R-3 insulation around distribution pipes in unconditioned spaces.

Credits

5.2 **Greatly Reduced Distribution Losses** (2 points). Keep the system (including boiler and distribution pipes) entirely within the conditioned envelope.

5.3 **Minimal Distribution Losses** (1 point). Install outdoor reset control (i.e., controls that modulate distribution water temperature based on outdoor air temperature).

Synergies and Trade-Offs

A project receiving points for EA 1.2 is not eligible for this credit, and vice versa. A project pursuing this credit must follow the prescriptive pathway and meet all of the prerequisites in EA 2–10. Prerequisite EA 1.1 should be skipped. See the pathway schematic at the beginning of the EA section.

EQ 6 requires proper duct design to ensure adequate air flow and includes credit for testing air flow into each room.

MR 1.2–1.5 address framing efficiency. HVAC and framing efficiency are closely linked; floor, ceiling, and roof framing layouts should be designed to use framing material efficiently and at the same time accommodate duct runs as efficiently as possible. Addressing both simultaneously provides an opportunity to achieve multiple resource efficiencies through one design exercise.

EQ prerequisite 10 prohibits the placement of ductwork in the garage.

EA 5.1: Reduced Distribution Losses

EA 5.2: Greatly Reduced Distribution Losses

EA 5.3: Minimal Distribution Losses

In typical new homes, duct leakage may account for 15% to 25% of total heating and cooling energy use. Leaky supply ducts running through unconditioned spaces may dump conditioned air outside or draw unconditioned outside air into the home. Leaky ducts may also cause pressure imbalances inside that will increase infiltration and exfiltration rates.

The air tightness of ducts is measured by the amount of conditioned air that leaks from the ducts to areas outside the conditioned space. A piece of equipment called a duct blaster is commonly used to measure total leakage. Since the size of a duct system varies with the size of a home, the measured leakage rate is often normalized by dividing it by the floor area of the home.

It is not uncommon for leakage rates in typical duct systems to reach 20 cfm per 100 square feet of conditioned floor area. The lower the value, the less leakage from the system. A home whose distribution ducts are all installed inside the thermal envelope will have zero leakage to the outside.

Reducing the duct leakage rate saves energy, but more importantly, properly designed and sealed duct systems deliver air more effectively within the home. Unevenly hot or cold rooms are often caused by leaky ducts. A well-sealed duct system delivers conditioned air to each room as intended, ensuring that the occupants are always comfortable.

Leaky ducts may also draw moisture, dust, and other contaminants into the house; draw hot, humid air into conditioned cavities; depressurize enclosed rooms sufficiently to cause backdrafting of fireplaces and atmospherically vented appliances; and pressurize house cavities with conditioned air and force moist air into unconditioned areas, causing moisture problems. Such problems can be greatly reduced and/or eliminated with tight duct systems.

Homes with radiative (ie hydronic) systems use water pipes to distribute heat throughout the home and usually have no leakage problems, but they must be properly designed to ensure that adequate heat is delivered to each room. A separate set of credits in this category addresses enhanced radiative systems.

This credit category rewards the installation of highly efficient distribution systems that are properly sized and have minimal leaks.

Approach and Implementation

Forced-Air Systems

During the design stage, limit the number of kinks and seams in the ductwork. This may require working with the framer, electrician, and other trades. Work with the mechanical contractor to keep all ductwork and equipment within conditioned space through the use of chases, bulkheads, designated wall cavities, and interior mechanical rooms. Use ACCA Manual D to properly design the system to minimize opportunities for noise and airflow issues.

Prior to duct testing, seal all duct system holes, seams, joints, transitions, cracks, and penetrations with water-based mastic. Seal seams and joints at the air handler and supply-return plenums with mastic and fiberglass mesh for added resistance to vibration. Test the ductwork and identify and seal any leaks.

Inform the HVAC contractor that the home will have tight ducts so that this fact can be entered into the design calculations. Otherwise, the HVAC equipment will likely be oversized (see also EA 6.1).

Hard-duct all returns; do not use wall cavities or panned floor joists.

Radiative Systems

Homes with radiant heating systems have no air leakage and cannot be evaluated using the criteria above. Efficient nonducted designs (i.e., hydronic systems) have piping and radiator layouts that ensure that the proper amount of heat is delivered to each room.

Insulate the hot water pipes to minimize uncontrolled heat losses. Keep all the piping within the conditioned space (inside the thermal envelope).

Provide multiple thermal zones to improve temperature control within the home and enable occupants to turn down the thermostat in rooms that are not being used.

Calculations

No calculations are needed for this credit.

Verification and Submittals

Verification Team or Qualified energy rater:

A. Forced-Air Systems

❑ Conduct on-site verification that installed distribution system is fully ducted.

❑ Conduct on-site verification that installed ductwork located in unconditioned spaces is insulated with R-6 or greater insulation.

❑ Verify duct leakage test results conducted by a qualified energy rater, or USGBC-approved alternative, according to the procedures set forth

in the National Home Energy Rating System Standards.

❑ For EA 5.3, part (b), conduct on-site verification that installed air handler unit and ductwork is located within conditioned envelope and verify envelope leakage test results conducted by a qualified energy rater, or USGBC-approved alternative (see EA 3.3)."

❑ For EA 5.3, part (c), conduct on-site verification that installed air handler unit and ductwork is located visibly within conditioned spaces.

B. Radiative Systems

❑ For EA 5.1, conduct on-site verification that R-3 insulation is installed around all distribution pipes in unconditioned spaces.

❑ For EA 5.2, conduct on-site verification that the entire heating and distribution system is located within the conditioned envelope.

❑ For EA 5.3, conduct on-site verification that an outdoor reset control is installed.

Exemplary Performance

No additional points are available for exemplary performance. Projects that exceed the credit requirements are encouraged to use the performance pathway in EA 1.2.

Considerations

Economic Issues

Locating ducts and pipes in conditioned space instead of in unconditioned attics and crawl spaces has little if any up front cost, but can substantially reduce energy bills, heating and cooling loads (up to 20%), and the size of the HVAC equipment.

Duct tightness is one of the primary factors used to assess the size of the heating and cooling equipment needed to meet peak heating and cooling loads. An additional investment in sealing the ducts will substantially reduce the home's energy expense and may permit smaller (and less expensive) heating and cooling equipment. The savings on the HVAC equipment may offset the additional cost of the duct sealing.

Regional Variances

Nonducted systems are used regionally. Find a local contractor who is familiar with both the design and the installation of these kinds of systems and can deliver ongoing maintenance services.

Resources

Web Sites

Advanced Energy Tech Tips: Duct Sealing

www.advancedenergy.org/buildings/programs/affordable_housing/documents/Duct%20Sealing%20[SV].pdf

This two-page PDF, published in 2005, provides simple, practical, visual installation instructions for properly sealing ductwork by using a series of construction site photos. Instructions are in English and Spanish.

An Introduction to Residential Duct Systems

Lawrence Livermore

www.ducts.lbl.gov

This site includes general discussions of duct leakage, duct sealing, installation in conditioned versus unconditioned space, duct sizing, and insulation. It also includes worst, good, and best practice examples and links to additional duct system resources.

Duct Sealing

U.S. Environmental Protection Agency ENERGY STAR® Program

www.energystar.gov/index.cfm?c=home_improvement.hm_improvement_ducts

Aimed primarily at the consumer and homeowner, this site provides sound basic information on the benefits of proper duct sealing and installation.

Air Distribution System Installation and Sealing

Toolbase Services

www.toolbase.org/Home-Building-Topics/Indoor-Air-Quality/proper-duct-installation

This site includes a link to a Department of Energy fact sheet on air distribution sealing, as well as other resources on HVAC equipment and duct design and installation.

Residential HVAC Design Software

Wrightsoft Corporation

www.wrightsoft.com

Wrightsoft produces automated and integrated residential and commercial HVAC design and sales software systems, including Manual J and Manual D design and calculations modules.

Print Media

Builder's Guide series for specific North American climate zones: *Cold Climates, Mixed-Humid Climates, Hot-Humid Climates* and *Hot-Dry & Mixed Dry Climates*, by Joseph Lstiburek, Ph.D., P.Eng. Building Science Press. See in particular the construction details and systems descriptions in Chapter 1: Design, and Chapter 12: HVAC. Using a systems approach to building design and construction, these extensive guides provide climate-specific details and guidelines for residential construction, incorporating most aspects of each construction phase, type of building system, and climate considerations.

Manual D: Residential Duct Systems. Air Conditioning Contractors of America. The manual describes duct sizing and design procedures that may be applied to constant volume systems and zoned, variable air volume systems and over the full range of duct construction materials. Manual D also includes comprehensive equivalent length data. The manual and other related HVAC publications may be purchased through the ACCA online bookstore, at

www.accaconference.com/Merchant2/merchant.mv.

"Smart and Cool—The Art of Air Conditioning," by John Proctor. *Home Energy Magazine*, 2005.

EA 6: Space Heating and Cooling Equipment

Intent

Reduce energy consumption associated with the heating and cooling system.

Requirements

Note: Both the space heating and the space cooling equipment must meet the requirements of this credit. If only one type of equipment qualifies, then half the points should be taken. Homes built either without air-conditioning or without heating should be modeled under EA 1, using the default (minimum efficiency allowed) in both the reference and the rated homes.

Prerequisites

6.1 **Good HVAC Design and Installation.** Meet each of the following requirements:

   a) Design and size HVAC equipment properly using ACCA Manual J, the ASHRAE 2001 Handbook of Fundamentals, or an equivalent computation procedure.

   b) Install HVAC equipment that meets the requirements of the ENERGY STAR for Homes national Builder Option Package (**Table 1**).

   c) Install programmable thermostat (except heat pumps and hydronic systems).

Credits

6.2 **High-Efficiency HVAC** (2 points). Design and install HVAC equipment that is better than the equipment required by the ENERGY STAR Builder Option Package (**Table 1**).

OR

6.3 **Very High-Efficiency HVAC** (maximum 4 points). Design and install HVAC equipment that is substantially better than the equipment required by the ENERGY STAR Builder Option Package (**Table 1**). Any piping designed as part of a heat pump system to carry water that is well above (or below) the thermostatic temperature settings in the home must have R-4 insulation or greater.

   Note: The maximum of 4 points is available only if a heat pump is installed. Furnace and boiler systems can earn a maximum of 3 points.

Synergies and Trade-Offs

A project receiving points for EA 1 is not eligible for this credit, and vice versa. A project pursuing this credit must follow the prescriptive pathway and meet all of the prerequisites in EA 2–10. Prerequisite EA 1.1 should be skipped. See the pathway schematic at the beginning of the EA section.

Substantial energy savings can be achieved by using heat recovery equipment. Heat or energy recovery systems are rewarded in EQ 4.2.

EQ 10 prohibits the placement of the air handler unit in the garage. EA 11 requires a refrigerant charge test and encourages the selection of preferred refrigerants.

Table 1(a). HVAC Requirements for IECC Climate Zones 4–8.

			HVAC equipment		Ground-source heat pumps		
	End use	Central AC and air source heat pumps	Furnaces (gas, oil, or propane)	Boilers (gas, oil, or propane)	Open loop	Closed loop	Direct expansion
EA 6.1: Good HVAC Design and Installation (prerequisite)	Cooling	≥ 13 SEER	≥ 90 AFUE	≥ 85 AFUE	≥ 16.2 EER	≥ 14.1 EER	≥ 15 EER
	Heating	≥ 8.2 HSPF			≥ 3.6 COP	≥ 3.3 COP	≥ 3.5 COP
EA 6.2: High-Efficiency HVAC (2 points)	Cooling	≥ 14 SEER	≥ 92 AFUE	≥ 87 AFUE	≥ 17.8 EER	≥ 15.5 EER	≥ 16.5 EER
	Heating	≥ 8.6 HSPF			≥ 4.0 COP	≥ 3.6 COP	≥ 3.9 COP
EA 6.3: Very High Efficiency HVAC (heat pump, 4 points; other systems, 3 points)	Cooling	≥ 15 SEER	≥ 94 AFUE*	≥ 90 AFUE	≥ 19.4 EER	≥ 17 EER	≥ 18 EER
	Heating	≥ 9.0 HSPF			≥ 4.3 COP	≥ 4.0 COP	≥ 4.2 COP

* Furnace with low electric energy use.

Table 1(b). HVAC Requirements for IECC Climate Zones 1–3.

			HVAC equipment		Ground-source heat pumps		
	End use	Central AC and air source heat pumps	Furnaces (gas, oil, or propane)	Boilers (gas, oil, or propane)	Open loop	Closed loop	Direct expansion
EA 6.1: Good HVAC Design and Installation (prerequisite)	Cooling	≥ 14 SEER	≥ 80 AFUE	≥ 80 AFUE	≥ 16.2 EER	≥ 14.1 EER	≥ 15 EER
	Heating	≥ 8.2 HSPF			≥ 3.6 COP	≥ 3.3 COP	≥ 3.5 COP
EA 6.2: High-Efficiency HVAC (2 points)	Cooling	≥ 15 SEER	≥ 90 AFUE	≥ 85 AFUE	≥ 17.8 EER	≥ 15.5 EER	≥ 16.5 EER
	Heating	≥ 8.6 HSPF			≥ 4.0 COP	≥ 3.6 COP	≥ 3.9 COP
EA 6.3: Very High Efficiency HVAC (heat pump, 4 points; other systems, 3 points)	Cooling	≥ 16 SEER	≥ 92 AFUE*	≥ 87 AFUE	≥ 19.4 EER	≥ 17 EER	≥ 18 EER
	Heating	≥ 9.0 HSPF			≥ 4.3 COP	≥ 4.0 COP	≥ 4.2 COP

* Furnace with low electric energy use.

EA 6.1: HVAC Design and Installation
EA 6.2: High-Efficiency HVAC
EA 6.3: Very High-Efficiency HVAC

Heating, ventilating, and air-conditioning (HVAC) equipment is a big energy user. Energy savings of 20% to 30% can be achieved by installing space heating and cooling equipment with the ENERGY STAR label. This equipment is designed with performance characteristics that greatly exceed the federal minimum requirements.

The HVAC system offers three opportunities to achieve energy savings: in the sizing of the equipment, in the selection of efficiency levels, and in the installation of refrigerants.

This credit category rewards the installation of heating and cooling equipment that meets or exceeds the performance levels required by the ENERGY STAR for Homes national Builder Option Package.

Approach and Implementation

EA 6 only applies to projects with both heating and cooling. Homes built without air conditioning or without heating must be modeled and meet the requirements of EA 1.1.

Compliance with this credit requires a three-step process. First, use ACCA Manual J, ASHRAE 2001 Handbook of Fundamentals, or an equivalent computation procedure to determine heating and cooling loads. Second, use ACCA Manual S to size the heating and cooling equipment, based on the Manual J calculation. And third, select, design, and install HVAC equipment that meets the performance specifications in the credit.

Manual J has a built-in 15% cushion to account for extraordinary loads. Accu-rately model the home you are designing; do not artificially increase the heating or cooling loads by manipulating design temperatures, adding occupants, changing the window orientation or area, or reducing enclosure R-values.

An oversized air-conditioner can compromise comfort, especially in humid climates. Since it has shorter run times, an oversized unit cannot dehumidify as effectively as a right-size air-conditioner.

The U.S. Environmental Protection Agency's ENERGY STAR HVAC labeling program covers most of the common types of space heating and cooling equipment used in new homes, including central air-conditioning, high-efficiency furnaces, air-source heat pumps, ground-source heat pumps, and high-efficiency boilers. Additional information about these products (including manufacturers and models that have been labeled) can be found at www.energystar.gov/index. cfm?c=heat_cool.pr_hvac.

The use of electric resistance heating will prevent a home from scoring well on the HERS index unless the home has practically no heating demand. If electric heating is preferred or natural gas is unavailable, consider using an electric heat pump.

If a heat pump is installed with a programmable thermostat, the thermostat must be equipped with adaptive recovery. This technology enables the heating equipment to gradually adjust when the thermostat setting changes, preventing overdependence on the less efficient backup heating system.

Calculations

Other than the ACCA Manual J equipment sizing calculation, no additional calculations are needed for this credit.

Verification and Submittals

Supporting Verification Materials, made available by the Project Team:

❑ Present design calculations related to the HVAC design to the Verification Team.

❑ Present any HVAC system equipment literature (e.g., user manuals, brochures, specifications) to the Verification Team.

❑ Include HVAC equipment literature in the occupant's operations and maintenance manual.

❑ Sign an Accountability Form to indicate that the system was designed and installed according to the prerequisite.

Verification Team:

❑ Visually verify that all HVAC design calculations are completed in compliance with the Verification and Submittal Guidelines..

❑ Visually verify (using equipment literature, labels, etc.) the type of equipment installed and its efficiency.

❑ Verify that an Accountability Form has been signed by the responsible party.

Exemplary Performance

No additional points are available for exemplary performance. Projects that exceed the credit requirements are encouraged to use the performance pathway in EA 1.2.

Considerations

Environmental Issues

Reduced demand for fossil fuel–based energy reduces emissions of air pollutants like carbon dioxide, nitrogen oxides, and sulfur dioxide.

Economic Issues

When selecting high-efficiency HVAC equipment, compare the incrementally higher cost of energy-efficient HVAC equipment with the long-term energy cost savings. Take into account continued increases in energy prices.

Regional Variations

Equipment efficiency requirements for IECC zones 1–3 and 4–8 are different (see **Table 1**) because high-efficiency air-conditioning equipment is less cost-effective in cold climates, and high-efficiency heating equipment is less cost-effective in hot climates. Since larger energy savings are expected in areas with more extreme climates, the cost-effectiveness of higher-efficiency HVAC equipment will be higher in these locations.

Resources

Web Sites

ARI Directory of Certified Product Performance

Air-Conditioning & Refrigeration Institute

www.aridirectory.org

ARI represents manufacturers that voluntarily participate in independent testing to ensure that their products perform according to published claims. Certified ratings are published in ARI's Directory of Certified Product Performance, a convenient source for finding product performance ratings based. The appropriate product for a particular job can be selected with the assurance that the product will perform as promised.

Heating and Cooling Efficiency

U.S. Environmental Protection Agency ENERGY STAR® Program

www.energystar.gov/index.cfm?c=heat_cool.pr_hvac

This site has general information on heating and cooling system efficiency along with the standards for meeting the ENERGY STAR efficiency requirements. There are also links to listings of ENERGY STAR–lified heating and cooling equipment.

Product Directory

GAMA, An Association of Appliance and Equipment Manufacturers

www.gamanet.org/gama/inforesources.nsf/vContentEntries/Product+Directories

This site has downloadable lists of space heating equipment eligible for federal tax credits, along with product ratings tested under the association's certification programs. Its database search engine allows users to retrieve information on equipment that meets various criteria, including equipment eligible for tax credits.

Residential Gas Heating

Consortium for Energy Efficiency

www.cee1.org/gas/gs-ht/gs-ht-main.php3

CEE has developed lists of residential gas furnaces and residential gas boilers that meet the specifications for its Residential Gas Heating Initiative.

Residential HVAC Design Software

Wrightsoft Corporation

www.wrightsoft.com

Wrightsoft produces automated and integrated residential and commercial HVAC design and sales software systems, including Manual J and Manual D design and calculations modules.

Specification of Energy-Efficient Installation and Maintenance Practices for Residential HVAC Systems

Consortium for Energy Efficiency

www.cee1.org/resid/rs-ac/rs-ac-main.php3

This 62-page document is a comprehensive guide to the selection, sizing, installation, and maintenance of residential HVAC equipment. The focus is on maximizing the efficiency of these systems.

Print Media

Manual J: HVAC Residential Load Calculation. Eighth edition. Air Conditioning Contractors of America. Manual J® is the industry standard residential load calculation method, required by most building codes around the country. This manual and other related HVAC publications may be purchased through the ACCA online bookstore, at www.acca.org/store

EA 7: Water Heating

Intent

Reduce energy consumption associated with the domestic hot water system, including improving the efficiency of both the hot water system design and the layout of the fixtures in the home.

Requirements

Prerequisites

None.

Credits

7.1 **Efficient Hot Water Distribution** (2 points). Design and install an energy-efficient hot water distribution system (see **Figure 1**). None of the branch length requirements below apply to cold water demand loads (e.g., toilets), washing machines, or tubs without showerheads. Select one of the following designs:

a) Structured plumbing system. The system must meet all of the following:

   i. The system must have a demand-controlled circulation loop that is insulated to at least R-4.

   ii. The total length of the circulation loop must be less than 40 linear feet of plumbing in one-story homes. Add 2x the ceiling height for two-story homes, and add 4x the ceiling height for three- or four-story homes.

   iii. Branch lines from the loop to each fixture must be ≤10 feet long and a maximum of ½-inch nominal diameter.

   iv. The system must be designed with a push button control in each full bathroom and the kitchen and an automatic pump shut-off.

b) Central manifold distribution system. The system must meet all of the following:

   i. The central manifold trunk must be no more than 6 feet in length.

   ii. The central manifold trunk must be insulated to at least R-4.

   iii. No branch line from the central manifold to any fixtures may exceed 20 feet in one-story homes. Add 1x the ceiling height for two-story homes, and add 2x the ceiling height for three- or four-story homes.

   iv. Branch lines from the manifold must be a maximum of ½-inch nominal diameter.

c) Compact design of conventional system. The system must meet all of the following:

   i. No branch line from the water heater to any fixtures may exceed 20 feet in one-story homes. Add 1x the ceiling height for two-story homes, and add 2x the ceiling height for three- or four-story homes.

   ii. Branch lines from the central header to each fixture must be a maximum of ½-inch nominal diameter.

7.2 **Pipe Insulation** (1 point). All domestic hot water piping shall have R-4 insulation. Insulation shall be properly installed on all piping elbows to adequately insulate the 90-degree bend.

7.3 **Efficient Domestic Hot Water (DHW) Equipment** (maximum 3 points). Design and install energy-efficient water heating equipment. Select one measure from **Table 1** below.

Figure 1(a). Sample Schematic of a Structured Plumbing System
Figure 1(b). Sample Schematic of a Central Manifold Distribution System
Figure 1(c). Sample Schematic of a Compact Design

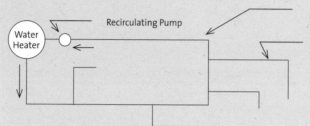

Recirculation loop must be insulated (≥R-4), and limited in length (see credit).

All branches from the recirculation loop to the fixture must be ≤10 feet and max 1/2" diameter.

Synergies and Trade-Offs

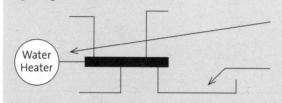

Trunk must be ≤6 feet from water heater and insulated to ≥R4

Home must have a tight plumbing core, with branches that are limited in length (see credit) and max 1/2" diameter

A project receiving points for EA 1 is not eligible for EA 7.3, and vice versa. A project

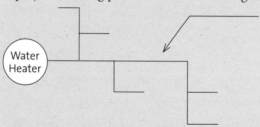

Home must have a tight plumbing core, with branches that are limited in length (see credit) and max 1/2" diameter

pursuing EA 7.3 must follow the prescriptive pathway and meet all of the prerequisites in EA 2–10. Prerequisite EA 1.1 should be skipped. See the pathway schematic at the beginning of the EA section. EA 7.1 and 7.2 are available to every project, whether the performance approach (EA 1) or the prescriptive approach (EA 2–10) is used.

Low-flow showerheads and faucets may also reduce demand for hot water and resulting energy use for water heating. Points for installing low-flow showerheads are available under WE 3. Additional reductions in hot water energy use achieved through efficient appliances are addressed in EA 9.

Table 1. High-Efficiency Water Heating Equipment

Water heater type and efficiency requirement	Description	Points
Gas water heaters		
EF ≥ 0.53 (80 gallon)	High-efficiency storage water heater	1
EF ≥ 0.57 (60 gallon)	High-efficiency storage water heater	1
EF ≥ 0.61 (40 gallon)	High-efficiency storage water heater	1
EF ≥ 0.8	Storage or tankless water heater	2
CAE ≥ 0.8	Combination water and space heaters	2
Electric water heaters		
EF ≥ 0.89 (80 gallon)	High-efficiency storage water heater	1
EF ≥ 0.92 (50 gallon)	High-efficiency storage water heater	1
EF ≥ 0.93 (40 gallon)	High-efficiency storage water heater	1
EF ≥ 0.99	Tankless water heater	2
EF ≥ 2.0	Heat pump water heater	3
Solar water heaters		
≥ 40% of annual DHW load	With preheat tank	2
≥ 60% of annual DHW load	With preheat tank	3

EF = Energy factor. Energy factors for equipment from various manufacturers are available at http://www.gamanet.org/gama/inforesources.nsf/vContentEntries/Product+Directories.

CAE = Combined annual efficiency.

EA 7.1: Efficient Distribution System

EA 7.2: Pipe Insulation

EA 7.3: Efficient Domestic Hot Water Equipment

As much as one-third of a home's total energy bill is spent on heating water. Energy is used to heat water from room temperature to 140 degrees, and that heat may be lost both in the piping system and at the storage tank.

Approximately 10% to 15% of energy use in hot water systems is wasted in distribution losses. Such losses can be greatly reduced by ensuring that all fixtures and appliances that use hot water are located as close as possible—within 10 to 20 feet—to the hot water heater. An additional 20% of hot water–related energy use is due to inefficiencies in the actual water heating equipment.

For each of the three credits in this category, the relevant metric is the energy and potable water consumption of the domestic water heating system. High-efficiency water heaters can reduce energy bills by 10% to 50%. Efficient hot water distribution can save both energy and water by reducing the need to run the shower while waiting for hot water to arrive.

These credits reward the design and installation of efficient hot water distribution systems and the selection of high-efficiency water heating equipment.

Approach and Implementation

One of the primary factors affecting homeowner satisfaction is the relative comfort associated with the hot water delivery system. The distance from the water heater has a great impact on the temperature of the water that arrives at a fixture and how long it takes for the hot water to be delivered.

The first step in designing an efficient hot water distribution system (see **Figure 1**) is to design the home with a central plumbing core, where the kitchen, the bathrooms, and the laundry room are in close proximity. This is easier for small homes but possible for any home size if it is attended to early in the design process.

Design the system so the water heater is centrally located beneath the central plumbing core, particularly if the water heater is located in a basement or crawlspace beneath the home. Design the system to minimize the total volume of pipe. EA 7.1 (a) can be met using multiple loops that extend from a single water heater. EA 7.1 (b) and (c) can bet met using multiple water heaters.

Limit run lengths and design the system in a tree-like structure with trunks, branches, and twigs, where longer pipe lengths (e.g., twigs) have a much smaller pipe diameter.

Coordinate all of the trades to ensure that the plumbing design can be installed as designed. Conflicts with the framing or HVAC installation can force the plumber to re-direct pipe, resulting in considerable system inefficiencies, wasted material, and poorer system performance.

If possible, design the kitchen and bathrooms with a designated space for water heating equipment. Designate locations for pipes in coordination with the needs of other trades. Minimize the distances between plumbing fixtures to shorten the lengths of the plumbing runs.

If a structured plumbing or manifold distribution system is intended, work with an experienced contractor to design the system.

Insulate the pipes to minimize heat losses in both the conditioned and unconditioned parts of the home. This helps reduce energy use and keep the water temperature as high as possible. Cavity insulation can be used to meet the pipe insulation requirements, but the pipe must be insulated on all sides (e.g., locate pipe in center of cavity or use additional exterior insulation).

Low-flow showerheads and faucets, awarded in WE 3, will reduce both the hot water consumption and the rate at which hot water reaches the fixtures. If low-flow showerheads and faucets are installed, a smaller water heater and smaller-diameter piping can be used. To make up for the lower flow rate associated with low-flow showerheads and faucets, design the water distribution system to be compact.

When selecting equipment, assess the relative lifetime cost of electric versus gas water heaters. Consider the incremental increase in the energy factor (EF) relative to the code requirements as well as the related energy savings over the life of the unit (approximately 15 years). The incremental cost of an efficient water heater can pay for itself in a short period.

In some locations, solar water heating systems may be very cost-effective, depending on annual hours of sunshine and financial incentives.

Projects using alternative water heating designs, such as small-tank, combination tankless/tank systems, or heat-pump preheat systems, should submit a Credit Interpretation Request or use the performance pathway in EA 1.

Calculations

For EA 7.1, determine ceiling height by measuring the floor-to-floor distance.

For EA 7.1 part (a-ii), calculate the allowable length for the circulation loop based on the number of stories in the home. Calculate the length of pipe in the installed circulation loop.

For EA 7.1 parts (a-iii), (b-iii), and (c-i), calculate the length of installed pipe from the circulation loop, manifold, or water heater to the furthest fixture. Any 3/8" diameter piping should be counted at half the length of ½" diameter pipe when calculating maximum branch length; check local code for compliance.

For EA 7.1 (c-i) in a multi-story home, the maximum allowable branch length differs for each story. Branches to 1st floor fixtures may not exceed 20 feet; branches to 2nd story fixtures may not exceed 20 feet + 1x the story height; branches to 3rd story fixtures may not exceed 20 feet + 2x the story height; etc.

For EA 7.3, if a solar water heater is installed, have the installer estimate the percentage of the total annual hot water load that will be met by the solar water heater, taking into consideration system design, climate and estimated consumption patterns.

Verification and Submittals

Supporting Verification Materials, made available by the Project Team:

EA 7.1 Efficient Distribution System

❑ Sign an Accountability Form to indicate that the hot water distribution system is installed according to the credit requirements.

EA 7.3 Efficient Domestic Hot Water Equipment

❑ Present any equipment literature related to the hot water distribution system (e.g., user manuals, brochures, specifications) to the Verification Team.

❑ Include equipment literature in the operations and maintenance occupant's manual.

❑ For a solar hot water heater, present calculations to the Verification Team demonstrating the percentage of the annual domestic hot water load being met.

Verification Team:

EA 7.1 Efficient Distribution System

☐ Visually verify the design of the hot water distribution system.

☐ Verify that an Accountability Form has been signed by the responsible party.

EA 7.2 Pipe Insulation

☐ Visually verify that pipes are insulated according to the credit requirements.

EA 7.3 Efficient Domestic Hot Water Equipment

☐ Visually verify (using equipment literature, labels, etc.) the type of equipment installed and its efficiency.

☐ For a solar hot water heater, visually verify that the calculations meet the requirements.

Partial Credit

Partial credit (1 point) is awarded for EA 7.1 if a project meets part (a) – structured plumbing system - sections i, iii, and iv.

Exemplary Performance

Projects that meet the requirements in EA 7.3 by installing a solar DHW system should be awarded one exemplary performance point for installing a back-up gas system with EF or CAE ≥ 0.8 or a back-up electric system with EF ≥ 0.99 for instantaneous water heaters or EF ≥ 2.0 for heat pump water heaters.

Considerations

Economic Issues

Electric tankless water heaters typically draw a substantial amount of electricity, and the electrical systems in homes with these tankless systems may need to be upgraded accordingly. Consider the cost of any necessary upgrade when selecting an electric tankless water heating system.

Environmental Issues

Reduced demand for fossil fuel–based energy reduces emissions of air pollutants like carbon dioxide, nitrogen oxides, and sulfur dioxide.

In selecting the fuel for a home's water heating system, consider the local CO_2 emissions rate of the local electric plant. Utilities with large hydro and nuclear generation capabilities have lower CO_2 emissions rates than those using fossil fuel–fired generators.

Regional Variances

Solar water heating systems are becoming more attractive as energy prices continue to rise. They are relatively cost-effective in the South, less so in northern states. Several tools are available to help assess the potential for using solar energy in locations across the United States; see "Resources," below.

Resources

Web Sites

Product Directory

GAMA, An Association of Appliance and Equipment Manufacturers

www.gamanet.org/gama/inforesources. nsf/vContentEntries/Product+Directories

In this GAMA and I=B=R efficiency rating certified product directories section, users will find downloadable lists of water heating equipment tested under the association's certification programs. Its database search engine allows users to retrieve information on equipment that meets various criteria, including the new GAMA Model ID.

Residential Hot Water Distribution

California Urban Water Conservation Council

www.cuwcc.org/res_hot_water.lasso

On this site, CUWCC has collected an extensive series of practical articles, reports, and government-funded studies on efficient water distribution, covering piping design and materials, insulation, on-demand systems, recirculation systems, and point-of-use systems.

Solar Water Heaters

U.S. Department of Energy

www.eere.energy.gov/consumer/ your_home/water_heating/index.cfm/ mytopic=12850

The site briefly describes the various types of solar hot water heating systems and provides links to more extensive information on solar hot water heating systems selection, components, systems design, product information, manufacturers, and government incentives.

Solar Hot Water

Florida Solar Energy Center

www.fsec.ucf.edu/en/consumer/solar_ hot_water/homes/index.htm

An excellent resource for information on solar hot water heating systems, sizing, installation, and collector and system ratings. FSEC also has an industry resources page that includes its 193-page Solar Heating Manual, a domestic solar hot water installation pictorial, and additional links to related resources, available at www.fsec.ucf.edu/en/industry/resources/ solar_thermal/index.htm.

EA 8: Lighting

Intent

Reduce energy consumption associated with interior and exterior lighting.

Requirements

Prerequisites

8.1 **ENERGY STAR Lights.** Install at least four ENERGY STAR labeled light fixtures or ENERGY STAR labeled compact fluorescent light bulbs (CFLs) in high-use rooms (kitchen, dining room, living room, family room, hallways).

Credits

8.2 **Improved Lighting** (1.5 maximum points). Select and install one or both of the following measures:

a) Indoor lighting (0.5 points). Install three additional ENERGY STAR labeled light fixtures or ENERGY STAR labeled compact fluorescent light bulbs (CFLs) in high-use rooms. These are in addition to the four ENERGY STAR lights required by EA 8.1.

b) Exterior lighting (1 point). All exterior lighting must have either motion sensor controls or integrated photovoltaic cells. The following lighting is exempt: emergency lighting; lighting required by code for health and safety purposes; and lighting used for eye adaptation near covered vehicle entrances or exits.

OR

8.3 **Advanced Lighting Package** (3 points). Install ENERGY STAR Advanced Lighting Package using only ENERGY STAR labeled fixtures. The Advanced Lighting Package consists of a minimum of 60% ENERGY STAR qualified hard-wired fixtures and 100% ENERGY STAR–qualified ceiling fans (if any).

OR

Install ENERGY STAR labeled lamps in 80% of the fixtures throughout the home. ENERGY STAR labeled CFLs are acceptable. All ceiling fans must be ENERGY STAR labeled.

Synergies and Trade-Offs

A project receiving points for EA 1 is not eligible for this credit, and vice versa. A project pursuing this credit must follow the prescriptive pathway and meet all the associated prerequisites in EA 2–10. Prerequisite EA 1.1 should be skipped. See the pathway schematic at the beginning of the EA section.

Improving the lighting efficiency may also reduce cooling loads and the energy consumption associated with air-conditioning.

EA 8.1: ENERGY STAR Lights

EA 8.2: Improved Lighting

EA 8.3: Advanced Lighting Package

Interior and exterior lighting accounts for about 5% to 15% of a new home's total energy use. High-efficiency indoor lighting fixtures, such as those with the ENERGY STAR label, use approximately 50% to 75% less energy than conventional incandescent fixtures. Additional energy savings can be achieved through the use of dimmer and occupant sensor controls.

Besides saving energy, high-efficiency lamps require less frequent replacement and generate less heat.

This credit category rewards the installation of ENERGY STAR labeled light fixtures, compact fluorescent bulbs, and exterior lighting control equipment.

Approach and Implementation

ENERGY STAR labeled lighting provides bright, warm light but uses about 75% less energy than standard lighting, produces 75% less heat, and lasts up to 10 times longer.

To save the most energy and money, install these energy-efficient lamps in the home's most-used fixtures: kitchen ceiling lights, living or family room table and floor lamps, and the outdoor porch or post lamp.

Many homes are designed with large numbers of recessed light fixtures, or cans. These lighting fixtures are either Type IC (for insulated ceilings) or Type Non-IC (for noninsulated ceilings). Typically, cans provide an air leakage pathway from the home's interior conditioned space, as well as cause moisture flows and condensation in the attic. IECC Section 502.1.3 now requires that Type IC recessed light fixtures be designed so that there are no penetrations between the inside of the recessed fixture and the ceiling cavity, and that they be sealed or gasketed to prevent air leakage into unconditioned space.

Select airtight cans labeled as Type IC. Install each can inside a sealed box constructed from a minimum 0.5-inch-thick gypsum wall or from a preformed polymeric vapor barrier, or other airtight assembly manufactured for this purpose. Maintain proper clearances of not less than 0.5 inch from combustible material and not less than 3 inches from insulation material.

For exterior fixtures, use infrared sensors that turn lights on only when motion is sensed and timers that automatically turn them off after a period of inactivity. Exterior lighting is usually installed with on–off controls and is often left on for extended periods when it is not actually needed. By operating only when illumination is needed, exterior lighting energy use may be reduced by half or more.

The criteria for ENERGY STAR light fixtures and lamps are presented in **Table 1**. Additional criteria for other types of fixtures are provided at www.energystar.gov/index.cfm?c=fixtures.pr_crit_light_fixtures.

Calculations

For EA 8.3, calculate the percentage of the home's light fixtures that are ENERGY STAR labeled OR calculate the percentage of the home's lamps (i.e. light bulbs) that are ENERGY STAR labeled.

Table 1. ENERGY STAR Sample Criteria for Light Fixtures and Lamps

Performance metric	ENERGY STAR specification
Combined lamp and ballast requirements	
System efficacy per lamp ballast platform, in lumens per watt (LPW)	≥ 50 LPW for all lamp types below 30 total listed lamp watts.
≥ 60 LPW for all lamp types that are ≤ 24 inches and ≥ 30 total listed lamp watts.	
≥ 70 LPW for all lamp types that are ≥ 24 inches and ≥ 30 total listed lamp watts.	
Lamp requirements	
Lamp life	For lamps shipped with fixtures, average rated life of lamp must be > 10,000 hours.
	For lamps not shipped with fixtures, product packaging must meet requirements set forth in the "Product Packaging for Consumer Awareness" specifications of ENERGY STAR.
Lumen maintenance	For lamps indicated on fixture packaging or shipped with fixtures, average rated lumen maintenance must be at least 80% of initial lamp lumens at 40% (4,000 hours minimum) rated lamp life.
Color rendering index	For lamps shipped with fixtures, color rendering index must meet following requirements:
	≥ 80 for compact fluorescent lamps;
	≥ 75 for linear fluorescent lamps.
	For lamps not shipped with fixtures, product packaging must meet requirements set forth in "Product Packaging for Consumer Awareness" specifications of ENERGY STAR.
Correlated color temperature	For lamps shipped with fixtures, the lamps must have one of the following designated correlated color temperatures (CCT): 2700K, 3000K, 3500K, 4100K, 5000K, or 6500K.
	For lamps not shipped with fixtures, product packaging must meet requirements set forth in "Product Packaging for Consumer Awareness," below.

Verification and Submittals

Supporting Verification Materials, made available by the Project Team:

EA 8.3: Advanced Lighting Package

❑ Present calculations to the Verification Team demonstrating the percentage of light fixtures or lamps that are ENERGY STAR labeled.

Verification Team:

EA 8.1: ENERGY STAR Lights

❑ Visually verify ENERGY STAR lights in the home.

EA 8.2: Improved Lighting

❑ For (a), visually verify ENERGY STAR lights.

❑ For (b), visually verify motion sensors and photovoltaic lights.

EA 8.3: Advanced Lighting Package

❑ Visually verify ENERGY STAR lights in the home.

❑ Visually verify the calculations for the percentage of ENERGY STAR labeled lights in the home.

Exemplary Performance

Projects that install at least 90% Energy Star labeled hard-wired fixtures should be awarded one exemplary performance point, to be counted under Innovation in Design 3.

ID	LL	SS	WE	**EA**	MR	EQ	AE
			8.1 – 8.3				

Considerations

Environmental Issues

Because compact fluorescent light bulbs contain trace amounts of mercury, they should be disposed of at recycling facilities. Additional information on disposing of compact fluorescents should be provided to occupants. Go to www.energystar.gov/ia/partners/promotions/change_light/downloads/Fact_Sheet_Mercury.pdf.

Resources

Web Sites

Alliance to Save Energy

www.ase.org/section/topic/lights

Along with a general description of the benefits to using compact fluorescent fixtures (CFLs), this Web site has several additional links to excellent related sites on CFL selection, government and utility incentive programs, and lighting controls.

ENERGY STAR Advanced Lighting Program

U.S. Environmental Protection Agency ENERGY STAR® Program

www.energystar.gov/index.cfm?c=bldrs_lenders_raters.ALP_Builder

This site includes complete information on EPA's Advanced Lighting Program specifications and requirements, along with extensive technical resources, qualified product and manufacturer lists and locators, case studies, and marketing support resources.

EA 9: Appliances

Intent

Reduce appliance energy consumption.

Requirements

Prerequisites

None.

Credits

9.1 **High-Efficiency Appliances** (maximum 2 points). Install appliances from the list below. To receive points for one type (e.g., refrigerator), every appliance of that type must meet the applicable requirement below.

   a) ENERGY STAR labeled refrigerator(s) (1 point).

   b) ENERGY STAR labeled ceiling fans (at least one in living or family room and one per bedroom) (0.5 point).

   c) ENERGY STAR labeled dishwasher(s) that uses 6.0 gallons or less per cycle (0.5 point).

   d) ENERGY STAR labeled clothes washer(s) (0.5 point).

9.2 **Water-Efficient Clothes Washer** (1 point). Install clothes washer with modified energy factor (MEF) ≥ 2.0 and water factor (WF) < 5.5. A clothes washer that meets these requirements and the requirement in EA 9.1 can be counted for both.

Synergies and Trade-Offs

A project receiving points for EA 1 is not eligible for this credit, and vice versa. A project pursuing this credit must follow the prescriptive pathway and meet all the prerequisites in EA 2–10. Prerequisite EA 1.1 should be skipped. See the pathway schematic at the beginning of the EA section.

EA 9.1: High-Efficiency Appliances
EA 9.2: Water-Efficient Clothes Washer

Household appliances are responsible for 20% to 30% of a home's total energy use and about 25% of its indoor water use. Efficient household appliances save substantial amounts of both energy and water.

The U.S. Environmental Protection Agency has developed the ENERGY STAR label for energy-efficient appliances. On average, ENERGY STAR labeled appliances consume 20% to 30% less water than conventional appliances, and horizontal-axis clothes washers use up to 50% less water than conventional clothes washers.

This credit rewards homes that are built with ENERGY STAR labeled appliances installed.

Approach and Implementation

This section addresses four types of appliances. The primary metrics used in rating the performance of these appliances are explained below.

Refrigerators

ENERGY STAR refrigerators require about half as much energy as models manufactured before 1993. The criteria for labeling ENERGY STAR refrigerators and freezers are presented in **Table 1**.

Ceiling Fans

Combination ceiling fan–light units that have earned the ENERGY STAR label are about 50% more efficient than conventional units. This can save $10 per year on the occupant's utility bills, as well as reduce air-conditioning or heating demand. The criteria for labeling ENERGY STAR ceiling fans are presented in **Table 2**.

Dishwashers

The performance of dishwashers is compared using the energy factor (EF), which

Table 1. ENERGY STAR Criteria for Refrigerators and Freezers

Type	Volume	Criteria
Full-size refrigerators	7.75 cubic feet or greater	At least 15% more energy efficient than minimum federal government standard (NAECA).
Full-size freezers	7.75 cubic feet or greater	At least 10% more energy efficient than minimum federal government standard (NAECA).
Compact refrigerators and freezers	Less than 7.75 cubic feet and 36 inches or less in height	At least 20% more energy efficient than minimum federal government standard (NAECA).

Table 2. ENERGY STAR Criteria for Ceiling Fans

Sample Specifications
Residential ceiling fan airflow efficiency is defined on a performance basis: Cubic feet per minute (cfm) of airflow per watt of power consumed by motor and controls. Efficiency is measured on each of three speeds.
At low speed, fans must have minimum airflow of 1,250 cfm and efficiency of 155 cfm/watt.
Qualifying ceiling fan models must have minimum 30-year motor warranty; one-year component(s) warranty; and two-year light kits warranty.
At high speed, fans must have minimum airflow of 5,000 cfm and efficiency of 75 cfm/watt.

is expressed in cycles per kWh and is the reciprocal of the sum of the machine electrical energy per cycle (M), plus the water heating energy consumption per cycle (W):

$$EF = \frac{1}{M + W}$$

This equation may vary based on dishwasher features such as water heating boosters or truncated cycles. The greater the EF, the more efficient the dishwasher. EF is the energy performance metric of both the federal standard and the ENERGY STAR program. The federal EnergyGuide label on dishwashers shows the annual energy consumption and cost. These figures use the energy factor, average cycles per year, and the average cost of energy to make the energy and cost estimates. The EF may not appear on the EnergyGuide label.

ENERGY STAR labeled dishwashers are at least 41% more energy efficient than those that meet the minimum federal government standards, as shown in **Table 3**.

Clothes Washers

The performance of clothes washers is compared using two metrics. One, the modified energy factor (MEF), has replaced EF for clothes washers; the higher the MEF, the more efficient the appliance.

The second metric is the water factor (WF), the number of gallons per cycle per cubic foot that the clothes washer uses; the lower the WF, the more efficient the washer. For example, if a clothes washer uses 30 gallons per cycle and has a tub volume of 3 cubic feet, the water factor is 10.

The ENERGY STAR criteria for clothes washers changed on January 1, 2007, as shown in **Table 4**. The new ENERGY STAR criteria require all qualified products to have an MEF of 1.72 or more, as well as a WF of 8.0 or less.

Most full-sized ENERGY STAR qualified washers use 18–25 gallons of water per load, compared with the 40 gallons used by a standard machine.

Calculations

No calculations are needed for this credit.

Verification and Submittals

Supporting Verification Materials, made available by the Project Team:

❑ Present any equipment literature related to the appliances (e.g., user manuals, brochures, specifications) to the Verification Team.

Table 3. ENERGY STAR Criteria for Dishwashers

	Federal EnergyGuide energy factor	ENERGY STAR energy factor
Standard (≥ 8 place settings + 6 serving pieces)	≥ 0.46	≥ 0.65
Compact (< 8 place settings + 6 serving pieces)	≥ 0.62	≥ 0.88

Table 4. ENERGY STAR Criteria for Clothes Washers

Type	Criteria before January 1, 2007	Criteria as of January 1, 2007
ENERGY STAR, top and front loading	MEF ≥ 1.42	MEF ≥ 1.72 WF ≤ 8.0
Federal standard, top and front loading	MEF ≥ 1.04	MEF ≥ 1.26

❑ Include appliance literature in the occupant's operations and maintenance manual.

Verification Team:

❑ Visually verify (using equipment literature, labels, etc.) the type of equipment installed and its efficiency.

Exemplary Performance

The energy models that are used for the performance pathway (EA 1) do not recognize the benefits of water-efficient clothes washers. A project using the performance pathway can earn exemplary performance points for meeting the requirements in EA 9.1 and 9.2 for clothes washers (1.5 points total).

Considerations

Economic Issues

Not all new homes are sold with the appliances installed. These credits are available only if the home includes the appliances. In some cases, washers and dryers are offered as options to new home buyers. By keeping margins on these ENERGY STAR labeled appliances at a reasonable level, builders can encourage homebuyers to purchase these optional appliances.

Resources

Web Sites

ENERGY STAR Qualified Appliances

U.S. Environmental Protection Agency ENERGY STAR® Program

www.energystar.gov/index.cfm?c=appliances.pr_appliances

This ENERGY STAR site includes links to lists of qualified dishwashers, clothes washers, refrigerators, and freezers, along with product and store locators, purchasing guides, and information about rebates and other incentive programs.

ENERGY STAR Qualified Ceiling Fans

U.S. Environmental Protection Agency ENERGY STAR® Program

www.energystar.gov/index.cfm?c=ceiling_fans.pr_ceiling_fans

This ENERGY STAR site includes links to lists of qualified ceiling fans, along with product and store locators, purchasing guides, and product selection.

Residential Dishwashers and High Efficiency Clothes Washers

California Urban Water Conservation Council

www.cuwcc.org/residential_dishwashers.lasso

www.cuwcc.org/efficient_clothes_washers.lasso

These sites provide detailed background information on their respective appliances, covering efficiency in both energy and water use, along with links to qualified products and product manufacturers, government studies, and appliance rebates in California.

EA 10: Renewable Energy

Intent

Reduce consumption of nonrenewable energy sources by encouraging the installation and operation of renewable electric generation systems.

Requirements

Prerequisites

None.

Credits

10 **Renewable Energy System** (maximum 10 points). Design and install a renewable electricity generation system. Use energy modeling to estimate both the energy supplied by the renewable energy system and the annual reference electrical load. Receive 1 point for every 3% of the annual reference electrical load met by the system.

Annual reference electric load is defined as the amount of electricity that a typical home (e.g., the HERS Reference Home) would consume in a typical year. The annual reference electric load must be determined using the procedures specified in the 2006 Mortgage Industry National Home Energy Rating Standards (HERS) Guidelines.

For example,

Annual reference electric load
= 10,000 KWh

Annual electricity consumption in LEED home
= 7,000 KWh

Annual electricity supplied by renewable energy system
= 1,800 KWh

Percentage of annual reference electric load supplied by renewable energy system
= 1,800 / 10,000

= 18.0%

LEED points, under EA 10
= 18.0 ÷ 3 = 6.0 points

Synergies and Trade-Offs

A project receiving points for EA 1 is not eligible for this credit, and vice versa. A project pursuing this credit must follow the prescriptive pathway and meet all of the prerequisites in EA 2–10. Prerequisite EA 1.1 should be skipped. See the pathway schematic at the beginning of the EA section.

Passive solar designs must be modeled and can take credit using the approach laid out in EA 1.

Solar hot water heating systems are rewarded in EA 7.3.

EA 10: Renewable Energy System

Several promising technologies are available for on-site generation of electricity from renewable energy sources, including wind and solar power. Such systems are becoming increasingly cost-competitive as fuel prices rise. In some areas, utility rebates and other incentives are available, reducing the payback period. They also substantially reduce the amount of greenhouse gases generated over the life of the renewable energy system (approximately 20 to 30 years).

This credit rewards the installation of renewable electricity generation systems that meet substantial portions of a home's annual electrical load, thereby reducing the consumption of nonrenewable energy sources.

Approach and Implementation

Renewable energy systems should bring an already efficiently designed home to a lower level of net energy use. Renewable energy should be a complement, not an alternative, to traditional energy-efficiency measures.

The renewable energy contractor should work with the qualified energy rater to design a system that meets the base energy load for the designed home. Installing a system to meet peak energy demand is not typically economical. The estimated energy output of the system should be based on models that reflect local conditions (e.g., solar radiation, wind).

Many types of renewable energy systems are available, including technologies that capture solar, wind, geothermal, water, or biomass energy to satisfy on-site electric power demand, and technologies that directly offset space heating, space cooling, or water heating energy consumption.

This credit category applies only to renewable electricity generation systems that produce electric power for use on-site. Photovoltaic, wind, microhydro, and biofuel-based systems are eligible for this credit.

Design the system to facilitate net metering back to the grid for periods when output exceeds the on-site demand. Make the home as energy efficient as possible to minimize the size (and initial cost) of the renewable energy system required.

The following other types of renewable energy systems are ineligible for EA 10; they are addressed in other credits:

❑ Architectural features. Architectural passive solar strategies provide significant energy savings that are chiefly efficiency related. Their contributions are eligible under EA 1.

❑ Geo-exchange systems (geothermal or ground-source heat pumps). Earth-coupled HVAC applications that do not obtain significant quantities of deep-earth heat or that use vapor-compression systems for heat transfer are not eligible. These systems are addressed in EA 6.

❑ Solar domestic water heating systems. Active solar domestic water heating systems that employ collection panels and a defined heat storage system, such as a hot water tank, are not eligible for this credit. These are addressed in EA 7.

❑ "Green power." Green power products (tradable renewable certificates, green TAGs, and renewable energy certificates) that are purchased from qualified contractual sources and delivered to the site via electric transmission lines are not builder-driven activities and hence are not explicitly included in the Rating System. Green power options should be addressed in the occupant's operations and maintenance manual.

Calculations

The number of points earned is not based on a traditional calculation of percentage of energy demand met by the system. Instead, for the sake of consistency with the performance pathway and the HERS methodology, points are earned by comparing the renewable energy output (kWh) with the energy demand in a hypothetical reference home.

This calculation requires four steps:

Step 1. Have the renewable energy contractor estimate the annual electricity output of the system.

Step 2. Have the qualified energy rater or Verification Team model the annual electricity demand of a HERS reference home.

Step 3. Calculate the percentage of the annual reference electric load that is met by the renewable energy system.

Step 4. Calculate the number of LEED points earned, where 1 point is awarded for every 3% of the annual reference electric load that is met by the renewable energy system.

A sample calculation is provided above.

Verification and Submittals

Supporting Verification Materials, made available by the Project Team:

❑ Present any equipment literature related to the renewable energy system (e.g., user manuals, brochures, specifications) to the Verification Team.

❑ Present calculations and/or modeling results to the Verification Team demonstrating the percentage of annual reference electric load being met by the renewable energy system.

❑ Include equipment literature in the occupant's operations and maintenance manual.

Verification Team:

❑ Visually verify the renewable energy system on-site.

❑ Visually verify that the calculations meet the requirements.

❑ Verify that an Accountability Form has been signed by the responsible party.

Exemplary Performance

No additional points are available for exemplary performance. Projects that exceed the credit requirements are encouraged to use the performance pathway in EA 1.2.

Considerations

Economic Issues

Use of on-site renewable energy technologies can reduce occupants' utility bills, particularly if peak-hour demand charges are high. Rising electricity costs make the additional up-front system expense more palatable and reduce the payback period. Utility rebates are often available to reduce first costs of renewable energy equipment. In some states, first costs can be offset by net metering, whereby excess electricity is sold back to the utility.

The reliability and lifetime of photovoltaic systems are also improving. Manufacturers typically guarantee their systems for up to 20 years.

Environmental Issues

Use of renewable energy reduces environmental impacts associated with utility energy production and use. These effects include natural resource destruction, air pollution, and water pollution. Reduced use of fossil fuel reduces emissions of air

ID	LL	SS	WE	EA	MR	EQ	AE
				10			

pollutants like carbon dioxide, nitrogen oxides, and sulfur dioxide.

Regional Variances

Three regional issues can significantly affect the suitability of renewable electricity generation systems: regional variations in the potential of solar or wind energy, regional electricity prices, and the availability of government and utility rebates. Investigate each factor before deciding whether to use a renewable energy system, and if so, how large a system to invest in.

Resources

Web Sites

American Solar Energy Society

www.ases.org

ASES is a nonprofit organization committed to a sustainable energy economy. ASES accelerates the development and use of solar and other renewable energy resources through advocacy, education, research, and collaboration among professionals, policymakers, and the public.

American Wind Energy Association

www.awea.org

AWEA is a national trade association representing wind power plant developers, wind turbine manufacturers, utilities, consultants, insurers, financiers, researchers, and others involved in the wind industry.

Database of State Incentives for Renewable Energy

www.dsireusa.org

The North Carolina Solar Center developed this database to collect information on state financial and regulatory incentives (e.g., tax credits, grants, and special utility rates) designed to promote the application of renewable energy technologies. DSIRE also offers additional features such as preparing and printing reports that detail the incentives on a state-by-state basis.

Florida Solar Energy Center

www.fsec.ucf.edu/en/consumer/solar_electricity/index.htm

An excellent resource for basic information on types of photovoltaic solar electric systems, sizing, installation, and system ratings. FSEC also has an industry resources page that includes its Photovoltaic System Design Course Manual, available at www.fsec.ucf.edu/en/industry/resources/pv/index.htm.

National Center for Photovoltaics

www.nrel.gov/ncpv

NCPV provides a clearinghouse on all aspects of photovoltaic (PV) solar cell systems.

National Renewable Energy Laboratory

www.nrel.gov

The National Renewable Energy Laboratory is a leader in the U.S. Department of Energy's effort to secure an energy future for the nation that is environmentally and economically sustainable.

Office of Energy Efficiency and Renewable Energy

U.S. Department of Energy

www.eere.energy.gov

The EERE Web site includes information on all types of renewable energy technologies and energy efficiency.

Print Media

Wind and Solar Power Systems, by Mukund Patel. CRC Press, 1999. This text offers information about the fundamental elements of wind and solar power generation, conversion, and storage, and about the design, operation, and control methods of both stand-alone and grid-connected systems.

Wind Energy Comes of Age, by Paul Gipe. John Wiley & Sons, 1995. This book provides extensive information on the wind power industry and is one of several books by the author covering general and technical information about wind power.

Guide to Photovoltaic (PV) System Design And Installation. California Energy Commission, 2001.

EA 11: Residential Refrigerant Management

Intent

Select and test air-conditioning refrigerant to ensure performance and minimize contributions to ozone depletion and global warming.

Requirements

Prerequisites

11.1 **Refrigerant Charge Test.** Provide proof of proper refrigerant charge of the air-conditioning system (unless home has no mechanical cooling system).

Credits

11.2 **Appropriate HVAC Refrigerants** (1 point). Do one of the following:

a) Do not use refrigerants.

b) Install an HVAC system with non-HCFC refrigerant (e.g., R-410a).

c) Install an HVAC system with a refrigerant that complies with the following equation. (See **Table 1** for examples of the equation applied to R410a used in different system sizes.)

$$LCGWP + LCODP \times 10^5 \leq 160$$

where

$$LCODP = [ODPr \times (Lr \times Life + Mr) \times Rc]/Life$$

$$LCGWP = [GWPr \times (Lr \times Life + Mr) \times Rc]/Life$$

LCODP = Lifecycle Ozone Depletion Potential (lb CFC11/ton-year)

LCGWP = Lifecycle Direct Global Warming Potential (lb CO_2/ton-year)

GWPr = Global Warming Potential of Refrigerant (0–12,000 lb CO_2/lbr)

ODPr = Ozone Depletion Potential of Refrigerant (0–0.2 lb CFC11/lbr)

Lr = Refrigerant Leakage Rate (0.5–2.0%; default of 2% unless otherwise demonstrated)

Mr = End-of-life Refrigerant Loss (2.0–10%; default of 10% unless otherwise demonstrated)

Rc = Refrigerant Charge (0.50–5.0 lbs of refrigerant per ton of cooling capacity)

Life = Equipment Life (10–35 years; default based on equipment type, unless otherwise demonstrated)

Synergies and Trade-Offs

Efficient air-conditioning systems are covered under EA 6.

This credit is available to every project, whether the performance approach (EA 1) or the prescriptive approach (EA 2–10) is used.

Table 1. Examples of Residential Refrigerants Eligible for EA 11.2

Refrigerant	Combined LCGWP+ LCODP score	System size	Refrigerant charge	Leakage rate	Equipment life
R410a	152	2 tons	3.7 lb/ton	1.5%	15 years
R410a	151	3 tons	3.0 lb/ton	2.0%	15 years
R410a	151	4 tons	3.0 lb/ton	2.0%	15 years
R410a	121	5 tons	3.0 lb/ton	2.0%	15 years

Refrigerant charge is the ratio of refrigerant required (pounds) to cooling capacity provided (tons) by a piece of installed cooling equipment. Field tests of residential cooling systems have shown that many systems have incorrect refrigerant charge levels. Data from one of these studies indicate that about one-third were undercharged and one-third were overcharged (Proctor 2000). Both undercharge and overcharge can reduce cooling equipment longevity, capacity, and efficiency. An undercharge of as little as 15% can reduce the equipment's total capacity by as much as 20% and the energy efficiency ratio by as much as 15%.

Most refrigerants commonly used in HVAC equipment are stable chemical compounds that, when released to the environment, contribute to deterioration of the earth's protective ozone layer and emit greenhouse gases.

Hydrochlorofluorocarbons (HCFCs, such as R22) have been the refrigerants of choice for residential heat pump and air-conditioning systems for more than four decades. Unfortunately for the environment, releases of HCFCs from system leaks contribute to ozone depletion and global warming.

Beginning in 2010, chemical manufacturers may produce HCFCs only for servicing existing equipment. Thereafter, HCFCs cannot be manufactured for use in new equipment.

This credit requires testing of the refrigerant charge and encourages the early selection of non-HCFC refrigerants in HVAC equipment.

Approach and Implementation

Standard refrigerant charge test procedures are provided by the California Energy Commission, Appendix RD to Title 24 (see "Resources," below), which outlines two alternative tests. Thermostatic expansion valves (TXVs) provide some relief for systems that may be undercharged. A thermostatic expansion valve controls the amount of refrigerant entering the evaporator coils. However, even HVAC systems with a TXV must have a refrigerant charge test to satisfy the prerequisite, EA 11.1.

Split systems, including those that are pre-charged, must have a refrigerant charge test to satisfy EA 11.1. This prerequisite is satisfied automatically by ground-source heat pumps that are pre-charged and sealed.

The easiest way to earn a point under EA 11.2 is not to use refrigerants. LEED projects that do not use refrigerants are automatically awarded this credit—no calculations or analysis required. Examples include a naturally ventilated building with no active cooling system (and therefore no refrigerants) and a green building design that eliminates the need for vapor-compression HVAC and refrigeration equipment.

Where mechanical cooling is used, install an HVAC system with non-HCFC refrigerant (e.g., R410a). Design HVAC equipment such that the unit has the smallest possible refrigerant charge. Locate the evaporator and the condenser close together to reduce the potential for leakage. Select equipment with an efficient refrigerant charge.

Provide guidance to help the occupant maintain equipment to prevent leakage of refrigerant to the atmosphere. Manufacturers may offer leakage rate guarantees for certain types of major HVAC and refrigeration equipment (such as chillers) as part of a long-term service contract.

If the home has an HVAC system that uses a refrigerant other than R410a, complete the required calculation. **Table 2** shows the ozone depletion potential and direct global warming potential of many common refrigerants (some used only in nonresidential applications). In accordance with the Montreal Protocol, all chlorinated refrigerants, including CFCs and HCFCs, will be phased out by 2030. In the meantime, the choice of an appropriate refrigerant for any given project and HVAC system may be constrained by available equipment, energy efficiency, budget, and other factors. Where options are available, select refrigerants with no or very little ozone depletion potential and minimal global warming potential.

Minimize refrigerant leakage. Refrigerants cannot damage the atmosphere if they are contained and never released to the environment. Unfortunately, in real-world applications, some or all of the refrigerant in HVAC equipment is leaked during installation, operation, servicing, and/or decommissioning.

Although this credit concerns refrigerants used in HVAC equipment, other types of home appliances have refrigerants as well, including refrigerators, freezers, and wine coolers. Consider using ozone-friendly refrigerants for these types of appliances.

Calculations

No calculations are needed for this credit if R410a is used. Otherwise, use the equation to determine whether the selected HVAC refrigerant qualifies.

Table 2. Environmental Effects of Common HVAC Refrigerants (100-year values)

Refrigerant	Ozone depletion potential	Global warming potential	Common applications
Chlorofluorocarbons			
CFC-11	1.0	4,680	Centrifugal chillers
CFC-12	1.0	10,720	Refrigerators, chillers
CFC-114	0.94	9,800	Centrifugal chillers
CFC-500	0.605	7,900	Centrifugal chillers, humidifiers
CFC-502	0.221	4,600	Low-temperature refrigeration
Hydrochlorofluorocarbons			
HCFC-22	0.04	1,780	Air-conditioning, chillers
HCFC-123	0.02	76	CFC-11 replacement
Hydrofluorocarbons			
HFC-23	~ 0	12,240	Ultra-low-temperature refrigeration
HFC-134a	~ 0	1,320	CFC-12 or HCFC-22 replacement
HFC-245fa	~ 0	1,020	Insulation agent, centrifugal chillers
HFC-404A	~ 0	3,900	Low-temperature refrigeration
HFC-407C	~ 0	1,700	HCFC-22 replacement
HFC-410A	~ 0	1,890	Air-conditioning
HFC-507A	~ 0	3,900	Low-temperature refrigeration
Natural refrigerants			
Carbon dioxide (CO_2)	0	1.0	
Ammonia (NH_3)	0	0	
Propane	0	3	

Verification and Submittals

Supporting Verification Materials, made available by the Project Team:

EA 11.1 Refrigerant Charge Test

❑ Present the refrigerant charge test results to the Verification Team.

EA 11.2 Appropriate HVAC Refrigerants

❑ For (b) and (c), present information related to the type of refrigerant (e.g., cooling system user manuals, brochures, specifications) to the Verification Team.

Verification Team:

EA 11.1 Refrigerant Charge Test

❑ Visually verify the refrigerant charge test results according to the Verification and Submittal Guidelines..

EA 11.2 Appropriate HVAC Refrigerants

❑ For (b) and (c), visually verify (using cooling system manuals, specifications, etc.) the type of refrigerant used.

Exemplary Performance

No additional points are available for exemplary performance.

Considerations

Environmental Issues

The LEED Technical and Science Advisory Committee makes the following observation:

An objective scientific analysis of trade-offs between global warming and ozone depletion is extremely complex and will only come from a full understanding of all interacting pathways and the effects on economic activities, human health and terrestrial and oceanic ecosystems.

Any quantitative credit scheme addressing both must involve some subjectivity in the relative weight given to each issue.

Proper management can minimize the negative effects of refrigerant use on ozone depletion and global warming. Strategies include designing homes that do not rely on chemical refrigerants, choosing equipment that uses energy efficiently, selecting refrigerants with zero or low ozone depletion potential and minimal direct global warming potential, and maintaining equipment to reduce refrigerant leakage.

Regional Variances

The availability of HVAC equipment that uses R410a may vary, depending on local demand. If your local suppliers do not stock this type of equipment, go to their national wholesale suppliers.

Resources

Web Sites

California Energy Commission, Title 24

ACM RESIDENTIAL MANUAL APPENDIX RD-2005, Procedures for Determining Refrigerant Charge for Split System Space Cooling Systems without Thermostatic Expansion Valves.

www.energy.ca.gov/title24/2005standards/residential_acm/2005_RES_ACM_APP_RD.PDF

Appendix RD-2005 defines two procedures, the Standard Charge Measurement Procedure in Section RD2 and the Alternate Charge Measurement Procedure in Section RD3.

EPA's Significant New Alternatives Policy

U.S. Environmental Protection Agency

www.epa.gov/ozone/snap/index.html

SNAP is an EPA program to identify alternatives to ozone-depleting substances.

The program maintains up-to-date lists of environmentally friendly substitutes for refrigeration and air-conditioning equipment, solvents, fire suppression systems, adhesives, coatings, and other substances.

What You Should Know about Refrigerants When Purchasing or Repairing a Residential A/C System or Heat Pump

U.S. Environmental Protection Agency

www.epa.gov/ozone/title6/
phaseout/22phaseout.html

This EPA Web site discusses the background on the phaseout of banned refrigerants, approved alternatives, system servicing requirements, and purchasing recommendations.

Print Media

"Field Measurements of New Residential Air Conditioners in Phoenix, Arizona," by J. Proctor. *ASHRAE Transactions* 103(1): 406–15, 1997.

"Monitored In-Situ Performance of Residential Air-Conditioning Systems," by J. Proctor. *ASHRAE Transactions* 104(1): 1833–40, 1998.

The Treatment by LEED of the Environmental Impact of HVAC Refrigerants

U.S. Green Building Council, 2004.

(202) 82-USGBC

www.usgbc.org/Docs/LEED_tsac/
TSAC_Refrig_Report_Final-Approved.
pdf

This report was prepared under the auspices of the U.S. Green Building Council's LEED Technical and Scientific Advisory Committee (TSAC), in response to a charge given TSAC by the LEED Steering Committee to review the atmospheric environmental impacts arising from the use of halocarbons as refrigerants in building HVAC equipment.

CFCs, HCFC and Halons: Professional and Practical Guidance on Substances that Deplete the Ozone Layer. CIBSE, 2000.

This booklet provides background information on the environmental issues associated with CFCs, HCFCs, and halons, design guidance, and strategies for refrigerant containment and leak detection.

Materials & Resources

The choice of building materials is important for sustainable homebuilding because of the extraction, processing, and transportation they require. Activities to produce building materials may pollute the air and water, destroy natural habitats, and deplete natural resources. Construction and demolition wastes constitute about 40% of the total solid waste stream in the United States.

Good design decisions, particularly in the framing of homes, can significantly reduce demand for framing materials, as well as the associated waste and embedded energy. Without even changing the home design, a builder can save framing materials and reduce site waste by planning appropriately and communicating the design to the framing team through detailed framing documents and/or scopes of work.

Sources should be evaluated when materials are selected for a project. Reclaimed (i.e., salvaged postconsumer) materials can be substituted for new materials, saving costs and reducing resource use. Recycled-content materials make use of material that would otherwise be deposited in landfills. Use of local materials supports the local economy and reduces the harmful impacts of long-distance transport. Use of third-party–certified wood promotes good stewardship of forests and related ecosystems. Use of low-emitting materials will improve the indoor air quality in the home and reduce demand for materials with volatile toxic compounds.

An increasing number of public and private waste management operations have reduced construction debris volumes by recycling these materials. Recovery activities typically begin at the job site, with separation into multiple bins or disposal areas. In some areas, regional recycling facilities accept commingled waste and separate the recyclable materials from those that must go to the landfill. These facilities can achieve waste diversion rates of 80% or greater.

The Materials & Resources (MR) category in the LEED for Homes Rating System has three components—Material-Efficient Framing, Environmentally Preferable Products, and Waste Management—which are summarized in **Table 1** and described in the following sections.

Table 1. Overview of Materials & Resources (MR) Category

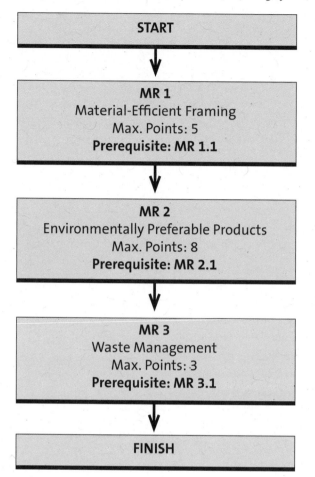

START

MR 1
Material-Efficient Framing
Max. Points: 5
Prerequisite: MR 1.1

MR 2
Environmentally Preferable Products
Max. Points: 8
Prerequisite: MR 2.1

MR 3
Waste Management
Max. Points: 3
Prerequisite: MR 3.1

FINISH

IMPORTANT NOTE:
*A minimum of **2 points** must be achieved in the MR category.*

MR 1: Material-Efficient Framing

Intent

Optimize the use of framing materials.

Requirements

Prerequisites

1.1 **Framing Order Waste Factor Limit.** Limit the overall estimated waste factor to 10% or less. If the waste factor on any portion of the framing order exceeds 10%, calculate the overall waste factor as shown in **Table 1**.

Waste factor is defined as the percentage of framing material ordered in excess of the estimated material needed for construction.

Table 1. Sample Framing Order Waste Factor Calculation

Framing component	Total cost	Waste factor	Waste cost
Random lengths	$1,000	15%	$150
Studs	$2,000	5%	$100
Beams and headers	$500	20%	$100
Roof deck	$2,000	0%	$0
Wall sheathing	$0	0%	$0
Rafters	$2,000	0%	$0
Ceiling joists	$1,500	10%	$150
Cornice work	$3,000	10%	$300
TOTAL	**$12,000**		**$1,000**
Overall waste factor (waste $ / cost $)			**8.3%**

Credits

1.2 **Detailed Framing Documents** (1 point). Prior to construction, create detailed framing plans or scopes of work and accompanying architectural details for use on the job site. Indicate the specific locations, spacing, and sizes of all framing members in the floors, walls, roof, and ceiling (if different from the roof).

1.3 **Detailed Cut List and Lumber Order** (1 point). The requirements in MR 1.2 must be met to earn this credit. Prior to construction, create a detailed cut list and lumber order that corresponds directly to the framing plans and/ or scopes of work.

AND/OR

1.4 **Framing Efficiencies** (maximum 3 points). Implement measures from **Table 2**.

OR

1.5 **Off-Site Fabrication** (4 points). Use either of the following alternatives to on-site framing:

a) Panelized construction. Wall, roof, and floor components are delivered to the job site preframed.

b) Modular, prefabricated construction. All principal building sections are delivered to the job site as prefabricated modules.

Table 2. Efficient Framing Measures

Measure	Points
Precut framing packages	1.0
Open-web floor trusses	1.0
Structural insulated panel (SIP) walls	1.0
SIP roof	1.0
SIP floors	1.0
Stud spacing greater than 16" o.c.	1.0
Ceiling joist spacing greater than 16" o.c.	0.5
Floor joist spacing greater than 16" o.c.	0.5
Roof rafter spacing greater than 16" o.c.	0.5
Implement any two of the following: ■ Size headers for actual loads ■ Use ladder blocking or drywall clips ■ Use 2-stud corners	0.5

Note: Alternative measures not listed in Table 2 may be eligible to earn points if they save comparable amounts of framing material. A formal credit interpretation request with full justification of any alternative measure's potential savings must be submitted by the Provider to USGBC.

Synergies and Trade-Offs

Reduced framing can reduce the number and size of thermal breaks and increase the amount of insulation installed, leading to better energy performance (EA 1 and 2).

Credit MR 1.2 is a prerequisite for MR 1.3. A home that earns points for MR 1.2, 1.3, and 1.4 cannot earn points for MR 1.5, and vice versa.

Optimizing the use of framing will reduce the amount of construction waste (MR 3.2).

When builders overestimate the amount of wood needed for framing, much of this wood ends up either going to a landfill or being unnecessarily incorporated into the house framing. According to one study of U.S. homebuilding, roughly one-sixth of the wood that was delivered to the building site ended up going to a landfill.[1] This wood represents wasted material, wasted energy, and an unnecessary waste management burden. Extra wood that is not sent to landfill is often needlessly incorporated into the framing of the home, resulting in thermal breaks, compacted insulation, and poor thermal performance for the envelope.

This prerequisite requires that all LEED for Homes projects have framing orders with less than a 10% waste factor.

Approach and Implementation

Work with architects, engineers, and/or framers to create an accurate estimate of the amount of lumber needed, taking into account the home design and any advanced framing measures being incorporated. Best practice is to create a detailed framing order and cut list, as per MR 1.2 and 1.3.

Order only as much framing lumber as the estimate calls for. Builders often assume that additional lumber may be needed because of mistakes in the field, loss, or theft, and they incorporate this anticipated waste into the framing order. Some builders purchase additional lumber in anticipation of using any leftover wood on future projects.

If theft is a concern, an alternative approach to meeting this prerequisite is to purchase less framing lumber than the home is expected to require and then purchase additional lumber as needed. This approach encourages conservation during construction and also saves lumber if the initial estimate was high.

The prerequisite does not require an audit of actual lumber use on the site, but efficient framing will reduce the amount of waste sent to landfill (see MR 3.2). Store lumber on level blocking and under cover to minimize warping and damage. Damaged wood is often wasted or requires reinforcement.

If panelized or prefabricated components are used (MR 1.5), order only as many modules as needed, cut to the requirements of the home. In this case, the framing waste factor is zero and the prerequisite is met.

Calculations

Waste factor is defined as the percentage of material purchased for a project that is planned to be waste.

Waste Factor = (Lumber Ordered – Lumber Needed) ÷ Lumber Needed

The waste factor can be calculated based on total material (board feet of wood) or total cost. Individual framing components may exceed 10% waste, but the overall waste factor must be less than 10%. A sample calculation is provided in **Table 2**.

Postconstruction calculations of actual framing waste are not required, except as part of the total waste management assessment for MR 3.1.

Exemplary Performance

No additional points are available for exemplary performance.

---

1 NRDC, "Efficient Wood Use in Residential Construction", 1998.

ID	LL	SS	WE	EA	MR	EQ	AE
			1.1				

Verification and Submittals

Supporting Verification Materials, made available by the Project Team:

❑ Present calculations for the framing waste factor to the Verification Team.

Verification Team:

❑ Visually verify that all calculations related to the framing waste factor have been completed.

Projects with a precut framing package (e.g. modular homes, kit homes) are awarded MR 1.2 and MR 1.3 automatically. Projects with non-wood frames can earn MR 1.2 and MR 1.3 if the requirements are met for the relevant structural material. For gut-rehab projects, if 90% of the interior and exterior framing for the final LEED home (i.e., not the original home) is salvaged or maintained, both MR 1.2 and MR 1.3 should be awarded automatically.

Considerations

Environmental Issues

Unless the wood being used for framing is reclaimed, recycled, or sustainably grown and harvested (see MR 2.2), the use of excess lumber in residential construction will contribute to deforestation and its associated environmental impacts.

Economic Issues

Reducing the demand for construction material through improved planning and design can save considerable money through reduced framing costs and, indirectly, reducing waste-hauling costs. Good framing practices can also save the occupants heating and cooling costs by improving the thermal performance of the envelope.

Resources

Please see the USGBC Web site, at www.usgbc.org/resources, for more specific resources on materials sources and other technical information.

Web Sites

Building America Best Practice Handbooks

www.eere.energy.gov/buildings/building_america

This site includes links to the Best Practice Handbooks, which include detailed information about design and construction practices following building science principles. There are five climate-specific volumes, all available for free download.

Print Media

Efficient Wood Use in Residential Construction. Natural Resources Defense Council, 1998. This NRDC handbook describes the advantages of several wood-efficient approaches to design, material selection, and construction for residential applications and includes extensive practical and resource information for builders, architects, engineers, and developers. It may be purchased online, at www.nrdc.org/cities/building/rwoodus.asp.

MR 1.2: Detailed Framing Documents

MR 1.3: Detailed Cut List and Lumber Order

A major challenge in new home construction is determining the amount of framing materials needed for a project. Often the amount of lumber ordered greatly exceeds what is actually needed. A detailed assessment of framing requirements will help prevent this waste.

This credit rewards projects that explicitly document exactly where framing materials are to be used and their related dimensions, thereby minimizing the potential for overestimating a framing lumber order. Indirectly, this may also help minimize overall construction waste.

MR 1.2 rewards projects with detailed framing documents (i.e., detailed drawings of framing layouts for all walls, floors, and roofs). These documents are a critical tool for ensuring that the efficient framing strategies in the design of the home are actually adopted during construction. Detailed framing documents give site managers specific direction about where and how framing members should be utilized.

MR 1.3 rewards projects with a detailed cut list that corresponds to the detailed framing documents. The detailed cut list makes it possible to order lumber accordingly, thus bringing onto the site only the lumber that is needed.

Approach and Implementation

Produce detailed framing documents by collaborating with the architect and HVAC engineer. These documents must be produced prior to construction and provide specific direction for the location, spacing, and sizing of all framing members.

Ensure that the HVAC engineer uses the plans provided by the architect to design the basic system layout. Detailed HVAC load analyses should inform the size and lengths of duct runs, which should in turn be used by the architect to improve the framing layout. Such an integrated approach reduces ad hoc design changes that lead to waste or performance problems (e.g., crushed ducts).

Incorporate any and all advanced framing measures in the detailed framing documents (MR 1.4) and use them to create a detailed cut list and lumber order (MR 1.3).

Provide detailed framing documents to the site manager. Train the framing crew in advance and provide supervision during construction.

In the detailed framing documents, include the following:

- ❑ Floor framing plan(s) to show the specific location and sizes of all floor framing members.

- ❑ Exterior wall framing elevations shown laid down adjacent to floor (or floor framing) plans, with the specific location and sizes of all wall framing members, including studs, headers, cripples, and blocking.

- ❑ Interior wall framing elevations keyed to floor (or floor framing) plans, showing the specific location and sizes of all wall framing members, including studs, headers, cripples, and blocking.

- ❑ Roof framing plan with specific locations and sizes of all roof framing members.

- ❑ Ceiling framing plan (if different from roof) with specific locations and sizes of all ceiling framing members.

Substitutes for those plans may be thorough scopes of work and architectural details. If using scopes of work, the directions must be clear, specific, and usable by the site manager and framing crew.

Develop framing plans through an integrated, iterative process that includes the architect, HVAC engineer, plumber, and other team members as appropriate.

Credit for the detailed cut list and framing order (MR 1.3) can be earned only if detailed framing documents or scopes of work are produced (MR 1.2). The cut list must correspond directly to the detailed framing documents, and the framing order must correspond directly to the cut list. The cut list should include a tabulation of every framing member shown in the framing plans, according to the nominal cross-section (2x4, 2x6, etc.) and length.

Provide the site manager and framing crew with training in using the precut framing lumber with the detailed framing documents. Clarify that precut framing members correspond to certain parts of the frame, as per the framing documents.

Calculations

No calculations are required.

Exemplary Performance

No additional points are available for exemplary performance.

Verification and Submittals

Supporting Verification Materials, made available by the Project Team:

MR 1.2: Detailed Framing Documents

❑ Provide detailed framing plans and/or scopes of work to the Verification Team.

MR 1.3: Detailed Cut List and Lumber Order

❑ Provide detailed framing cut list and lumber order to the Verification Team.

Verification Team:

MR 1.2: Detailed Framing Documents

❑ Visually verify detailed framing plans and/or scopes of work.

MR 1.3: Detailed Cut List and Lumber Order

❑ Visually verify detailed framing cut list and lumber order.

Considerations

Environmental Issues

The proper use of detailed framing documents can minimize the waste of excess lumber, the associated burden on landfills, and contributions to deforestation and other negative environmental impacts.

Economic Issues

The cost of producing detailed framing documents will vary with the type of builder and project (e.g., custom vs. production). Detailed framing documents can be costly to produce the first time but can be reused or modified for future projects. The proper use of detailed framing documents can significantly reduce the cost of lumber and waste hauling on a project.

The cost of producing a detailed cut list and detailed lumber order is moderate, as is the additional cost of custom lumber orders. These costs will also vary with the type of builder and project (e.g., custom, production, affordable).

Having each piece of lumber cut according to the needs of the framing plans can reduce the costs for framing lumber, minimize waste hauling costs, and also reduce the time and labor required to frame the home.

Resources

Please see the USGBC Web site, at www.usgbc.org/resources, for more specific resources on materials sources and other technical information.

Web Sites

Building America Best Practice Handbooks

www.eere.energy.gov/buildings/building_america

This site includes links to the Best Practice Handbooks, which include detailed information about design and construction practices following building science principles. There are five climate-specific volumes, all available for free download.

Print Media

Efficient Wood Use in Residential Construction. Natural Resources Defense Council, 1998. This NRDC handbook describes the advantages of several wood-efficient approaches to design, material selection, and construction for residential applications and includes extensive practical and resource information for builders, architects, engineers, and developers. It may be purchased online, at www.nrdc.org/cities/building/rwoodus.asp.

MR 1.4: Framing Efficiencies

Conventional framing techniques use about 15% to 20% more framing material than is structurally needed. This credit focuses on wood framing because approximately 90% of U.S. housing stock is wood-framed.

Efficient framing measures can be easily incorporated into the home design, providing the necessary structural support with much less framing material. Decisions about efficient framing strategies should be made early in the design process so that they can be included in any detailed framing plans (MR 1.2) and reflected in framing cut lists and lumber orders (MR 1.3). Multiple framing strategies can be used together to maximize savings.

Although efficient framing practices may indirectly reduce the amount of construction waste from a project, that issue is addressed in MR 3.

This credit rewards builders who purchase and use less lumber by implementing efficient (or advanced) framing practices.

The requirements of MR 1.4 only apply to exterior framing, although material-efficient framing techniques are strongly encouraged for interior framing.

Approach and Implementation

Include framing considerations in the design of the home. Where possible, design the home in 2-foot modules, to correspond with stud spacing and typical sheathing, drywall, and lumber dimensions. Design the framing so that floor, wall, and roof framing members are vertically aligned to ensure optimal load bearing.

Advanced framing techniques can in some cases affect the installation of ductwork, piping, electrical, and insulation. Include all relevant trades in the advanced framing decisions (Innovation in Design 1.2). Show them how advanced framing strategies can improve insulation and shorten ductwork and pipe runs.

Framing crews may hesitate to increase spacing in studs, joists, and rafters or use less lumber for headers, corners, and blocking. Employ framing crews familiar with these technologies or train them prior to construction.

Use precut framing packages and open-web floor trusses. These assembled components, available from various manufacturers, can be integrated into an otherwise conventional framing design. A builder can choose only the structural components or obtain a nearly complete home with windows, doors, and siding.

Use structural insulated panels (SIPs) for walls, roof, or floors. These engineered, factory-produced, load-bearing components consist of polystyrene foam in a metal frame or bonded to oriented-strand board with structural adhesives similar to those used for other engineered wood products. SIPs give strength and stiffness to a structure and facilitate longer clear spans than can be achieved with conventional framing. SIPs provide superior and uniform insulation compared with more traditional construction methods (stud or "stick frame") and can generate energy savings of 12% to 14%.

Space studs, ceiling joists, floor joists, and roof rafters at greater than 16 inches on center. 24-inch spacing may require use of 2x6 instead of 2x4 studs but reduces the amount of framing lumber needed in a typical home. It will also enable more efficient use of sheathing and drywall sheets and allow for greater insulation.

Implement two of the following three

design strategies to earn ½ point:

1. Size headers for actual loads, eliminating headers in nonload-bearing walls where possible.

2. Use ladder blocking or drywall clips.

3. Use two-stud corners.

Calculations

No calculations are required.

Partial Credit

If the requirements are met in only 50% of the walls (by area), half credit can be awarded.

Exemplary Performance

Projects that install measures from MR 1.4 such that more than 3 points are earned may be awarded exemplary performance points, to be counted under Innovation in Design 3.

Verification and Submittals

Verification Team:

❏ Visually verify the use of advanced framing measures in the home.

Considerations

Environmental Issues

Efficient framing measures reduce the demand for framing materials and significantly reduce landfill waste. Advanced framing measures can also reduce thermal bridging, enable better insulation installation, and reduce energy usage for space heating and cooling.

Economic Issues

Incorporating advanced framing techniques into the design and training contractors in these techniques may increase costs for the first home. However, these practices can save hundreds or even thou-

sands of dollars once designs have been refined and crews are familiar with them. SIP costs are at the high end, but design changes such as using two-stud corners cost almost nothing.

Overall, these techniques reduce lumber, labor, and shipping costs and potentially save on tipping fees.

Using efficient framing techniques can reduce cut-off waste from standard-sized building material. The use of 2x6s at 24-inch-on-center wall studs and exterior load-bearing walls and the reduction in the number of studs in building corners improve insulation and lower energy costs.

Higher energy efficiency can result from decreased thermal bridging across structural members, which has a measurable impact on heating and cooling costs.

Regional Variances

Efficient framing measures are generally applicable throughout the country. However, some advanced framing techniques, such as 24-inch-on-center spacing, may be prohibited by code under certain circumstances (e.g., high wind or earthquake zones) or in some localities. Consult local building officials early in the design phase to verify compliance and obtain approval for advanced techniques.

Resources

Please see the USGBC Web site, at www.usgbc.org/resources, for more specific resources on materials sources and other technical information.

Web Sites

Building America Best Practice Handbooks

www.eere.energy.gov/buildings/building_america

This site includes links to the Best Practice Handbooks, which include detailed information about design and construc-

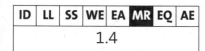

tion practices following building science principles. There are five climate-specific volumes, all available for free download.

Energy & Environmental Building Association, Builders' Guides

www.eeba.org/bookstore

The EEBA Builders' Guides, written by Joe Lstiburek, provide detailed step-by-step guidance on design and construction based on building science and best practice construction techniques. There are four climate-specific guides: hot and humid, cold, mixed humid, and mixed dry.

Toolbase.org, Advanced Framing Techniques

NAHB Research Center

www.toolbase.org/TechInventory

The Technology Inventory includes "Advanced Framing Techniques." This site includes frequently asked questions, case studies and reports, and various links. It also has illustrations that help explain advanced framing techniques.

Print Media

Efficient Wood Use in Residential Construction. Natural Resources Defense Council, 1998. This NRDC handbook describes the advantages of several wood-efficient approaches to design, material selection, and construction for residential applications and includes extensive practical and resource information for builders, architects, engineers, and developers. It may be purchased online, at www.nrdc.org/cities/building/rwoodus.asp.

Advanced Wall Framing. U.S. Department of Energy, Office of Energy Efficiency and Renewable Energy. The "Technology Fact Sheet" includes information and illustrations for advanced framing techniques. Available online, at www.eere.energy.gov/buildings/info/publications.html.

MR 1.5: Off-Site Fabrication

Off-site, prefabricated component construction provides a controlled factory environment that achieves resource efficiencies at the fabrication site and minimizes or even eliminates on-site job waste. This method also ensures a consistent, high-quality product and reduces assembly time and associated costs.

This credit is an alternative to MR 1.2, 1.3, and 1.4.

Approach and Implementation

To achieve this credit, use either of two approaches:

a) Wall, roof, and floor are preframed using panelized construction components.

b) All building sections are delivered to the site as prefabricated modules.

Panelized, or modular, prefabricated homebuilding systems are produced off-site and then delivered by truck to the site for assembly. These systems can include only the structural components of a home or be a nearly completed home with windows, doors, and siding.

Modular or manufactured homes qualify for this credit, to reflect the efficiencies in a production plant. Modular or manufactured homebuilders are encouraged not to reinforce home framing or otherwise overengineer structures, which is a common practice intended to reduce damage during delivery.

Projects that achieve this credit are not eligible for MR 1.2, 1.3, or 1.4. However, modular and manufactured homebuilders are encouraged to use efficient framing measures, such as those listed in MR 1.4.

This credit should only be awarded if the walls, roof, and floor are all fabricated off-site. The credit can alternatively be awarded for the use of panelized walls, roof trusses, and floor trusses throughout the home.

This credit should be awarded to homes that install only pre-cut SIPs in the walls, roof, and floor. If SIPs are cut on-site, or only used in walls and/or the roof, no points should be awarded for this credit; points may be awarded in MR 1.4 instead.

This credit should be awarded to homes with concrete panelized wall systems, if they are formed and poured off-site."

Calculations

No calculations are required.

Exemplary Performance

No additional points are available for exemplary performance.

Verification and Submittals

Verification Team:

❑ Visually verify the use of panelized or modular, prefabricated construction on-site.

Considerations

Economic Issues

Using manufactured components saves time and materials. The slightly higher cost is largely offset by savings from reduced warping, twisting, and shrinking, as well as improved thermal performance and fewer drywall call-backs. Faster job completion can result in lower carrying costs and an opportunity to build more units per year.

Regional Variances

The availability and cost of panelized and prefabricated components vary regionally.

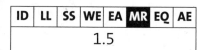
Resources

Please see the USGBC Web site, at www. usgbc.org/resources, for more specific resources on materials sources and other technical information.

Web Sites

Considerations for Contractors Building with Wall Panels

WTCA—Representing the Structural Building Components Industry

www.sbcindustry.com/images/ publication_images/ttbwall.pdf

Based on a comparison study between a stick-frame and component-built house, this report highlights the construction and economic benefits and installation procedures for component-built homes.

National Association of Homebuilders

www.nahb.org/panel

This site contains basic information about panelized construction, as well as a directory of manufacturers.

Manufactured Housing Institute

www.manufacturedhousing.org

This site contains information about manufactured homes, including what they are, how they are built, and how to find a manufacturer. This site also contains links and resources.

MR 2: Environmentally Preferable Products

Intent

Increase demand for environmentally preferable products and products or building components that are extracted, processed, and manufactured within the region.

Requirements

Prerequisites

2.1 **FSC-Certified Tropical Wood.** Meet the following two requirements, as applicable:

a) Provide all wood product suppliers with a notice (see **Figure 1**, below) containing all of the following elements:

  i. a statement that the builder's preference is to purchase products containing tropical wood only if it is FSC-certified;

  ii. a request for the country of manufacture of each product supplied; and

  iii. a request for a list of FSC-certified tropical wood products the vendor can supply.

b) If tropical wood is intentionally used (i.e., specified in purchasing documents), use only FSC-certified tropical wood products. Reused or reclaimed materials are exempt.

Note: A species of wood is considered tropical for the purposes of this prerequisite if it is grown in a country that lies between the Tropics of Cancer and Capricorn.

Credits

2.2 **Environmentally Preferable Products** (0.5 point each, maximum 8 points). Use building component materials that meet one or more of the criteria below. Except as noted in **Table 1**, a material must make up 90% of the component, by weight or volume. A single component that meets each criterion (i.e., environmentally preferable, low emissions, and local sourcing) can earn points for each.

a) Environmentally preferable products (0.5 point per component). Use products that meet the specifications in **Table 1**.

*Note: Recycled content products must contain a minimum of 25% postconsumer recycled content, except as noted in **Table 1**. Postindustrial (preconsumer) recycled content must be counted at half the rate of postconsumer content.*

AND/OR

b) Low emissions (0.5 point per component). Use products that meet the emissions specifications in **Table 1**.

AND/OR

c) Local production (0.5 point per component). Use products that were extracted, processed, and manufactured within 500 miles of the home.

Table 1. Environmentally Preferable Products

Assembly	Component	EPP specifications (0.5 point per component)	Emission specifications (0.5 point per component)	Local production (0.5 point per component)
Exterior wall	Framing/wall structure	Concrete wall structure: Use 30% fly ash or slag wood frame: FSC-certified or reclaimed or finger joint studs	N/A	Eligible
Exterior wall	Siding or masonry	Recycled content, reclaimed, or FSC-certified	N/A	Eligible
Floor	Flooring (45% of total floor area)	Linoleum, cork, bamboo, FSC-certified or reclaimed wood, sealed concrete, recycled-content flooring, *or combination*	Carpet & pad: ½ point if all carpet complies with Carpet & Rug Institute (CRI) Green Label Plus program and all pad complies with CRI Green Label program. Hard flooring: ½ point if 90% of the floor area is hard-surface flooring.	Eligible
Floor	Flooring (90% of total floor area)	Meet specifications above to receive *additional* 0.5 point	Hard flooring: ½ point for using a product that is SCS FloorScore certified for 90% of floor area.	Eligible *(additional 0.5 point)*
Floor	Framing	FSC-certified or reclaimed	N/A	Eligible
Foundation	Aggregate	N/A	N/A	Eligible
Foundation	Cement	Use 30% fly ash or slag	N/A	Eligible
Interior wall	Framing	FSC-certified or reclaimed	N/A	Eligible
Interior walls AND ceilings	Gypsum board	N/A	N/A	Eligible
Interior walls AND ceilings AND millwork	Paints and coatings	Recycled paint that meets Green Seal standard GS-43	Use products that comply with all applicable standards in Table 2.	Not eligible
Landscape	Decking or patio material	Recycled content, FSC-certified, or reclaimed	N/A	Eligible
Other	Cabinets	Recycled content, FSC-certified, or reclaimed AND composite materials must contain no added urea-formaldehyde resins	N/A	Eligible
Other	Counters (kitchens and bathrooms)	Recycled content, FSC-certified, or reclaimed AND composite materials must contain no added urea-formaldehyde resins	N/A	Eligible
Other	Doors (not including garage or insulated doors)	Recycled content, FSC-certified, or reclaimed	N/A	Eligible
Other	Interior trim	Recycled content, FSC-certified, or reclaimed AND composite materials must contain no added urea-formaldehyde resins	N/A	Eligible
Other	Adhesives and sealants	N/A	Use products that comply with all applicable standards in Table 3.	Not eligible
Other	Window framing	Recycled content, FSC-certified, or reclaimed	N/A	Eligible
Roof	Framing	FSC-certified	N/A	Eligible
Roof	Roofing	Recycled content	N/A	Eligible
Roof AND floor AND wall	Cavity insulation (i.e. not rigid foam insulation)	Recycled content of 20% or more	Comply with California "Practice for Testing of VOCs from Building Materials Using Small Chambers". www.dhs.ca.gov/ehib/IAQ/VOCS/Practice.htm	Eligible
Roof, floor, wall (2 of 3)	Sheathing	Recycled content, FSC-certified, or reclaimed	N/A	Eligible

Figure 1. Example Notice to Wood Products Suppliers

Notice to Vendors: [The company] is required to purchase products that contain tropical wood only if they are certified according to the guidelines of the Forest Stewardship Council (FSC). Please provide the country of manufacture of each product you expect to supply to us. Also please provide a list of FSC-certified products you can supply.

Table 2. Standards for Environmentally Preferable Paints and Coatings

Types of Paints and Coatings	Applicable standard (VOC content)	Reference
Architectural paints, coatings, and primers applied to interior elements	Flats: 50 g/L Nonflats: 150 g/L	Green Seal Standard GS-11, Paints, 1st Edition, May 20, 1993
Anticorrosive and antirust paints applied to interior ferrous metal substrates	250 g/L	Green Seal Standard GC-03, Anti-Corrosive Paints, 2nd Edition, January 7, 1997
Clear wood finishes	Varnish: 350 g/L Lacquer: 550 g/L	South Coast Air Quality Management District Rule 1113, Architectural Coatings
Floor coatings	100 g/L	
Sealers	Waterproofing: 250 g/L Sanding: 275 g/L All others: 200 g/L	
Shellacs	Clear: 730 g/L Pigmented: 550 g/L	
Stains	250 g/L	

Synergies and Trade-Offs

Products with low emissions of volatile organic compounds (VOCs) may improve indoor air quality. Such products are included in this credit rather than in the EQ section in order to consolidate information pertaining to materials selection, specification, and purchase.

A substantial amount of energy is used to transport materials from product manufacturing plants to home construction sites. Choosing local products will reduce the embedded transportation energy usage associated with construction.

Table 3. Standards for Low-Emissions Adhesives and Sealants (meet South Coast Air Quality Management District Rule #1168)

	Applicable standard (VOC content, g/L less water)
Architectural applications	
Indoor carpet adhesives	50
Carpet pad adhesives	50
Wood flooring adhesives	100
Rubber floor adhesives	60
Subfloor adhesives	50
VCT and asphalt adhesives	50
Drywall and panel adhesives	50
Cove base adhesives	50
Multipurpose construction adhesives	70
Structural glazing adhesives	100
Ceramic tile adhesives	65
Specialty applications	
PVC welding	510
CPVC welding	490
ABS welding	325
Plastic cement welding	250
Adhesive primer for plastic	550
Contact adhesive	80
Special-purpose contact adhesive	250
Structural wood member adhesive	140
Sheet-applied rubber lining operations	850
Top and trim adhesive	250
Substrate-specific applications	
Metal to metal	30
Plastic foams	50
Porous materials (except wood)	50
Wood	30
Fiberglass	80
Sealants	
Architectural	250
Nonmembrane roof	300
Roadway	250
Single-ply roof membrane	450
Other	420
Sealant primers	
Architectural nonporous	250
Architectural porous	775

MR 2.1: FSC-Certified Tropical Woods

Poor forestry practices continue to degrade many tropical rain forests, resulting in significant climate change impacts as well as irreversible harm to biological diversity. Many tropical woods can be replaced by nontropical woods. Where tropical woods are required to serve a particular function, the use of sustainably grown and harvested woods is required.

Certification by the Forest Stewardship Council (FSC) is a "green" seal of approval awarded to forest managers who adopt environmentally and socially responsible forest management practices and to companies that manufacture and sell products made from certified wood. This seal enables consumers to identify and procure wood products from well-managed sources and thereby use their purchasing power to influence and reward improved forest management activities around the world.

Tropical wood content can end up in a wide variety of products, unbeknownst to the purchaser. Providing a notice of intent to wood products suppliers clarifies the pursuits of the project team and raises exposure and awareness.

Approach and Implementation

Include FSC purchasing preference language (**Figure 1**) in all purchasing contracts and purchase orders.

In the early stages of design, identify any components of the home that might contain tropical woods. Identify lumber suppliers that have FSC chain-of-custody and work to procure certified tropical woods.

If FSC-certified tropical woods are unavailable or impractical, determine whether and how tropical woods might be avoided through the use of alternative products. Where tropical wood was included to serve a functional purpose, such as strength or pest resistance, consider alternative engineered designs or borate treatments.

Wood species can be identified accurately only by scientific (botanic) name and not by either common or proprietary name. A species of wood is considered tropical for purposes of this credit if it is grown in a moist tropical country that lies either in part or in its entirety between the Tropics of Cancer and Capricorn (23.5 degrees latitude north and south, respectively). See **Table 4** for a reference list by continent.

Table 4. Tropical Countries, by Continent

Continent	Tropical countries
Africa	All except Morocco, Tunisia, Algeria, Egypt, and Libya
Asia and Southeast Asia	All except Japan, North Korea, South Korea, and Russia
Australia and Oceana	All except New Zealand
Central America and Caribbean	All countries
Europe	None
Middle East	None
North America	Mexico
South America	All except Uruguay

"Resources," below, lists Web sites that can help project teams identify tropical species, locate FSC products, and determine a product's country of origin.

Calculations

No calculations are required.

Exemplary Performance

No additional points are available for exemplary performance.

Verification and Submittals

Supporting Verification Materials, made available by the Project Team:

❑ Provide the required notice to all wood products suppliers.

❑ Present the wood supplier notice to the Verification Team.

❑ Sign an Accountability Form confirming that no tropical woods were used except those that were FSC-certified or reclaimed.

Verification Team:

❑ Visually verify that the wood supplier notice has been provided to vendors and that it meets the stated requirements.

❑ Verify no wood used in the project is from a tropical country, unless FSC-certified, using information provided by suppliers and vendors.

❑ Verify that an Accountability Form has been signed by the responsible party.

Considerations

Environmental Issues

Poor forestry practices have numerous negative environmental impacts, including climate change, soil degradation, and loss of biodiversity. These impacts are even more pronounced in tropical areas, where rain forests hold significant biological wealth and local laws and regulations are difficult to enforce. The Forest Stewardship Council sets standards for sustainable forest management and certifies sustainable forests and products from those forests.

Economic Issues

The limited supply of FSC-certified tropical wood in the United States has raised costs for certified wood products. Efforts are being made to increase the FSC-certified land base in the United States to make it more possible to buy FSC wood locally. Certified tropical wood also may generally cost more because of the associated costs of growing and harvesting wood in a sustainable manner.

Regional Variances

Lumber with the FSC logo, which warrants that the wood was harvested from a well-managed forest, can be obtained across the world from a variety of mills, manufacturers, and distributors. Many well-known national retailers also stock FSC products. Local retailers can provide information on their FSC-certified products.

FSC Chain-of-Custody Requirements

FSC chain-of-custody (COC) certification enables tracking of wood that originates in FSC-certified forests all the way through the value chain into final products. All companies that take legal ownership of FSC products and produce, sell, promote, or trade them need to be certified for COC. Thus, all FSC-certified wood products in LEED projects must be supplied by vendors that have the FSC COC certification. Vendors are defined as those companies that sell products to the project contractor or subcontractors.

For this prerequisite, in order to ensure

that the requirements have been met, the project team will need to verify that all vendor invoices for any permanently installed tropical wood products purchased for the project conform to the following requirements:

- ❑ Each wood product, whether tropical or not, must be identified on a line-item basis and must state the product's country of manufacture;

- ❑ All wood products manufactured in moist tropical countries (i.e., countries that lie, either in part or in their entirety, between the Tropics of Cancer and Capricorn) must be FSC-certified and must be identified as such on a line-item basis;

- ❑ Any tropical wood products must be FSC certified. Certification under any of the FSC labels (e.g., FSC Pure, FSC Mixed, FSC Mixed [NN]%, FSC Recycled) is acceptable.

- ❑ The vendor's COC certificate number must be shown on any invoice that includes FSC-certified products.

Contractors and subcontractors are considered end consumers and do not need to have COC.

Resources

Please see the USGBC Web site, at www. usgbc.org/resources, for more specific resources on materials sources and other technical information.

Web Sites

Rainforest Alliance

SmartGuide to Green Building Wood Sources

www.rainforestalliance.org/smartguides

This site lists U.S. suppliers, manufacturers, and distributors of FSC-certified building products.

U.S. Forest Service

www2.fpl.fs.fed.us/TechSheets/tropical-wood.html

This is a free database of tropical hardwoods, listed both by common name and by genus and species. This list is not comprehensive, but each species of wood has a fact sheet.

Forest Stewardship Council

www.findfsc.org

For help in locating FSC-certified products, fill out the form on this Web site and submit it to FSC-US; FSC will circulate it to certified companies, who then will contact you if they have your desired product(s) available.

The Wood Explorer

www.toolcenter.com/wood/index.html

This CD covers 1,650 wood species. It includes scientific and common names, origins, and properties.

ID	LL	SS	WE	EA	MR	EQ	AE
					2.1		

MR 2.2: Environmentally Preferable Materials

Environmentally preferable products have reduced environmental impact compared with conventional alternatives. Many new products are less harmful to the environment and to humans because they are sustainably produced, include recycled content, are rapidly renewable, or have lower emissions. Products procured from local sources require less transportation.

The use of these materials in place of conventional products can significantly improve the overall environmental performance of the home. Qualifying materials have one or more of the following attributes:

a) FSC-certified wood products, or recycled or reclaimed content.

b) Low or no emissions of volatile organic compounds (VOCs).

c) Local production (the product was extracted, processed, and manufactured within 500 miles of the site).

This credit rewards the significant use of materials that have one of these attributes and can be shown to meet one of the environmentally preferable specifications shown in **Table 1**.

Approach and Implementation

Additional measures have been approved for credit under MR 2.2. Ask your LEED for Homes Provider for details.

Early in the design process, review each component with the project team to identify possible opportunities for replacing conventional materials with preferable materials, as listed in **Table 1**.

Identify suppliers that carry environmentally preferable products, including FSC-certified wood, recycled-content wood, and locally produced materials. If possible, use products that meet both the Environmentally Preferable Products and

Local Production requirements; a single component that meets both requirements is worth 1 LEED point.

Work with suppliers to help them understand what is needed to fulfill the Environmentally Preferable Products and Local Production requirements and encourage them to expand their offerings to meet the growing demand for green products.

a) Environmentally Preferable Products

In LEED for Homes, an environmentally preferable product is a material or product that causes less environmental damage than the conventional alternative. Since the basis for comparison (the conventional alternative) varies by building component, the list of qualifying products differs by component (see **Table 1**). Points can be earned for each component. For example, if FSC-certified lumber is used for interior wall framing, floor framing, and exterior wall framing, 1.5 points are awarded (0.5 point for each component).

Recycled content is material that includes at least 25% postconsumer or 50% preconsumer (postindustrial) recycled material. In the case of cabinets, counters, and trim, recycled-content materials must also contain no added ureaformaldehyde resins to earn the 0.5 point.

Reclaimed content is material that has been recovered from a demolition site. Reclaimed material can be considered locally produced and earn points accordingly if the reclamation takes place within 500 miles of the LEED home site. Only postconsumer material can be counted as reclaimed material, not construction leftovers.

FSC-certified wood comes from suppliers that have been granted chain-of-custody by the Forest Stewardship Council. See

"Resources," below, for Web sites that can help project teams locate FSC-certified products.

b) Low-Emissions Materials

This part of the credit applies to four types of materials: adhesives and sealants; paints and coatings; carpet and floor systems; and insulation.

For paints and coatings and for adhesives and sealants, limits are set on the amount of volatile organic compounds (VOCs) per given volume of the product. The threshold limits and the content within a particular product are generally expressed in grams per liter (g/L). Refer to **Tables 2 and 3** when selecting products tested for emissions and check emissions levels on product labels. Pre-finished surfaces are assumed to meet the emissions specification.

For carpet and floor systems, products that meet the requirements of either the Green Label Plus program or the Floor-Score program can earn points. These programs use rigorous protocols to test products for emissions and maintain a high level of consistency.

For insulation, products must comply with California's Practice for Testing of VOCs from Building Materials Using Small Chambers. Insulation products that meet the standard are certified by either the California Collaborative for High Performance Schools (CHPS) program or the GreenGuard Environmental Institute Children & Schools program.

c) Local Production

Early in the design process, determine the availability of products that have been extracted, harvested, recovered, and manufactured locally (within 500 miles of the project site).

Work with subcontractors and suppliers to verify availability of local materials.

Reclaimed material can be considered locally produced if the reclamation takes place within 500 miles of the home site. In the case of gut rehab projects, material that is refurbished and reused on-site can be counted as reclaimed. Only postconsumer waste can be counted as reclaimed material.

Calculations

To earn 0.5 point, at least 90% of a given component (by weight or volume) must meet the requirements for Environmentally Preferable Products, Low-Emissions Materials, or Local Production. This can be achieved with multiple products that each meet the requirement. For example, if a project has 70% FSC-certified counters and 20% reclaimed counters, the project earns 0.5 point.

For example, in order to earn credit for the component "Interior Walls AND ceiling AND millwork", at least 90% of all paints and coatings used on these surfaces must meet the requirements.

The only exception to the 90% requirement is for flooring:

- ❑ 45% of the floor area must meet the Environmentally Preferable Products requirements to earn 0.5 point;

- ❑ 90% of the floor area must meet the Environmentally Preferable Products requirements to earn 1 point; and

- ❑ 90% of the floor area must meet the Low-Emissions Materials requirements for hard flooring or for carpet and pad to earn 0.5 point.

Detailed calculations are not required for each component. Approximations are acceptable, and no calculations are necessary if the entirety of a component meets the requirements of the credit.

For this calculation, all garage floor area (for both conditioned and unconditioned garages) should be excluded.

Both ICFs and SIPs should be treated as two different components – framing

ID	LL	SS	WE	EA	**MR**	EQ	AE
					2.2		

and insulation. If the requirements for either or both components are met, points should be awarded accordingly.

Both ICFs and SIPs should be treated as two different components – framing and insulation. If the requirements for either or both components are met, points should be awarded accordingly .

When calculating distances for Local Production, use either driving distance or "as the crow flies" distance. The latter is shorter, but the former may be easier to calculate. Averaging is not allowed; if any step in the production process (extraction, processing, or manufacturing) for a particular component is outside a 500-mile radius from the home, the credit cannot be awarded for that component.

Exemplary Performance

Projects that install more than 16 of the measures listed in MR 2.2 should be awarded exemplary performance points, to be counted under Innovation in Design 3. Each additional measure is worth 0.5 point, with a maximum of 4 exemplary performance points total.

Verification and Submittals

Supporting Verification Materials, made available by the Project Team:

❏ Present any relevant product stamps, certification labels, web links, and/or literature to the Verification Team as needed to demonstrate that the credit requirements were met.

❏ Sign an Accountability Form to indicate that each product being counted in this credit represents the required minimum percentage of the applicable component.

Verification Team:

❏ Visually verify (using product stamps, labels, web links, and/or literature, as needed) that all products counted in this credit meet the relevant requirements and were used in the project.

❏ Verify that an Accountability Form has been signed by the responsible party.

Considerations

Environmental Issues

The use of materials with recycled content reduces demand for virgin materials (and the associated impacts of extraction or harvesting) and diverts material that would otherwise be sent to landfill. Choosing low-emitting materials will improve the health and comfort of occupants and reduce the demand for toxic materials that affect human health and the environment "upstream," at the manufacturing site. Volatile organic compounds in particular contribute to smog and can react with sunlight and nitrogen oxides in the atmosphere to form ground-level ozone, a chemical that has a detrimental effect on human health and the local environment. The use of local building materials reduces transportation energy usage and the accompanying pollution associated with delivering materials to the job site.

Economic Issues

Currently, the cost of FSC-certified wood products is equal to or higher than that of conventional wood products, and availability varies by region. The price of FSC-certified wood products is expected to become more competitive as the industry adjusts. Many commonly used products are now available with recycled content. Most recycled-content products exhibit performance similar to products made with virgin-only materials and can be incorporated into building projects with ease and minimal cost. The cost of reclaimed material depends on the cost to refurbish the material. Reclaiming material from demolition projects reduces waste-hauling costs.

The construction market increasingly offers low-VOC alternatives to conventional building products. These low-VOC products are generally competitive with conventional materials, but some, particularly new products, are more expensive. Some types of low-VOC products may also be difficult to obtain. However, these problems will recede as application of low-VOC products becomes more commonplace.

Locally produced building materials should cost the same as or less than materials transported from long distances.

Regional Variations

Lumber with the FSC logo, which warrants that the wood came from a certified, well-managed forest, can be obtained across the world from a variety of mills, manufacturers, and distributors. Many well-known national retailers now stock FSC products. Local retailers can provide information on their FSC-certified products.

The availability of local building materials depends on the project location. In some areas the majority of products needed for the project can be obtained within a 500-mile radius. In other areas few materials may be locally sourced.

Chain-of-Custody Requirements

FSC COC certification is designed to enable tracking of wood that originates in FSC-certified forests all the way through the value chain into final products. All companies that take legal ownership of FSC products and produce, sell, promote, or trade them need to be certified for COC. Thus, all FSC-certified wood

products in LEED projects must be supplied by vendors that have FSC COC certification. Vendors are defined as those companies that sell products to the project contractor or subcontractors.

In order to earn credit for the use of FSC-certified wood products, project teams must compile all vendor invoices for materials, both FSC-certified and non-certified, used in the component in question (e.g., roof framing). Each vendor invoice used for verification must conform to the following requirements:

❑ Each individual product must be identified on a line-item basis;

❑ FSC-certified products must be identified as such on a line-item basis;

❑ The quantity (e.g., number of units, square feet, lineal feet) of each line item must be shown;

❑ The vendor's COC certificate number must be shown on any invoice that includes FSC-certified products.

Except as otherwise noted in **Table 1** (e.g., for flooring, where the required minimum is 45 percent), at least 90 percent of a component must be FSC-certified in order to earn credit. Wood products that are identified on invoices as "FSC Pure" and "FSC Mixed Credit" should be counted at 100 percent. Wood products identified as "FSC Mixed [NN]%" should be counted at the indicated percentage, e.g., a product identified as "FSC Mixed 75%," should be counted at 75 percent. Wood products identified as "FSC Recycled" or "FSC Recycled Credit" may not be counted as FSC-certified but can be counted as recycled content.

Contractors and subcontractors are considered end consumers and do not need to have COC.

ID	LL	SS	WE	EA	MR	EQ	AE
					2.2		

Resources

Web Sites

a) Environmentally Preferable Products

Green Building Pages

www.greenbuildingpages.com/main_a.html

Green Building Pages, Inc., is an online, sustainable design and decision-making tool for building industry professionals and environmentally and socially responsible consumers. It includes articles, white papers, case studies, and other links and resources regarding green building practices, along with an extensive directory of products.

Green Building Resource Guide

www.greenguide.com/about.html

A database of more than 600 green building materials and products selected specifically for their usefulness to the design and building professions, rather than merely their green material content.

Green HomeGuide

www.greenhomeguide.com

GreenHomeGuide is a web-based resource that includes a combination of tips, case studies, expert Q&A articles, and regional directories of products and services.

Green Seal

www.greenseal.org/index.cfm

An independent nonprofit organization dedicated to safeguarding the environment and transforming the marketplace by promoting the manufacture, purchase, and use of environmentally responsible products and services. Products and manufacturers that comply with its published paint standards are listed on the site.

Oikos Green Building Source

www.oikos.com/green_products/index.php

A Web site dedicated to sustainable and energy-efficient construction: Green Building News, Product Database, Product Gallery, Energy Source Builder Newsletter, and more.

Rainforest Alliance

SmartGuide to Green Building Wood Sources

www.rainforestalliance.org/smartguides

This site lists U.S. suppliers, manufacturers, and distributors of FSC-certified building products.

U.S. Forest Service

www2.fpl.fs.fed.us/TechSheets/tropical-wood.html

This is a free database of tropical hardwoods, listed both by common name and by genus and species. This list is not comprehensive, but each species of wood has a fact sheet.

Salvaged Building Materials Exchange

Green Building Resource Guide

www.greenguide.com/about.html

A searchable database of salvaged building materials.

Used Building Materials Exchange

www.build.recycle.net

(519) 767-2913

A free marketplace for buying and selling recyclables and salvaged materials.

National Wood Recycling Directory

American Forest and Paper Association

www.afandpa.org/recycling/recycling.html

(202) 463-2700

A searchable directory of outlets for recycling construction lumber. Also find the AF&PA directory of wastepaper dealers and recycling centers on this site.

Reuse Development Organization

www.redo.org

(410) 669-7245

ReDO is a national nonprofit in Indianapolis that promotes reuse as an environmentally sound, socially beneficial, and economical means of managing surplus and discarded materials. See the "Find a ReUse Center" link for state-by-state lists of reuse and recycling centers.

Forest Stewardship Council

www.fscus.org/faqs/fsc_products.php

www.findfsc.org

For help in locating FSC-certified products, fill out the form on this Web site and submit it to FSC-US; FSC will circulate it to certified companies, that then will contact you if they have your desired product(s) available.

The Wood Explorer

www.toolcenter.com/wood/index.html

This CD covers 1,650 wood species. It includes scientific and common names, origins, and properties.

b) Low Emissions Materials

CRI Green Label

The Carpet and Rug Institute

www.carpet-rug.org/commercial-customers/green-building-and-the-environment/green-label-plus/index.cfm

CRI has created its own set of standards for rating low-emitting carpets, adhesives, and pads. This site describes the standards and has a directory of products that meet them.

Greenguard Environmental Institute's Children & Schools Certified Products

www.greenguard.org

This site includes a listing of all products that are certified according to the Greenguard Children & Schools program. Any insulation products that have earned this certification automatically meet the low emissions criteria for LEED for Homes, as stipulated in an agreement between Greenguard and the State of California.

California Collaborative for High Performance Schools (CHPS) Program

www.chps.net/manual/lem_table.htm

This site includes a list of products that have been certified to meet the CHPS low-emitting materials criteria. This list includes insulation, carpet, rug, and flooring products that meet the requirements of LEED for Homes.

Carpet & Rug Institute Green Label Plus Program

www.carpet-rug.org

This Web site includes information about the CRI Green Label Plus and Green Label programs. Details are provided under "Commercial Customers," within "Green Building and the Environment."

Scientific Certification System FloorScore Program

www.scscertified.com/iaq/floorscore.html

This Web site includes information about the SCS FloorScore program, as well as a list of certified products that is updated regularly.

Print Media

Green Building Products: The GreenSpec Guide to Residential Building Materials. BuildingGreen, Inc., and New Society Publishers. Available online, at www.buildinggreen.com/ecommerce/gbp.cfm

Making Better Concrete: Guidelines to Using Fly Ash for Higher Quality, Eco-Friendly Structures, by Bruce King, P.E. Green Building Press. Learn more at www.greenbuildingpress.com/mbc/index.htm

ID	LL	SS	WE	EA	MR	EQ	AE
					2.2		

MR 3: Waste Management

Intent

Reduce waste generation to a level below the industry norm.

Requirements

Prerequisites

3.1 **Construction Waste Management Planning.** Complete the following tasks related to management of construction waste:

a) Investigate and document local options for diversion (e.g., recycling, reuse) of all anticipated major constituents of the project waste stream, including cardboard packaging and household recyclables (e.g., beverage containers).

b) Document the diversion rate for construction waste. Record the diversion rate for land clearing and/or demolition, if applicable (e.g., on gut rehab project), separately from the rate for the new construction phase of the project.

Credits

3.2 **Construction Waste Reduction** (maximum 3 points). Reduce or divert waste generated from new construction activities from landfills and incinerators to a level below the industry norm. Use either of two options:

a) Reduced construction waste. Generate 2.5 pounds (or 0.016 cubic yards) or less of net waste (not including waste diverted for reclamation or recycling) per square foot of building floor area. Use column 1 or 2 and column 5 of **Table 1** to determine the score.[2]

b) Increased waste diversion. Divert 25% or more of the total materials taken off the construction site from landfills and incinerators. Use column 3 or 4 and column 5 of **Table 1** to determine the score; calculate the percentage using either weight or volume.

Note: Land clearing and demolition waste (e.g., from removal of preexisting structures on the site) should not be counted in this calculation.

Synergies and Trade-Offs

Waste can be minimized by creating a detailed framing plan and using advanced framing techniques or off-site fabrication (MR 1).

The use of products with reclaimed or recycled content (MR 2.2) reduces both the production of new materials and the burden on landfills.

---

2 The industry average is 4.2 pounds (0.0265 cubic yards) of waste per square foot of conditioned floor area, based on data provided by the National Association of Home Builders' Research Center.

Table 1. Waste Diversion

Amount to landfills and incinerators				
Reduced construction waste		Increased waste diversion		
Pounds / ft²	Cubic yards / 1,000 ft²	Percentage waste	Percentage diverted	Points
4.0	25.5	100%	0%	0.0
3.5	22.3	87.5%	12.5%	0.0
3.0	19.1	75%	25%	0.5
2.5	15.9	62.5%	37.5%	1.0
2.0	12.8	50%	50%	1.5
1.5	9.6	37.5%	62.5%	2.0
1.0	6.4	25%	75%	2.5
0.5	3.2	12.5%	87.5%	3.0

Because landfill space is rapidly diminishing, incineration produces pollutants, and waste of materials in itself carries negative environmental impacts, waste should be avoided to the extent possible.

The National Association of Home Builders estimates that the construction of a "typical" 2,000-square-foot home generates about 8,000 pounds of waste that occupies roughly 51 cubic yards of landfill space. This equates to an average of about 4 pounds of waste per square foot of conditioned space and a cost of roughly $500 per house for construction waste disposal.

Although recycling requires collecting, sorting, and converting the waste to a useful product, it is frequently more efficient than throwing away money in disposal costs. Recycling and reusing construction waste can help the economy by creating jobs related to salvaging and recycling of construction waste.

These credits reward projects for reducing construction waste and diverting unavoidable waste into the recycling stream.

Approach and Implementation

Two primary strategies can help project teams earn credit for waste reduction and diversion: Design the home and manage materials purchasing and construction to reduce the production of waste; and identify and utilize methods for diverting waste.

To minimize waste, develop detailed framing documents, create an accurate cut list and framing order, adopt efficient framing techniques, use prefabricated components, and generally purchase only as much material as needed for the job.

To divert waste from landfills, develop and document a construction waste management plan by assessing waste types, quantities, and disposal costs. Identify licensed haulers and processors of recyclables. Identify markets for salvaged materials. Employ deconstruction, salvage, reuse, and recycling strategies and processes, including waste auditing. Document the cost for recycling, salvaging, and reusing materials.

Partner with local businesses and community groups, such as local salvage centers and used material exchanges (used building supply outlets) and others, to sell or donate lumber, fixtures, appliances, masonry, and roofing. Donate large pieces of scraps or other usable materials to housing programs (e.g., Habitat for Humanity) and community groups (e.g., local theaters).

Acceptable strategies for waste diversion include:

❑ Recycling

❑ Third-party scrap reuse

❑ On-site grinding of engineered lumber, untreated cellulosic material, and gypsum for use as a soil amendment.

Strategies that cannot be counted as diversion include:

❑ Scrap reuse by the builder

❑ Burying unground material on-site

❑ Packing unused material into wall cavities

❑ Grinding treated / finished wood as soil amendment

❑ Incineration, even waste-to-energy applications

Outline procedures, expectations, and results for monitoring, collecting, and promoting waste management planning.

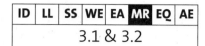
Make sure construction crews understand and participate, with updates throughout the building process.

Measure waste by either weight or volume. Documenting weight is more likely to produce reliable estimates because compaction can alter volume dramatically when a waste container is loaded. Require that the weight of the waste be calculated and documented.

Research recycling options and evaluate the cost-effectiveness of recycling or reusing rigid insulation, engineered wood products, and other materials. Reuse or recycle materials found at the job site, including any demolition materials from preexisting structures (e.g., wood scraps for bracing, drywall scraps as fillers in closets). Recycle corrugated cardboard, metals, concrete, brick, asphalt, land-clearing debris, clean dimensional wood, plastic, glass, gypsum board, and carpet. Collect beverage containers from crews.

Identify construction haulers and recyclers to handle the designated materials; they can serve as valuable partners in this effort.

Mark and designate containers. Have the waste management company provide separate containers for different types of waste based on its destination (reclamation, recycling, or landfill) or arrange for the waste management company to separate the waste after hauling.

Avoid contaminating recyclable materials with other construction debris and food waste products. Beverages and other liquids can be particularly harmful to porous materials, eliminating their potential to be recycled.

Sort and set aside, in a marked and designated area, lumber, plywood, and oriented-strand board cut-offs that can be used as fire blocking, as spacers in header construction, and in other ways. Separate clean sawdust and lumber cut-offs to be chipped for use in compost piles or around planting areas.

Track the quantities and cost savings of diverted materials. Obtain and retain verification records (waste haul receipts, waste management reports, spreadsheets) to confirm that materials have been recycled or salvaged as planned.

Minimize and properly dispose of any hazardous materials.

Calculations

Do not include demolition or land-clearing debris. Document the waste totals with receipts from the waste hauling company, or keep track of waste hauling totals using a simple inventory like that provided in **Table 2**.

Calculate waste reduction and waste diversion as follows.

Reduced Construction Waste

Step 1. Calculate the net construction waste (in weight or volume):

Net Waste = Waste Sent to Landfill + Waste Incinerated

Table 2. Waste Reduction Record

Load tag date	Volume hauled (cubic yards)	Weight hauled (pounds)
TOTAL		
Home size (SF)		
Weight hauled / SF		

OR

Net Waste = Total Waste Hauled – (Material Reclaimed + Material Recycled)

Step 2. Calculate the waste rate from construction:

Waste Rate (lbs/ft^2) = Net Waste / Home Size

OR

Waste Rate (yds^3/1000 ft^2) = Net Waste / Home Size ÷ 1000

Increased Waste Diversion

Step 1. Calculate the amount of waste diverted from the landfill or incinerator:

Waste Diverted = Total Waste Hauled – (Waste Sent to Landfill + Waste Incinerated)"

OR

Waste Diverted = Material Reclaimed + Material Recycled

Step 2. Calculate the percentage of waste diverted from the landfill or incinerator:

Waste Diverted (%) = Waste Diverted / Total Waste Hauled

If waste is processed by a waste management facility, the average monthly or annual diversion rate for the entire facility may be used for the purposes of this credit. This option is only acceptable if the annual waste facility data is available and verified by the Verification Team.

Exemplary Performance

Projects that can demonstrate that 100% of the waste was diverted can earn an additional 0.5 point, to be counted under Innovation in Design 3.

Verification and Submittals

Supporting Verification Materials, made available by the Project Team:

MR 3.1: Construction Waste Management Planning

❑ Present documentation to the Verification Team of local waste diversion options.

❑ Present calculations to the Verification Team demonstrating construction waste diversion rates, using documentation from the waste management company.

MR 3.2: Construction Waste Reduction

❑ Present calculations to the Verification Team demonstrating average waste (in pounds or cubic yards per square foot) for the project, using documentation from the waste management company.

❑ Present calculations to the Verification Team demonstrating construction waste diversion rates, using documentation from the waste management company.

Verification Team:

MR 3.1: Construction Waste Management Planning

❑ Verify documentation of local waste diversion options.

❑ Verify calculations of construction waste diversion rate.

MR 3.2: Construction Waste Reduction

❑ Verify calculations of average construction waste.

❑ Verify calculations of construction waste diversion rate.

ID	LL	SS	WE	EA	**MR**	EQ	AE
			3.1 & 3.2				

Considerations

Environmental Issues

Efforts to reduce, reuse, and recycle construction waste may save money, reduce liability, keep job sites cleaner and safer, and conserve valuable landfill space. Preventing waste also reduces demand for natural resources, such as trees, oil, and minerals.

Reclamation or recycling of construction waste reduces demand for virgin resources and, in turn, reduces the environmental impacts associated with resource extraction, processing, and transportation. Landfills pollute groundwater and encroach upon green space. Construction waste management makes it possible to extend the lifetime of existing landfills.

Economic Issues

Strategies to minimize waste through improved design and planning will save money from reduced material use and reduced waste-hauling fees.

In the past, when landfill capacity was readily available and disposal fees were low, reclamation or recycling of construction was an extra cost burden. The economics of recycling continue to improve, especially as disposal costs have increased and disposal regulations have tightened.

Today, the costs associated with waste management vary considerably by location. In some cases, recycling—particularly metals, concrete, asphalt, and cardboard—can reduce project costs by significantly reducing landfill tipping fees. Commingled recycling may simplify the waste management effort on-site but increase recycling costs.

Regional Variances

The availability of recycling opportunities varies by region. In urban areas, recycling resources are typically more developed, and builders can choose between separating waste on-site and hiring commingled waste recyclers.

Recycling opportunities are expanding rapidly in many communities. Metal, vegetation, concrete, and asphalt recycling opportunities have long been available and economical in most communities. Paper, corrugated cardboard, plastics, and clean wood markets vary by regional and local recycling infrastructure but are recycled in most communities.

Some materials, such as gypsum wallboard, can be recycled only in communities where reprocessing plants exist or where soil can handle the material as a stabilizing agent.

Resources

Web Sites

Toolbase.org, Best Practices for Construction Waste Management

NAHB Research Center

www.toolbase.org/Best-Practices/Construction-Waste/waste-mgmt-field-guide

This page includes frequently asked questions, case studies, reports, and various links. It also includes "A Builder's Field Guide," which includes guidance for creating a step-by-step construction waste management and recovery plan.

Cardboard Packaging Council

www.corrugated.org

The Corrugated Packaging Council can help locate local outlets for cardboard.

American Forest & Paper Association

www.afandpa.org/recycling

AF&PA publishes a directory of wastepaper dealers and recycling centers.

U.S. EPA WasteWise Program

www.epa.gov/wastewise/targeted/challenge/cbres.htm

1-800-EPA-WISE

This site has information about the WasteWise Building Challenge program, including articles, publications, and various links and resources for more information.

California Integrated Waste Management Board

www.ciwmb.ca.gov/publications

This site provides links to numerous publications on topics related to waste management.

Construction and Demolition Debris

U.S. Environmental Protection Agency

www.epa.gov/epaoswer/non-hw/debris-new/index.htm

This site includes basic information on construction and demolition debris disposal practices, regional and state programs, publications, and links.

Construction Materials Recycling Association

www.cdrecycling.org

Includes links to Web sites on recycling concrete, asphalt roof shingles, and drywall, as well as a state-by-state listing of construction waste reusers and recyclers.

Building Materials Reuse Association

www.ubma.org

Formerly the Used Building Materials Association, BMRA is a nonprofit, membership-based organization that represents companies and organizations involved in the acquisition and/or redistribution of used building materials.

California Materials Exchange

California Integrated Waste Management Board

www.ciwmb.ca.gov/CalMAX

A program of the California Integrated Waste Management Board, this site allows users to exchange nonhazardous discarded materials online.

Reuse Development Organization

www.redo.org

ReDO is a national nonprofit in Indianapolis that promotes reuse as an environmentally sound, socially beneficial, and economical means of managing surplus and discarded materials. See the "Find a ReUse Center" link for state-by-state lists of reuse and recycling centers.

Print Media

On-Site Grinding of Residential Construction Debris: The Indiana Grinder Pilot. NAHB Research Center, 1999. Available online, at www.epa.gov/epaoswer/non-hw/debris-new/pubs/indiana.pdf.

Residential Construction Waste Management: A Builder's Field Guide. NAHB Research Center, 1997. This guide may be used to create a step-by-step construction waste management and recovery plan. Go to www.nahbrc.org/bookstore/cw0503w.aspx.

Efficient Wood Use in Residential Construction. Natural Resources Defense Council, 1998. This NRDC handbook describes the advantages of several wood-efficient approaches to design, material selection, and construction for residential applications and includes extensive practical and resource information for builders, architects, engineers, and developers. It may be purchased online, at www.nrdc.org/cities/building/rwoodus.asp.

Indoor Environmental Quality

Americans spend on average 90% of their time indoors, where levels of pollutants may run two to five times—and occasionally more than 100 times—higher than outdoors, according to the U.S. Environmental Protection Agency.[1] Similarly, the World Health Organization reported in its Air Quality Guidelines for Europe[2] that most of an individual's exposure to many air pollutants comes through inhalation of indoor air. Many of the pollutants found indoors can cause health reactions in the estimated 17 million Americans who suffer from asthma and 40 million who have allergies, contributing to millions of days absent from school and work.

Homeowners are just beginning to realize the link between their health and their homes. Hazardous household pollutants may include carbon monoxide, radon, formaldehyde, mold, dirt and dust, pet dander, and residue from tobacco smoke and candles. Many homeowners also store various chemicals inside their homes as well, including pesticides, fertilizers, solvents, grease, oils, degreasers, gasoline, antifreeze, strong detergents, thinners, and oil-based paints.

Over the past 20 years, research and experience have improved our understanding of what is involved in attaining high indoor environmental quality and revealed manufacturing and construction practices that can prevent problems from arising. Preventing indoor air quality problems is generally much less expensive than identifying and solving them after they occur. Generally, there are three types of strategies: source removal, source control, and dilution.

Source removal is the most practical way to ensure that harmful chemical compounds are not brought into the home. Evaluating the properties of adhesives, paints, carpets, composite wood products, and furniture and selecting materials with low levels of potentially irritating off-gassing can reduce occupants' exposure. Scheduling deliveries and sequencing construction activities can reduce exposure of materials to moisture and absorption of off-gassed contaminants. (Low emissions materials are addressed under Materials & Resources.)

Source control strategies focus on capturing pollutants that are known to exist in a home. For example, filtering the supply air stream removes particulates that would otherwise be continuously recirculated through the home. Protection of air-handling systems during construction and a building flushout prior to occupancy further reduce the potential for problems.

Dilution involves the use of fresh outside air to ventilate a home and exhaust pollutants to the outdoors. This may also help control moisture within the home. Most new homes in the United States do not have mechanical fresh-air ventilation systems. The typical air-handling systems in new homes merely recirculate the air within the home, continuously pumping indoor pollutants through the rooms rather than exhausting them.

Another aspect of indoor air quality is occupant comfort. The proper installation of automatic sensors and controls to maintain proper temperature, humidity,

---

1 United States Environmental Protection Agency. *Healthy Buildings, Healthy People: A Vision for the 21st Century.* October 2001. www.epa.gov/iaq/hbhp/hbhptoc.html

2 World Health Organization. *Air Quality Guidelines for Europe, Second Edition.* 2000. www.euro.who.int/document/e71922.pdf

and ventilation in occupied spaces helps maintain optimal air quality. Surprisingly, sensors to alert a home's occupants to deadly carbon monoxide concentrations are frequently not required by current codes but should be included in all new homes. Letting occupants fully and effectively control their thermal environment can reduce hot–cold complaint calls and generally raise satisfaction levels.

The Indoor Environmental Quality (EQ) credit category encourages builders to prevent air pollution and improve air quality and comfort in the homes they build.

Alternative Compliance Pathways

The two parallel pathways through the 10 EQ credits in the LEED for Homes Rating System are illustrated in **Table 1** and summarized below.

Pathway 1: EPA Indoor airPLUS

Projects that participate in the U.S. Environmental Protection Agency's Indoor airPLUS (IAP) initiative automatically qualify for 13 points. Projects that meet IAP are exempt from the prerequisites in EQ 2–10, since IAP includes comparable requirements. Up to 8 additional points are available if the following credits are also completed:

EQ 4.2: Enhanced Outdoor Air Ventilation

EQ 5.2: Enhanced Local Exhaust

EQ 5.3: Third-Party Testing

EQ 7.2 or 7.3: Better or Best Air Filters

EQ 8.2: Indoor Contaminant Control

Pathway 2: Prescriptive Approach

Pathway 2 also has a maximum of 21 points, distributed throughout EQ credits 2–10:

EQ 2: Combustion Venting

EQ 3: Moisture Control

EQ 4: Outdoor Air Ventilation

EQ 5: Local Exhaust

EQ 6: Distribution Systems

EQ 7: Air Filtering

EQ 8: Contaminant Control

EQ 9: Radon Protection

EQ 10: Garage Pollutant Protection

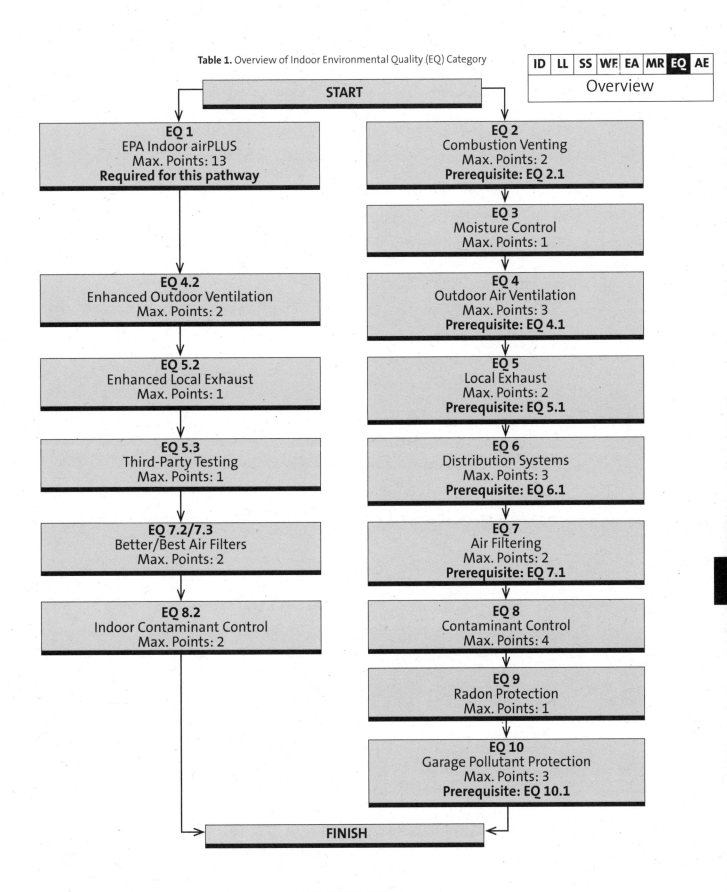

IMPORTANT NOTE:
*A minimum of **6 points** must be achieved in the EQ category.*

EQ 1: EPA Indoor airPLUS

Intent

Improve the overall quality of a home's indoor environment by installing an approved bundle of air quality measures.

Requirements

Prerequisites

None.

Credits

1 **EPA Indoor airPLUS** (13 points). Complete all the requirements of the U.S. Environmental Protection Agency's EPA Indoor airPLUS (IAP).

Synergies and Trade-Offs

A project receiving points for this credit may skip the prerequisites in EQ 2–10 and is not eligible to earn points in EQ 2.2, 3, 4.3, 6, 8.1, 8.3, 9, and 10.

Achieving the measures in EPA's Indoor airPLUS may qualify a home to receive points in other categories of the LEED for Homes Rating System. See **Table 1** for equivalencies.

Table 1. Applicability of EPA Indoor airPLUS Measures to LEED for Homes

LEED for Homes prerequisites / credits	Relevant Indoor airPLUS measures	Applicability
Innovation in Design Process 2.1, 2.2	Various	Meeting Indoor airPLUS specifications will address many durability issues listed in durability inspection checklist template.
Sustainable Sites 5	3.1, 3.2	Depending on project location, meeting Indoor airPLUS specifications may earn up to 2 LEED points.
Energy & Atmosphere 6.1 (a) and EA 11.1	4.1, 7.1	Meeting Indoor airPLUS specifications achieves prerequisites EA 6.1(a) and EA 11.1.
Materials & Resources 2.2	6.1–6.3	Depending on project details, meeting Indoor airPLUS specifications may earn up to 2 LEED points.

EQ 1: EPA Indoor airPLUS

The U.S. Environmental Protection Agency's Indoor airPLUS is a labeling program designed to encourage healthier indoor air quality in new homes. Implementing its comprehensive set of measures for ventilation, source control, and source removal earns 13 LEED points. The program requires verification and documentation by an accredited third party trained by EPA.

Approach and Implementation

EPA's Indoor airPLUS is not currently available in all areas of the country. Qualified energy raters are the principal third-party inspectors. Ask your qualified energy rater whether this program is available in your area and whether he or she has been trained in its application and verification.

In 2009, the EPA released the Indoor airPLUS program as a replacement for the original Indoor Air Package program. LEED for Homes projects that register after June 23, 2009 must use the Indoor airPLUS program to earn EQ 1; projects that registered prior to that date are encouraged to use Indoor airPLUS, but they may use Indoor airPLUS instead.

Project teams may choose between participation in this program and the alternative pathway, EQ 2–10. Review the requirements of both approaches with a certified qualified energy rater and choose the more appropriate path for the project. If a project pursues EPA Indoor airPLUS, additional LEED points can be earned in EQs 5.2, 5.3, 7.2, 7.3, and 8.2. If the EPA program is not available, the alternative pathway must be used, including all prerequisites.

The Indoor airPLUS measures should be addressed during the design stage and included in building plans and documentation. Many of these measures should also be included as part of the durability planning effort for Innovation in Design 2.

Calculations

Please see the requirements of the EPA Indoor airPLUS for details.

Exemplary Performance

No additional points are available for exemplary performance.

Verification and Submittals

Supporting Verification Materials, made available by the Project Team:

❑ Present EPA Indoor airPLUS certification to the Verification Team.

Verification Team:

❑ Verify that EPA Indoor airPLUS certification has been achieved.

Considerations

Environmental Issues

The EPA program includes a broad set of measures that target most types of indoor pollutants. It offers a well-crafted package for homebuyers interested in purchasing a healthful home.

Economic Issues

EPA created the Indoor airPLUS to help builders meet the growing consumer preference for homes with improved indoor air quality and energy efficiency. By constructing homes that meet these stringent specifications, forward-thinking builders can distinguish themselves and offer homes that display the EPA Indoor airPLUS label.

Regional Variances

EPA Indoor airPLUS is a one-size-fits-all approach to indoor environment problems. Innovation in Design 2 offers more regional flexibility in addressing some of these issues.

Resources

Please see the USGBC Web site, at www. usgbc.org/resources, for more specific resources on materials sources and other technical information.

Web Sites

EPA Indoor airPLUS Program

U.S. Environmental Protection Agency

www.epa.gov/indoorairplus

This Web site provides all the necessary information on the EPA Indoor airPLUS.

EQ 2: Combustion Venting

Intent

Minimize the leakage of combustion gases into the occupied space of the home.

Requirements

Prerequisites

2.1 **Basic Combustion Venting Measures.** Meet all the following requirements.

   a) No unvented combustion appliances (e.g., decorative logs) are allowed.

   b) A carbon monoxide (CO) monitor must be installed on each floor.

   c) All fireplaces and woodstoves must have doors.

   d) Space and water heating equipment that involves combustion must meet one of the following. Space heating systems in homes located in IECC-2007 climate zone 1 or 2 are exempt.

   i. it must be designed and installed with closed combustion (i.e., sealed supply air and exhaust ducting);

   ii. it must be designed and installed with power-vented exhaust; or

   iii. it must be located in a detached utility building or open-air facility.

Credits

2.2 **Enhanced Combustion Venting Measures** (maximum 2 points). Install no fireplace or woodstove, or design and install a fireplace or woodstove according to the requirements in **Table 1**.

Conducting a Back-Draft Potential Test

Using the results from a blower-door test, measure the pressure difference created by the presence of a chimney-vented appliance. To ensure a limited risk of back-drafting, the pressure difference (ΔP) must be less than or equal to 5 Pascals, where

$$\Delta P = (Q/C)^{1/n} \text{ (must be} \leq 5 \text{ Pascals)}$$

and Q is equal to the sum of the rated exhaust provided by the two biggest exhaust appliances in the home, and C and n are both constants produced by the blower-door test results.

Synergies and Trade-Offs

A project receiving points for EQ 1 is not eligible to earn points in EQ 2.2. A project pursuing EQ 2.2 must meet all the prerequisites in EQ 2–10.

Table 1: Fireplace and Stove Combustion-Venting Requirements

Fireplace or stove	Enhanced combustion-venting measures	
	Better practice (1 point)	Best practice (2 points)
None	See "best practice".	Granted automatically.
Masonry wood-burning fireplace	Install masonry heater as defined by American Society for Testing and Materials Standard E-1602 and International Building Code 2112.1.	Meet requirement for "better practice", and conduct back-draft potential test to ensure $\Delta P \leq 5$ Pascals (see "Conducting a Back-Draft Potential Test" below).
Factory-built wood-burning fireplace	Install equipment listed by approved safety testing facility (e.g., UL, CSA, ETL) that either is EPA certified or meets the following: equipment with catalytic combustor must emit less than 4.1 g/hr of particulate matter, and equipment without catalytic combustor must emit less than 7.5 g/hr of particulate matter.	Meet requirement for better practice, and conduct back-draft potential test to ensure $\Delta P \leq 5$ Pascals (see "Conducting a Back-Draft Potential Test" below).
Woodstove and fireplace insert	Install equipment listed by approved safety testing facility that either is EPA certified or meets following requirement: equipment with catalytic combustor must emit less than 4.1 g/hr of particulate matter, and equipment without catalytic combustor must emit less than 7.5 g/hr of particulate matter.	Meet requirement for better practice, and conduct back-draft potential test to ensure $\Delta P \leq 5$ Pascals (see "Conducting a Back-Draft Potential Test" below).
Natural gas, propane, or alcohol stove	Install equipment listed by approved safety testing facility that is power-vented or direct-vented and has permanently fixed glass front or gasketed door.	Meet requirement for better practice, and include electronic (not standing) pilot.
Pellet stove	Install equipment that is either EPA certified or listed by approved safety testing facility to have met requirements of ASTM E 1509-04, "Standard Specification for Room Heaters, Pellet Fuel-Burning Type."	Meet requirement for better practice, and include power venting or direct venting.

The leakage of toxic combustion exhaust gases into the home can cause poor indoor air quality and human health impacts, particularly in homes that are well constructed and well sealed. Closed combustion through direct or power venting can dramatically reduce the risk that combustion gases will be drawn into the home under conditions of negative pressure. The best way to block combustion gases from fireplaces and wood-burning stoves is to avoid installing them; fireplace doors provide a minimal reduction in back-drafting. Although closed combustion reduces back-drafting, the use of monitors is an easy and effective way to mitigate the risk of unforeseen exposure to carbon monoxide from leaks, equipment failures, and unanticipated occupant behavior.

Approach and Implementation

If a fireplace or woodstove is installed, ensure that it is vented and has tight-fitting doors or a solid glass enclosure. The requirement for doors is met if the fireplace has a solid glass enclosure. Install carbon monoxide monitors on each level or floor of the house, in or near any spaces that are above or next to combustion appliances or garages. In multi-family buildings, CO monitors must be installed in each unit.

Work with the HVAC contractor to identify combustion appliances that suit the needs of the home, meet the energy goals of the project, and are designed for closed combustion or power-vented exhaust. If the project requires appliances that are not direct-vented or power-vented, include plans for a detached or open-air space for the appliances. The common practices of installing a chimney-vented furnace and locating the water heater in an attic or attached garage do not meet the requirements for this credit.

Closed combustion requires that both the supply air and the exhaust air are fully ducted and sealed. Power-vented exhaust systems use fans to blow air out of the house and prevent back-drafting of combustion gases. Both options eliminate the need for a conventional chimney.

All furnace and water heater manufacturers offer a wide range of direct- and power-vented alternatives. Most high-efficiency furnaces (i.e., 90% AFUE or higher) are direct-vented through sealed plastic pipe. A standard midefficiency furnace usually vents into a conventional natural-draft chimney and therefore does not meet the intent of this requirement.

The noise associated with a power-vented water heater may be objectionable if the appliance is installed within the home. Select a power-vented water heater with a quiet motor or install the unit away from living areas. An alternative to closed-combustion furnaces or water heaters is the use of electric heat pumps and electric water heaters, which do not involve combustion.

Kitchen stoves and ovens are not considered unvented combustion appliances, as kitchens are required to have local exhaust under EQ 5.

Projects with masonry wood-burning fireplaces can earn 1 point for either meeting the requirements for a masonry heater OR passing the backdraft potential test. These projects must meet the requirements for a masonry heater AND pass the backdraft potential test to earn 2 points.

Calculations

No calculations are required for this credit.

The BPI Worst Case Combustion Zone Test is an acceptable method for meeting the requirements of the back-draft test, as long as all exhaust appliances (e.g. bathroom fan, clothes dryer, range hood) are included.

Exemplary Performance

No additional points are available for exemplary performance.

Verification and Submittals

Verification Team:

❑ Visually verify that all requirements of the prerequisite have been met.

Considerations

Economic Issues

The use of direct-vented furnaces offers flexibility in installation because they can be installed not only in the same location as conventional furnaces but also in closets, and they are usually multipositional.

Regional Variances

Homes in very hot climates (IECC climate zones 1 and 2) are exempt from the closed-combustion requirement because the use of fireplaces and furnaces in these areas is infrequent and therefore poses less of a human health risk. Homes in these areas are still encouraged to use direct-vented or electric water heaters.

Resources

Web Sites

Combustion Gases and Carbon Monoxide

U.S. Environmental Protection Agency

www.epa.gov/iaq/combust.html

www.epa.gov/iaq/co.html

These two extensive EPA sites describe the sources of carbon monoxide and other combustion gases, their health effects, steps to reduce exposure, related standards and guidelines, and additional resources and links.

Canada Mortgage and Housing Corporation

www.cmhc-schl.gc.ca/en/co/maho/yohoyohe/inaiqu/inaiqu_004.cfm

This site is part of CMHC's "About Your House" series of educational articles. It includes information about combustion gases, the effects of exposure, and strategies for limiting exposure.

Product Safety Tips: CO Alarms

Underwriters Laboratories

www.ul.com/consumers/co.html

This site provides a basic overview of the problems associated with carbon monoxide, as well as tips about purchasing and installing carbon monoxide alarms.

EQ 2.2: Enhanced Combustion-Venting Measures

Indoor air quality and human health are adversely affected by leakage of exhaust combustion gases into the home. Having no fireplace or stove is the most effective way to reduce the risk associated with combustion gases. Meeting EQ 2.1 for fireplaces and woodstoves provides minimal back-draft protection. Better practice is installation of efficient appliances that achieve a more complete burn and therefore produce fewer pollutants and reduce human health risks. Best practice provides improved appliance efficiency and the highest level of back-draft protection.

Approach and Implementation

The only way to completely eliminate the risks associated with harmful combustion gases from fireplaces and wood-burning stoves is not to install these appliances. The next best option is to install a system that burns cleanly and minimizes the risk of back-drafting into the house. Natural gas and propane fireplaces that are designed properly with direct-venting pose fairly little risk. Masonry heaters are designed to burn efficiently and are an effective method for space heating.

A conventional site-built open-hearth fireplace is not eligible for points in this credit. Such fireplaces are very inefficient, in part because they draw a large amount of combustion air from within the home. Consequently, they tend to pull air through envelope leaks, making the home cold and drafty.

If a traditional wood-burning fireplace or stove is desired, select a UL-listed factory-built fireplace or factory-built insert that meets EPA standards for particulate matter emissions. Such appliances are designed to burn solid fuel more fully and more cleanly, which means improved efficiency, safety, and indoor air quality.

Fireplaces with 60% to 80% efficiency are readily available in the marketplace.

Provide a source of air to the fireplace or stove and limit the number and size of exhaust fans in the house. Even factory-built wood-burning fireplaces and stoves with tight-fitting doors can result in some back-draft of combustion gases into the home. The greatest risk of back-drafting comes from running large exhaust fans (e.g., kitchen, bathroom, or other ventilation with high cfm ratings), which can depressurize the home and pull air from the fireplace back inside. Back-draft potential tests should be conducted by an qualified qualified energy rater.

For gas fireplaces, use an electronic ignition rather than a continuously operating pilot light to save energy throughout the year.

Seal air leaks at the joint between the chimney and the wall by removing the trim (if necessary) and applying heat-resistant caulking.

Install a carbon monoxide detector near all combustion appliances.

Calculations

To meet the best practice requirements and earn 2 points, a home with a wood-burning stove or fireplace must pass a back-draft potential test, to be conducted by the qualified energy rater. This calculation requires a blower-door test.

Using the results from a blower-door test, test the pressure difference created by the presence of a chimney-vented appliance. The pressure difference (ΔP) must be less than or equal to 5 Pascals, where

$$\Delta P = (Q/C)^{1/n} \ (\leq 5 \text{ Pascals})$$

and Q is equal to the sum of the rated exhaust provided by the two biggest exhaust appliances in the house, and C and n are both constants produced by the blower-door test results.

Exemplary Performance

No additional points are available for exemplary performance.

Verification and Submittals

Supporting Verification Materials, made available by the Project Team:

❑ Present any fireplace or stove equipment literature (e.g., user manuals, brochures, specifications) to the Verification Team for visual inspection.

❑ Include fireplace or stove equipment literature in the occupant's operations and maintenance manual.

❑ For best practice with a wood-burning stove or fireplace, present back-draft calculations to the Verification Team.

❑ For masonry heaters, sign Accountability Form to indicate that the product meets the credit.

Verification Team:

❑ Visually verify that all applicable standards and certifications have been met: check safety listing in the appliance user manual, check EPA certification on the EPA Web site (www.epa.gov/woodstoves/index.html) or in the user manual, and check pellet stove compliance with ASTM E1509-04 in the appliance user manual. (See labels, **Figure 1**.)

❑ For best practice with a wood-burning stove or fireplace, visually verify that back-draft calculations are completed.

❑ Visually verify all applicable equipment in the home.

❑ For masonry heaters, verify that an Accountability Form has been signed by the appropriate party.

Figure 1. Safety Laboratory and EPA Certification Labels

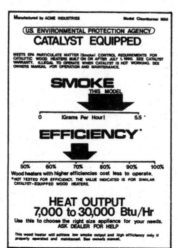

Considerations

Environmental Issues

Inefficient, poorly designed fireplaces and stoves not only increase the risk of exposure to combustion gas within the house, they also have higher emissions of harmful particulates and other combustion products. Poorly designed systems can depressurize the home, causing backdraft of gases.

Economic Issues

Poorly designed fireplaces can cause air to be pulled into the house through cracks and seams, leading to increased infiltration and increased space-heating costs.

Resources

Web Sites

Combustion Gases and Carbon Monoxide

U.S. Environmental Protection Agency

www.epa.gov/iaq/combust.html

www.epa.gov/iaq/co.html

These two extensive EPA sites describe the sources of carbon monoxide and other combustion gases, their health effects, the steps to reduce exposure, related standards and guidelines, and additional resources and links.

Canada Mortgage and Housing Corporation

www.cmhc-schl.gc.ca/en/co/maho/yohoyohe/inaiqu/inaiqu_004.cfm

This site is part of CMHC's "About Your House" series of educational articles. It includes information about combustion gases, the effects of exposure, and strategies for limiting exposure.

Environmental Protection Agency

www.epa.gov/woodstoves/index.html

This site focuses on clean-burning fireplaces and woodstoves and includes information on wood-burning efficiency and safety, as well as EPA-certified products.

Hearth, Patio, and Barbecue Association

www.hpba.org

This site contains product and safety information about masonry heaters, factory-built fireplaces, and fireplace inserts.

Masonry Heater Association of North America

www.mha-net.org/html/library.htm

This site provides information about masonry heaters, including descriptions, specifications, and articles.

ID	LL	SS	WE	EA	MR	EQ	AE
				2.2			

ID	LL	SS	WE	EA	MR	EQ	AE
			2.2				

U.S. Green Building Council

288

EQ 3: Moisture Control

Intent

Control indoor moisture levels to provide comfort, reduce the risk of mold, and increase the durability of the home.

Requirements

Prerequisites

None.

Credits

3 **Moisture Load Control** (1 point). Install dehumidification equipment with sufficient latent capacity to maintain relative humidity at or below 60%. This must be achieved through one of the following:

a) Additional dehumidification system(s).

b) A central HVAC system equipped with additional controls to operate in dehumidification mode.

Note: LEED for Homes does not encourage active dehumidification for all projects. Work with the HVAC contractor to determine whether this credit is appropriate and/or necessary.

Synergies and Trade-Offs

A project receiving points for EQ 1 is not eligible to earn points in EQ 3. A project pursuing EQ 3 must meet all the prerequisites in EQ 2–10.

Water leakage through the building envelope can cause mold and other indoor environmental problems. Improved foundation, exterior walls, and roof water management should be addressed in the durability inspection checklist (ID 2).

In hot and humid climates, dehumidification can reduce the energy demands associated with air-conditioning (EA 1, 6).

EQ 3: Moisture Control

Traditional HVAC designs do not typically include moisture balance considerations. Extremely high or low humidity levels can create an uncomfortable living space and lead to premature durability failures. High humidity levels can foster mold growth, leading to human health problems. This credit rewards projects that manage the moisture balance in the home during both summer and winter conditions.

Approach and Implementation

The best approach for moisture control depends on the typical humidity levels and peak humidity levels (high and low) throughout the year. Dehumidification may not be worthwhile for every project. If the home is in a warm, humid area of the country or if the sensible heat ratio is less than 0.70, then dehumidification may be an important strategy. Humidity control is important in cold climate areas, too, because indoor moisture can lead to condensation but excess ventilation results in high space-heating costs.

It can be difficult to determine ideal humidity levels because thermal comfort for individuals is affected by air temperature, humidity level, air movement, and personal preference or health conditions. Good practice is to keep relative humidity (RH) levels between 25% and 45% in the winter and below 60% in the summer.

Dehumidification equipment is not required to maintain RH <60% for every hour of the year; projects are granted some discretion. When determining latent loads to include, use ASHRAE Fundamentals or a comparable standard. Loads should include outdoor loads from ventilation and air leakage, as well as indoor loads from showers, cooking, etc.

This credit can be earned only through the use of dehumidification systems or additional dehumidification controls on the HVAC equipment that will maintain humidity levels at or below 60% RH. Some projects—particularly those located in dry climates—may not need dehumidification to maintain a low RH, in which case this credit may not be appropriate or applicable.

Indoor humidity is affected by infiltration and ventilation. An engineer or HVAC contractor should use infiltration and ventilation rates to calculate the amount of moisture removed in winter and added in summer. Use this estimate, together with industry estimates (e.g., ASHRAE data) of indoor moisture loads from occupants, to determine whether additional moisture control measures are necessary.

Indoor moisture levels are influenced by both external humidity and indoor activities. In a house with reduced outside air infiltration, human respiration, cleaning, showering, and other activities can have a considerable impact on humidity levels. Indoor loads can be significant enough to require dehumidification even during dry periods (e.g., winter).

Avoid oversizing air-conditioning systems. Oversized AC units cost more money and short-cycle, never allowing proper moisture control. Encourage HVAC contractors to select AC coils that have high latent ratios (the ability to remove more moisture).

Simple controls can be very effective. For example, in cold climates, use a dehumidistat on an exhaust fan, and in warm, humid climates, use a thermostat that also has a humidity control allowing the AC unit to operate for either air cooling or dehumidification.

Mechanical ventilation systems should be sized appropriately to help ensure proper moisture control. Include energy-recovery ventilators (ERVs) on the ventilation system. ERVs transfer moisture between outgoing exhaust streams and incoming supply air streams and thus help moderate indoor moisture levels in dry winters or humid summers.

Efficient stand-alone or ducted dehumidifiers can be used to maintain acceptable humidity levels in parts of the home that experience excess humidity, such as the basement.

Table 1 provides guidance on the appropriate humidity levels necessary for thermal comfort at different warm-weather temperatures. If humidity levels exceed these values, occupants will be. uncomfortable and reduce thermostat settings, wasting energy.

Calculations

An engineer or HVAC contractor should use infiltration and ventilation rates to calculate the amount of moisture removed in winter and added in summer. Use this estimate, together with industry estimates (e.g., ASHRAE data) of indoor moisture loads from occupants, to determine whether moisture control measures in addition to dehumidistats and advanced thermostats are necessary.

Even the best calculations, however, require assumptions about occupant loads and design infiltration rates that may not reflect actual conditions. Calculations for this credit therefore cannot guarantee adequate moisture control in individual houses under all circumstances.

Exemplary Performance

No additional points are available for exemplary performance.

Verification and Submittals

Supporting Verification Materials, made available by the Project Team:

❑ Present calculations of latent capacity to the Verification Team.

❑ Include dehumidification equipment literature in the occupant's operations and maintenance manual.

Verification Team:

❑ Visually verify that all calculations related to latent capacity are completed.

❑ Visually verify all applicable equipment in the home.

Considerations

Environmental Issues

Improved moisture control creates a greatly improved indoor environment. By eliminating condensation, mold, and odor problems, builders can construct more comfortable homes that pose fewer health risks to the occupants.

Economic Issues

High humidity levels encourage occupants to change air-conditioning thermostat settings to temperatures that are lower than necessary, wasting energy and money. A dehumidification system or simple moisture control measures can

Table 1. Maximum Comfortable Humidity at Summer Temperatures

Indoor temperature (degrees F)	Relative humidity (%)	Humidity ratio (lb water / lb dry air)
70	76	0.012
74	66	0.012
78	58	0.012
82	50	0.012

reduce the burden on the air-conditioner, permitting installation of a smaller, less expensive system and reducing operating costs.

Regional Variances

Although moisture control is of greatest concern in hot and humid climates, excess humidity from indoor moisture loads can be a problem in any tight house. During cold weather, indoor moisture can cause damaging condensation and mold growth.

Resources

Web Sites

Building America Best Practice Handbooks

www.eere.energy.gov/buildings/building_america

This site includes links to the Best Practice Handbooks, which include detailed information about design and construction practices following building science principles. The focus of these handbooks is to emphasize indoor moisture control through good envelope design.

ENERGY STAR Program Dehumidifiers

U.S. Environmental Protection Agency

www.energystar.gov/index.cfm?c=dehumid.pr_dehumidifiers

This Web site provides information on ENERGY STAR–labeled dehumidifiers, including the advantages of the label, criteria for earning the label, and a list of products.

Energy & Environmental Building Association, Builders' Guides

www.eeba.org/bookstore

The EEBA Builders' Guides, written by Joe Lstiburek, provide detailed step-by-step guidance on design and construction

based on building science and best practice construction techniques. There are four climate-specific guides: hot and humid, cold, mixed humid, and mixed dry. These guides emphasize indoor moisture control through good envelope design.

Moisture: Build to Keep It Out of Homes in Warm, Humid Climates

Clemson University

www.clemson.edu/psapublishing/PAGES/FYD/HL258.pdf

This short report describes the relationships between moisture, comfort, and performance and explains the causes and remedies of excess moisture in the home.

Mold Resources

U.S. Environmental Protection Agency

www.epa.gov/mold/moldresources.html

This Web site is a comprehensive review of mold growth in the home, covering causes, risks, and preventive measures. In addition to overview content, there are links to various articles and technical papers, including the EPA report "A Brief Guide to Mold, Moisture, and Your Home."

Residential Dehumidification Systems Research for Hot-Humid Climates

U.S. Department of Energy, Building America Program

www.nrel.gov/docs/fy05osti/36643.pdf

This report, published by DOE, describes a two-year empirical study of dehumidification systems in a hot-humid climate. The report includes goals, methods, and lessons learned from the study.

Print Media

ASHRAE Standard 55-2004: Thermal Environmental Conditions for Human Occupancy. ASHRAE, 2004.

ASHRAE Standard 62-2004: Ventilation for Acceptable Indoor Air Quality in Low-Rise Buildings. ASHRAE, 2004.

Humidity Control Design Guide, by L.
Harriman, G.W. Brundett, and R. Kittler.
ASHRAE, 2000.

EQ 4: Outdoor Air Ventilation

Intent

Reduce occupant exposure to indoor pollutants by ventilating with outdoor air.

Requirements

Prerequisites

4.1 **Basic Outdoor Air Ventilation.** Design and install a whole building ventilation system that complies with ASHRAE Standard 62.2-2007. A summary of alternatives is provided below, but the HVAC contractor should review and follow the requirements of ASHRAE Standard 62.2-2007, Sections 4 and 7.

a) Mild climate exemption. A home built in a climate with fewer than 4,500 infiltration degree-days[3] is exempt from this prerequisite.

b) Continuous ventilation. Meet the ventilation requirements in **Table 1** below.

c) Intermittent ventilation. Use Equation 4.2 of ASHRAE Standard 62.2-2007 to demonstrate adequate ventilation air flow.

d) Passive ventilation. Have a passive ventilation system approved and verified by a licensed HVAC engineer as providing ventilation equivalent to that achieved by continuous ventilation systems as described in **Table 1**.

Credits

4.2 **Enhanced Outdoor Air Ventilation** (2 points). Meet one of the following:

a) In mild climates (fewer than 4,500 infiltration degree-days), install a whole-building active ventilation system that complies with ASHRAE Standard 62.2-2007.

OR

b) Install a system that provides heat transfer between the incoming outdoor air stream and the exhaust air stream, such as a heat-recovery ventilator (HRV) or energy-recovery ventilator (ERV). The heat recovery system must be listed by a certified testing lab (e.g., UL, ETL).

4.3 **Third-Party Performance Testing** (1 point). Have a third-party test the flow rate of air brought into the home, and verify that the requirements of ASHRAE Standard 62.2-2007 are met. In exhaust-only ventilation systems, install exhaust ducts according to Table 7.1 of ASHRAE Standard 62.2-2007, and either test the flow rate out of the home or conduct air flow tests to ensure back-pressure of ≤ 0.20 inches w.c.

---

3 It is assumed that in mild climates (areas with fewer than 4,500 infiltration degree-days), the minimum outdoor air ventilation needs can be met with open windows and doors. Homes in these areas are also exempt from meeting the air filtering requirements of ASHRAE Standard 62.2 under EQ 7.1.

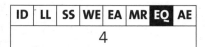

Table 1. Minimum Air Flow Requirements for Continuous Ventilation Systems, in cfm

Conditioned floor area (ft²)	Bedrooms				
	0, 1	**2, 3**	**4, 5**	**6, 7**	**> 7**
≤ 1,500	30	45	60	75	90
1,501–3,000	45	60	75	90	105
3,001–4,500	60	75	90	105	120
4,501–6,000	75	90	105	120	135
6,001–7,500	90	105	120	135	150
> 7,500	105	120	135	150	165

Credit: ASHRAE Standard 62.2, 2007. ©American Society of Heating, Refrigerating and Air Conditioning Engineers, Inc., www.ashrae.org <http://www.ashrae.org/>

Synergies and Trade-Offs

A project receiving points for EQ 1 is not eligible to earn points for EQ 4.3, but may earn points for EQ 4.2. A project pursuing EQ 4.3 must meet all the prerequisites in EQ 2–10.

Natural air leakage through the envelope contributes to the overall ventilation rate of the home (EA 3.1–3.3). From a health perspective, it is important not to underventilate a home. From an energy perspective, it is important not to overventilate.

Exhaust fans, which also provide the local exhaust required by EQ 5.1, can simultaneously provide the outdoor air ventilation system for the home.

A heat-recovery system can substantially reduce the energy used by the heating and cooling equipment (EA 6).

Outdoor air has historically been provided through leaks in the house envelope, but energy concerns have led to construction practices with reduced natural infiltration. This is compounded by changes in lifestyle—people today spend more time indoors with windows and doors closed—and increased awareness of the risks associated with poor indoor air quality. Homes with insufficient outdoor air have problems with humidity, odors, and pollutants that can lead to discomfort and increased health risks. Designed ventilation systems help reduce occupants' exposure to indoor pollutants and improve comfort.

Even well-designed ventilation systems sometimes fail to operate properly because of installation errors, equipment problems, or accidental interference by other trades. Third-party testing provides assurance that the ventilation system will operate as designed.

Approach and Implementation

There are various ways to meet the prerequisite in EQ 4.1, but having a whole-building ventilation design is important in all regions of the country and all types of homes.

Relying solely on natural ventilation does not sufficiently address air quality concerns where occupants may keep doors and windows closed during cold, hot, or humid weather. This approach is reliable only in mild climates. Homes in areas with fewer than 4,500 infiltration degree-days are exempt from the prerequisite because it is assumed that occupants in such mild climates will keep windows and doors open more often.

ASHRAE Standard 62.2 allows passive ventilation designs provided the design is approved by an HVAC professional and ensures adequate air-flow rates through the home. For EQ 4.1 (d), Green Raters must verify some evidence (e.g., model results, calculations, or on-site test results) that the design will yield air flows equivalent to those required by ASHRAE Std. 62.2. Operable windows and natural infiltration is not sufficient, because the air flows in Std. 62.2 already assume natural infiltration (i.e., the Std. 62.2 air flows are above natural infiltration).

Projects using passive ventilation must submit their strategies to the USGBC for research purposes. Even in areas with little heating and cooling loads, a quiet bathroom fan with a simple timer control is a great opportunity to provide occupants with improved indoor environmental quality.

Standard 62.2 addresses minimum ventilation capacity. Additional capacity may be required if there will be high occupant loads or additional indoor pollutants from a home office, crafts, or other activities.

The HVAC contractor should follow the requirements in ASHRAE Standard 62.2, Section 4.1.3, to ensure that natural and mechanical ventilation is properly integrated and the house has neither too little nor too much ventilation. The HVAC contractor should not rely on the language in the LEED credit but should carefully review all of Standard 62.2 related to ventilation. The minimum air-flow requirements listed in **Table 1**, above, are applicable only to systems designed for continuous operation.

When locating the fresh-air intake for a ventilation system, consider pollutant sources, such as exhaust from vehicles, dryers, or other appliances or gas vents.

Locate the fresh-air intake at least 6 feet from pollutant sources.

Projects using intermittent ventilation systems must compensate by installing fans with a greater flow rate. Review the requirements of ASHRAE Standard 62.2, Section 4.4, for details.

The EQ 4.1 mandatory measures can be met with one of three basic strategies:

1) Exhaust-only ventilation. Install a quiet bathroom fan, sized in accordance with Standard 62.2, with a timer switch to allow for continuous or extended run times, and install exhaust ducts according to Standard 62.2, Table 7.1. This approach depressurizes the house, pulling air in through leaks in the home. In hot, humid climates, exhaust-only ventilation systems draw in humid air, creating a risk of condensation within wall cavities. For this reason, exhaust-only systems are most suitable for cold climates.

2) Supply-only ventilation. Install a properly sized fresh-air duct tied into the return air system of a furnace or an air handler with a timer or controller that allows the air-handler fan to operate continuously or for sufficient time to ensure the introduction of fresh air. Supply-only systems are most suitable for hot climates.

3) Balanced ventilation with or without heat recovery. Install a system of supply and exhaust fans that operate simultaneously to ensure an exchange of air between inside and outside. Heat-recovery or energy-recovery ventilators use the waste energy from the exhaust air stream to preheat the ventilation air in winter and precool it in summer. HRVs and ERVs are addressed in EQ 4.2.

Specify timer controls that ensure the ventilation system will operate during peak occupancy periods (early morning and evening) and also allow occupants to extend the run times.

Common problems with exhaust-only systems are undersized fans, crushed or ruptured exhaust ducts, and clogged or broken fans. Use rigid ducts to reduce the risk that workers will accidentally crush ducts. Seal ductwork during construction to prevent puncturing the ducts and clogging the system with paint and particulates.

Ventilation is most effective if air is provided directly to every room. Otherwise, some rooms (e.g., bedrooms) may get insufficient outside air.

Only systems that are quiet, efficient, and simple to operate will be used by occupants. Choose fans that have a sound rating of less than 1.5 sones, preferably under 1 sone.

Some building types (e.g., nursing homes, dormitories, buildings with more than three stories) fall outside the scope of ASHRAE Standard 62.2. Such buildings should follow the ventilation requirements in ASHRAE Standard 62.1.

Performance testing is important for identifying any equipment failures or installation problems. HVAC contractors should conduct their own performance testing, but this does not qualify as third-party testing for the purposes of EQ 4.3.

Third-party testing must be performed by a qualified qualified energy rater, Verification Team, or a third-party testing and balancing company. If testing indicates insufficient air flow rates, the HVAC contractor should investigate and fix the problem. Once the problem is fixed, the air flow rates must be re-tested and the requirements of the credit must be met before EQ 4.3 can be awarded.

Calculations

The number of infiltration degree-days is equal to the sum of the cooling degree-days plus the heating degree-days for a particular location. These exemptions are based on ASHRAE Std. 62.2-2004, which references ASHRAE Std. 119-1988 (RA 2004). Following this standard, LEED for Homes uses a base of 65ºF for heating degree-days and 78ºF for cooling degree-days.

ASHRAE prescribes a simple calculation for determining the minimum amount of mechanical ventilation. See Equations 4.1a and 4.1b in Standard 62.2, Section 4. As an example, a three-bedroom home with a conditioned floor area of 2,500 square feet requires a minimum ventilation rate of 60 cfm.

Equation 4.2 in ASHRAE Standard 62.2 covers intermittent ventilation systems.

Exemplary Performance

No additional points are available for exemplary performance.

Verification and Submittals

Supporting Verification Materials, made available by the Project Team:

EQ 4.1 Basic Outdoor Air Ventilation

❑ For EQ 4.1(b) and (c), present calculations to the Verification Team demonstrating that the ventilation system is designed to meet the requirements.

❑ For EQ 4.1(d), present calculations, test results, or equivalent that demonstrates that the proposed designs meet ASHRAE Standard 62.2.

❑ Include equipment literature in the occupant's operations and maintenance manual.

❑ For EQ 4.1(b), (c) and (d), sign an Accountability Form to indicate that the system is installed according to the design specifications.

Verification Team:

EQ 4.1 Basic Outdoor Air Ventilation

❑ For EQ 4.1(b), (c) and (d), visually verify that all calculations related to outdoor air ventilation are completed.

❑ For EQ 4.1(b), (c), and (d), verify that an Accountability Form has been signed by the responsible party.

EQ 4.3 Third-Party Inspection

❑ Test the outdoor ventilation air flow into the home and verify that it meets the requirements.

Considerations

Environmental Issues

Design the home with natural ventilation strategies (screened, operable windows located on opposite walls to provide cross-ventilation, etc.) to minimize the need for mechanical ventilation when outside air temperatures and humidity are moderate.

Economic Issues

Proper ventilation will always cost more in terms of energy use but is a critical component of healthy indoor environments. The energy savings component of HRVs and ERVs will minimize the cost of operation and offset the capital cost of equipment.

Supply-only systems that use the central air-handler fan to bring in and distribute fresh air should include timer controls or ECM fan motors to reduce the power consumption of the comparatively large air-handler fan.

Regional Variances

As explained above, supply-only systems are most appropriate in hot, humid climates; exhaust-only systems are most appropriate in cold climates. Balanced systems are suitable for any climate.

An exemption is made for homes in areas with fewer than 4,500 infiltration degree-

ID	LL	SS	WE	EA	MR	**EQ**	AE
4.1 & 4.3							

days because residents in these mild climates are assumed to rely on natural ventilation.

Resources

Web Sites

American Society of Heating, Refrigerating and Air-Conditioning Engineers

www.ashrae.org

(404) 636-8400

ASHRAE advances the science of heating, ventilation, air-conditioning, and refrigeration for the public's benefit through research, standards writing, continuing education, and publications.

ASHRAE Standard 62.2-2007

www.ashrae.org/technology/page/548

This site provides a viewable version of ASHRAE Standard 62.2-2007, as well as Standards 62.1-2007 and 90.1-2007. The online version cannot be printed or saved but can be previewed.

Ventilation Systems and Controls

Home Ventilating Institute

www.hvi.org/

www.hvi.org/assets/pdfs/HVIGuide-2006Low.pdf

AND

www.hvi.org/assets/pdfs/Ventilation_Controls_for_Life-Styles.pdf

HVI provides consumers an assurance of product performance. It also works to increase public awareness of the need for good ventilation and provides resources for selecting the proper ventilation products.

Recommended Ventilation Strategies for Energy-Efficient Production Homes

Lawrence Berkeley National Laboratory

www.enduse.lbl.gov/projects/ESVentilation

Review of Residential Ventilation Technologies

Building Science.com

www.buildingscience.com/documents/reports

This page provides a link to "Review of Residential Ventilation Technologies," a report that reviews current and potential ventilation technologies for residential buildings, with particular emphasis on North American climates and construction.

U.S. Environmental Protection Agency, Indoor Air Quality

www.epa.gov/iaq

(800) 438-4318

EPA offers a wide variety of tools, publications, and links to address indoor air quality concerns in schools and large buildings.

Print Media

Builder's Guide series for specific North American climate zones: *Cold Climates, Mixed-Humid Climates, Hot-Humid Climates* and *Hot-Dry & Mixed Dry Climates*, by Joseph Lstiburek, Ph.D., P.Eng. Building Science Press. Refer to the Design and HVAC chapters within each guide for discussion of construction details on proper outdoor air ventilation techniques. Available at www.eeba.org/bookstore/default.asp.

Ventilation Guide, by Armin Rudd. Building Science Press, 2006.

This guide presents a variety of recommendations for improving indoor air quality in residential buildings through controlled mechanical ventilation. Available at www.eeba.org/bookstore/default.asp.

ASHRAE Standard 62.2-2007: Ventilation for Acceptable Indoor Air Quality in Low-Rise Buildings. ASHRAE, 2007.

ASHRAE Standard 119-1988, ASHRAE, 1998.

EQ 4.2: Enhanced Outdoor Air Ventilation

Projects located in mild climates can still benefit from designed ventilation systems, since occupants do not always open windows and doors when weather conditions are favorable.

Two kinds of ventilation enhancements are appropriate: balanced ventilation and heat or energy recovery from the exhausted air.

Simple ventilation systems are often designed only to bring outside air in (thereby pressurizing the home) or only to exhaust air out (thereby depressurizing the home). Balanced ventilation systems provide both supply and exhaust air flows, thereby maintaining a more controlled ventilation rate in the home.

Heat-transfer ventilators (HRVs) allow incoming ventilation air to be heated (or cooled) by exhaust air, reducing the energy costs associated with space heating (or cooling). Energy-recovery ventilators (ERVs) also transfer moisture between outgoing exhaust streams and incoming supply streams, which helps moderate indoor moisture levels in dry winters or humid summers.

Approach and Implementation

Have the HVAC contractor install an HRV or ERV system that is listed by a certified third-party laboratory (UL, ETL, CSA, etc.); the Home Ventilation Institute maintains a list of certified equipment on its Web site. Size the HRV or ERV properly for the whole-house ventilation system. HRVs or ERVs provide an all-in-one package system designed to run quietly and efficiently on a continuous basis. These systems vary in efficiency.

Projects located in mild climates (fewer than 4,500 infiltration degree-days) can earn this point by simply putting in a ventilation system. These exemptions are based on ASHRAE Std. 62.2-2004, which references ASHRAE Std. 119-1988 (RA 2004). Following this standard, LEED for Homes uses a base of 65ºF for heating degree-days and 78ºF for cooling degree-days. Whole-house ventilation systems are not required in mild climates under EQ 4.1 because it is assumed that the occupants will use windows and doors to bring in adequate outside air. However, whole-house ventilation has value even in mild climates because occupants may choose not to open windows and doors because of the temperature, humidity, noise, or security concerns.

The heat exchanger is usually a single transfer unit made from special conductive materials. Incoming and outgoing airflows pass through the unit but are not mixed, causing the outgoing conditioned air to raise or lower the temperature of the incoming fresh air. After passing through the heat exchanger, the outgoing exhaust air is carried out of the home and the incoming air goes through the air-handler unit or is sent directly to living spaces.

HRVs and ERVs can be installed by qualified HVAC contractors using conventional ductwork, tools, and materials. The heat-exchange unit is typically installed in an attic, crawlspace, or storage or utility area, often adjacent to air handlers.

Heat recovery is not an option if the EQ 4.1 requirement is met with passive, exhaust-only or supply-only ventilation designs. It is possible only with a balanced ventilation system.

Homes with exhaust-only systems and heat-recovery ventilation systems are exempt from EQ 7.1, but project teams are still encouraged to use a filtration system if possible.

Calculations

No calculations are required for this credit.

Exemplary Performance

No additional points are available for exemplary performance.

Verification and Submittals

Supporting Verification Materials, made available by the Project Team:

❑ For EQ 4.2(a), present calculations to the Verification Team demonstrating that the ventilation system is designed to meet the requirements.

❑ Include any ventilation system equipment literature in the occupant's operations and maintenance manual.

❑ For EQ 4.2(a), sign an Accountability Form to indicate that that system has been installed according to the design specifications.

Verification Team:

❑ For EQ 4.2(a), visually verify that all calculations related to outdoor air ventilation have been completed.

❑ Visually verify all applicable equipment in the home.

❑ For EQ 4.2(a), verify that an Accountability Form has been signed by the responsible party.

Considerations

Environmental Issues

Heat- and energy-transfer systems can save energy associated with space heating or cooling.

Economic Issues

Heat or energy transfer reduces the costs associated with space heating or cooling.

Regional Variances

HRVs and ERVs can save energy everywhere but are more cost-effective in climate zones with large heating or cooling loads or in areas where energy prices are comparatively high. ERV systems are more appropriate for warm, humid climates. Balanced ventilation systems with HRVs or ERVs are very common in many markets, and HVAC contractors can be easily trained to install and maintain them.

Resources

Web Sites

American Society of Heating, Refrigerating and Air-Conditioning Engineers

www.ashrae.org

ASHRAE advances the science of heating, ventilation, air conditioning, and refrigeration for the public's benefit through research, standards writing, continuing education, and publications.

ASHRAE Standard 62.2-2007

www.ashrae.org/technology/page/548

This site provides a viewable version of ASHRAE Standard 62.2-2007. The online version cannot be printed or saved but can be previewed.

Ventilation Systems and Controls

Home Ventilating Institute

www.hvi.org/

www.hvi.org/assets/pdfs/HVIGuide-2006Low.pdf

and

www.hvi.org/assets/pdfs/Ventilation_Controls_for_Life-Styles.pdf

HVI provides consumers an assurance of product performance. It also works to increase public awareness of the need for good ventilation and provides resources for selecting the proper ventilation products.

Common Questions about Heat and Energy Recovery Ventilators

University of Minnesota

www.extension.umn.edu/distribution/housingandclothing/DK7284.html

This site provides a brief, easy-to-understand overview of heat- and energy-recovery ventilators.

Review of Residential Ventilation Technologies

Building Science.com

www.buildingscience.com/documents/reports

This page provides a link to "Review of Residential Ventilation Technologies," a report that reviews current and potential ventilation technologies for residential buildings with particular emphasis on North American climates and construction.

Print Media

Builder's Guide series for specific North American climate zones: *Cold Climates, Mixed-Humid Climates, Hot-Humid Climates,* and *Hot-Dry & Mixed Dry Climates*, by Joseph Lstiburek, Ph.D., P.Eng. Building Science Press. Refer to the Design and HVAC chapters within each guide for discussion of construction details on proper outdoor air ventilation techniques. Available at www.eeba.org/bookstore/default.asp.

Recommended Ventilation Strategies for Energy-Efficient Production Homes. Lawrence Berkeley Labs, December, 1998. Report LBNL-40378. Available online, at www.enduse.lbl.gov/Info/LBNL-40378.pdf.

Ventilation Guide, by Armin Rudd. Building Science Press, 2006.

This guide presents a variety of recommendations for improving indoor air quality in residential buildings through controlled mechanical ventilation. Available at www.eeba.org/bookstore/default.asp.

ASHRAE Standard 62.2-2004: Ventilation for Acceptable Indoor Air Quality in Low-Rise Buildings. ASHRAE, 2004.

ASHRAE Standard 119-1988. ASHRAE, 1998.

EQ 5: Local Exhaust

Intent

Reduce moisture and exposure to indoor pollutants in kitchens and bathrooms.

Requirements

Prerequisites

5.1 **Basic Local Exhaust.** Meet all the following requirements:

a) Design and install local exhaust systems in all bathrooms (including half-baths) and the kitchen to meet the requirements of Section 5 of ASHRAE Standard 62.2-2007. Sample requirements that relate to minimum intermittent local exhaust flow rates are shown in **Table 1**, below.

b) Design and install the fans and ducts to meet the requirements of Section 7 of ASHRAE Standard 62.2-2007.

c) Exhaust air to the outdoors (i.e., exhaust to attics or interstitial spaces is not permitted).

d) Use ENERGY STAR labeled bathroom exhaust fans (except for exhaust fans serving multiple bathrooms).

Credits

5.2 **Enhanced Local Exhaust** (1 point). Use one of the following strategies in every bathroom to control the use of the local exhaust fan:

a) An occupancy sensor.

b) An automatic humidistat controller.

c) An automatic timer to operate the fan for a timed interval after occupant leaves the room.

d) A continuously operating exhaust fan.

5.3 **Third-Party Performance Testing** (1 point). Perform a third-party test of each exhaust air flow rate for compliance with the requirements in Section 5 of ASHRAE Standard 62.2-2007.

Synergies and Trade-Offs

A project receiving points for EQ 1 is eligible to earn points for EQ 5.2 and EQ 5.3.

If designed properly, exhaust fans can also provide sufficient outdoor air ventilation system for the entire home, as required by EQ 4.1.

Table 1: Minimum Air Flow Requirements for Intermittent Local Exhaust

Location	Minimum air flow
Kitchen	100 cfm; vented range hood required if exhaust fan flow rate is less than 5 kitchen air changes per hour.
Bathroom	50 cfm

EQ 5.1: Basic Local Exhaust

EQ 5.2: Enhanced Local Exhaust

EQ 5.3: Third-Party Performance Testing

This credit addresses the specific need for removal of potential pollutants from bathrooms and kitchens—two kinds of rooms that produce considerable moisture and odors. It is always most effective to control pollutants at their source. Proper ventilation of these rooms increases the functionality of the rooms and assists in overall indoor air quality control.

Bathroom and kitchen fans are often underutilized by occupants. Occupancy sensors, automatic humidistats, and timers are effective ways to ensure that local exhaust systems are used effectively.

Equipment failure, installation errors, and incidental damage caused during construction can all lead to underperforming local exhaust systems. Third-party testing ensures that the systems function properly.

Approach and Implementation

All kitchens and bathrooms in all climate zones need provision for mechanical exhaust. In many cases, a simple bathroom fan with a timer can also be used as part of the overall fresh-air ventilation strategy, as noted in EQ 4.

Work with the electrician to ensure that kitchens and bathrooms have exhaust systems with minimum air flow, as listed in **Table 1**. Duct exhaust fans directly outside through a dedicated exhaust vent, not into soffit or roof vents in the attic. Recirculating kitchen range hoods do not remove moisture and pollutants, and do not satisfy the prerequisite in EQ 5.1.

Specify the use of ENERGY STAR–labeled bathroom fans that are properly sized to meet the minimum air-flow re-quirements. It is acceptable to install bathroom fans that are slightly oversized for large bathrooms or those where excessive moisture production is expected. In most cases, a properly installed 50-cfm fan will provide proper ventilation even for large bathrooms.

The requirement of part d (i.e., ENERGY STAR labeled bathroom fans) is waived for bathrooms with an ERV or an HRV.

There is currently no ENERGY STAR labeling program for kitchen range fans. Avoid oversized range fans, which can depressurize homes, cause back-drafting of combustion appliances and fireplaces, and lead to higher energy bills. For most kitchen applications, a range hood fan that is sized to meet the requirements in ASHRAE Std. 62.2 will suffice.

Have the HVAC contractor size the ducts properly and install duct runs as straight as possible. Undersized ducts can cause the exhaust system to underperform and the fan to operate less efficiently. For example, a 50-cfm fan requires a 5-inch-diameter sheet metal duct for typical directly routed installations. Increase the duct size to 6-inch-diameter for long duct runs or if flexible ducting is used.

In many markets, electricians purchase and install bathroom and kitchen fans and HVAC contractors do the venting. This can sometimes lead to confusion in ensuring the proper fan with the proper size vent is installed. Be sure to specify this measure to both the electrician and the HVAC contractor.

If the kitchen fan is estimated to provide fewer than five kitchen air changes per hour, locate it above the range as a vented range hood so that it pulls air from the room's primary source of humidity.

Best practice is to use fans with a sound rating of 1 sone or less. Quieter fans are often larger or deeper and may not fit in standard ceiling cavities. Check the depth of the fans to ensure they fit.

Look for fans labeled for sound rating and air-flow capacity. The Home Ventilating Institute tests and verifies the air flow and sound performance of bathroom fans and kitchen range fans, and it maintains a list of manufacturers and fan ratings on its Web site, at www.hvi.org. An HVI-tested fan bears a sticker listing the sound rating and air flow capacity.

Credit EQ 5.2 can be awarded if the requirements are met for all bathrooms with showers, bathtubs, or spas. Half-baths can be excluded.

Specify timer controls or occupancy sensors on bathroom fans to ensure they operate when the bathroom is in use and for a period of time after the occupant has left the room. Humidistat controls or other humidity sensors are the best option to ensure that moisture is exhausted.

Performance testing is important for identifying any equipment failures or installation problems. HVAC contractors should conduct their own performance testing, but this does not qualify as third-party testing for the purposes of EQ 5.3.

Third-party testing must be performed by a qualified qualified energy rater, Verification Team, or a third-party testing and balancing company. If testing indicates insufficient air flow rates, the HVAC contractor should investigate and fix the problem. Once the problem is fixed, the air flow rates must be re-tested and the requirements of the credit must be met before EQ 5.3 can be awarded.

Calculations

Use the following equation to determine the total kitchen air changes per hour provided by the kitchen fan:

$$ACH_{kitchen} = \text{Fan Capacity} * 60 \text{ Minutes} \div \text{Kitchen Size}$$

where ACH is air changes per hour, fan capacity is measured in cfm, and kitchen size is measured in cubic feet. If $ACH_{kitchen}$ is less than 5, install the kitchen fan as a vented range hood.

Exemplary Performance

No additional points are available for exemplary performance.

Verification and Submittals

Supporting Verification Materials, made available by the Project Team:

EQ 5.1: Basic Local Exhaust

❑ Present calculations to the Verification Team demonstrating that the local exhaust system is designed to meet the requirements.

❑ Include any equipment literature in the occupant's operations and maintenance manual.

❑ Sign an Accountability Form to indicate that the local exhaust system is installed according to the design specifications.

EQ 5.2: Enhanced Local Exhaust

❑ Include equipment literature on occupancy sensors, automatic humidistat controllers, automatic timers, or continuously operating exhaust fans in the occupant's operations and maintenance manual.

Verification Team:

EQ 5.1: Basic Local Exhaust

❑ Visually verify that all calculations for local exhaust are completed.

❑ Visually verify all applicable equipment in the home.

- Verify that an Accountability Form has been signed by the responsible party.

EQ 5.2: Enhanced Local Exhaust

- Visually verify all applicable equipment in the home.

EQ 5.3: Third-Party Performance Testing

- Test exhaust air flow from the home and verify that it meets the requirements.

Considerations

Environmental Issues

Large exhaust fans can back-draft gases from combustion appliances that vent via conventional chimneys. Under EQ 2, Combustion Venting, the depressurization test includes the operation of exhaust appliances to ensure safe venting under all conditions.

Adequate local exhaust helps reduce moisture in kitchens and bathrooms, which reduces the risk of mold growth. Mold is a significant health concern in homes.

Economic Issues

ENERGY STAR–labeled quiet fans are more expensive than conventional fans but are still a moderate-cost measure. Adequate local exhaust can reduce the risk of moisture damage and associated repair costs.

Resources

Web Sites

ASHRAE Standard 62.2-2007

www.ashrae.org/technology/page/548

This site provides a viewable version of ASHRAE Standard 62.2-2007. The online version cannot be printed or saved but can be previewed.

ENERGY STAR® Program, Ventilating Fans

U.S. Environmental Protection Agency

www.energystar.gov/index.cfm?c=vent_fans.pr_vent_fans

Describes the advantages of ENERGY STAR–labeled bathroom, utility room, and kitchen exhaust fans and provides product and manufacturer lists.

Ventilation Systems and Controls

Home Ventilating Institute

www.hvi.org/

www.hvi.org/assets/pdfs/HVIGuide-2006Low.pdf

and

www.hvi.org/assets/pdfs/Ventilation_Controls_for_Life-Styles.pdf

HVI provides consumers an assurance of product performance. It also works to increase public awareness of the need for good ventilation and provides resources for selecting the proper ventilation products.

Review of Residential Ventilation Technologies

Building Science.com

www.buildingscience.com/documents/reports

This page provides a link to "Review of Residential Ventilation Technologies," a report that reviews current and potential ventilation technologies for residential buildings with particular emphasis on North American climates and construction.

Print Media

Builder's Guide series for specific North American climate zones: *Cold Climates, Mixed-Humid Climates, Hot-Humid Climates*, and *Hot-Dry & Mixed Dry Climates*, by Joseph Lstiburek, Ph.D., P.Eng. Building Science Press. Refer to the Design and HVAC chapters within each guide for discussion of construction

ID	LL	SS	WE	EA	MR	EQ	AE
5.1 – 5.3							

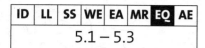

ID	LL	SS	WE	EA	MR	EQ	AE
			5.1 – 5.3				

details on proper ventilation techniques. Available at www.eeba.org/bookstore/default.asp.

Ventilation Guide, by Armin Rudd. Building Science Press, 2006.

This guide presents a variety of recommendations for improving indoor air quality in residential buildings through controlled mechanical ventilation. Available at www.eeba.org/bookstore/default.asp.

ASHRAE Standard 62.2-2004: Ventilation for Acceptable Indoor Air Quality in Low-Rise Buildings. ASHRAE, 2004.

EQ 6: Distribution of Space Heating and Cooling

Intent

Provide appropriate distribution of space heating and cooling in the home to improve thermal comfort and energy performance.

Requirements

A. Forced-Air Systems:

Prerequisites

6.1 **Room-by-Room Load Calculations.** Perform design calculations (using ACCA Manuals J and D, the ASHRAE Handbook of Fundamentals, or an equivalent computation procedure) and install ducts accordingly.

Credits

6.2 **Return Air Flow or Room-by-Room Controls** (1 point). Ensure that every room (except baths, kitchens, closets, pantries, and laundry rooms) has adequate return air flow through the use of multiple returns, transfer grilles, or jump ducts. Meet one of the following requirements:

a) Size the opening to 1 square inch per cfm of supply (this area may include free area undercut below door).

b) Demonstrate that the pressure differential between closed rooms and adjacent spaces with return is no greater than 2.5 Pa (0.01 inch w.c.).

6.3 **Third-Party Performance Test** (2 points). Have the total supply air flow rates in each room tested using a flow hood with doors closed or one of the other acceptable methods cited by the ACCA Quality Installation Specifications. Supply air flow rates must be within +/– 15% (or +/– 10 cfm) of calculated values from ACCA Manual J (as required by EA 6.1).

B. Nonducted HVAC Systems (e.g., Radiative Systems):

Prerequisites

6.1 **Room-by-Room Load Calculations.** Perform design calculations (using ACCA Manual J and D, the ASHRAE Handbook of Fundamentals, or an equivalent computation procedure) and install system accordingly.

Credits

6.2 **Room-by-Room Controls** (1 point). Design the HVAC system with flow control valves on every radiator.

6.3 **Multiple Zones** (2 points). Install nonducted HVAC system with at least two distinct zones with independent thermostat controls.

Synergies and Trade-Offs

A project receiving points for EQ 1 is not eligible to earn points for EQ 6.2 or EQ 6.3. A project pursuing EQ 6.2 or EQ 6.3 must meet all the prerequisites in EQ 2–10.

The choice of air filter (EQ 7) should be made prior to duct design, to ensure adequate air flow. Filters with a high MERV can create a large pressure drop that should be accommodated during system design.

Space heating and cooling loads and room air flow rates must be calculated using ACCA Manual J (EA 6.1). The design calculations conducted for this credit should be based on those Manual J calculations.

Duct installation should be visually inspected during the predrywall insulation inspection (EA 5).

EQ 6.1: Room-by-Room Load Calculations
EQ 6.2: Return Air Flow or Room-by-Room Controls
EQ 6.3: Third-Party Performance Test

Proper distribution of heating and cooling is expected by today's homebuyer. When spaces are perceived to be too hot or cold, occupants adjust thermostat settings to achieve the comfort they desire, which can result in system inefficiencies. Proper heating and cooling distribution is very important in the control of humidity and surface temperatures to avoid localized condensation (mainly on windows) in cold weather.

Proper room-by-room sizing using accepted industry methods, such as ACCA Manual J, is required, and extra points are available for third-party verification of the as-built delivery of heating and cooling to each room.

Adequate return air flow is a critical part of managing the distribution of conditioned air to spaces. Insufficient return air flow can cause back-pressure, leading to insufficient air flow into the room and excess air distribution (and discomfort) to other rooms.

Third-party testing can identify problems with the design and installation of the distribution system. Even a system that has been well designed and well installed by the HVAC contractor can underperform if ducts are blocked, crushed, or punctured by other trades during construction. An ineffective distribution system can result in occupant discomfort and wasted energy.

Flow controls and zoning with separate thermostatic controls can ensure thermal comfort and save energy in homes with radiative heating systems.

This credit is meant to ensure that each room in the home has adequate heating and cooling.

Approach and Implementation

Heat loss and heat gain calculations should be performed by the HVAC contractor or qualified energy rater, taking into account such critical information as wall and ceiling insulation values, air tightness estimates, and window solar heat gain values. This information should be used by the HVAC contractor when sizing equipment, ducts, and grilles, based on the method provided in ACCA Manuals J and D, the ASHRAE Handbook of Fundamentals, or other design guides.

All forced-air heating and cooling systems should be sized in accordance with local winter and summer design data, as found in ASHRAE or ACCA manuals. Using rules of thumb or worst-case scenarios will result in oversized equipment, which is wasteful and less efficient to operate.

Install balancing dampers in each branch line of a duct system to allow adjustment and balancing of air flows throughout the system. Dampers and grilles should be installed in each room but are not an acceptable substitute for balancing dampers.

Projects are prohibited from using floor, ceiling, or wall cavities as a substitute for ductwork.

HVAC contractors sometimes bump up the size of equipment or ducts to prevent complaints by occupants. Although it is acceptable to oversize equipment by up to 10% for air-conditioning and up to 25% for heating to accommodate "pick-up" loads—getting the house to temperature quickly if setback thermostats are used—do not allow contractors to oversize by more than these amounts. Oversized systems result in just as many comfort complaints as undersized systems. Many

HVAC equipment manufacturers make small furnaces with "oversized" blower capacities to overcome this problem.

In some cases, two-speed (dual-stage) or variable-output air-handler units can help achieve proper design loads. However, HVAC contractors should not use such air handlers as an excuse for oversizing equipment.

Consider using a hot-water air handler rather than a conventional furnace to provide heating. Hot-water coils can be sized more accurately to design heat losses.

Qualified energy raters should have the proper equipment to measure and verify air flows in each room. The qualified energy rater should compare the actual tested results with the original design. The best method is to use properly calibrated balometers or flow hoods for air-flow measurements at individual grilles. Anemometers may be used for air-flow measurements in ducts in certain cases.

Performance testing is important for identifying any equipment failures or installation problems. HVAC contractors should conduct their own performance testing, but this does not qualify as third-party testing for the purposes of EQ 6.3.

Third-party testing must be performed by a qualified qualified energy rater, Verification Team, or a third-party testing and balancing company. If test results deviate significantly from the design air flow rates, ductwork may be crushed, punctured, or obstructed. In this case, the HVAC contractor should investigate and fix the problem. Once the problem is fixed, the air flow rates must be re-tested and the requirements of the credit must be met before EQ 6.3 can be awarded.

Air-flow testing should be done with the room dampers completely open and room doors completely closed. If test results deviate slightly from the design air-flow

rates, adjust the balancing dampers and retest.

Nonducted systems must also be designed to provide sufficient heating and cooling to each space. Use design calculations to determine the proper sizing of radiators in each room.

Flow-control valves and thermal zoning give the occupant control over temperature settings, which can improve thermal comfort and save energy. Provide instruction on how to use flow-control valves and separate zoning in the occupant's operations and maintenance manual, and highlight these technologies during the occupant walkthrough.

Calculations

A full, detailed ACCA Manual D calculation is strongly recommended but may be more than is necessary. Various software programs can assist with HVAC distribution design. Have the HVAC contractor prepare design calculations or software printouts for the Verification Team's review.

Exemplary Performance

No additional points are available for exemplary performance.

Verification and Submittals

Supporting Verification Materials, made available by the Project Team:

EQ 6.1 Room-by-Room Load Calculations

❑ Present design calculations to the Verification Team.

❑ Include any equipment literature (e.g., user manuals, brochures, specifications) in the occupant's operations and maintenance manual.

- Sign an Accountability Form to indicate that the system is installed according to the design specifications.

EQ 6.2 Return Air Flow or Room-by-Room Controls

- For ducted systems, provide calculations to the Verification Team demonstrating that the credit requirements have been met.

Verification Team:

EQ 6.1 Room-by-Room Load Calculations

- Collect the Manual J & D calculations and verify that they were fully and properly completed, per LEED for Homes Verification and Submittal Guidelines.

- Verify that an Accountability Form has been signed by the responsible party.

EQ 6.2 Return Air Flow or Room-by-Room Controls

A. Forced-Air Systems

- For EQ 6.2, part (a), conduct on-site verification that every room has a return, transfer grille, jump duct, or door undercut."

- For EQ 6.2, part (b), conduct pressure differential test between closed rooms and adjacent spaces and confirm pressure difference is less than 2.5 Pa.

B. Radiative Systems

- Verify that each radiator or radiative heating segment has a flow control installed.

EQ 6.3 Third-Party Performance Test or Multiple Zones

- For ducted systems, conduct testing of supply air-flow rates in each room and verify that the requirements are met.

- For nonducted systems, visually verify zones and thermostat controls.

Considerations

Environmental Issues

An ineffective distribution system wastes energy by overheating or overcooling. Uneven space conditioning can prompt occupants to set the thermostat to excessively high or low temperatures or open windows in the winter to offset localized overheating, thereby wasting energy.

Economic Issues

Larger heating and cooling systems are more expensive, so having the system properly sized can save money up front. This is particularly true if energy efficiency measures are implemented to reduce heating and cooling loads.

Third-party testing can reduce call-backs. Any necessary repairs of ducts located behind walls are less expensive to complete during rather than after construction.

Ensuring comfort through proper distribution design, installation, and third-party verification will reduce heating and cooling costs for the occupant.

Resources

Web Sites

American Society of Heating, Refrigerating and Air-Conditioning Engineers

www.ashrae.org

(404) 636-8400

ASHRAE advances the science of heating, ventilation, air conditioning, and refrigeration for the public's benefit through research, standards writing, continuing education, and publications.

Air Conditioning Contractors of America

ID	LL	SS	WE	EA	MR	EQ	AE
6.1 – 6.3							

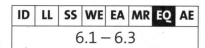

ID	LL	SS	WE	EA	MR	EQ	AE
			6.1 – 6.3				

Manual D: Residential Duct Design

www.acca.org/tech/codes/Manual_D_verification.pdf

Air Conditioning Contractors of America

Manual J: Residential Load Calculation

www.acca.org/tech/manualj/

Air Conditioning Contractors of America

HVAC Quality Installation Specification

www.acca.org/tech

This Web site provides a free link to the ACCA Standard: "HVAC Quality Installation Specification: Residential and Commercial Heating, Ventilating, and Air Conditioning Applications." The site also includes a link to various articles and other ANSI and ACCA standards.

California Energy Commission

Procedures for HVAC System Design and Installation

www.energy.ca.gov/efficiency/qualityhomes/procedures.html

This site provides an overview of good practices for designing and installing the HVAC system, as well as detailed strategies and measures for the "house as a system" approach to construction.

EQ 7: Air Filtering

Intent

Reduce particulate matter from the air supply system.

Requirements

A. Forced-Air Systems:

Prerequisites

7.1 **Good Filters.** Install air filters with a minimum efficiency reporting value (MERV) ≥ 8 and ensure that air handlers can maintain adequate pressure and air flow. Air filter housings must be airtight to prevent bypass or leakage.

Non-ducted units such as PTACs and mini-splits are exempt from this prerequisite per the requirements of ASHRAE Standard 62.2-2007, section 6.7, Minimum Filtration.

Credits

7.2 **Better Filters** (1 point). Install air filters ≥ MERV 10 and ensure that air handlers can maintain adequate pressure and air flow. Air filter housings must be airtight to prevent bypass or leakage.

OR

7.3 **Best Filters** (2 points). Install air filters ≥ MERV 13 and ensure that air handlers can maintain adequate pressure and air flow. Air filter housings must be airtight to prevent bypass or leakage.

B. Nonducted HVAC Systems (e.g., Radiative Systems):

Prerequisites

7.1 **Good Filters.** Install air filters ≥ MERV 8 and maintain adequate pressure and air flow in any mechanical ventilation systems. A home in a climate with fewer than 4,500 infiltration degree-days or a home that uses only passive or exhaust-only ventilation is exempt from this requirement.

Credits

7.2 **Better Filters** (1 point). Install air filters ≥ MERV 10 and maintain adequate pressure and air flow for any mechanical ventilation systems.

OR

7.3 **Best Filters** (2 points). Install air filters ≥ MERV 13 and maintain adequate pressure and air flow for any mechanical ventilation systems.

Synergies and Trade-Offs

A project receiving points for EQ 1 is eligible to earn points for EQ 7.2 or EQ 7.3.

The choice of air filter should be made during or prior to duct design (EQ 6) to ensure adequate air flow. Filters with a high MERV can create a large pressure drop that should be accommodated during system design.

7.1: Good Filters

7.2: Better Filters

7.3: Best Filters

Inadequate air filtration can have adverse health effects. Improved air filters that are installed properly remove more particles from the supply air stream.

The industry standard for comparing mechanical air filters is the minimum efficiency reporting value (MERV) rating. MERV ratings are determined by independent test labs using ASHRAE Standard 52.2, and they characterize the effectiveness of a mechanical air filter based on the number and size of the particles that can get through the filter under normal conditions.

Filters with higher MERV ratings remove both a greater percentage of total airborne dust and a greater percentage of fine airborne particles. Fine particulates float in the air longer and, when inhaled, go deeper into the respiratory system of the human body. Filters that capture a higher percentage of small particles help create healthier indoor environments for occupants.

Filters must be installed properly or unfiltered air will bypass the filter and enter the living space. If the HVAC system isn't designed for the higher MERV filter, the system may provide insufficient air to the living space and/or suffer damage and inefficiency.

This credit is aimed at improving the effectiveness of air filters in furnaces, air handlers, and ventilation systems.

Approach and Implementation

Work with the HVAC contractor to choose an air filter that is suitable to the project. Make sure the system is designed with the filter in mind. The choice of air filter should be made prior to duct design (see EQ 6) to ensure adequate air flow.

The mandatory measure is MERV 8; points are available for higher MERV ratings. Check manufacturers' labels or obtain the manufacturer's documentation of the MERV rating.

True HEPA filters, not "HEPA-type" filters, meet the highest rating using the ASHRAE Standard 52.2 test and can be treated as equivalent to MERV-16. Electronic filters cannot be MERV rated, so it is impossible to evaluate their effectiveness. Unlike mechanical filters, which become more effective with use, electronic air filters actually operate less effectively over time and can fail to operate altogether without adequate maintenance. For these reasons, electronic filters are not acceptable for meeting the prerequisite or credit requirements.

Because a high-efficiency air filter can restrict air flow, the HVAC system needs to account for the additional resistance. Work with the HVAC contractor to choose an air filter that is suitable to the project. Make sure the system is designed with the filter in mind. Select the air filter before the duct design to ensure adequate air flow. Filters with a high MERV can create a large pressure drop, which should be accommodated during system design.

To facilitate proper duct sizing to accommodate high-MERV–rated filters, have the HVAC contractor conduct air-flow measurements with the air filter in place. Be sure that the air filter housings are airtight to ensure that unfiltered air does not bypass the filter.

If the ventilation system is separate from the heating and cooling system, use a separate filter that meets the prerequisite and the requirements for any credit being sought. Homes located in mild climates (fewer than 4,500 infiltration degree-days) built with a nonducted HVAC system or a passive or exhaust-only ventilation strategy are exempt from the prerequisite. Heat- or energy-recovery ventilators are currently exempt from Prerequisite EQ 7.1, although air filters of some kind are strongly recommended.

Higher-rated mechanical filters capture more dust and therefore get dirtier sooner. To minimize maintenance, specify filters with more surface area—those with deep pleats or large filter boxes. A wide range of pleated media filters with different MERV ratings are available in configurations to match most HVAC system requirements. Larger or deeper filters may require modest modification to ductwork, return grilles, or filter boxes.

Educate occupants on the need for filter replacement or cleaning every 3 to 12 months (follow manufacturer's recommendations). Infrequent filter replacement or cleaning can lead to clogged filters and heavily restricted air flow, which in turn reduces the ability of the HVAC system to provide thermal comfort. If the air handler–furnace–ventilation system is not easy to access, install the filter in the return air grille for ease of maintenance.

Include in the operations and maintenance manual information on where to buy replacement filters, since some sizes and types are not sold at retail hardware or building supply stores. If possible, provide replacement filters.

Filters with higher MERV ratings are typically more expensive to replace. Washable MERV-8 filters are available; they cost more initially but eliminate the need to find and buy replacements.

Calculations

No calculations are required for this credit.

Exemplary Performance

No additional points are available for exemplary performance.

Verification and Submittals

Supporting Verification Materials, made available by the Project Team:

- ❏ Present any air filter product literature to the Verification Team.
- ❏ Include product literature in the occupant's operations and maintenance manual.

Verification Team:

- ❏ Visually verify (using product literature, labels, etc.) that the applicable MERV rating has been met.
- ❏ Visually verify air filters and housings in the home.

Considerations

Environmental Issues

The efficiency of heating and cooling systems can be adversely affected by the improper sizing or selection of filters, leading to unnecessary energy use. Washable filters and deep-pleated filters require less frequent replacement.

Economic Issues

Duct modifications may be required to house a larger air filter. The efficiency of heating and cooling systems can be adversely affected by the improper sizing or selection of filters, increasing costs to the occupant. Filters with high MERV ratings are typically more expensive to replace. Washable MERV-8 filters cost more initially but eliminate the need to buy replacements.

Regional Variances

These credits may not apply in mild and dry climates where no central heating,

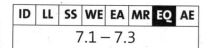

cooling, or mechanical ventilation system is installed.

Resources

Web Sites

American Lung Association

Residential Air Cleaning Devices

www.lungusa.org/site/pp.asp?c=dvLUK9O0E&b=39289

This site links to an ALA report on air cleaning devices for residential applications. This report explains the types of air cleaning devices, how they work, and how consumers should choose among the available options.

Guide to Air Cleaners in the Home

U.S. Environmental Protection Agency

www.epa.gov/iaq/pubs/airclean.html

This site links to an EPA report on air-cleaning devices for residential applications. The report explains the types of air quality problems and their associated risks, and reviews the different types of air-cleaning devices and their effectiveness in removing indoor contaminants.

EQ 8: Contaminant Control

Intent

Reduce occupants' and construction workers' exposure to indoor airborne contaminants through source control and removal.

Requirements

Prerequisites

None.

Credits

8.1 **Indoor Contaminant Control during Construction** (1 point). Upon installation, seal all permanent ducts and vents to minimize contamination during construction. Remove any seals after all phases of construction are completed.

8.2 **Indoor Contaminant Control** (1 point each, maximum 2 points). Select from the following measures:

a) Design and install permanent walk-off mats at each entry that are at least 4 feet in length and allow accessibility for cleaning (e.g., grating with catch basin).

b) Design a shoe removal and storage space near the primary entryway, separated from living areas. This space may not have wall-to-wall carpeting, and it must be large enough to accommodate a bench and at least two pairs of shoes per bedroom.

c) Install a central vacuum system with exhaust to the outdoors. Ensure that the exhaust is not near any ventilation air intake.

8.3 **Preoccupancy Flush** (1 point). Flush the home with fresh air, according to the following guidelines:

a) Flush prior to occupancy but after all phases of construction are completed.

b) Flush the entire home, keeping all interior doors open.

c) Flush for 48 total hours; the hours may be nonconsecutive, if necessary.

d) Keep all windows open and run a fan (e.g., HVAC system fan) continuously or flush the home with all HVAC fans and exhaust fans operating continuously at the highest flow rate.

e) Use additional fans to circulate air within the home.

f) Replace or clean HVAC air filter afterward, as necessary.

Synergies and Trade-Offs

A project receiving points for EQ 1 is not eligible to earn points for EQ 8.1 or EQ 8.3, but may earn points for EQ 8.2.

Products with low VOC emissions greatly benefit indoor air quality. Source control of these kinds of emissions is addressed in MR 2.

EQ 8.1: Indoor Contaminant Control during Construction

Open ductwork can get clogged with paint, debris, dust, and other particulates. This not only leaves residues in the ducts, with eventual exposure to occupants, but also damages the ducts, fans, and systems.

Approach and Implementation

Require the HVAC contractor to tape off or install dust covers on all rough-in openings to the HVAC system. For many contractors, this is common practice. Ask the HVAC supplier for reusable dust covers for standard-size grilles. This saves time and money.

Communicate the purpose of this credit to crews so that workers do not remove covers. Use fans in summer, space heaters in winter, and other techniques to keep crews comfortable so that they do not need to use the space-conditioning equipment during construction.

Control pollutants created during construction by regularly cleaning all systems and spaces. Flushing the home after construction helps remove certain kinds of pollutants, and this practice is rewarded in EQ 8.3.

Calculations

No calculations are required for this credit.

Exemplary Performance

No additional points are available for exemplary performance.

Verification and Submittals

Supporting Verification Materials, made available by the Project Team:

❑ Sign an Accountability Form to indicate that the system is installed according to the design specifications.

Verification Team:

❑ During construction, visually verify that ducts are sealed at the termination point.

❑ After construction, conduct a visual inspection and swipe of duct interiors.

❑ Verify that an Accountability Form has been signed by the responsible party.

Considerations

Economic Issues

Dust covers are inexpensive and can save money by preventing damage to the systems.

Resources

Web Sites

Air Quality in the Home

American Lung Association

www.lungusa.org

This site includes an entire section devoted to indoor air quality in the home. Choose "Air Quality" at the bottom of the screen and then click "Indoor Air Quality" and "Air Quality in the Home" to find numerous articles and educational pieces about maintaining a healthy indoor environment.

U.S. Environmental Protection Agency, Indoor Air Quality Division

www.epa.gov/iaq

This site has numerous resources related to indoor air quality in homes, including reports and web links.

A majority of the dirt and dust in homes is tracked in by occupants. Debris carried into the house from shoes often contains lead, asbestos, pesticides, and other hazardous materials. Shoes also track moisture into the home, leading to mold growth in carpeting near entryways. Walk-off mats trap some dirt at the entryway that would otherwise be tracked into the home. One of the most effective approaches to reducing indoor contaminants is removing shoes upon entry. Central vacuums exhaust collected dust and particulates to the outdoors.

Approach and Implementation

To encourage occupants and visitors to remove shoes at the door, design and incorporate a convenient space for the removal and storage of shoes near the primary entryway to the house. Select hard-surface, easy-to-clean flooring for this area.

Make design changes to allow space for shoe removal and storage. For a small home, where space is at a premium, simple cabinetry can create an attractive combination bench-and-shoe-storage area that takes up very little room. Carpet should not be used in this space because it will absorb moisture and dirt; Innovation in Design 2.1 prohibits the use of carpet within 3 feet of any exterior doors, and Materials & Resources 2.2 rewards homes for not using any carpet in the home.

Design walk-off mats as permanent features of the home, incorporated into the aesthetic of the entry. Make mats long enough to capture dirt from regular walking strides—at least 4 feet. Walk-off mats are particularly effective in multifamily buildings, where they can be placed in indoor communal areas (i.e., in the lobby);

do not place them in any living spaces.

Make walk-off mats accessible for cleaning, and use the operations and maintenance manual to inform occupants that mats lose their effectiveness unless regularly cleaned.

Discuss central vacuum options with the electrician or central vacuum contractor or supplier. Central vacuum systems require a rough-in of pipes similar to that for electrical or plumbing systems. All central vacuum systems use common piping and low-voltage electrical components, so the rough-in components are the same for all manufacturers.

Central vacuum systems have become very common in many markets. Typically, the vacuum unit itself is installed in a garage, and small-diameter exhaust pipes are run to central locations throughout the house. Because vacuum hoses can reach 25 feet or more, only one or two outlets may be required per floor. Air-seal around the exhaust pipe leading to the garage, and specify that the vacuum exhaust be vented directly outside, not into the garage.

This credit should not be awarded automatically to projects with nonducted systems. To earn this credit, projects with nonducted systems must submit a proposal to their Provider for submission to the USGBC. Within the proposal, the project must demonstrate an effort to reduce construction pollutant exposure to occupants. Examples include covering radiators or mini-split air handler units during construction, and implementing a thorough cleaning program of all equipment.

Calculations

No calculations are required for this credit.

Exemplary Performance

Projects that implement all three measures in this credit can earn 1 additional point, to be counted under Innovation in Design 3.

Verification and Submittals

Supporting Verification Materials, made available by the Project Team:

❑ Include any filtration system equipment literature in the occupant's operations and maintenance manual.

Verification Team:

❑ Visually verify walk-off mats, shoe storage area, and/or central vacuum system on home site.

Considerations

Economic Issues

The use of walk-off mats and a shoe removal and storage area will reduce moisture damage and wear-and-tear on the floors in the home. These strategies will reduce the need for cleaning and delay the need to replace or refinish the floors.

Regional Variances

Mud rooms are common in cold climates because of snow and salt, but the strategy of installing a shoe storage area is valuable in all climates.

Resources

Web Sites

Air Quality in the Home

American Lung Association

www.lungusa.org

This site includes an entire section devoted to indoor air quality in the home. Choose "Air Quality" at the bottom of the screen and then click "Indoor Air Quality" and "Air Quality in the Home" to find numerous articles and educational pieces about maintaining a healthy indoor environment.

Indoor Air Quality Division

U.S. Environmental Protection Agency

www.epa.gov/iaq

This site has numerous resources related to indoor air quality in homes, including reports and web links.

Controlling Pollutants and Sources

U.S. Environmental Protection Agency

www.epa.gov/iaq/schooldesign/controlling.html

EPA offers detailed information on entry or walk-off mats and flush-out ventilation practices after construction activity.

EQ 8.3: Preoccupancy Flush

Many materials finish off-gassing their volatile chemical constituents within a relatively short time, but certain pollutants will remain in the home until removed. Flushing the house removes VOCs, ureaformaldehyde, and other air pollutants that remain after construction. These pollutants are mostly caused by off-gassing paints, adhesives, and sealants. Flushing the home also removes some of the dust and particulates that remain from construction, especially if the ductwork was not sealed.

Approach and Implementation

A preoccupancy whole-house flush is an easy way to remove volatile pollutants. The flush must take place prior to occupancy but after all construction, including paint touchups, has been completed.

The best approach is to leave the windows open and run all local and whole-house ventilation fans for an extended period, using additional fans within the home to circulate air. Keep all interior doors open during the flush, including cabinet and closet doors.

An extended flush with the windows open may not be practical because of weather or security concerns. Consequently, this credit can also be achieved by flushing the house with windows closed for at least 48 hours. In this case, all HVAC fans (including local exhaust) should be run at their maximum air flow for the full 48 hours, and additional internal fans should be used to circulate air. The 48 hours of flushing does not have to be consecutive; for example, flushing the house for six hours each day over eight days is acceptable.

Even after flushing, certain materials and chemicals may remain in the home. Flushing for longer than 48 hours is preferable, but in some cases even an extended flush may not eliminate all volatile pollutants.

Choose products with low or no VOCs, ureaformaldehyde, or other pollutants to reduce the risk of exposure to the occupant. Some of these strategies are rewarded in Materials & Resources 2.2.

Have the construction crew clean the site regularly to reduce dust and dirt.

Calculations

No calculations are required for this credit.

Exemplary Performance

No additional points are available for exemplary performance.

Verification and Submittals

Supporting Verification Materials, made available by the Project Team:

❑ Sign an Accountability Form to indicate that the preoccupancy flush has been conducted according to the requirements.

Verification Team:

❑ Verify that an Accountability Form has been signed by the responsible party.

❑ Verify the dates, duration, and methods used to conduct the preoccupancy flush.

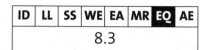

ID	LL	SS	WE	EA	MR	EQ	AE
			8.3				

Resources

Web Sites

Air Quality in the Home

American Lung Association

www.lungusa.org

This site includes an entire section devoted to indoor air quality in the home. Choose "Air Quality" at the bottom of the screen and then click "Indoor Air Quality" and "Air Quality in the Home" to find numerous articles and educational pieces about maintaining a healthy indoor environment.

Indoor Air Quality Division

U.S. Environmental Protection Agency

www.epa.gov/iaq

This site has numerous resources related to indoor air quality in homes, including reports and web links.

EQ 9: Radon Protection

Intent

Reduce occupant exposure to radon gas and other soil gas contaminants.

Requirements

Prerequisites

9.1 **Radon-Resistant Construction in High-Risk Areas.** If the home is in EPA Radon Zone 1, design and build the home with radon-resistant construction techniques as prescribed by EPA, the International Residential Code, Washington State Ventilation and Indoor Air Quality Code, or some equivalent code or standard.

Credits

9.2 **Radon-Resistant Construction in Moderate-Risk Areas** (1 point). If the home is outside EPA Radon Zone 1, design and build the home with radon-resistant construction techniques as prescribed by EPA, the International Residential Code, Washington State Ventilation and Indoor Air Quality Code, or some equivalent code or standard.

Note: Radon-resistant construction does not guarantee that occupants will not be exposed to radon. The Surgeon General and EPA recommend that every home in the country be tested for radon. Information about radon testing is available at the EPA Web site, at www.epa.gov/radon/radontest.html.

Synergies and Trade-Offs

A project receiving points for EQ 1 is not eligible to earn points for EQ 9.2.

EQ 9.1: Radon-Resistant Construction in High-Risk Areas
EQ 9.2: Radon-Resistant Construction in Moderate-Risk Areas

According to Environmental Protection Agency estimates, radon is the number-one cause of lung cancer among nonsmokers in the United States, and the second leading cause of lung cancer overall. It is estimated that radon causes 5,000 to 20,000 lung cancer deaths each year. The risk associated with radon is directly related to the concentration of radon exposure, so designing the home to reduce exposure to radon can significantly reduce health risks.

In areas of the country that have been designated as high-risk areas for radon, LEED for Homes (and often local codes) requires use of radon-resistant construction techniques. In other areas, the known risk of radon may be lower, but radon-resistant construction techniques are still encouraged. In addition to reducing exposure to radon, the construction techniques required for this credit also reduce exposure to other ground-source chemicals and pollutants and are generally considered good practice.

Approach and Implementation

Radon protection has been well documented, and many materials and techniques are available in most regions of the country.

Consult EPA's radon map to determine whether the site is in Zone 1 (high risk). If so, radon-protection measures are mandatory under this credit. In all other zones, radon resistance measures earn 1 point.

Incorporate radon-resistant new construction techniques at the beginning of the design process. Follow the techniques and strategies outlined in EPA's "Building Radon Out: A Step-by-Step Guide on How to Build Radon-Resistant Homes"

or the practices in ASTM E2121-03, "Standard Practice for Installing Radon Mitigation Systems in Existing Low-Rise Residential Buildings." Similar guidelines are provided in Appendix F of the International Residential Code and the Washington State Ventilation and Indoor Air Quality Code.

Radon-resistant construction strategies include five components: a gas-permeable layer, heavy-gauge plastic sheeting, sealing and caulking of all penetrations through the concrete slab, and a vent pipe to exhaust gases from under the home.

The use of heavy-gauge plastic between concrete slab and soil provides both radon protection and a capillary break for moisture control. A 4- to 6-inch layer of stone on grade under slabs with a perforated drainage pipe vented to a passive vent stack provides both additional radon protection and moisture control.

Radon-resistant new construction requires the sub-slab pipe to be vented to the outside, either through the side wall or roof. It is not acceptable to cap the pipe inside the home.

Best practice is to install radon-resistant construction and conduct radon testing after construction. Radon testing methods are published by EPA (see www.epa.gov/radon/radontest.html). If tests for radon are positive, install an active radon mitigation system, which includes an exhaust fan incorporated with the vent stack to pull gases out from below the house. After the mitigation system is installed, re-test for radon to ensure that the system is functioning properly to remove radon.

Testing is not an alternative to radon-resistant construction. The presence of radon can change over time, so a negative radon test does not ensure the long-term absence of any radon. EPA recommends regular testing of radon, especially in high-risk areas.

Gut-rehab projects should use the new residential construction guidance in EPA's Indoor airPLUS, or existing residential buildings language in ASTME-2121. Post-occupancy tests are strongly encouraged. See www.epa.gov/radon/pubs/mitstds.html.

For multifamily buildings, an acceptable alternative to radon-resistant construction is to build above an open-air garage.

Calculations

No calculations are required for this credit.

Exemplary Performance

No additional points are available for exemplary performance.

Verification and Submittals

Supporting Verification Materials, made available by the Project Team:

❑ Sign an Accountability Form to indicate that the home was built with radon-resistant construction.

Verification Team:

❑ Visually verify radon-resistant construction.

❑ Verify that an Accountability Form has been signed by the responsible party.

Considerations

Environmental Issues

If radon proves to be a significant problem in the future, implementing active radon mitigation methods is much more effective in a home with radon-resistant

construction than in a conventionally constructed home.

Some areas have soil gases other than radon. Radon mitigation systems can also help minimize penetration of these soil gases into homes.

Economic Issues

The costs of implementing radon-resistant construction are moderate. If radon becomes a problem in the future, implementing more aggressive radon mitigation methods will be less expensive in a home with radon-resistant construction. The radon measures also help control moisture movement through slabs and reduce flooring problems.

Regional Variances

Radon measures may already be required by local code in high-risk areas. If code dictates specific practices for radon protection, these measures can be used to satisfy the prerequisite or credit requirements.

Resources

Web Sites

Radon-Resistant New Construction

U.S. Environmental Protection Agency

www.epa.gov/radon/construc.html

This site contains general information on radon, including the health risks associated with radon and the common techniques for radon-resistant construction. This site includes a link to the report "Building Radon Out: A Step-by-Step Guide on How to Build Radon-Resistant Homes."

EPA Map of Radon Zones

U.S. Environmental Protection Agency

www.epa.gov/radon/zonemap.html

This site includes a county-by-county map of the United States indicating the relative radon risk levels.

Radon Fact Sheet

American Lung Association

www.lungusa.org/site/
pp.asp?c=dvLUK9O0E&b=35420

This is a general overview of the health risks associated with radon exposure.

American Association of Radon Scientists and Technologies

www.aarst.org

This organization is dedicated to radon research and education. Its site includes links to educational material as well as technical scientific reports.

Washington State Ventilation and Indoor Air Quality Code

Builder's Field Guide

www.energy.wsu.edu/pubs

Chapter 2 of this field guide provides tips, procedures, and schematics for understanding how to mitigate radon risks during new construction.

Print Media

Builder's Guide series for specific North American climate zones: *Cold Climates, Mixed-Humid Climates, Hot-Humid Climates*, and *Hot-Dry & Mixed Dry Climates*, by Joseph Lstiburek, Ph.D., P.Eng. Building Science Press. Refer to the discussion and construction details regarding passive and active radon mitigation. Available at www.eeba.org/bookstore/default.asp.

Building Radon Out: A Step-by-Step Guide on How to Build Radon-Resistant Homes. U.S. Environmental Protection Agency, 2001. Available at www.epa.gov/radon/pdfs/buildradonout.pdf.

Standard Practice for Installing Radon Mitigation Systems in Existing Low-Rise Residential Buildings. U.S. Environmental Protection Agency. Available at www.epa.gov/radon/pubs/mitstds.html.

ASTM E2121-03 Standard Practice for Installing Radon Mitigation Systems in Existing Low-Rise Residential Buildings. ASTM International, Active Standards. Available at www.astm.org/standards.

EQ 10: Garage Pollutant Protection

Intent

Reduce occupant exposure to indoor pollutants originating from an adjacent garage.

Requirements

Prerequisites

10.1 **No HVAC in Garage.** Place all air-handling equipment and ductwork outside the fire-rated envelope of the garage.

Credits

10.2 **Minimize Pollutants from Garage** (2 points). Tightly seal shared surfaces between garage and conditioned spaces, including all of the following:

a) In conditioned spaces above the garage:

    i) seal all penetrations; and

    ii) seal all connecting floor and ceiling joist bays.

b) In conditioned spaces next to the garage:

    i) weather-strip all doors;

    ii) place carbon monoxide detectors in adjacent rooms that share a door with the garage;

    iii) seal all penetrations; and

    iv) seal all cracks at the base of the walls.

AND/OR

10.3 **Exhaust Fan in Garage** (1 point). Install an exhaust fan in the garage that is rated for continuous operation and designed to be operated in one of the following ways. Nonducted exhaust fans must be 70 cfm or greater, and ducted exhaust fans must be 100 cfm or greater.

a) Fan must run continuously; or

b) Fan must be designed with an automatic timer control linked to an occupant sensor, light switch, garage door opening–closing mechanism, carbon monoxide sensor, or equivalent. The timer must be set to provide at least three air changes each time the fan is turned on.

OR

10.4 **Detached Garage or No Garage** (3 points).

Synergies and Trade-Offs

A project receiving points for EQ 1 is not eligible to earn points for EQ 10.2, EQ 10.3, or EQ 10.4. A project receiving points EQ 10.4 is not eligible to earn points for EQ 10.2 or 10.3, and vice versa.

EQ 10.1 should be taken into consideration when designing the HVAC and heating and cooling distribution system (EA 5, 6; EQ 4, 6).

10.1 No HVAC in Garage

10.2 Minimize Pollutants from Garage

10.3 Exhaust Fan in Garage

10.4 Detached Garage or No Garage

Occupants' health may be adversely affected by car emissions, such as carbon monoxide, leaking from the garage into the home. Recent studies have demonstrated the potential for pollutants from attached garages to affect the quality of air in occupied spaces. Of special concern are vehicle exhaust, moisture, and off-gassing from stored chemicals, power tools, and other items commonly stored in garages. Locating the HVAC system or ductwork in the garage can pull this polluted air into the system and circulate it throughout the home.

Sealing off the garage helps reduce exposure, since air from the garage can otherwise be pulled into the house by localized depressurization. Installing fans in the garage helps reduce the concentrations of pollutants, particularly airborne car emissions.

Approach and Implementation

Best practice is to build a detached garage or no garage (EQ 10.4). If a home is constructed with no garage, consider building a shed or some other vented space where occupants can store paint, adhesives, and other materials that are unwanted in the living space.

There cannot be a door from an air handling unit closet that opens into the garage. The access door to an air handling unit must open into the living space, or the exterior of the building.

If the project includes a garage, work with the architect and HVAC contractor to find a space outside the garage to install the HVAC equipment. In regions where HVAC equipment is commonly located in garages, this credit may require significant changes to the home design. Address this concern early in the process so that retrofitting is not required.

HVAC equipment with closed combustion (as required by EQ 2.1) can be installed in conditioned space—a closet, a dropped ceiling, a conditioned crawl space or basement, or a conditioned room in the attic. Although an attic installation of HVAC equipment is possible, it is always best to keep HVAC systems entirely within conditioned space. Start by sizing the equipment properly: right-sized systems are generally small and thus easier to locate.

The garage is defined by its fire-rated envelope. Ductwork that runs outside this envelope (e.g., in the interstitial spaces around the garage) is allowed but discouraged. If this is done, special care should be taken to seal off the ductwork.

Proper and thorough air sealing between the house and garage is awarded and strongly encouraged. This can be achieved using standard caulking, sealants, and weather-stripping, but the use of spray foam insulation in the walls and ceiling of the garage is also encouraged for both improved indoor air quality and energy efficiency.

An qualified energy rater using a blower door and a technique known as series leakage can measure the effectiveness of air sealing and direct the placement of air-sealing insulation and air barriers on garage walls adjacent to living space.

This kind of testing is encouraged but not required for this credit.

If an exhaust fan is installed in the garage, choose a fan that is appropriate for the space and will not disturb the occupants. Larger fans may produce more sound but operate for a shorter period; small fans may be quieter but may have to operate continuously or for extended periods. Continuous operation is not necessarily worse for comfort and energy use if the fan is quiet and efficient. If possible, choose a fan that is ENERGY STAR–labeled and has a sound rating of less than 1.5 sones.

Calculations

If installing an exhaust fan in the garage, use the following equation to calculate the length of time, in minutes, that the garage fan must run to provide three air changes:

Operating Time = Garage Size * 3 ÷ Fan Capacity

where garage size is measured in cubic feet and fan capacity is measured in cfm.

Sample calculation: A 20x20x10-foot garage has 4,000 cubic feet. Three air changes is 12,000 cubic feet. A 100-cfm fan must therefore be set to run 120 minutes.

Exemplary Performance

No additional points are available for exemplary performance.

Verification and Submittals

Supporting Verification Materials, made available by the Project Team:

EQ 10.3: Exhaust Fan in Garage

❑ Provide calculations to the Verification Team demonstrating that the garage exhaust fan provides the necessary air changes.

❑ Include garage exhaust fan equipment literature in the occupant's operations and maintenance manual.

Verification Team:

EQ 10.1: No HVAC in Garage

❑ Visually verify that the requirements have been met.

EQ 10.2: Minimization of Pollutants from Garage

❑ Visually verify that the requirements have been met.

EQ 10.3: Exhaust Fan in Garage

❑ Visually verify the calculations for garage air changes.

❑ Visually verify that the appropriate garage exhaust equipment has been installed.

EQ 10.4: Detached Garage or No Garage

❑ Visually verify that the home has no attached garage.

Considerations

Economic Issues

Air sealing is inexpensive. Installing an exhaust fan should be a moderate cost. Relocating HVAC equipment will be at least moderate cost. Offset the cost of relocating the HVAC system by properly sizing the system and redesigning framing layouts to accommodate ductwork within conditioned space.

Resources

Web Sites

Air and Pollutant Transport from Attached Garages to Residential Living Spaces

National Institute of Standards and Technology Report

www.fire.nist.gov/bfrlpubs/build03/art068.html

This report provides an overview of the major issues, as well as a review of relevant scientific studies and a series of field studies.

Print Media

Builder's Guide series for specific North American climate zones: *Cold Climates, Mixed-Humid Climates, Hot-Humid Climates*, and *Hot-Dry & Mixed Dry Climates*, by Joseph Lstiburek, Ph.D., P.Eng. Building Science Press. Refer to the discussion and construction details regarding air sealing and connected garages. Available at www.eeba.org/bookstore/default.asp.

Awareness & Education

The LEED for Homes Rating System addresses the design and construction of new green homes—roles that are the responsibility of the home designer and the builder, respectively. But the environmental impact of a home continues throughout its life cycle, well beyond the initial design and construction decisions. Most new homes are expected to last 50 to 100 years, during which the occupants will consume energy, water, and other resources. They therefore play a substantial role in the resource use of a home over its lifetime.

Some homebuyers may know very little about green home construction. They may be unaware of the green features in the home, or they may be unfamiliar with how to use and maintain them. Without adequate training, the full benefits of the LEED measures likely will not be achieved.

This credit category promotes broad awareness among homebuyers and tenants that LEED Homes are built differently and need to be operated and maintained accordingly. Because the operations and maintenance tasks in multifamily buildings may be performed by a building manager, this credit also addresses the need for appropriate education of building managers.

The two Awareness & Education (AE) categories in the LEED for Homes Rating System—Education of the Homeowner or Tenant and Education of the Building Manager—are summarized in **Table 1** and described in the following sections.

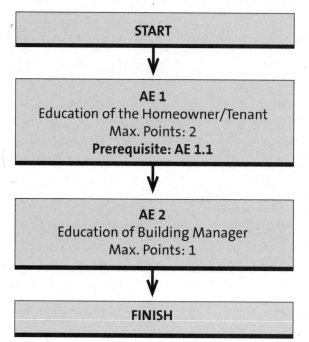

Table 1. Overview of Awareness & Education (AE) Category

START

AE 1
Education of the Homeowner/Tenant
Max. Points: 2
Prerequisite: AE 1.1

AE 2
Education of Building Manager
Max. Points: 1

FINISH

AE 1: Education of the Homeowner or Tenant

Intent

Maintain the performance of the home by educating the occupants (i.e., the homeowner or tenant) about the operations and maintenance of the home's LEED features and equipment.

Requirements

Prerequisites

1.1 **Basic Operations Training.** Provide the home's occupant(s) with the following:

a) An operations and maintenance manual or binder that includes all the following items:

  i. The completed checklist of LEED for Homes features.

  ii. A copy of each signed Accountability Form.

  iii. A copy of the durability inspection checklist.

  iv. The product manufacturers' manuals for all installed equipment, fixtures, and appliances.

  v. General information on efficient use of energy, water, and natural resources.

  vi. Operations and maintenance guidance for any LEED for Homes–related equipment installed in the home, including

  ❑ space heating and cooling equipment;

  ❑ mechanical ventilation equipment;

  ❑ humidity control equipment;

  ❑ radon protection system;

  ❑ renewable energy system; and

  ❑ irrigation, rainwater harvesting, and or graywater system.

  vii. Guidance on occupant activities and choices, including the following:

  ❑ cleaning materials, methods, and supplies;

  ❑ water-efficient landscaping;

  ❑ impacts of chemical fertilizers and pesticides;

  ❑ irrigation;

  ❑ lighting selection; and

  ❑ appliance selection.

  viii. Educational information on "green power."

b) A minimum one-hour walk-through of the home with the occupant(s), featuring the following:

i. Identification of all installed equipment.

ii. Instruction in how to use the measures and operate the equipment.

iii. Information on how to maintain the measures and equipment.

Credits

1.2 **Enhanced Training** (1 point). Provide two hours of training for the occupant(s) in addition to the training provided for AE 1.1. Examples of eligible trainings include:

a) An additional walk-through or training held in another home that has similar green measures and equipment.

b) A builder- or developer-sponsored meeting of potential homebuyers that informs participants of the unique features of a LEED home.

c) A group homebuyer training that includes discussion of the required items in the occupant's operations and maintenance manual, including information on efficient use of resources, appropriate use of measures and systems, and proper maintenance of measures and systems.

d) A homebuyer DVD with operations and maintenance information on the home's LEED for Homes measures.

1.3 **Public Awareness** (1 point). Promote general public awareness about LEED for Homes by conducting at least three of the following activities:

a) Hold an advertised, attended public open house that lasts at least four hours per day on at least four weekends or participate in a green building exhibition or tour. The home or building must display at least four informational stations about the LEED for Homes features (and/or offer a guided tour that highlights at least four LEED for Homes features).

b) Publish a Web site with at least two pages that provides detailed information about the features and benefits of LEED homes.

c) Generate a newspaper article on the LEED for Homes project.

d) Display LEED for Homes signage, measuring six square feet or more, on the exterior of the home or building.

Synergies and Trade-Offs

Many of the measures in the Rating System should be addressed in the operations manual and the on-site training, particularly any measures that require routine maintenance (e.g., air filters) or instruction for proper operation (e.g., heat-recovery systems).

AE 1.1 Basic Operations Training

AE 1.2 Enhanced Training

AE 1.3 Public Awareness

The performance and durability of a LEED home depend on the proper use of its features and the maintenance of its systems throughout its service life. Thus, awareness and education of the occupants are critical to achieving long-term sustainability goals in the residential sector.

Home occupants need general information about their new LEED home: its unique features, the value that a sustainable home provides, and the appropriate use and proper maintenance of its measures and equipment.

This credit requires builders to provide an occupant's manual and conduct a walk-through and rewards those who further educate their homebuyers, rental tenants, and the public.

Approach and Implementation

For AE 1.1, which is required, prepare an operations and maintenance manual covering all the green features installed in the LEED Home. The manual must be presented to the homebuyer or rental tenant by the builder. Design the manual for ease of use, with particular emphasis on aspects of the home that require regular maintenance. Where possible, include the names of vendors where the homeowner can purchase replacements parts (e.g., air filters) or have systems serviced.

Design the manual for long-term use, so the manual can change hands and still be useful twenty years after the home has been constructed.

Design standard elements of the operations and maintenance manual that can be reused for multiple homes, then swap out information that is specific to each home or project.

Conduct a minimum one-hour walk-through of the building with the home-buyer or rental tenant, with explanation of the proper operation and maintenance procedures for all the green features installed in the building. Use the operations and maintenance manual as the walk-through is conducted to familiarize the occupants with the manual and its utility.

For AE 1.2, offer additional training as indicated in the credit language, above.

For AE 1.3, create public awareness of the features and benefits of a specific LEED for Homes project, inviting the public to visit and possibly choose to purchase a LEED Home. Public awareness activities that are not included in the credit may be counted if a Credit Interpretation Request is submitted and approved.

Verification and Submittals

Builder / Project Team:

AE 1.1 Basic Operations Training

❑ Present the operations and maintenance manual to the Green Rater for review.

❑ Provide the operations and maintenance manual to the occupant.

❑ Sign an Accountability Form to indicate that a walk-through has been conducted with the occupant.

AE 1.2 Enhanced Training

❑ Sign an Accountability Form to indicate that additional training that meets the requirements has been provided to the occupant.

AE 1.3 Public Awareness

❑ Provide open-house dates, Web site address, and/or newspaper citation to the Green Rater.

Verification Team:

AE 1.1 Basic Operations Training

❑ Visually verify that the operations and maintenance manual meets the requirements.

❑ Verify that an Accountability Form has been signed by the responsible party.

AE 1.2 Enhanced Training

❑ Verify that an Accountability Form has been signed by the responsible party.

AE 1.3 Public Awareness

❑ Visually verify the list of open-house dates, Web site page, newspaper article, and LEED for Homes signage.

Calculations

No calculations are required for this credit.

Exemplary Performance

No additional points are available for exemplary performance.

Resources

Web Sites

Canadian Mortgage and Housing Corporation

www.cmhc-schl.gc.ca/en/co

This site provides tips on home repair and maintenance, including a maintenance checklist.

Connecticut Department of Environmental Protection, Health Home Brochure

www.ct.gov/dep/lib/dep/p2/individual/healthyhome.pdf

This site links to the "A Green Home Is a Healthy Home" brochure, a good example of a simple brochure with a readable layout and presentation.

Minnesota Building Industry Foundation, Home-Smart

www.home-smart.org

This site provides information for homeowners on maintaining their home. It includes seasonal checklists and step-by-step instructions for general maintenance, as well as special instructions for new-home buyers on maintaining their home during its first year.

AE 2: Education of Building Manager

Intent

Maintain the performance of the home by educating the building manager about the operations and maintenance of the home's LEED features and equipment.

Requirements

Prerequisites

None.

Credits

2   **Education of Building Manager** (1 point). For multifamily buildings (more than five units), provide the building manager with the following:

a)   A building owner's manual or binder that includes these items:

i.   The completed checklist of LEED for Homes features.

ii.   A copy of each signed Accountability Form.

iii. A copy of the durability inspection checklist.

iv.   The product manufacturers' manuals for all installed equipment, fixtures, and appliances.

v.   General information on efficient use of energy, water, and natural resources.

vi.   Operations and maintenance guidance for any LEED for Homes–related equipment installed in the home, including:

❏   space heating and cooling equipment;

❏   mechanical ventilation equipment;

❏   humidity control equipment;

❏   radon protection system;

❏   renewable energy system; and

❏   irrigation, rainwater harvesting, and/or graywater system.

vii. Guidance on occupant activities and choices, including the following:

❏   cleaning materials, methods, and supplies;

❏   water-efficient landscaping;

❏   impacts of chemical fertilizers and pesticides;

❏   irrigation;

❏   lighting selection; and

❏   appliance selection.

viii. Educational information on "green power."

b) A minimum one-hour walk-through of the building before occupancy, featuring the following:

   i.   Identification of all installed equipment.

   ii.   Instruction in how to use the measures and operate the equipment in each unit.

   iii.   Information on how to maintain the measures and equipment in each unit.

Synergies and Trade-Offs

Many of the measures in the Rating System should be addressed in the building manager's manual and on-site training, particularly any measures that require routine maintenance (e.g., air filters) or specific instruction for proper operation (e.g., heat-recovery systems).

AE 2: Education of Building Manager

The performance and durability of a LEED-certified multifamily building can be significantly influenced through proper operations and maintenance of its green equipment and systems. The manager has a critical role in the long-term sustainability goals for a multifamily building and needs to know about its unique features, the value that green features provide, and the appropriate use and maintenance of the equipment.

This credit rewards builders who educate building managers and provide them with a building manager's manual.

Approach and Implementation

Prepare an operations and maintenance manual for all the green features installed in the building. Present this manual to the building manager.

An operations and maintenance manual for a building manager will differ from the manual provided to occupants. Give particular emphasis to measures or maintenance items that affect the performance of the home and focus on systems or features that are unusual or unique to green homebuilding.

Complete a minimum one-hour walk-through with the building manager and explain the proper operation and maintenance procedures for all the green features installed in the building.

If the builder hires the manager or has input into the hiring decision, identify candidates who have experience and familiarity with the principles and concepts of energy efficiency, water-efficient landscape maintenance, indoor air quality, and other aspects of green buildings.

Calculations

No calculations are required for this credit.

Verification and Submittals

Builder / Project Team:

❑ Present the operations and maintenance manual to the Green Rater for review.

❑ Provide the operations and maintenance manual to the building manager.

❑ Sign an Accountability Form to indicate that a walk-through has been conducted with the building manager.

Green Rater:

❑ Visually verify that the operations and maintenance manual meets the requirements.

❑ Verify that an Accountability Form has been signed by the responsible party.

Exemplary Performance

No additional points are available for exemplary performance.

Resources

Web Sites

Canadian Mortgage and Housing Corporation

www.cmhc-schl.gc.ca/en/co

This site provides tips on home repair and maintenance, including a maintenance checklist.

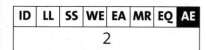

ID	LL	SS	WE	EA	MR	EQ	**AE**
			2				

Connecticut Department of Environmental Protection, Health Home Brochure

www.ct.gov/dep/lib/dep/p2/individual/healthyhome.pdf

This site links to the "A Green Home Is a Healthy Home" brochure, a good example of a simple brochure with a readable layout and presentation.

Minnesota Building Industry Foundation, Home-Smart

www.home-smart.org

This site provides information for homeowners on maintaining their home. It includes seasonal checklists and step-by-step instructions for general maintenance, as well as special instructions for new-home buyers on maintaining their home during its first year.

Glossary

Abbreviations and Acronyms

AFUE	annual fuel utilization efficiency
ALP	ENERGY STAR Advanced Lighting Package
CFA	conditioned floor area
COC	chain of custody
COP	coefficient of performance
CRI	Carpet & Rug Institute
CZ	climate zone
DOE	US Department of Energy
HOA	homeowner's association
HSPF	heating season performance factor
IAP	ENERGY STAR Indoor airPLUS
IAQ	indoor air quality
IRC	International Residential Code
ACCA	Air Conditioning Contractors of America
AE	Awareness & Education section credit category
AP	LEED Accredited Professional (LEED)
ASHRAE	American Society of Heating, Refrigerating, and Air Conditioning Engineers
ASME	American Society of Mechanical Engineers
ASTM	American Society for Testing and Materials
CAE	combined annual efficiency
CFC	chlorofluorocarbon
CFL	compact fluorescent light
cfm	cubic feet per minute
CFR	U.S. Code of Federal Regulations
CIR	credit interpretation request
CO	carbon monoxide
DHW	domestic hot water
DU	distribution uniformity
EA	Energy & Atmosphere section
EER	energy efficiency rating
EERE	U.S. Office of Energy Efficiency and Renewable Energy

Glossary

EF	energy factor
EPA	U.S. Environmental Protection Agency
EQ	Indoor Environmental Quality section
ET	evapotranspiration
FEMA	U.S. Federal Emergency Management Agency
FSC	Forest Stewardship Council
gpf	gallons per flush
gpm	gallons per minute
HCFC	hydrochlorofluorocarbon
HEPA	high-efficiency particle absorbing
HERS	Home Energy Rating Standards
HET	high-efficiency toilet
HVAC	heating, ventilation and air -conditioning
ICF	insulated concrete form
ID	Innovation in Design section
IDR	innovative design request
IECC	International Energy Conservation Code
kW	kilowatt
kWh	kilowatt-hour
LED	light-emitting diode
LEED	Leadership in Energy and Environmental Design
LL	Location & Linkages section
MEF	modified energy factor
MERV	minimum efficiency reporting value
MR	Materials & Resources section
NFRC	National Fenestration Rating Council
OSB	oriented-strand board
RESNET	Residential Energy Services Network
SCS	Scientific Certification Systems
SEER	seasonal energy efficiency rating
SHGC	solar heat gain coefficient
SIP	structural insulated panels
SRI	solar reflectance index
SS	Sustainable Sites section
TASC	Technical Advisory Sub-Committee
UL	Underwriter's Laboratory
USGBC	U.S. Green Building Council

VOC	volatile organic compound
WE	Water Efficiency section
WF	water factor
WFA	window-to-floor area ratio

Glossary

adapted plant a groundcover, perennial, shrub, or tree that, once established, reliably grows well in a given habitat with minimal winter protection, pest protection, irrigation, or fertilization. Adapted plants are considered to be low maintenance but not invasive.

adhesive any substance used to bond one surface to another by attachment. Adhesives include adhesive bonding primers, adhesive primers, adhesive primers for plastics, and any other primer.

albedo surface reflectivity. High-albedo materials are very reflective.

anticorrosive paint a coating formulated and recommended for use in preventing the corrosion of ferrous metal substrates.

assembly recycled content the weight of recycled material, including both postconsumer and preconsumer (postindustrial) material, divided by the overall weight of the assembly.

balancing damper an adjustable plate that regulates air flow within ducts.

bedroom in LEED for Homes, any room or space that could be used or is intended to be used for sleeping purposes and meets local fire and building code requirements.

biomass plant material, such as trees, grasses and crops, that can be converted to heat energy to produce electricity.

black water wastewater that is generated from toilets and kitchen sinks and contains high levels of bacterial pollutants.

borate a wood preservative that is nontoxic to humans but highly toxic to wood-boring insects, such as termites.

buildable land the portion of a site where construction can occur. Buildable land excludes public streets and other public rights-of-way, land occupied by nonresidential structures, public parks and land excluded from residential development by law.

built environment the manmade alterations to a specific area, including its natural resources. On a home site, this includes everything that has been disturbed during construction.

catchment the surface area of a roof that intercepts rainwater for a rainwater harvesting system.

central vacuum system a network of tubing with inlets throughout the house designed to remove dust and debris to a remote receptacle. A central vacuum system is more efficient than a traditional vacuum cleaner.

chain-of-custody in forest certification, the path taken by raw materials, processed materials, and products from the forest to the consumer, including all successive stages of processing, transformation, manufacturing and distribution. A chain-of-custody certificate number on invoices for nonlabeled products indicates that the certifier's guidelines for product accounting have been followed. A chain-of-custody certification is not required by distributors of a product that is individually labeled with the Forest Stewardship Council logo and manufacturer's chain-of-custody number.

charrette an intensive, collaborative session in which a project team discusses design options related to all aspects of a building construction.

chlorofluorocarbon (CFC) a compound of carbon, hydrogen, chlorine and fluorine, once commonly used in refrigeration, that depletes the stratospheric ozone layer.

circulation loop a system that returns cold water to the water heater (instead of down the drain) until hot water reaches the faucet. A circulation loop is one component of a structured plumbing system.

climate zones the climate of a project's location can have a significant effect on environmental design and construction (particularly in terms of heating and cooling); thus the LEED for Homes rating system awards credit to projects that include sustainable goals appropriate for the local climate.

closed combustion a design for furnaces and water heaters in which the supply air is ducted from the outside and exhaust gases are ducted to the outdoors. All elements of the system are sealed to prevent combustion exhaust from leaking into the home.

combustion exhaust gases the most common gases resulting from fossil fuel combustion, including carbon dioxide, carbon monoxide, sulfur dioxide and nitrogen oxides. These gases pose health hazards at high concentrations.

composite wood a product consisting of wood or plant particles or fibers bonded together by a synthetic resin or binder. Examples include plywood, particleboard, oriented-strand board (OSB), medium-density fiberboard (MDF) and composite door cores.

conditioned space interior area that utilizes any method of air-conditioning or heating to control temperature and/or humidity levels, usually measured in cubic feet.

conventional turf grass, typically a monoculture, that requires considerable watering, mowing, and/or fertilizers. What is considered conventional turf may vary by region.

cool pavement a road, driveway, parking lot, sidewalk or other hard surface that has reduced absorption, retention and emittance of solar heat. Techniques to achieve cool pavement include coloration, porosity and other factors that promote solar reflectivity and cooling through augmented air filtration and evaporation.

credit interpretation request in LEED for Homes, a project team's request for clarification on the Rating System. A request is submitted to the Provider, which then forwards it to the appropriate technical advisory sub-committee for action.

daylighting the controlled admission of natural light into a space through glazing. Daylighting reduces the need for electric lighting.

degree-day the difference between the mean outdoor temperature on a given day and a reference temperature, used to estimate heating and cooling requirements.

demand-controlled circulation the automatic circulation of water, triggered by a switch or motion sensor, through a looped system to ensure that hot water is immediately available while keeping unused cold water in the system, saving both water and energy.

density the quantity of structures on a site, measured for residential buildings as dwelling units per acre of buildable land available for residential uses, and for nonresidential buildings as floor area ratio per net acre of buildable land available for nonresidential uses.

designed landscape the arrangement of features on a site, including softscapes (e.g., grass, shrubs) and hardscapes (e.g., patios, fountains) but not driveways or areas under roof. Preserved natural areas are not considered part of the designed landscape.

development the homes and building lots that surround the new LEED home project that is to be built. A development may be new or preexisting. Also known as community.

distribution uniformity the consistency with which irrigation water is applied to an area. Distribution uniformity (DU) ranges between 0 and 1, where 1 indicates that the irrigation system is providing perfectly equal coverage. A higher DU means less likelihood of overwatering or underwatering.

disturbed lot area the part of a site that is directly affected by construction activity, including any activity that would compact the soil or damage vegetation.

diverted waste debris from construction or demolition that is not sent to a landfill or incinerator. Strategies for diverting waste include reclamation, recycling and, for certain materials, mulching.

drip irrigation system a network of pipes and valves that rest on the soil or underground and slowly deliver water to the root systems of plants. Drip irrigation saves water by minimizing evapotranspiration and topsoil runoff.

drywall clip a device that supports drywall at a corner with minimal contact with the studs. Drywall clips eliminate the need for additional framing members.

dry well an underground structure that collects runoff and distributes it over a large area, increasing absorption and preventing erosion.

dual-flush toilet a toilet with two flush volumes, one for solid waste and a reduced volume for liquid waste.

durability the ability of a building component to perform its function over a long period without extra maintenance or unanticipated repair.

edge development generally, a group of homes that extend an existing community beyond its borders but remain connected to it. In LEED for Homes, at least 25% of an edge development's perimeter borders land that has been previously developed..

ENERGY STAR home a U.S Department of Energy and Environmental Protection Agency program that certifies energy-efficient dwellings (at least 15% more efficient than the International Energy Conservation Code).

envelope see *thermal envelope.*

EPA Indoor airPLUS a certification program that recognizes homes with systems to ensure high standards of indoor air quality that is also an ENERGY STAR Qualified Home.

erosion a process in which materials of the earth's surface are loosened, dissolved or worn away and transported by natural agents, such as water, wind or gravity.

flat coating a paint or varnish that registers a gloss of less than 15 on an 85-degree meter or less than 5 on a 60-degree meter.

fly ash the fine ash residue from coal combustion. Fly ash can be substituted for Portland cement, a bonding material in concrete.

formaldehyde a naturally occurring volatile organic compound used as a preservative.

When present in high concentrations, formaldehyde is an irritant to most people—causing headaches, dizziness, mental impairment, and other symptoms—and may be a carcinogen.

graywater wastewater that comes from household baths and clothes washers and is neither clean nor heavily soiled. More specifically, (1) "untreated house-hold wastewater which has not come into contact with toilet waste. Graywater includes used water from bathtubs, showers, bathroom wash basins, and water from clothes-washer and laundry tubs. It shall not include wastewater from kitchen sinks or dishwashers" (Uniform Plumbing Code, Appendix G, "Grey Water Systems for Single-Family Dwellings); (2) "wastewater discharged from lavatories, bathtubs, showers, clothes washers, and laundry sinks" (International Plumbing Code, Appendix C, "Grey water Recycling Systems"). Some states and local authorities allow kitchen sink wastewater to be included in graywater.

hardscape "elements added to a natural landscape, such as paving stones, gravel, walkways, irrigation systems, roads, retaining walls, sculpture, street amenities, fountains, and other mechanical features" (American Society of Landscape Architects). Hardscapes are often impermeable, but they are not impermeable by definition.

high-efficiency particulate absorbing (HEPA) filter an air filter that removes nearly all particulates.

high-efficiency toilet (HET) a toilet that uses no more than 1.3 gallons per flush.

Home Energy Rating System (HERS) index a system for evaluating the energy efficiency of a home using an energy simulation model. A HERS index of 100 represents the energy efficiency of a reference home that meets basic IECC code requirements; each index point below 100 represents a 1% decrease in energy use, down to 0, which is a net zero energy home.

hydrochlorofluorocarbon (HCFC) a organic compounds composed of carbon, fluorine, chlorine and hydrogen, used as a refrigerant. HCFCs deplete the stratospheric ozone layer but to a lesser extent than chlorofluorocarbons (CFCs).

hydronic system a heating or cooling system that uses circulating water as the heat-transfer medium, such as a boiler with hot water circulated through radiators or radiant floor heat.

infill site a lot in an existing community. In LEED for Homes, an infill site is defined as having at least 75% of its perimeter bordering land that has been previously developed.

infiltration degree-days the sum of the heating degree-days and the cooling degree-days.

innovative design request in LEED for Homes, a project team's request for receiving LEED points for installing a measure that meets the intent of a credit but of which details are not currently listed the Rating System. A request is submitted to the Provider, which then forwards it to the appropriate technical advisory sub-committee for action.

insulated concrete form (ICF) foam forms that are filled with reinforced concrete to create insulated structural walls.

invasive species "an alien species whose introduction does or is likely to cause economic or environmental harm or harm to human health" (Executive Order 13112). Not all nonnative species are considered invasive, and invasive species differ by region. Regional agencies that list invasive species are available at www.invasivespeciesinfo.gov/unitedstates/state.shtml.

ladder blocking a method of framing in which an interior partition wall butts up against a perpendicular exterior wall and is connected by horizontal pieces of lumber - rather than vertical studs - which allows additional insulation to be installed behind the horizontal lumber on the exterior wall.

light fixture illumination that is permanently fixed to the home. A fluorescent light fixture has an integrated ballast. A compact fluorescent lamp (CFL) is not a light fixture.

local heat island effect the incidence of higher air and surface temperatures caused by the absorption of solar energy and its reemission from roads, buildings and other structures.

lot the individual building lot where the qualifying LEED Home is to be built.

microirrigation a watering system with small sprinklers and microjets or drippers designed to apply small volumes of water. The sprinklers and microjets are installed within a few centimeters of the ground; drippers are laid on or below grade.

minimum efficiency reporting value (MERV) the effectiveness of a mechanical air filter based on the number and size of the particles that pass through it under normal conditions. The higher the rating, the more effective the filter.

native plant a plant that has evolved within a particular habitat and is not invasive within its natural range. Native plants provide food and shelter to indigenous wildlife and grow in balance with surrounding plant and animal species.

net metering an arrangement that allows on-site generators to send excess electricity flows to the regional power grid and offset a portion of the electricity flows drawn from the grid.

no-disturbance zone an area that is preserved during construction.

nonflat coating a paint or varnish that registers a gloss of 5 or greater on a 60-degree meter and a gloss of 15 or greater on an 85-degree meter.

pedestrian-oriented design an arrangement of features in the urban landscape that promote walking. Examples include wide sidewalks that are shaded and buffered from the street, short pedestrian crossings, and street-level pedestrian access to buildings (as opposed to access from parking lots).

postconsumer recycled content material used and then recycled by consumers, as distinguished from the recycled by-products of manufacturing, called preconsumer (postindustrial) recycled content.

postconsumer waste material generated by households or by commercial, industrial and institutional facilities that can no longer be used for its intended purpose. Examples include construction and demolition debris, materials collected through recycling programs, broken pallets (from a pallet refurbishing company, not a pallet-making company), discarded cabinetry and decking, and home maintenance waste (leaves, grass clippings, tree trimmings).

potable suitable for drinking. Potable water is generally supplied by municipal water systems.

power-vented exhaust a system that uses active exhaust to pull combustion gases out of the home. Combustion equipment with power venting can use indoor air as the combustion supply air.

preconsumer content material diverted from the waste stream during the manufacturing process. Formerly known as postindustrial content. Examples include planer shavings, plytrim, sawdust, chips, bagasse, culls, trimmed materials and obsolete inventory. Excluded is reutilization of materials such as rework, regrind or scrap generated in a process and capable of being reclaimed within the same process that generated it (Source ISO 14021).

previously developed a site with preexisting paving, construction or other types of altered landscapes. This does not apply to altered landscapes resulting from current agricultural use, forestry use, or use as preserved natural area.

previously developed site in LEED for Homes, a lot consisting of at least 75% previously developed land.

prime farmland "land that has the best combination of physical and chemical characteristics for producing food, feed, forage, fiber, and oilseed crops, and is also available for these uses" (U.S. CFR, Title 7, Part 657.5).

project the design and construction of a LEED home. A project may include multiple homes in a development.

Provider local organizations selected by USGBC based on demonstrated experience and expertise in supporting builders in the construction of high-performance, sustainable homes in their market. A LEED for Homes Provider has three primary roles: marketing LEED to builders; providing green home rating support services to builders; and training, coordinating and overseeing Green Raters.

radon a radioactive gas that naturally vents from the ground. High levels of radon are known to be carcinogenic.

rain garden a swale, or low tract of land into which water flows, planted with vegetation that requires or tolerates high moisture levels. A rain garden can reduce the volume of water entering storm drains and replenish groundwater.

rated power the nameplate power on a piece of equipment, representing the capacity of the unit and the maximum wattage it will draw.

receptacle load the total demand on an electrical system from all power equipment.

reclaimed material building components that have been recovered from a demolition site and are reused in their original state (i.e., not recycled). Also known as salvage.

recycling the collection, reprocessing, marketing and use of materials that were diverted or recovered from the solid waste stream.

refrigerant a fluid that absorbs heat from a reservoir at low temperatures and rejects heat at higher temperatures.

reuse the return of salvaged materials to use in the same or a related capacity.

R-value a measure of thermal resistance, most often used for rating insulation products and installations. The greater the R-value, the greater the resistance to heat transfer. R-value is the inverse of U-value (i.e., R = 1/U).

sealant a substance that prevents passage of air or moisture. Sealants are used on wood, fabric, paper, corrugated paperboard, plastic foam and other materials with tiny openings, often microscopic, that may absorb or discharge gas or fluid.

sedimentation the deposition of soil and other natural solids in waterbodies. Sedimentation decreases water quality and accelerates the aging process of lakes, rivers and streams.

siltation the deposition and accumulation of very fine particles in waterbodies. Siltation is often harmful to lake, river and stream ecosystems.

site the individual building lot where a home is to be built. A site may include all of the lots that a builder is responsible for.

smart growth various urban planning policies and land-use strategies that seek to provide the greatest benefit to the community and preserve the natural environment. Smart growth often includes high-density development, mixed-use buildings and a strong consideration of transportation issues.

softscape the natural elements of a landscape, such as plant materials and soil. Softscapes can include hard elements, such as rocks.

solar heat gain coefficient (SHGC) "the fraction of incident solar radiation admitted through a window, both directly transmitted, and absorbed and subsequently released inward. SHGC is expressed as a number between 0 and 1. The lower a window's solar heat gain coefficient, the less solar heat it transmits." (Efficient Windows Collaborative)

solar window screen mesh used to block light and heat from the sun, as well as insects.

structural insulated panel (SIP) panels made from a thick layer of foam that is sandwiched between two layers of sheathing, often Oriented Strand Board (OSB), plywood or fiber-cement.

subdivision the homes and building lots that immediately surround the new LEED home project that is to be built. A subdivision may be new or preexisting, and belongs to a larger development.

sustainable forestry the practice of managing forest resources to meet the long-term forest product needs of humans while maintaining the integrity of forested landscapes and sustaining a full range of forest values—economic, social and ecological.

technical advisory sub-committee in LEED for Homes, a group of specialists who rule on credit interpretation requests and innovative design requests.

termite a wood-eating social insect (order Isoptera) that can cause serious structural damage to buildings in many regions of the United States. Also known as white ant.

thermal bridge a part of a building envelope that has high thermal conductivity, lowering the average R-value of the assembly. Studs are common thermal bridges.

thermal envelope the border on a building where conditioned air meets unconditioned space. The thermal envelope must be both continuous and contiguous with the pressure envelope: there must be an air barrier that continuously touches the insulation.

topsoil the uppermost layer of soil, containing high levels of nutrients and organic matter. Healthy topsoil promotes plant growth.

tree/plant preservation plan a scheme that seeks to preserve existing plants on a project site.

ureaformaldehyde a combination of urea and formaldehyde used in some glues and adhesives, particularly in composite wood products. At room temperature, ureaformaldehyde emits formaldehyde, a toxic and possibly carcinogenic gas.

U-factor a measure of thermal conductivity that is the inverse of R-value, often used to measure the performance of windows. A lower U-value means a more energy-efficient window. Also known as U-value.

vegetated roof a roof partially or fully covered by vegetation, used to manage water runoff and provide additional insulation in winter and cooling in summer.

vegetated swale see *rain garden*.

volatile organic compound (VOC) a carbon compound that vaporizes (becomes a gas) at normal room temperatures. VOCs contribute to air pollution directly and through atmospheric photochemical reactions to produce secondary air pollutants, principally ozone and peroxyacetyl nitrate.

walk-off mat an interior pad designed to trap dust and debris.

wetland an area inundated or saturated by surface or ground water at a frequency and duration sufficient to support, and that under normal circumstances does support, a prevalence of vegetation typically adapted for life in saturated soil conditions (U.S. Code of Federal Regulations, Title 40, Part 232). Wetlands generally include swamps, marshes, bogs, and similar areas.